MONASH'S MASTERPIECE

Peter FitzSimons

The Battle of Le Hamel and the
93 Minutes that Changed the World

hachette
AUSTRALIA

hachette
AUSTRALIA

Published in Australia and New Zealand in 2018
by Hachette Australia
(an imprint of Hachette Australia Pty Limited)
Level 17, 207 Kent Street, Sydney NSW 2000
www.hachette.com.au

10 9 8 7 6 5 4 3 2 1

NATIONAL
LIBRARY
OF AUSTRALIA
A catalogue record for this
book is available from the
National Library of Australia

ISBN 978 0 7336 4008 7

Cover design by Luke Causby/Blue Cork
Cover photographs: State Library of Victoria, H32850, portrait of Sir John Monash;
Australian War Memorial, B01959, RE8 reconnaissance bomber; E02690, American and
Australian troops dug in together during the battle of Hamel; E02666, Australians searching
for wounded amongst the ruins of Hamel the day following the capture of the village
Author photo courtesy Peter Morris/Sydney Heads
Typeset in 11.2/15.12 pt Sabon LT Pro by Bookhouse, Sydney
Printed and bound in Australia by McPherson's Printing Group

To Sir John Monash
A hundred years on, Sir, we dips our lids

CONTENTS

LIST OF MAPS

ACKNOWLEDGEMENTS AND AUTHOR'S NOTE

Yes, I know I called my last book, on the Battle of Villers-Bretonneux, the 'third of my trilogy' on the great battles Australians were involved in during the Great War, but in the course of writing them I kept hearing about the Battle of Hamel – a tactical masterpiece by our own General Sir John Monash that changed the course of warfare and shortened the war. My eldest brother David – fortuitously, like Monash, a civil engineer – was the first one to explain the whole thing to me in detail and, after sitting transfixed for an hour listening to him, I decided to explore further. While researching my book on Villers-Bretonneux, and visiting the battlefield, I ducked over to Hamel, just three kilometres away, and first started to get an appreciation for how the battle rolled. When I read the moving words of French Prime Minister Georges Clemenceau praising the Australians for their efforts, just three days after the battle – now emblazoned on the memorial for all eternity – I knew I had to do the book, and sooner rather than later, beginning with the briefest of reprises from the trilogy, concerning the Americans entering the war. It is simply not right that such a battle, such a monumental feat, does not resonate with Australians 100 years later.

And so it began . . .

As I detailed in my trilogy, I have tried to bring the *story* part of this hi*story* alive, by putting the whole account in present tense, and constructing it in the manner of a novel, albeit with 1000 odd footnotes as the pinpoint pillars on which the story rests. For the sake of the storytelling, I have occasionally created a direct quote from reported speech in a newspaper, diary or letter, and changed pronouns and tenses to put that reported speech in the present tense – every now and then assuming generic emotions where it is obvious, even though that emotion is not necessarily recorded in the diary entries, letter, etc. I have also occasionally restored swear words that were blanked out in the original newspaper and diary accounts due to the sensitivities of the time. Always, my goal has been to determine what were the words used, based on the documentary evidence presented, and what the feel of the situation was. For the same reason of remaining faithful to the language of the day, I have stayed with the imperial system of measurement and used the contemporary spelling.

I also note that for the sake of simplicity, Lieutenant-Generals and Major-Generals are referred to simply as Generals. Brigadier-Generals are referred to as Brigadiers. Similarly, Lieutenant-Colonels and Colonels are both described as Colonels. I also advise that 'left' and 'right' flank is always viewed from the position of a person within the unit under discussion and facing the enemy. German translations have been lightly edited to make the meaning clearer in English.

While British, Australian and German formations are all different, here is the rough size of the units that made up their armies in the Great War:

> One Army Group (German only) = three or more armies, up to 1,200,000 men
>
> One Army = three to five Corps = up to 500,000 men
>
> One Corps = two to five Divisions, plus Corps troops = 50,000 to 150,000 men
>
> One Division = three Brigades of infantry and artillery = 16,000 men
>
> One Brigade or Regiment = three or four Battalions, plus machine guns and mortars = 3000 to 4000 men
>
> One Battalion = four Companies plus Battalion headquarters = 600 to 900 men
>
> One Company = four platoons = 150 to 200 men. (Owing to an influenza epidemic and lack of replacements for casualties, German, British and Australian companies were frequently only 100 strong.)

While I prized primary documents above all else, many books were wonderful sources, and none more – as ever – than the combined works of Charles E. W. Bean, including most particularly his *Official History*, as well as his diaries and notebooks. On that subject, I express here my deep gratitude to Edward Bean LeCouteur and Anne Marie Carroll, the grandchildren of Charles Bean and owners of the copyright in his diaries and papers, for their kind permission to quote from the great man.

All books used are listed in the Bibliography, but of the works beyond Bean, I drew particularly heavily on Monash's *Australian Victories in France in 1918*, Pedersen's *Hamel*, Serle's *Monash* and the histories of the 10 Australian battalions most involved in the battle. Sheffield and Bourne's *Douglas Haig, War Diaries and Letters* was also very valuable. I particularly enjoyed my friend Ross Coulthart's biography of Charles Bean, and appreciated his personal counsel on a couple of esoteric points concerning the friendship of Bean and Keith Murdoch.

In Germany, deep thanks to Carmen Böhm from Bayerisches Armeemuseum (Bavarian Army Museum) in Ingolstadt, who again went way above and beyond the call of duty. Special thanks to the helpful staff at Staats-und Universitätsbibliothek Hamburg, especially Monika Lachnik in the *Medienlieferdienste*, Media Delivery Services department, Christoph Albers at Staatsbibliothek zu Berlin, Preußischer Kulturbesitz, Heidrun Fink at Deutsches Literaturarchiv Marbach, and Lisa Weber at Landesarchiv Baden-Württemberg, Hauptstaatsarchiv Stuttgart.

In the USA I'd like to thank the staff at the National Archives and Records Administration, Washington, DC. In the United Kingdom the Bovington Tank Museum, the Churchill Archives Centre at Cambridge and the Liddell Hart Centre for Military Archives in London were ever helpful to my researchers and I am in their debt.

Just as with all my books for the last decade, I have relied heavily on a great team of researchers, most of whom have worked with me, and substantially with each other, for many years. For this one, my principal researcher was Dr Peter Williams, who worked with me on it from first to last. Beyond his innate and studied knowledge of Hamel, time and again I relied on his wider depth and width of military knowledge and lore to inform my writing – his 40 years of study in the field, not to mention his extensive library of wartime literature, were invaluable. He was a great font of knowledge, a constant guide, and indefatigable in getting to the bottom of things. His role included producing the first draft of the maps and liaising with other researchers: in the UK, the excellent Lieutenant-Colonel Renfrey Pearson of the British Army; in the USA, Eulalia and Jeff Wiltrout, First World War author Ed Lengel, and Gunnar Lopez; in Germany, Sonja Görnitz; and in Australia, Katarina Welborn.

I was also helped by my cousin Angus FitzSimons, a great researcher, who received more than his fair share of our family's intellectual acuity and who I frequently gave tasks to late at night, which I would find wonderfully resolved and back in my in-tray by the time I woke up.

Meanwhile, beyond the aforementioned researchers around the world, who I also warmly thank, I particularly cite *meine liebe Freundin*, Sonja Göernitz, a dual German–Australian citizen, who first started working with me for my book on Tobruk in 2005. Sonja was, as ever, invaluable in bringing the German side of the story to life. Now living back in Germany, she liaised with military archives and libraries and turned up great accounts that she panned for gold (and) then translated into English.

As ever, I also relied on other specialists in their fields, including my wonderfully assiduous long-time researcher at the Australian War Memorial, Glenda Lynch; my dear friend Dr Michael Cooper, for medical history; Peter Finlay on all matters of military aviation; Gregory Blake, for his assistance in all matters to do with firearms and artillery; and Mat McLachlan, of Battlefield Tours, for vetting the whole manuscript and suggesting additional angles and stories. Completing the circle, I also had my brother David go through from first to last – as he does with all of my books – giving his views as to what works and what doesn't.

My thanks also to the descendants of the Australian soldiers Henry Dalziel, Jack Axford, Cliff Geddes and 'Bertie' Englert – who gave me their blessing to use their diaries to strengthen my account, as well as giving me some oral history from their families. I am particularly grateful for the help of David Dalziel, Don Axford, Linda Geddes,

Graham Geddes, Greg Englert and Pam Caddy. Thanks, too, to Paul Stephenson, historian of the Gordon Cricket Club for his help with Cliff Geddes. As to illustrations and maps, I am once more indebted to Jane Macaulay whose great work you will see throughout. I have always been of the view that if a picture is worth a thousand words, then a good map in a book on a military battle must be worth at least two thousand, and this book is all the stronger for Jane's fine work.

Meanwhile, as she has done for yonks, and very nearly two yonks, my dear friend of thirty years at *The Sydney Morning Herald,* Harriet Veitch – now retired – did all the preliminary copyediting, spotting inconsistencies and errors while also untangling hopelessly twisted sentences and eliminating many grammatical errors.

My thanks also, as ever, to my highly skilled editor Deonie Fiford, who has honoured my request that she preserve most of the sometimes odd way I write, while only occasionally insisting that something come out because it just doesn't work.

I am grateful, as ever, to my friend and publisher, Matthew Kelly of Hachette, who I have worked with many times over the last three decades, and who was enthusiastic and supportive throughout, always giving great guidance.

Peter FitzSimons
Neutral Bay, Sydney
12 August 2017

The only general of creative originality produced by the First World War.[1]

A. J. P. Taylor, writing in 1963 on Sir John Monash

A perfected modern battle plan is like nothing so much as a score for a musical composition, where the various arms and units are the instruments, and the tasks they perform are their respective musical phrases. Each individual unit must make its entry precisely at the proper moment and play its phrase in the general harmony.[2]

General Sir John Monash, *Australian Victories in France in 1918*

The Australians, die australischen, *are very quick and cunning . . . They creep up in the night like cats to our trenches so that we don't notice them. Last night they were in our trench and killed two men and dragged one away with them.*[3]

German soldier's letter to his mother dated 5 May 1918

DRAMATIS PERSONAE

British Military
Field Marshal Douglas Haig, Commander of the British Expeditionary Force.
General William Birdwood, Commander of Australian Corps.
General Henry Rawlinson, Commander of the Fourth Army.
General Herbert Lawrence, Haig's Chief of Staff.

Australians
Prime Minister Billy Hughes.
Senator George Pearce, Minister for Defence.
Hannah Victoria Monash, nee *Moss*, 'Vic' was married to John Monash in 1891.
General John Monash, Commander of 3rd Australian Division, who became Commander of the Australian Corps.
General Sir Cyril Brudenell White, Chief of Staff to General Birdwood.
Brigadier Harold 'Pompey' Elliott, Commander of 15th Australian Brigade.
Captain Charles Bean, Official War Correspondent to the Australian Imperial Force.
Keith Murdoch, journalist, Managing Editor of the London cable service for the *Sydney Sun* and the *Melbourne Herald*.
Captain Lawrence Wackett, No. 3 Squadron, Australian Flying Corps, 22 years old.
Private Henry Dalziel, 15th Australian Infantry Battalion, civilian profession: railway operator, 25 years old.

Corporal Jack Axford, 16th Australian Infantry Battalion, civilian profession: labourer, 24 years old.

Corporal Cliff Geddes, 13th Australian Infantry Battalion, civilian profession: bank clerk, 30 years old.

Corporal Frank Shaw, 43rd Australian Infantry Battalion, civilian profession: farmer, 22 years old.

Americans

General John 'Black Jack' Pershing, Commander of the American Expeditionary Force.

General George Read, Commander of II US Corps.

Corporal Henry Zyburt, 131st Regiment, attached to 43rd Battalion.

Corporal Thomas Pope, 131st Regiment.

Sergeant Walter Corning, 131st Regiment.

French Political and Military

Georges Clemenceau, Prime Minister.

Field Marshal Ferdinand Foch, Supreme Commander of all the Allied forces on the Western Front.

A REPRISE OF AMERICA ENTERING THE GREAT WAR

7 May 1915, off the coast of Ireland, the *Lusitania* mania begins
Sehrohr hoch. Up periscope.

There it is!

On this sunny early afternoon, just 11 miles off the Old Head of Kinsale on the coast of Ireland, *Kapitänleutnant* Walther Schwieger, the 30-year-old commander of the German U-boat *U-20* – a man of notably calculating and ruthless disposition – can see the most extraordinary vessel. It is the *Lusitania*, a British cruiser that is the mightiest of Cunard's ocean liners. Due to berth at Liverpool tonight, on her way from New York on her 202nd crossing of the Atlantic, laden with meat, medical supplies, copper, oil, machinery and also, Schwieger suspects – correctly – secreted war *matériel*. He knows she would boast about 700 crew, and be carrying,[1] perhaps 1300[2] passengers. She's a 32,000-ton beauty, 786 feet long, with engines of 68,000 horsepower that are pushing her gracefully through the water at some 21 knots – and not for nothing is she the current holder of the fastest Atlantic crossing at just four days, 16 hours and 40 minutes.

But can he *actually* fire at least one of the nine torpedoes the *U-20* is carrying, through one of its four torpedo tubes, two in the bow and two in the stern, at a ship filled with innocent humanity?

He can.

500 metres . . . 400 metres . . . 350 metres . . . 325 metres . . .

'Three hundred metres,' *Kapitänleutnant* Schwieger keeps calling off the distance calmly. 'Standby . . . standby . . . fire bow torpedo.'

On board the U-boat, all is silent bar the humming of the engines, as everyone in the submarine waits for the result. Suddenly, it is as if two giant cymbals have struck on both sides of their vessel, making everything shake!

Bullseye.

The torpedo has hit the *Lusitania* just below the bridge on the starboard side, and instantly explodes, blowing an enormous hole in her hull. Most catastrophically, that first explosion causes a second, even bigger, one as the ship's boiler blows – and possibly even detonates the 175 tons of munitions the ship is secretly carrying. Within 30 seconds the ship is listing badly to starboard as tons of water rush into her shattered hull, while also sinking bow first.

Within minutes, and with one last blast of steam, the *Lusitania* heads straight to the ocean floor.

Satisfied, *Kapitänleutnant* Walther Schwieger gives the orders.

'*Auf 24 Meter tauchen!*'

'Dive to 24 metres.'[3]

●

In the Oval Office in Washington, just six hours later, President Woodrow Wilson is having a cup of tea when he is handed an urgent telegram that has been sent by American Ambassador Walter Page, in London: 'The Lusitania was torpedoed off the Irish coast and sank in half an hour. No news yet of passengers.'[4]

Ashen-faced, though still calm, Wilson calls for more details as they come to hand, and the broad contours of the catastrophe are soon apparent. For the preliminary estimates are devastating. Over a thousand of the 2000 souls on board are thought to have died, and over 100 of them are Americans.

●

Despite the outrage, for the moment America remains out of a war that continues to set new and appalling records of carnage. From February to November 1916, the Battle of Verdun would engage three million combatants, of whom one million are killed or wounded. In a separate action, on 1 July 1916, the Battle of the Somme was launched – as British forces, with a French contribution, totalling over a million men, attempt to break through the strong German trench system east of Albert, in a campaign that would last four months. At campaign's end, the British and French had suffered 600,000 casualties with 200,000 of them killed, while the Germans, similarly, had 500,000 casualties for 180,000 dead.

All for what?

The border of the Western Front – a 450-mile complex of trenches, stretching from Nieuport on the English Channel in Belgium, across the north and east of France, to the Swiss border, with four million men on each side defending it – had moved no more than 40 miles either way since September 1914, in the first months of the war. In most places it *hadn't moved at all*, as an otherwise unstoppable force met an immovable object, and the most tangible result apparent at the time had been the shedding of oceans of blood . . .

•

The final straw for America came on 19 March 1917.

Mr President? We regret to inform you that another three American ships, *Illinois, City of Memphis* and *Vigilancia*, have been sunk by German U-boats. No fewer than 14,500 tons of shipping is now at the bottom of the Atlantic, and 15 further American lives have been lost.

President Wilson sank back into his seat. This was the end then. After everything he had done to keep America out of this dreadful war, Germany was now forcing his hand. There was no option but to go to war.

It would take over a fortnight from this point, but Congress finally agreed, and before lunchtime on Good Friday, 6 April, President Wilson is informed that the War Resolution, requiring only his signature to become valid, is on its way to the White House.

'Stand by me, Edith,' he says to his wife, after she hands him the gold pen he had recently given her as a gift.

Clenching his jaw, Wilson affixed his florid signature, and rose.

'In an instant, wireless operators were transmitting the news to the world. For only the fourth time, the United States of America had declared war on a foreign nation.'[5]

Ultimately, however, the German leadership was not *too* alarmed. It was one thing for faraway America to declare war on them, but quite another for America to raise an army, train it, and transport it across the ocean through waters controlled by the U-boats. All that will take at least 18 months.

The tone is set by Admiral Müller, the friend and senior advisor to the Kaiser, who calmly noted in his diary on the day: 'News from America that Wilson has carried his proclamation of a state of war through the Senate and the Congress. So we are actually at war with the United States. No one can say where this will lead, but we hope that the U-boat campaign will bring about the end of the war in Europe before America can take a serious hand.'[6]

Yes, that is the key. They must finish the war before the Americans can arrive in force.

And they try, they really try, and all the harder when the U-boat campaign fails to end the war, and so they must rely on their army . . .

On 21 March 1918, the *Kaiserschlacht*, the war for *der Kaiser*, is launched, with no fewer than one million German soldiers going over the top against the British forces, who have their backs to the French coast, defending the Channel ports and the key railway hub and supply town of Amiens, just ten miles to the west. And if the Germans can't get to Amiens, they should be able to at least destroy it, if they can get their artillery perched atop Villers-Bretonneux.

Now, though advances had been initially spectacular as the exhausted and overwhelmed British forces had crumbled and withdrawn, the Australians had been sent for and thrown into the line.

In the ensuing six weeks, the Diggers fought 12 pitched battles against the Germans and won – let's see – all 12.

General Ewen George Sinclair-Maclagan's 4th Division had held the line at Dernancourt, while General Sir John Monash's 3rd Division stopped the Germans cold on Morlancourt Ridge, between the Ancre and the Somme, and then south of the Somme there were two extraordinary Australian victories which had saved Villers-Bretonneux, the last on Anzac Day 1918.

For the moment Fritz had been halted, and the crisis had passed.

But how long would it be before the Germans attacked again?

CHAPTER ONE

MONASH MANOEUVRES

[Haig] was certainly keen to bring on talent. Some highly competent men benefited from his patronage, such as Byng . . . and John Monash. Haig thought little of Birdwood as a general, and [Birdie's] promotion to command [the] Fifth Army in 1918 may have owed something to Haig's desire to promote Monash to command the Australian Corps.[1]

Gary Sheffield, *The Chief: Douglas Haig and the British Army*

We do not want Australia represented by men mainly because of their ability, natural and in-born among Jews, to push themselves . . .[2]

Charles Bean

We relieved the Australians. Loose was the word that seemed to fit these troops. Physically strong but loosely built in contrast to our stockier types, looser in the outer show of discipline, yet with an instinct for battle, brilliantly led by the ablest soldier of the war, General Monash. It is no surprise that the enemy had rather be anywhere else in the world than facing the Anzacs.[3]

Captain Anthony Eden, King's Royal Rifle Corps, later to be UK Prime Minister 1955–1957

Early May 1918, the Western Front, a digger diarises, a piano is poached

Just as there is a calm before the storm, a trough before a wave, so too is there a lull after the storm is over, a serenity of sorts after the last receding rumble of the major battle has gone, leaving only the recurring echoes.

Such is the situation for the Australian forces, in the first days of May 1918, in France. For, oh, what a battle the *Kaiserschlacht* had been, and how well the Australians had done! But it had come at a huge cost: 12,000 casualties. For the moment the Australians must lick their wounds, rebuild their forces, and wait while Berlin works out what to do next. Given that the Germans retain a large reserve of troops, there is every chance that they will launch once more and the only questions are when, and where? As ever, the most likely answers are 'soon', and 'at Amiens or Paris'.

Across the Australian Corps it is really only General Sir John Monash's 3rd Division who, restless for more action, continue to push their line forward.

'The Third Division had had enough of stationary warfare, and the troops were athirst for adventure,' Monash would later recount. 'They were tired of raids, which mean a mere incursion into enemy territory, and a subsequent withdrawal, after doing as much damage as possible. Accordingly I resolved to embark on a series of minor battles, designed not merely to capture prisoners and machine guns, but also to hold onto the ground gained.'[4]

Typically of Monash-organised excursions, they go well, with four small battles between 30 April and 7 May yielding several hundred prisoners who 'impart a mass of valuable information',[5] numerous machine guns, and a net mile of gained territory!

'During the last three days,' Field Marshal Haig admiringly records in his diary after the last successful raid, '[the Australian 3rd Division] advanced their front about a mile . . . The ground gained was twice as much as they had taken at Messines last June, and they had done it with very small losses; some 15 killed and 80 wounded; and they had taken nearly 300 prisoners.'[6]

There is only one problem. The further Monash's men push the Germans back to the east, in their positions just north of the Somme, the more it exposes their right flank to the Germans on the south.

'I was in possession of much the higher ground,' Monash would recount, 'and was able to look down, almost as upon a map, on to the enemy in the Hamel basin, yet I was beginning to feel very seriously the inconvenience of having, square on my flank, such excellent concealed artillery positions as . . . Hamel Woods.'[7]

The obvious solution – and Monash attempts to persuade the Australian Corps Commander, General Sir William Birdwood, to do it – is to have the Corps attack south of the Somme as well, and take the village of Hamel and the basin it is positioned in. Alas, it is decided that for the moment the Australian forces there need more time to recover from their exertions of the previous six weeks.

At least, while the bulk of Diggers wait for the next move to be made, they are in a fine part of the world to be so waiting, with none appreciating it more than the gnarled veterans among them.

Training in Cairo they'd been in the blistering deserts. At Gallipoli they had been in bloody trenches. For two years on the Western Front they'd lived like moles in bloody, muddy trenches, *stormed at with shot and shell* . . . and *now*? Now, it is springtime in France! After their heroic efforts at Villers-Bretonneux and the subsequent German retreat, things are relatively quiet, as the Australian task is merely to hold the Western Front defending the key town of Amiens.

It places them in one of the most picturesque parts of France, a dreamy patchwork of wheat and maize fields, sheep and cattle paddocks, abandoned small villages with cobblestone streets . . . and many cellars still stocked with wine.

Yes, life does offer better things, but not for an Australian soldier it doesn't. There is even a bit of shooting to be done, to keep them interested, and therein lies a tale.

For after the Germans' failed attempt to take Amiens, the most forward elements of the German Army have come to a halt at the point where their offensive force has been equalled by defensive resistance. It means that rather than holding a well-thought-out, superbly engineered major system of built-up trenches, the exhausted Germans have simply dug in the best they can in the chalky soil, wherever they can, as they work out their next move. They no longer hold their own line with a combination of concrete pill-boxes, dugouts, rolls of barbed wire and carefully positioned machine-gun posts that can deliver devastating fire on any intruder within 400 yards. Instead they occupy a series of non-continuous trenches, with dangerous gaps between, guarded by rolls of barbed wire here and there, and machine-gun posts scattered sporadically rather than bristling from every part.

And there is no effort to strengthen their line! This is, in part, a measure of the Germans' exhaustion and diminished resources, and also because their commander, Erich Ludendorff, has forbidden such consolidation on the reckoning they must keep the Allies guessing about whether they intend to advance once more, stay, or retreat.

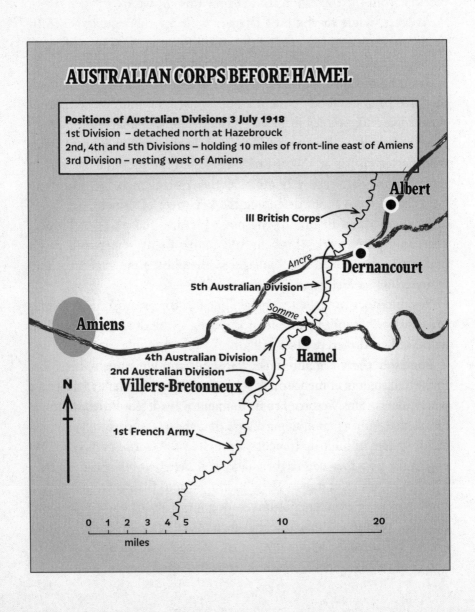

AUSTRALIAN CORPS BEFORE HAMEL

Positions of Australian Divisions 3 July 1918
1st Division – detached north at Hazebrouck
2nd, 4th and 5th Divisions – holding 10 miles of front-line east of Amiens
3rd Division – resting west of Amiens

Albert

III British Corps

Ancre

Dernancourt

5th Australian Division

Somme

Amiens

4th Australian Division

Hamel

2nd Australian Division

Villers-Bretonneux

N

1st French Army

0 1 2 3 4 5   10   20

miles

Hence, what the Australians are up to now – holding the ten miles of the Western Front that they have just so wonderfully held over the last six weeks, with three Divisions in the front-line trenches at any time, and one Division in reserve for two weeks at a time before rotating. Far and away the most important part of the line they are holding is that which lies in front of the French town of Amiens, stretching from the River Somme, to the Roman Road, a cobblestoned thoroughfare – first built by the Romans nearly two millennia earlier – which goes east from Villers-Bretonneux to Saint Quentin. From atop the highest point of the Australian section – Hill 104, just 3000 yards back from the front-lines – you can see the full gloriousness of the French countryside, the rich mosaic of ancient villages, even more ancient farmlands boasting clover and wheat fields, and out to the left the timeless Somme, in a marshy valley winding its majestic way through the dreamy landscape. Ah, and of course, from here you can look straight across to German-held territory, including a dangerous bulge in their line around the village of Hamel and, just behind it, the hill of Wolfsberg, nearly as high as Hill 104 and covered with German observers watching them in turn.

They'll keep.

For now, the tone is set by a few sentences in the diary of one Australian soldier occupying his trenches in this early part of May.

'I wonder if I'll ever see Australia again,' he writes. 'This life seems so unreal at times and one can see no end of the war in sight. The wood in front of us looks so beautiful in the sunlight and life seems so good, yet there is death in the . . . shells and whistling bullets.'[8]

Even though in comparison to what these men have lately known, it is all quiet on the Western Front, in many ways it is a little *too* quiet.

So quiet, in fact, if you cock your ear to the wind right now, you will hear something extraordinary.

For, yes, now, in the area a mile or so back from those front-line trenches, what is this that the Diggers have dragged out of an abandoned chateau, put on a 'shell-torn cart' and dragged back here to the Diggers' dugout? Why, it is a grand piano! A huge one. A *grand* grand piano.

Well, yes, it had been found midst 'sheets of music . . . strewn all over the floor, pictures & costly ornaments broken by shell fire, lovely cushioned chairs broken', and has taken a bit of a hit, suffering '4 shrapnel holes in the woodwork'.⁹ But while the chateau itself looked fine from a distance and was ruined up close . . . this, *this* is quite the reverse!

For now look.

Up steps a Digger with intent, and with the grand theatricality of the maestro he maybe once was, his fingers stretching skywards before gliding downward, he starts to play.

And play, and play, and *play!* See his fingers flow over the keyboard with impossible speed. Hear the music float out over the bloody trenches that serve as ugly slashes through the fields of dandelions, daisies and daffodils, and watch what happens now.

For as his chords float forth, and the battered piano delivers a pitch-perfect performance, heads start to bob up in yonder trenches. The bloke on latrine duty throws down his shovel, and walks on over. Passing platoons stop their weapons check and gather round. The bloke hauling the mess-cart stops, and comes on over. Diggers in dugouts come on out, like moles from a hole after the winter is over, and springtime has arrived. A crowd of mud-men gathers around the messy maestro, as still he keeps on playing.

Is it Brahms? Beethoven? Liszt? Mozart? Chopin? One of them German or Austrian coves, anyway?

Buggered if they know, most of them. But they know the Digger can play and play extraordinarily well, as the birds sing, and bombs burst in the distance.

A passing English major is so impressed, he asks will they sell the piano.

No.

Can the Germans in their trenches over yonder hear it, too?

They hope so. For they, too, must surely say, Play on, young man, play on. *Das ist gute Musik!*

Still the Digger does not look up, transported to a place far away, just as they all are, magically transported to a place where men aren't set on killing each other, where you can see your families, and go out on a Saturday night with your best girl, and the following day have Sunday roast with Mum and Dad and Auntie Dot. Where you can go to bed every night, with full confidence that you will see the sunrise.

Oh, play, Digger, play, as these Australians far from home soak up every note, many of them luxuriating in the finest silk panties beneath their muddy strides, their luscious drawers purloined from the drawers of Madame who had left yonder chateau a few days before. One of them stands there dressed for a joke as a combination of a fine French gentleman *and* lady with 'a tall black hat & white lace parasol'[10] that he has also 'souvenired', as the Australians are pleased to call looting.

'Lor' isn't it funny,' one Digger notes admiringly in his diary of his brothers-in-arms. 'They take nothing, not even war, seriously, though in the trenches Fritz learns what they are made of.'[11]

And yet while it is one thing to be such brothers-in-arms and feel that deep bond that comes with fighting for your life and the man beside you, while he does the same for you . . . it is quite another when your brothers-in-arms are your *actual* brothers, flesh of your flesh, blood of your blood, spirit of your spirit.

The Geddes brothers of the 13th Battalion are a case in point, and the middle one, Cliff, is right here, right now, soaking up the music. Originally from Warialda, up Moree way, the brothers Geddes – 35-year-old Sergeant Aubrey Geddes, 30-year-old Corporal Cliff Geddes and 24-year-old Sapper Stanley Geddes – had all been bank clerks before enlisting, and have been in the thick of the heavy fighting ever since. Aubrey, known as 'Boo' to the family, is with B Company of the 13th Battalion, while Cliff is with D Company of the same, and Stanley is with Brigadier Pompey Elliott's 15th Brigade, serving with the 15th Company Field Engineers.

Like his brothers, Cliff – a distinguished looking fellow, who is neat, as Diggers go, and careful with his presentation, just as he had been raised – is dead keen to finish this damn war, and get home as soon as possible. Like them all, he is proud of Australia's accomplishments in these parts, but a little pissed off that so often the Australians seem to be on their Pat Malone when the heavy lifting is to be done against Fritz.

'It was a great performance of our Australian lads to drive Fritz out of this town of Villers Bretonneux,' Cliff writes in his diary this evening. 'Lately it seems always a case of the Pommies losing a position, & our chaps holding Fritz, or having to win back what the Pommies lost.'[12]

And it is dangerous, make no mistake. A bloke could be killed at any moment. Oddly, Cliff worries more about his brothers – particularly Boo even though he is in the same Battalion – than himself, but that is just the way it is.

'Haven't seen Boo since Monday night, trust he's OK, they are not getting the shells in the front line we are back here, & if there's no hop over, I think he's pretty right, though one never knows what minute he'll be hit at this game.'[13]

The two key questions that a lot of the Diggers want answered right now are: firstly, what will the Germans do next?; and secondly, when will the bloody Yanks dip *their* bloody oars in?

You see, it seems clear that the Germans are girding their iron loins for their next attack, which will be a big one, there can be no doubt. Since Russia pulled out of the war after the Bolsheviks took over late the previous year, German forces previously on the Eastern Front have been flooding into France at the rate of 20,000 a week, and as the *Kaiserschlacht* showed, Germany is eager to win the war before the weight of the Americans, who, in turn, are now flooding into France at the rate of 60,000 a week, can be felt.

But while the Germans arriving are fighting, the bloody Yanks aren't and it is a real problem for those, like the Australians, who are holding the line.

Typical is the view of the British officer, Captain Hubert Essame of the 8th Division, who had recently fought by the side of the Australians as they re-took Villers-Bretonneux. His experience has convinced him that the Australian troops are the best in the war. But great boon that they are to the exhausted British forces, they will not be remotely enough.

'A year had now passed since the Americans had entered the war,' Essame would note, 'and yet, apart from four good divisions in quiet sectors on the French front, they had contributed virtually nothing to the death struggle . . .'[14]

•

But, let's get to grips.

How to find out exactly what the enemy intends to do now?

Obviously, grab a few and ask them!

For the word has gone out to the front-line Australian Battalions that 'talkative *Boche*'[15] are needed and a series of raids must be conducted on enemy lines to find the men they want. Every Fritz they capture builds more information as the Australians work out what Division they are from, how long they have been there, what activities they have been engaged in, how many troops they saw assembling in rear areas, and so forth. It will enable HQ to build a real picture of what Fritz is up to, and the Diggers are eager to hop to it. For to have the Squareheads so close, and so poorly defended, really does present an opportunity too good to miss, and so the Diggers embark on what they call 'peaceful penetration'. (Clearly, the phrase has an etymological root that grows on the Allied side of the line, because on the German side, 'peaceful' it is not.)

Night after night, as part of this policy of peaceful penetration, groups of Diggers venture forth across No Man's Land. Small patrols rather than large-scale attacks, they probe rather than assault, raid on the fly rather than seek to occupy permanently, dice delicately rather than slice savagely, take prisoners for interrogation – looking for 'talkative *Boche*'[16] just like HQ has been requesting – rather than try to wipe out entire battalions, infiltrate enemy posts by slipping between them before attacking from behind, rather than launch full-on frontal charges.

'The *Boche* is no match,' the 15th Brigade's esteemed Commanding Officer, Brigadier Pompey Elliott, would note, 'when it comes to personal combat. The Intelligence reports of these patrol encounters are joyful reading. I feel like going out myself for a rough and tumble, for the sport seems harmless for us as chasing and rounding up barn door fowls.'[17]

For all that, it really does require derring-do, the desire to hit hard and get out quickly, the capacity to quickly grab whatever opportunities present themselves.

Look here, for example, as on this sweltering May morning right in front of the Australian 18th Battalion's position near Morlancourt, one of the sentries on duty with the Company of Lieutenant Alex Irvine[18] has noticed something interesting.

'When [Fritz] is awake,' he tells Irvine, 'he's always chucking bottles and tins out of his post. There hasn't been one come over the parapet for two hours now.'[19]

And it is true that this usually noisy German machine-gun post has fallen remarkably silent. Say, you don't suppose that, after an exhausting night on the lookout for our usual night-time raids, Fritz is having a bit of a kip, do you?

Risking showing his head to have a 'dekko' above the Australian parapet, Lieutenant Irvine can't help but notice that a volley of shots does *not* ring out. So he rises up fully, his flesh tingling, ready to dive back down at the first sign that the Germans are still at their post. Still nothing.

And so he ducks back down, rouses his own platoon and in short order the whole lot of them, 18 Australian soldiers strong, are in a mad dash across No Man's Land! Their Australian compatriots in the front-lines watch them go with awe, ready to give heavy covering fire if the German machine-gun post suddenly starts spitting death. And yet, *still* there is nothing!

The Australians in the front-lines wait, not knowing what might be about to happen.

There.

No more than ten minutes later, the raiding party under Lieutenant Irvine re-emerges, this time with a couple of dozen sleepy German prisoners – and they have the German *Maschinengewehr 08* machine gun in tow!

•

No Divisional commander pushes such raids more than Monash, for they fit neatly into his whole military philosophy: 'A passive defence involved just as great an average daily wastage of fighting strength as active offensive operations, if well planned and executed.'[20]

So why not attack?

'Feed your troops on victory,'[21] is Monash's favourite maxim, and he would later expand upon the theme:

'The aim and end of all the effort and of all the heavy sacrifices of the Australian nation was victory in the field. Nothing that could be done would lead more swiftly and more directly to its fulfilment than an energetic offensive policy. The troops themselves recognised this. They learned to believe, because of success heaped upon success, that they were invincible. They were right, and I believe that I was right in shaping a course which would give them the opportunity of proving it.'[22]

Not for Monash keeping his troops in safe harbours. He wants them out there, in the field, looking for opportunities, getting used to the feeling of advancing, growing in self-confidence, in trust of each other, in belief that nothing could stop them – and accordingly he now insists on an 'energetic offensive policy'. Lethargy must give way to action.

Of course, the frequency of such raids, and their success – inevitably pushing the German lines back – is noted.

Haig is not remotely surprised that, once again, it is the 3rd Division doing so well, for he has long noted that their Commanding Officer, General Sir John Monash[23] – just recently on 1 January 1918, made Knight Commander of the Order of the Bath – is 'a clear headed, determined commander'.[24] When they had first met, back in December 1916, Haig had inspected the 3rd Division as they marched past in heavy mud, 'neath pouring rain, and at march's end Haig had put his arm around Monash's shoulder and said with entirely uncharacteristic warmth: 'You have a very fine division. I wish you all sorts of good luck, old man.'[25]*

Everything he has witnessed since of Monash's work with the 3rd Division has confirmed this opinion, through all the triumphs of Messines, Passchendaele and Morlancourt, Monash's men had been to the fore, executing extraordinarily well organised battles. Haig had been so impressed that in September of the previous year he had invited Monash to dine with him, in the company of GHQ Chief of Staff and Deputy Chief of Staff – an extremely rare honour for a mere Divisional Commander – and shortly thereafter Haig had told the influential Australian journalist Keith Murdoch that it was his intention 'that Monash should get an army corps'.[27]

---

* Speaking of 'old man', that is exactly the way Monash views the British commander himself, noting in a letter the same day, that 'Douglas Haig looked grey and old'.[26] But he is very pleased with Haig's commendation for all that.

For his part, Monash, while gratified by the Commander-in-Chief's clear appreciation of his worth, is quietly underwhelmed by this most senior British officer.

'Haig,' he would later note, 'was, technically speaking, quite out of his depth in regard to the minutiae of the immense resources which were placed in his hands to wield. I was, at first, quite dismayed to find that he obviously did not know the composition in detail of his own formations . . .'[28]

(Charles Bean would agree that much of the modern ways of warfare had passed Field Marshal Haig by at this stage, noting, 'I suppose Haig is one of those British soldiers – old-fashioned simple gentlemen to the backbone – who abide till their death in the beliefs which they learnt at their mother's knee.'[29])

The point remains, however. In the here and now, Field Marshal Haig has had his eye on the Australian General and his Division for some time. Now, here they are again, these extraordinary Australians seemingly effortlessly pushing the Germans back. The Germans themselves, of course, *more* than notice the Australian successes.

'The enemy, who has grown up in the Australian bush,' a German soldier informs the papers at home, 'wriggles to our posts with great dexterity from flank and rear in the high crops in order to overwhelm them. It has often happened that complete pickets [of our soldiers] have disappeared from the forward line without trace.'[30]

The Australian soldiers are also *hugely* encouraged when one of their disconsolate newly taken German prisoners says to them in remarkably good English: 'You bloody Australians, when you are in the line you keep us on pins and needles; we never know when you are coming over.'[31]

All up, they are an impressive bunch these Australians, and not just because of their recent derring-do and sheer grit in successfully defending Villers-Bretonneux and Amiens. No, it's the way they carry themselves, the confidence they project.

What *is* it?

Charles Bean thinks he has it.

'The sergeants,' he chronicles proudly, 'are every one of them strong men who give whatever orders are given in the yard in a downright voice which admits no hesitancy. The officers move in the crowd with absolute confidence . . . a weak man, or an undetermined man would have no chance at all of having authority in that crowd. The officers are the sergeants of last year, and the sergeants are officers in embryo; and the corporals are budding sergeants.'[32]

That might be it?

There is a certain *classlessness* about them. Now, in the Australian forces, no-one becomes an officer and rises through the ranks because of the school they went to, or because of who they know in the higher tiers of the hierarchy. No, this far into the war the only way to become an Australian officer is to start on the bottom tier as a Private, and work your way up from there, rising on the respect of both the men around you and your immediate superiors. The idea of a good officer, under Monash, is not to be what the men call a 'Brasso King', and put all your energy into making sure your men are spick and span, and shine all the time – but to focus on what counts, fighting well, and often!

All up, they are an experienced mob, with just over half of the infantry and a little under three quarters of the artillery having served on the Western Front since 1916, and they know what they are doing. The only real problem is . . . there are just not quite enough of them.

In the course of their last battles in the *Kaiserschlacht*, the Australian Corps had lost 12,000 men in casualties, a number which had not been remotely replaced by 'reinstoushments', as the Diggers call[33] those scattered few 'deep thinkers' who have at last arrived from home to bolster their dwindling numbers. But nearly all mature Australians who had wanted to volunteer for the war have already done so. In 1915, 165,000 volunteered, but in the first third of 1918 only 12,000. The best way forward thus, to rebuild the Corps back to full strength, is to keep the casualty rate low.

•

In the wake of the cataclysmic *Kaiserschlacht* battle – with so many forces battered, no few shattered, some officers discredited, some with minds broken – it is inevitable that there be a movement of respected officers to units requiring a kick up the backside. One of those tagged to be promoted, to take over and rebuild the all but destroyed Fifth Army, is General William Birdwood, the Englishman who has been commanding the Australian forces since the days of Gallipoli and through the trials and tribulations, tragedies and triumphs of the Western Front.

But with 'Birdie' due to leave within weeks, just who will take his place?

The only thing certain is that it will at last be an Australian officer, with the Australian government now insisting that, for the first time in the Great War, an Australian be appointed to command his fellow Australians. The days of automatically assuming that an English officer would be better suited for the role are gone.

There are two likely candidates.

Firstly there is General John Monash, the Commanding Officer of the 3rd Division which had done so well since coming into the line in November 1916 – specifically in the battles of Messines, Passchendaele and Morlancourt.

There is no doubt that Monash's 3rd Division is the best performing of the Australian Corps, and that Monash is of a different mould from most Australian Generals. Quietly spoken, urbane, he had been a highly accomplished engineer before the war, with such iconic Victorian constructions as the Anderson Street Bridge across the Yarra River and the Fyansford Bridge at Geelong to his credit – among over 40 large bridges he had overseen the construction of, not to mention Melbourne's Outer Railway Line and the iconic Melbourne Wool Exchange.

A fluent German speaker with degrees in arts and law, the Jewish intellectual had been born and raised in Jerilderie, a town that had first come to wider fame when the Kelly Gang had laid siege to it for two days in early February 1879. The then 14-year-old John Monash had been present at the time, on holidays from Scotch College in Melbourne, and had briefly talked to Ned Kelly. As a matter of fact, he would later be quoted as saying not only was the bushranger the most impressive man he'd ever met, but that, 'a Sunday school superintendent couldn't have given me better advice as to human conduct'.[34] Certainly, as a leader of men, Monash had always displayed extraordinary skill ever afterwards, bringing a certain cerebral quality to his military planning – a superlative attention to *detail* – which has seen his plans proceed like smoothly oiled juggernauts sweeping all before them, rather than the mobile mincing machines used by other Generals. Monash's men know that he values their lives, and they value him in turn.

The other candidate is General Sir Cyril Brudenell Bingham White, the highly regarded long-time Chief of Staff of General Birdwood, who has many achievements under his name in the service of the Australian Army, none greater than being the principal architect of the brilliant evacuation of Gallipoli, whereby 36,000 ANZACs had been able to steal away in under a week, including 10,000 soldiers on the final night – all without losing a man.

The most favoured of the two to get the job is General Monash, and his admirers include Brudenell White himself, who will have no problems if Monash succeeds – but there are several notable dissenters, most particularly among such journalists as Australia's first official War Artist, Will Dyson, and Charles Bean himself.

For Monash, Dyson tells Bean, has 'the advertising strength which insists on thrusting or insinuating itself into the front rank. Monash will get there – he must get there all the time on account of the qualities of his race: the Jew will always get there.'[35]

•

On the face of it, what Field Marshal Haig would really like to do is precisely what the French would like to do, too: unleash the Americans. After America had declared war on Germany in April 1917, the first of the American troops had arrived in Europe in June, and as of now there are some one million American soldiers here! But they are *yet* to fight. Oh, they'd been involved in one or two small operations, but as yet they had refused to take part in any large-scale offensive operation. Their Commanding Officer, General John 'Black Jack' Pershing, insists his army is not only not yet ready to fight, but he really doesn't want them thrown into the war until 1919, the year he expects the war to be won. For while there are currently 16 US Divisions in France, there are now eight more arriving *every month*, at a rate of 10,000 men every day, and by early 1919 the American Army would be larger than Britain's. So why attack now, when in just six months he would have an unstoppable force of two million American soldiers? In the meantime, he does *not* want bits and pieces of his forces attached to other Allied forces in an effort to get them involved, get them blooded for action, despite the best efforts of the likes of Field Marshal Haig to convince him to do so.

It has been an issue for some time, close to coming to a head.

Back in late December of the previous year, Haig had gone riding with Pershing to press the Americans into action, and Pershing had at least conceded that, 'If the situation becomes critical I am ready to break up American divisions and employ battalions and regiments to fill up your divisions.'[36]

Which was something. The problem had been that even when the Germans had launched their *Kaiserschlacht* in March 1918, shattering the British defences, Pershing had clearly not regarded the situation as critical *enough*, and the day had only been saved by the Australians.

For his part, General Sir Henry Rawlinson of the Fourth Army thinks that, for the moment, it is no great loss.

'The Americans are beginning to arrive in large numbers,' he records in his diary, 'but they sadly lack training and their officers are far from good.'[37]

So, in the absence of other shock troops being available for the fresh fight, Haig must call on the Australians to do the honours.

16 May 1918, Australian Corps HQ, Bertangles, 'a little Birdie' gives Bean news

Charles Bean is never one to give himself airs. He does not throw his weight around as a Captain of the Australian Imperial Force, or – far more significantly – as Australia's Official War Correspondent, a man who holds the reputation of the country's fighting forces in his hands and, specifically, at the ends of his typing fingers. And yet still he could wish, sometimes, that *some* people might regard him with just a tinge of awe. Specifically, on this day he means his driver, 'Boddy', who, while polite to Bean, is positively deferential to every other bloody vehicle on the road!

'Boddy does not drive the car as if I were a major-general,' Bean would confide to his diary. 'He generally waits upon any old lorry, box car, Ford, or Flying Corps tender, or even a steam roller, as if one were a sanitary corporal.'[38]

Irritating at the best of times, when Bean always has so much to do, it is positively frustrating on days like today, when he is about to engage in one of his favourite activities – visiting the highest officers of the Australian Corps HQ in their well-appointed chateau at Bertangles. There, as ever, among the 72 AIF officers and 230 other ranks housed in its gracious confines and nearby, he will have every chance of finding out precisely what the situation is in terms of coming plans, coming battles, casualty rates, numbers of returning wounded expected, as well as seeing the latest air photos taken by the airmen of the mighty No. 3 Squadron, Australian Flying Corps.

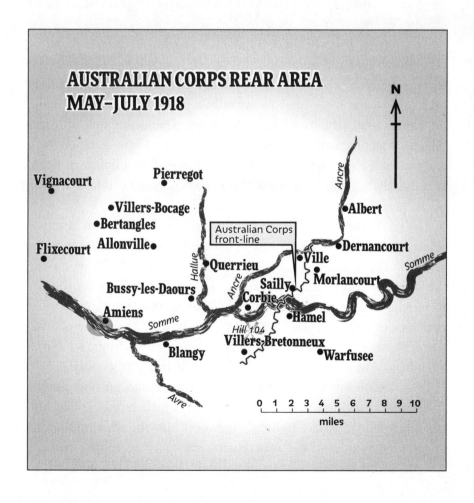

AUSTRALIAN CORPS REAR AREA MAY–JULY 1918

As it happens, Bean is only a short time in this three-storey 1734 masterpiece of French architecture, nestled in minutely manicured grounds, talking to this officer and that, as officious underlings scurry hither and thither, when the Sydneysider hears a clipped English voice summoning him. It can only belong to one person, and sure enough it is him, General Sir William Birdwood, who has heard Bean's dulcet tones, and now asks him to come into his study for a moment, and close the door behind him.

Yes, General?

The two men get on well, and always have. There is a quiet capability about the English General, together with a quite *un*-English informality that has always appealed to Bean, just as it has appealed to the Australian soldiers, who refer to the diminutive 52-year-old as 'good old Birdie'.[39]

And for his part, Birdwood has always admired Bean's blend of professionalism and gumption: his strong work ethic placed at the service of getting the story right, his courage harnessed to regularly take him to the front-lines to actually understand what was going on, rather than rely, as so many 'war correspondents' did, on press releases together with interviews conducted at a safe distance from danger. (Not everyone agrees. Monash is less of an admirer of Bean, very quietly expressing the view that the Sydneysider's style of writing is, 'the apotheosis of banality'.[40])

The relationship between Bean and Birdwood, thus, is an intimacy whereby the General knows he can tell the journalist important pieces of news which will help guide his coverage, without risking having that news appear in the newspapers, until such time as it is officially released. And this news is strong, ol' Bean, so you must lean in close even as our conversation is regularly rumbled by the drone of low-flying planes overhead, heading to and from the aerodrome for No. 3 Squadron, Australian Flying Corps, which is just a mile away.

In this conversation, the previously swirling rumours are now coming in to land as solid fact. And it is not just 'a little birdie' telling him so, it is *the* little Birdie, General Birdwood himself, advising that his job as Commander of the Australian Corps is to be split in two. At the end of the month, Birdwood will take leave of his command, to become Commander of the Fifth Army, elsewhere in France. While he will stay in charge of the whole of the AIF – which includes the Diggers in Palestine and Great Britain – command of the Corps in battle is to be handed to another, and General Birdwood has already written a formal recommendation to Defence Minister George Pearce as to who it should be.

Bean leans closer still.

Obviously, the Commanders of the five Australian Divisions, and Birdwood's own Chief of Staff, General Sir Cyril Brudenell White, are the six candidates. Of these, Birdwood is quick to reject Harold Walker because he is an Englishman, while Ewen Sinclair-Maclagan is a Scot, and in no small way the whole point of this exercise – as pushed by Prime Minister Billy Hughes himself – is that the Australian Corps will be commanded by an actual Australian. Birdwood also rejects John Gellibrand, the Tasmanian who is notoriously 'sensitive and often difficult',[41] as Bean describes him.

Which means . . .

'White, Hobbs and Monash,' Birdwood had already formally advised the Australian government, 'must all be considered for Corps Commander.'

Now, though General J.J. Talbot Hobbs[42] had done an excellent job with the 5th Division, Birdie is doubtful he is up to running an entire Corps, which leaves White and Monash. Of them all, he knows White's great capacity better than anyone, and would be inclined to advise his promotion if Monash could be passed over.

As Bean recounts in his diary, 'But Monash could not, Birdwood says. He had undoubted ability and success had met his work. Therefore he recommended Monash to command the Corps, White to come with him as Chief of Staff of the 5th Army.'[43]

Quietly, because it simply would not do to show his shock, and extreme disappointment, Bean reels. His worst fears risk being realised.

Monash in charge of the Corps!

His greatest friend, and richest source of information, Brudenell White, to depart with Birdie!

'This is a very great blow,'[44] Bean would confide to his diary, hurt, too, that he had not heard it from his great friend first. And beyond the loss of Brudenell White as a journalistic source, Bean, as an ever more proud and even proprietorial Australian, thinks it quite *improper*.

> That White should leave the Corps is simply to make a misuse of the staff of the AIF. If White has a great value to the British Army he has a greater value to Australia. I have been thinking out the straightest strongest telegram I can [send] to Pearce.[45]

It will have to be good to change things. For the Defence Minister is already in possession of General Birdwood's formal recommendation,

> Of his ability, there can be no possible doubt, nor of his keenness and knowledge . . . I don't think we could in justice overlook in any way his undoubted claims and equally undoubted ability to fill the appointment.[46]

Exactly. However great Brudenell White was as Chief of Staff, he had never actually been a front-line commander, while Monash had been leading men in battle since the days of Gallipoli onwards and had shone from the first, getting ever better as the war had progressed.

Charles Bean takes his leave of Birdwood with much to think about. In some ways, this day was always coming, and, as it happens, he has just been working to *delay* it for the last six months.

For yes, not long after the battle of Passchendaele, Bean had been granted an audience with no less than Field Marshal Douglas Haig, who had himself commented: 'You have some very capable commanders in the Australian force . . . General Monash for example. He is a very capable man. He has made a great success of everything he has touched – a very solid man.'[47]

Knowing that Haig had already suggested to Bean's supremely well connected colleague Keith Murdoch – later described by one of his biographers as Billy Hughes' 'voice . . . in Fleet Street . . . personal publicist, guide-to-the-British-mind, fixer, speech editor and errand boy'[48] – that Monash might be given command of the Australian Corps, Bean had been quick to pounce.

'Yes but if it meant any change in the position of General Birdwood it seems to me it would be a great pity. Gen. Birdwood has an independent position and standing which is of the utmost value to us. The Australians trust him . . .'

'I know General Birdwood's value but it seems to me that Australia should have [an Australian] Corps Commander,' replies Haig.

'Yes, sir, you know we look upon General White as the greatest soldier we have by a long way, we consider him the man whom Australia has produced in this war [. . .] It would be a very great pity if General Birdwood's position were altered – he [knows] Australians as few men [do] . . .'[49]

In desperation, Bean does indeed go through with the extraordinary step of sending a cable to Defence Minister George Pearce – who is also acting Prime Minister in the absence of Hughes – urging him to take steps to ensure that General Brudenell White not be lost to the Corps, as he is 'universally considered greatest Australian soldier'.[50]

The only thing that could be accomplished, however, would be to reverse the decision taken, and give Brudenell White command of the Australian Corps, at the expense of Monash.

Ultimately, however, the only man who can undo the decision, or at least sway the Cabinet to look at it again, is Prime Minister Billy Hughes, who is on the high seas, bound for Great Britain via Canada and the United States. After arriving in Vancouver, he is due to travel to Washington, DC, to meet with President Wilson, before catching a fast ship from New York across the Atlantic, arriving in London in mid-June in time to attend a meeting of the Imperial War Cabinet.

17 May 1918, Fourth Army HQ, Flixecourt, a commander performance

Conversations between Field Marshal Douglas Haig, the Commanding Officer of all British Empire Forces in France, and General Henry Rawlinson, the Commander of the Fourth Army, are not always the easiest. For you see, while there is no doubt Haig is Rawlinson's Commanding Officer, there is likely some doubt on both their parts as to whether indeed Haig is the superior officer.

Either way, there can be little doubt as to which is more modern in his thinking.

Two years earlier, when they had been building up to the opening day of the Battle of the Somme on 1 July 1916, the two had strongly disagreed as to whether it was better to attempt to burst through all the German lines at once, or to concentrate on just shattering the key first line. Haig, typically, preferred they attempt the glorious headline-grabbing breakthrough; Rawlinson would have much preferred his 'bite and hold' tactics – hammering the first line, securing it, and then, and only then, moving forward.

Haig, typically, had insisted on his way prevailing – and had been demonstrably wrong. At the end of a disastrous day, the British forces had made few advances, and had lost almost 20,000 dead and 40,000 wounded. Thereafter, Rawlinson's 'bite and hold' had become the tactic of choice. Yet, despite such things, when they meet they have clearly brought their moustaches from the same outfitter, for they are exactly the same thickness and shape. As ever, it is Haig's moustache that bristles a little menacingly and Rawlinson's that droops a little sadly and tiredly.

On this morning, however, as the two talk at General Rawlinson's HQ at Flixecourt – which would have been a pleasant little village on the western side of Amiens, but for the overpowering smell coming from the local jute-weaving factory – they are in broad agreement.

With the immediate crisis having passed and the *Kaiserschlacht* stalled, it is time to begin planning the next step – attacking the Germans, beginning the push on their lines to break them. Now that the Germans' big attack has been foiled, there is a growing sense of German exhaustion, and even of despair, and the right attack at the right place might just shatter them.

But where should the British make that attack?

'I told Rawlinson,' Haig would recount, 'to begin studying in conjunction with General Marie-Eugene Debeney [commanding the neighbouring French First Army], the question of an attack eastwards from Villers-Bretonneux . . . I gave him details of the scheme.'[51]

A single glance at the map reveals then, the obvious target.

An attack on the German line at Le Hamel?

It makes a lot of sense. Though the Australians had done extraordinarily well to beat off the German attack around Villers-Bretonneux on

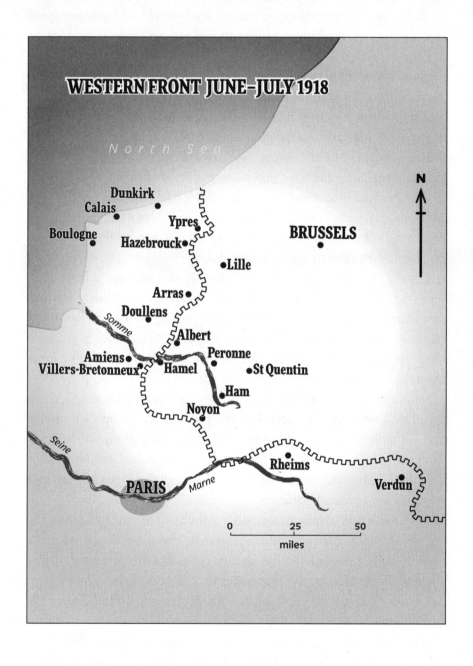

5 April, and then retake the town on 25 April, after the Germans had taken it from the British, in the final analysis Fritz had made one good gain for the day: the bulge in the map represented by their occupation of Hamel, just a mile to the north-east of Villers-Bretonneux and 1500 yards south of the Somme. It was a small red-brick village of just 300 people before the war, positioned in a saddle of land formed between two hills – the 240 foot high Wolfsberg, now held by the Germans, and a lesser hill, a low extension of Hill 104 a mile closer to Villers-Bretonneux, held by the Allies. Now, of course, all the villagers have fled, and the Germans have taken possession of Hamel and converted its many cellars into strongpoints. Taking it back will not be easy, not least because with Wolfsberg towering over it, any force building up before the village risks being spotted by the German artillery observers on high, and pounded out of existence.

Beyond the bulge being merely unsightly on the map, it is troublesome for the fact that it allows the Germans to spy on Allied positions on either side, as well as bringing devastating enfilading fire upon them. Aside from that, if Fritz is building to have another go, then the pointy end of their spear could be Hamel, which is only nine miles from Amiens – still a vital railway junction for the Allies.

So if the Allies can take back Hamel, it would dull the German spear, thus helping to protect Amiens. It would also stop their spying and enfilading fire; force Fritz to reinforce his line along the Somme, weakening his thrust on Paris; and make future Allied assaults on the German line in these parts much easier. A single advance in that spot would bring *myriad* benefits.

Now, when it comes to deciding which forces should make the attack, the most obvious choice would be the Australians, who not only hold that part of the line at this time, but are proven first-rate soldiers. Rawlinson knows that better than anyone, for the Australians have been here, in the post of honour protecting Amiens, since the end of March.

'I feel happier about the general situation, as I now have three brigades of Australians in reserve,' General Rawlinson had noted in his diary six weeks earlier at the height of the *Kaiserschlacht* crisis, 'so I think I shall be able to keep the *Boche* out of Amiens. I am to take over the Australian Corps on the 8th, with a front up to Albert. Hurrah!'[52]

Everything that had happened since had only confirmed his high opinion.

'They are a splendid body of men, and Hobbs and Monash are both very good commanders,' he had noted in his diary. 'They are ready for any emergency, which is comforting.'[53]

Field Marshal Haig could not agree more and, as a matter of fact, is looking forward to once more meeting modern Australian General Monash this afternoon.

First, however, he must make a brief visit to see General Birdwood at the Australian Corps HQ, where he is able to congratulate 'Birdie' on his forthcoming appointment to take over the Fifth Army.

Birdwood is thrilled at the visit, writing in his diary, 'Lovely Day. Very hot. Chief came to see me and was very nice about my becoming army commander, especially about my retaining GOC AIF.'[54]

Still, Field Marshal Haig does not stay long. For the main business of the day awaits, the meeting that he has been looking forward to.

•

As a broad rule, the Australian soldier has rarely impressed in this war when it comes to parade ground presentations. There is just something *about* him, which tends to the slightly slovenly in dress, the lacking in sharpness of salute, the ever so lightly tarnished when it comes to what should be gleaming brass and an extraordinary informality when it comes to interacting with officers.

It has been noticed, often with some envy, by the British soldiers.

'Their total lack of swank of class distinctions among them is most refreshing,' Private Reginald Wilkes, 16th Royal Warwickshires, would record of the Australians he'd come across the month before, near Hébuterne. 'It is fine to hear their officers calling their men by their Christian names. It is very funny to see one of these colonials go up to a young English officer and say "Mate, can you tell us the time, please?" Their conventions and ways of speaking to officers would send some of our old soldiers crazy. It's Tom, Dick and Harry with them, no Sirring and saluting.'[55]

For all that, on this day, the Diggers of the 10th Brigade of the 3rd Australian Division, formed up in a field east of the village of Allonville – just five and a half miles north-east of Amiens – really have made an effort to spruce up the best they can. 'Cos it's not every day is it, cobber, that you get inspected by the Commander of the entire British Expeditionary Force?

And so they stand there at 2 pm, at strict attention, as a convoy of gleaming cars pulls up, and out steps Field Marshal Sir Douglas Haig himself to be greeted warmly by the 3rd Division's Commanding Officer, General Sir John Monash. The two briefly exchange pleasantries, before General Monash introduces Sir Douglas to the Commanding Officer of the 10th Brigade, Brigadier Walter McNicoll – the former headmaster of Geelong High, who looks like exactly that in a military uniform. Monash and McNicoll carefully lead Sir Douglas Haig along the front row of soldiers, as the great man inspects them, pausing occasionally to chat to this soldier or that. Reaching the end, the expectation is that Field Marshal Haig will simply turn back, or go back along the second row, but an old hand to beat all hands at this kind of thing – and knowing that Brigadiers always put their best and brightest in the front rank, with the less impressive men further to the back – the good General promptly heads along one of the lines further back, where he is surprised, and pleased, to see no diminution in the quality and presentation of the soldiers.

Returning to the front with Brigadier McNicoll so the soldiers can do a march past, he is impressed once more, and amazed at just how far the AIF soldiers have come from the early days of the war.

'It was a grand sight,' Haig wrote in his diary that evening. 'Troops marched well, and were well turned out. The transport too was well cleaned and animals well-groomed and in good condition. The Australian is a different individual now to when he first came, both in discipline and smartness. Altogether it was . . . most inspiring . . .'[56]

What impresses him most, however, is Monash.

The more the two talk, the more Field Marshal Haig likes the cut of his jib, his obvious technical expertise, his logical way of thinking, the way he projects a confidence that whatever task he is asked to do, he and his men will be capable of it. Yes, it all confirms an opinion that

Field Marshal Haig had noted down in his diary the previous year, after first meeting him. This really is a man to watch, and support: 'General Monash, [is] in my opinion a clear headed determined commander.'[57]

To have Haig's total support is no small thing, and as a matter of fact the Commander-in-Chief of all His Majesty's forces in Western Europe has even expressed the view to Monash that if the Australians do not put him in charge of the Australian Corps, Haig would put him in charge of one of the *British* Corps.

'Cables have gone to Australia . . .' Monash had already written to his wife, 'to get the approval of the Government to the arrangement, but I do not think that it will affect my appointment to the Corps, because that is a matter on which Sir Douglas Haig will insist on making his own appointment, and I am proud to say that he has selected me.'[58]

Monash knows that to have Haig's support to this extent could even be a trump card to play at a later date, should Monash ever come under pressure from lesser forces.

•

'Brewery Farm' – a place which provides the modern former upon the ancient latter – sits right by the Hallue River on the outskirts of the small village of Querrieu, some seven miles north-east of Amiens, and is a wonderful base for the Allied war correspondents to make their sorties from, and return to.

On this late evening, Charles Bean is sitting alone at a table, gazing out the window and watching the river flow, still stewing over the news he had received from General Birdwood the day before.

Monash? It is just not right and . . .

And after a sudden outcry from the farm dogs, there is something of a commotion in the hallway, as three of his esteemed colleagues – the artist Will Dyson, the photographer Hubert Wilkins and his admired fellow journalist Fred Cutlack – return from what has likely been a well-lubricated dinner . . .

Bean blurts out the news: Birdie is to take command of the Fifth Army, taking White with him, and Birdie is recommending to the Australian government that *Monash* is promoted to take charge of the Australian Corps!

There was immediately a great consternation – war correspondents, artist and photographer sitting back around the table with their caps on the back of their heads discussing what was best to be done.[59]

In essence, their conversation centres on 'the relative merits of White who does not advertise, and Monash who does'.[60]

By evening's end, they are all, as Bean will record, of the one mind. They want White to take command of the Australian Corps.

They want a man who 'left others to appreciate his work, and left it to them whether he was good enough for any high position' . . . [rather than] 'Monash, who would leave no stone unturned and no underground channel untried'.[61]

Charles Bean is not above trying to take matters into his own hands, to actually try to alter the course of events by intervening outside the journalistic domain. Yes, in addition to writing to Pearce, Bean decides he must go to London with Will Dyson to lobby for a man who would never lobby for himself, Brudenell White . . .

Much later, Bean would expand on his reasoning: 'Though a lucid thinker, a wonderful organiser, and accustomed to take endless pains, he [Monash] had not the physical audacity that Australian troops were thought to require in their leaders, and it was for his ability in administration rather than for tactical skill that he was then reputed. Moreover, a few of those who knew both men doubted whether Monash's judgment would be as resistant as White's to the promptings of personal ambition or whether he was as well equipped to overbear a wrongly insistent superior or the strain of a great disaster. They knew that Monash had an almost Napoleonic skill in transmitting the appearance of his capacity, and there was some belief . . . that he had sought his appointment by every means in his power.'[62]

17 May 1918, front-lines, east of Villers-Bretonneux, on the Roman Road, Boo to the Germans

'What a strange existence!'

All day long, Cliff Geddes has been lying at the bottom of his trench. 'There I was with my boots & equipment off, sleeping in the front line, blue sky overhead, bright sunshine, & skylarks singing in the air; &

yet this cursed war goes on month after month, with good men dying daily in hundreds. Though it is so quiet here, we know any minute his guns could open & it would turn to Hell itself.'[63]

Indeed, even as Cliff is lying there, Fritz continues to 'send over those horrible whizz-bangs, which are on you with a "swish" before you know they're coming. They seemed to be just on top of our heads, but hit the edge of the town in rear, am glad he didn't shorten his range by 150 yards.'[64]

This sense that life could end at any moment is not confined to himself. That morning, before dawn, he'd watched his elder brother Boo head out on patrol into No Man's Land and for two whole hours had been on tenterhooks until Boo safely returned and he could breathe again. The very idea of what it would do to their parents if Boo is killed chills his soul as fast as a southerly buster in winter.

•

This is *not* just another cable.

For, coming from Acting Prime Minister and Defence Minister George Pearce, and addressed to General Birdwood, it gives the final imprimatur of official Cabinet approval to the recommendation made by Birdwood a week earlier, that his replacement as Commanding Officer of the Australian Corps be General Sir John Monash:

```
I approve all your recommendations as to appointments
(stop) ... Confirmed by Cabinet 21/5/18 (stop).
```
[65]

There is no stopping it now. General Monash will take over from General Birdwood as Commander-in-Chief of the Australian Corps before the end of the month.

Late May 1918, Washington, DC, not so silly, Billy

A meeting of minds it isn't. On the one hand, President Woodrow Wilson, the urbane former President of Princeton University. On the other, the irascible and outspoken Prime Minister of Australia, Billy Hughes, who – with his ever-present ear trumpet to help overcome his deafness – has stopped by Washington, DC, and the Oval Office, on his way to London. At particular issue on this day is what the post-war world will look like, specifically on this occasion, the fate of New Guinea, which, before the war, had been a German territory. Though the Australians now occupy it, having captured it in September 1914, Woodrow Wilson forcefully puts the view that New Guinea should become a Japanese protectorate, while Hughes is equally insistent that it should remain under Australian control. No matter what Hughes says, however, Wilson 'sat as unresponsive as a sphinx in the desert',[66] and the meeting does not go long.

Returning to his Washington hotel, Hughes receives a cable from his friend Keith Murdoch, drawing his attention to the fact that he is very unhappy that Monash has taken over as Commander of the Australian Corps in France.

Keith also points out, with alarm, that his own preferred candidate of Brudenell White has gone with Birdwood to London to have administrative command only of the wider AIF. Prime Minister, you must act to change this, for . . .

> Some officers . . . claim that in operations, strategy and under-standing of Australians [White] is immensely superior to Monash whose genius is for organization and administration and not akin to the true AIF genius of front line daring and dash.[67]

In response, Prime Minister Hughes is unsure. He has nothing against Monash at all personally, but a very high regard for Keith Murdoch and his views. This will bear some looking at when he gets to London in the middle of June.

•

Did someone say daring and dash?

Monash's men of the 3rd Division would be surprised at any assertion that he and they lacked it as in their last four weeks on the Somme they have, with some help from 2nd Division, in a series of small attacks and 'peaceful penetrations', advanced the line between the Somme and the Ancre some 2000 yards on a 5000 yard wide front, at the loss of precious few casualties.

Typical of Monash, though he knows he will soon be taking over the entire Australian Corps, his efforts with the 3rd Division do not waver for a moment, as, leading into the final week of May, he and his 3rd Division relieve the 4th Division in their positions on the Western Front – holding down the far southern flank of the British section of the line – and Monash takes up residence at the old 4th Division HQ at Glisy, right by Villers-Bretonneux.

On the first night there, settling in to his chair in the large and gracious study, the incoming Commander-in-Chief of the Australian Corps takes the opportunity to write a few notes to those in the know, who have sent him quiet congratulations on his appointment. His second note is to the highly influential Keith Murdoch, who had been most gracious in his praise. True, Monash does not remotely trust Murdoch, but so Machiavellian is he in his manoeuvres, it is better to maintain at least a façade of civility.

> *When replying to your previous letter . . . [I] failed to appreciate . . . that the main purpose was to tender me promise of personal support and help me in the responsibilities which are about to be imposed on me . . . I now take the opportunity of thanking you very sincerely for your proffered assistance . . . I am thoroughly assured that we both have one purpose in view, and that is the welfare of our Australian troops and the interests of Australia . . . You may be sure that I will gladly avail myself of your great experience and your patriotism . . .*
>
> *Yours very sincerely,*
> *John Monash*[68]

27 May 1918, Laon, Paris in peril

Now the Allies know.

The Germans do have another battle plan – take Paris!

It begins in the early hours with a fearful bombardment on the French forces positioned 40 miles south-east of Amiens, between Soissons and Rheims, and continues throughout the day with some 1,000,000 German soldiers pouring through the old French lines and advancing with an ease that is quite shocking. By sundown they have advanced six miles, to be within 52 miles of Paris. By sundown of the next day, another five miles. And another and another! In the first week of Operation Blucher, as the Germans call it, the front-line has advanced a spectacular 30 miles – even more than the first days of Operation Michael, which had begun the *Kaiserschlacht* back on 21 March.

Paris watches, agog, as the Germans are now just 30 miles from the city's outskirts.

What can be done to stop the monstrous German advance?

The driving force behind the German offensive, General Erich Ludendorff, had, in fact, initially planned this move on Paris as more of a feint than anything else, knowing that if his forces could get within striking distance of Paris, the Allies would be forced to move troops away from the fighting in Flanders – where German soldiers are within 30 miles of the crucial Channel ports. And yet, both he and the Allies had been startled by how well the push on Paris had worked – feint or not – as the German forces had broken through, captured no fewer than 50,000 Allied troops and now actually threaten the French capital!

Forget Flanders, they actually could take *Paris*, in which case France would have to surrender! The only pause for the Germans now comes not because of Allied resistance, but because the German supply line is so stretched it cannot quite catch the foremost troops. A tipping point has been reached, but for whom?

•

Not for nothing will General Monash put all his correspondence over the machinations to remove him as Commander-in-Chief of the Australian Corps in his personal files under the title of 'Keith Murdoch's Intrigue'.[69]

Not for nothing will General Monash write to Prime Minister Hughes, directly questioning Murdoch's right to be the spokesman of the AIF.[70]

For he is not only aware of Murdoch's machinations – word gets around among senior circles of the Australian Corps very quickly – but deeply aggrieved by them.

And he is not the only one.

One who is notably appalled at the injustice of it is Colonel Thomas Dodds, who is on General Birdwood's personal staff.

Taking it upon himself, he quietly contacts the Australian Defence Minister George Pearce to 'positively assure'[71] the powers back home in Australia that the views of Murdoch, and Bean for that matter, are not remotely reflective of the views of the many senior officers in France he has personally consulted on the matter, and for that matter are also 'entirely opposed to the feeling of the whole AIF'.[72]

•

At least not all of the press are against General Monash.

A case in point is the Australian journalist Arthur O'Connor, of the *Weekly Despatch*, who is ushered into the Victorian's presence in the last gasp of May, at the Bertangles HQ, in order to write a profile of him for Australian home consumption. Already, of course, O'Connor knows a fair bit of his subject's background, including his fame as an engineer in Melbourne, and that even in 'the heyday of his success he conceived the idea that a knowledge of law would be helpful. Monash never hit on a good idea without translating it into action. So he became a barrister and solicitor.'[73]

He also knows how quickly Monash had risen through the ranks, once the war had begun, how from beginning as a mere military censor, he had gone to Gallipoli, where he had commanded the 4th Brigade, only being evacuated on the last day; and then in 1916 he had been given command of the 3rd Division, where he had added to his wonderful reputation thereafter, being particularly outstanding in the Battle of Messines in 1917.

More recently of course, in his role as 'the personification of the offensive spirit', Monash had thrown one of his brigades at the Germans who had first captured Villers-Bretonneux, 'and with unexampled dash they drove the *Boche* clean over the horizon'.

But the *feel* of the man, in person, his aura, is really something. Carved out of granite, 'his broad shoulders and deep chest are surmounted by a big head thickly covered with tawny grey hair, brown eyes, alert yet kindly, moderately heavy moustache, a strong mouth'.

Of course in journalism there is a general ideal, in serious newspapers, not to gush in too overwhelming a manner, but, in this case, this journalist decides to give himself the day off.

'To the newspaper interviewer he is an ideal subject,' O'Connor will tell his readers. 'He speaks quietly, deliberately, unhesitatingly, and displays a masterly grip of every detail in the splendid organisation which he has created and maintained. First and last Monash is a *strong man*. He is intellectual, original, democratic – a confirmed believer in the system of promotion from the ranks – he is a born organiser, though pleasant socially, he is no seeker after cheap popularity, and if I am any judge of character he can be ruthless when the occasion calls for ruthlessness.'[74]

A small parenthesis here. On the subject of promotion from the ranks, Monash is passionate.

'From almost the earliest days of the war,' he will later recount, 'violence was done to a deep-rooted tradition of the British Army, which discouraged any promotion from the ranks, and stringently forbade, in rare cases where it was given, promotion in the same unit . . . The Australian Imperial Force changed all that. There was thus no officer caste, no social distinction in the whole force. In not a few instances, men of humble origin and belonging to the artisan class rose, during the war, from privates to the command of battalions. The efficiency of the force suffered in no way in consequence. On the contrary, the whole Australian Army became automatically graded into leaders and followers according to the individual merits of every man, and there grew a wonderful understanding between them. No officer dared to look after his own comfort until every man . . . had been fed and quartered. If the Australians hate anything, it is the superior airs which put a gap between them and their leaders . . . . artificial distinctions irk them badly.'[75]

Close parenthesis.

But, worry about Monash taking over from Birdwood. Never! Quite the contrary. For O'Connor those who criticise Monash entirely miss the point.

'Sir John Monash is a native-born Australian [and] that counts for much in the AIF. Some of our rabidly imperialistic politicians would probably deny that it makes any difference. But as one who gets close to the soul of the Australian soldier, one who watches daily the growth of his national sentiment and his pride in everything that is purely and genuinely Australian, I know that the name of the little old town on Monash's birth certificate is going to help the new commander from the jump.'[76]

•

Bean has gone in search of his old friend, journalist Keith Murdoch, in London, where he has resided since 1916. If anyone can get Prime Minister Billy Hughes – shortly to arrive in London – to change his mind, it is the supremely well connected Murdoch. Alas, for Bean, Murdoch proves to be away on a trip to Scotland for a few days and, in any case, it seems he is too late – the decision has been made.

With his only hope being to have the decision *reversed*, Bean writes a strong memorandum to Hughes, to be delivered by Murdoch when the Prime Minister arrives in London. For his part, Murdoch, when he arrives back in London, agrees to try his influence on the Prime Minister, sending him a cable asserting that the AIF is united in its view that Monash getting the Corps over White would be a bad mistake, and it is furthermore dead against Birdwood keeping administrative command of the AIF. Hughes agrees at least to delay any final decision until such times as he arrives in London in the middle of June . . .

30 May 1918, Le Havre, enter the Yanks

Some 300 years earlier, some of their forebears had fled the tyranny of Europe for the Americas, where they had been able to prosper and grow. Now, many of their descendants are returning to Europe to do their part to quell a new tyranny.

And so it is on this hot morning for the soldiers of the US Army's 131st Regiment – mostly farm boys from the back-blocks of Illinois together with clerks from Chicago, aboard SS *Leviathan*, as, after a two-week journey across the Atlantic, they wake this morning to see towering cliffs ahead, tiny villages clinging to the tops of them from which dark crucifixes sprout like mushrooms perfectly silhouetted against the pristine skies by the rising sun.

France!

Coming closer now, they can see an old fortress with round black towers and bristling guns, dozens of tiny 'fighting vessels with three-cornered reddish-brown sails', and a crowd of Frenchies on the wharves waiting for them!

Goggle-eyed, the American troops impatiently wait for their ship to dock, and then file down the gang-plank, where they are given a proper French welcome.

Vive l'Amerique!

Vive les soldats de les Etats-Unis!

Bienvenue!

Whatever that means.

Soon enough they are formed up into something approaching marching order, and begin to make their way to their billets behind, bizarrely enough, a Scotch band of bagpipers making a sound like cats fighting and dying.

The soldiers look around them, gathering impressions that will last the rest of their lives – even if, for some, that is now only a matter of weeks.

'The little narrow, winding streets up steep hills,' one soldier would recall, '. . . mobs of chattering, shouting, jabbering, quaintly-dressed townspeople . . . one last look across the Atlantic where more men and ships were making ready . . . dainty houses with gardens resplendent with flowers . . .'[77]

Ah, and there will be many more such impressions as they slowly move, if not to the front, at least to within a bull's roar of it, to towns just back from the main event.

'Pigs living in the same house with peasants . . . jerky trains with strange compartments . . . women wearing black . . . convalescent soldiers . . . Germans working near a wire-enclosed prison camp . . . the faint rumble of guns . . . kids asking for cigarette for pa-pa . . . the ground trembled like an earthquake as the war raged . . . it made us think . . . we were going into it . . . Red Cross trains filled with wounded going to the rear . . .'[78]

CHAPTER TWO

MONASH TAKES COMMAND

General Monash, on the other hand, brought to every military situation a fresh, vigorous and agile mind. To him it was a problem to which a solution had to be found. And he no more thought of pursuing the tactics that had served in the Sudan or the Boer War than he would have of using the tools of the Stone Age for some great engineering work.[1]

Billy Hughes in 1941, looking back

The defensive attitude which the situation thus forced on us, did not for long suit the temper of the Australian troops and I sought for a promising enterprise on which again to test their offensive power ... there had been no Allied offensive, of any appreciable size, on any of our fronts ... It was high time that some commanders on our side of No Man's Land should begin to 'think offensively' ... I was ambitious that any such kick should be administered first, at any rate, by the Australians.[2]

General Monash

I profoundly distrust this man [Murdoch].[3]

General Monash, to his wife, Vic, 31 May 1918,
the day he takes over the Australian Corps

31 May 1918, Australian Corps HQ, Bertangles, Birdwood ducks out

No nation does the 'changing of the guard' better, or at least more impressively, than the English. As anyone who has witnessed the traditional ceremony at Buckingham Palace can attest – it involves resplendently uniformed men, polished to within an inch of their lives and then half an inch, a series of guttural commands, much swivelling on heels, stamping of boots in unison, more swivelling, and a *preeeeeeeesent*-ing of arms, until it is all done and the new guard is in place.

When, however, the changing of the guard also involves Australians, and it is done at a very high level, it is all rather more informal. To farewell the men, General Birdwood – after presenting some Distinguished Conduct Medals and Military Crosses to a worthy few Australian soldiers – addresses a wider group at Bertangles for the occasion, bidding them all *adieu*, while noting the Commander-in-Chief had promised him the Australians would stay in his care. (Such occasions have not always gone well, with one soldier having noted previously, 'General Birdwood who came with a pocket full of medals and a cartload of B.S.'[4] but, on this occasion, the troops give him the benefit of the doubt.)

Looking back over the three-and-a-half years he had had the honour to command them, he is proud to say, 'The Australian soldiers have done more for the name of Australia than all the politicians since the days of Adam.'[5]

Bravo, Birdie, and see ya, and here is a slouch hat for you to wear, as we march past in farewell.

But the final goodbye? The actual handover of command? There is precious little hoo-ha.

For it is on this morning of 31 May that – with no more than a few handshakes – not only does General Birdwood cede command of the Australian Corps to an Australian in the person of General Monash, but so too do other Englishmen in General Harold Walker and General Nevill Smyth, VC, who hand the AIF's 1st Division and 2nd Division, respectively, to two Australians in Major-General Thomas Glasgow and General Charles Rosenthal.

For the same dynamic of rising national identity and pride, which has deemed it is time for an Australian to run the Australian Corps, also operates on the Divisions, with a desire that they, too, be run by those born, or at least living, beneath the Southern Cross.

Significantly, among those senior English officers leaving, there appears to be no hard feeling, with one of them, General Smyth, VC – who had commanded the AIF's 1st Brigade at Lone Pine and 2nd Australian Division on the Western Front – even penning the incoming Commander-in-Chief a note:

> *Dear Sir John,*
> *. . . I rejoice to think that you will lead that Corps to further victories and that the ambition is being realised of placing it upon a strictly territorial Australian basis throughout, including every branch of the staff. The fortune of war has indeed treated me kindly in enabling me to have the honour of being associated with your historic force.*
>
> *Yours most sincerely,*
> *Nevill M. Smyth.*[6]

Many of the Australian Brigadiers who now fall under General Monash's command feel the same way, with even the famously irascible Commanding Officer of the 15th Brigade, Brigadier Pompey Elliott, writing to his wife of the appointment of his fellow Melburnian to replace General Birdwood, noting he 'was never so delighted with anything in my life'.[7]

With the exit of such British officers, the 'Australianisation' of the Australian Corps is now complete. After nearly four years of being run by a surfeit of English officers, 1st Division is now run by General Thomas Glasgow, the 2nd Division by Sydney architect General Charles Rosenthal, while Brigadier John Gellibrand, an orchardist from Tassie, takes over Monash's 3rd Division and Generals Ewen Sinclair-Maclagan and Talbot Hobbs, also an architect, from Perth, continue to lead the 4th and 5th Divisions respectively.

It is an enormous thrill for Monash to at last have command of the Australian Corps, which he regards as no less than 'the finest Corps Command in the British Army'.[8]

Yes, it is one of 25 Corps now fighting for the Allies in France, but with 166,000 men, his is the largest.

And *he* is in charge!

'To be the first native born Australian Corps Commander is something to have lived for,' he had told his wife Victoria on first being told the news, 'and will not be forgotten in Australian history.'[9]

On this auspicious day, he feels the honour even more keenly.

> *For all practical purposes I am the supreme Australian commander, and thus, at long last the Australian nation has achieved its ambition of having its own commander in chief, a native born Australian.*[10]

The key, now, will be to *do* something with this command, to prove what an Australian Corps, led by Australian officers, can do, and to show up his detractors, who, he is keenly aware, may well be doubling their efforts to oust him, despite his appointment.

Aware, for example, that Prime Minister Hughes has cooled on his appointment and there is even some possibility that it will be rescinded, General Monash is quick to write to the PM, now *en route* to London, to invite him to come and visit the troops and to see for himself how they are situated, before they discuss it. Whatever else, however, he is insistent on one thing: 'Upon *every* ground, and in the best interests of the A.I.F . . . the present organization should be left undisturbed.'[11]

⁕

On this, the fifth day since the start of Operation Blucher, the Germans are advancing across a 25-mile front, having already captured 50,000 French soldiers and 800 guns, and are now within 40 miles of Paris!

Events are being very closely watched by the Australian officers and soldiers.

'The enemy offensive still continues with success,' writes Lieutenant William Thomas of the AIF's 14th Battalion. 'When is our own counter-offensive to start?'[12]

Also observing the advance with singular intensity is General Sir Henry Rawlinson – under whose command Monash's Australian Corps falls – who writes in his diary on this evening, 31 May, referring to the river some 40 miles from Paris. 'The *Boche* is up to the Marne but so far no report of his having crossed it . . . Paris will be in a great state of alarm I fancy.'[13]

⁕

Paris *is* in a great state of alarm, and following the broad rule that the more you know in this crisis, the more alarmed you are, few are more alarmed – albeit of unwavering resilience – than *Le Premier Ministre*, Georges Clemenceau, who is also the Minister of War. Known as '*Le Tigre*' for the sustained ferocity of his political manoeuvrings, not to mention his terrifying roar and complete lack of mercy for his enemies, the 76-year-old might remain the picture of unbowed virility – the lack of hair atop his head more than made up for by his bushy eyebrows and absurdly luxurious white moustache – but he is in no doubt that the entire war hangs in the balance.

This is his second stint as Prime Minister, having taken the reins again last November, at a time so dark it seemed no other politician wanted to lead, and he has pursued his policy of total war, war to the end, war at whatever cost, '*la guerre jusqu'au bout,* war until the end', ever since.

Politically, this had included having one of his predecessors as Prime Minister, Joseph Caillaux, arrested and thrown into prison for treason, once he had been discovered to have been secretly working for a possible peace settlement with the Germans. Clemenceau will not have *any* talk of surrender. He wants, and he means it, *la guerre jusqu'au bout,* the problem being that that end actually looks like it is remorselessly bearing down upon them.

On the one hand, he relishes the toughness. Duels were his preferred way of settling arguments when he was a younger man. One famous story was often quoted to show his wit and sangfroid. He and his second were leaving Paris, on their way to a countryside destination to duel, far from the intervening arm of the law. At the train station, Clemenceau ordered only a one-way ticket. 'Isn't that a little pessimistic?' asked his startled second. 'Not at all,' replied Clemenceau. 'I always use my opponent's return ticket for the trip back.'[14]

But, on the other hand, he is not a young man any more and neither he nor the French can fight the duel against Germany alone. Each day the news is worse, the battlelines come closer and closer to Paris itself. What France needs, most obviously, is the Americans to throw their weight behind actually attacking the Germans, but Clemenceau has little faith that they will. As a matter of fact, he has little faith in

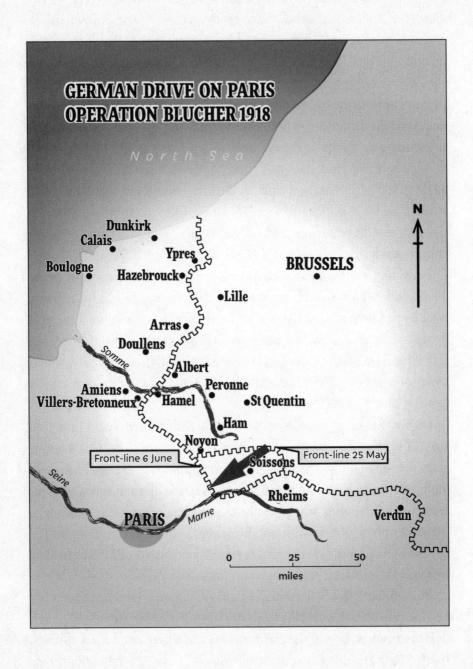

GERMAN DRIVE ON PARIS
OPERATION BLUCHER 1918

North Sea

N

Dunkirk
Calais
Ypres
Boulogne
Hazebrouck
BRUSSELS
Lille
Arras
Doullens
Somme
Albert
Peronne
Amiens
Villers-Bretonneux
Hamel
St Quentin
Ham
Noyon
Front-line 6 June
Front-line 25 May
Soissons
Seine
Rheims
PARIS
Marne
Verdun

0   25   50
miles

Americans in general, later noting, 'America is the only nation in history which miraculously has gone directly from barbarism to degeneration without the usual interval of civilization.'[15]

31 May 1918, Allonville, Bertie's last post

Oh, the sheer pleasure of it!

This evening, after a long day's march, from their last billet at Vignacourt, the men of the AIF's 14th Battalion arrive in Allonville, nine miles north-west of Villers-Bretonneux, and a good ten miles back from the Western Front.

Tomorrow, early, both the 13th and 14th are due to head to the front-line to relieve the 54th and 55th Battalions, and conditions in those trenches are likely to be tough. But that's *tomorrow*. Tonight the 14th, too, can enjoy the shelter, the rest, the camaraderie, all in the relative safety of some barns, one of which is so large it is able to accommodate nearly all of the 14th's A Company, no fewer than 170 men, while other Companies are scattered around in barns nearby.

Yes, some of the German long-range guns are technically capable of reaching them, but it remains highly unlikely they can do any real damage. So, let's enjoy the evening!

As it happens, the arrival of the 14th means the 'Smart Set', the 4th Division's Concert Party, is now complete, and they can put on a show in the largest barn of all, an all-singing, all-dancing revue for the lads – with a troupe that includes four soldiers in drag and the rest in top hat, white tie and tails, making the men laugh and relax. Oh, how the men roar with appreciation.

'They were splendid,' a delighted Cliff Geddes records, 'every item very good. One chap was very clever, dressed as a woman, wore some nice frocks & it was an excellent impersonation.'[16]

True, there is one moment of tension as a sudden whistling grows louder, before a German shell explodes just a coupla hundred yards away, but that's just the way it is. If you want to be within coo-ee of the Western Front, then worrying about shells would be like worrying about flies in an Australian summer.

Still, the near explosion sets up the man they fondly refer to as the 'Old Brig', Brigadier-General Charles Brand, Commander of the mighty 4th Brigade at the age of 45 – though he looks *much* younger – who addresses the men at intermission to give them 'the latest "oil"'.[17]

Though Fritz has not yet been stopped in his drive on Paris, the Yanks have, if not quite moved to stop him, at least not got out of the way and are now doing some fighting themselves at Cantigny! (*Cheers and shouts of, 'You bloody beauty!' and 'About time!'*). Meantime you all will be going into the line just east of Corbie and Villers-Bretonneux, at a spot near that little village of Hamel, you know the one – the tiny burgh that lies at the foot of that hill, Wolfsberg. As ever, your job will be to beat the bastards back if ever they attack, and beyond that seek every opportunity to harass them. Good luck.

When it is all over, the men return to their billets to have their dinner of fried eggs, washed down by billy tea, before some of them – enjoying the late light of summer, go out for something of an evening constitutional.

Among them is Cliff Geddes, who heads off to B Company to have a yarn to Boo and his mates, before they go off to look at the massive hole made by the shell they'd heard during the show.

'Lor' it was awful to look at it,' Cliff chronicles, 'a huge hole in the earth you could bury a horse & buggy in. French kiddies were in it after souvenirs, & big clods of earth thrown everywhere. On looking at it, it makes one curse the war to think men have to face things like that, I've never seen a shell hole like it. Every one is now fed up of war, & the sooner the Hun is outed the better.'[18]

Indeed. I mean, *look* at that bloody hole! I mean, what would a shell like that do to a Company of men? It just doesn't bear thinking about, though Cliff can't stop himself. As ever, he is more worried about what it might do to Boo and B Company than himself and D Company – as his protective family instinct outweighs his own sense of self-preservation and camaraderie.

But, enough. Time for some kip.

The brothers head back to their respective billets in the village of Allonville and soon, all over the area, the Australian soldiers of the 4th Brigade start to settle down a little, in preparation for turning in.

In the big barn where the 14th Battalion's A Company are staying, the men sit around, talking quietly, writing letters, playing cards, some occasionally guzzling from wine bottles they have purloined from abandoned cellars to smuggle forward. Others are off in a world of their own, a world actually on the other side of where they are, as they stare at photos of loved ones.

Most of the men are fairly rough nuts – wharfies, labourers, jackaroos – but not all. One standout for his rather sensitive, artistic nature is the bloke they all call 'Bertie' Englert, a painter and bugler from Manilla in regional New South Wales. Just a couple of years before, he had married the love of his life, Ruth Higgins, bought a house for her in Drummoyne in Sydney, then joined up. (Only five foot one, he had to wait till the AIF was desperate enough for manpower that they would lower their height restrictions to allow even such as him in.) Of course, he hasn't seen Ruth since, and misses her terribly, but what Ruth has lost for the moment, the AIF has gained in spades as Bertie is a beauty of a bloke to have in the Battalion, always ready to play a tune for the boys, have a laugh, lend a shoulder to both the wheel and to a troubled comrade to cry on, all while being a good soldier. And there is a certain *elan* about him. When the troopship Bertie had been sailing to England on, the *Ballarat*, had been torpedoed in the English Channel on Anzac Day 1917 – after the soldier who spotted the torpedo heading their way had a stammer, and couldn't get out the word in time[19] – one of the survivors in a life-raft had been a cornet player, who, as the ship started to sink, had played riffs of ironic song choices to keep their spirits up, like 'So Long Letty', 'Fall in the Band' and 'Defaulters'. As reported by *The New York Times* a 'little bugler', at that point still on board, had stood on the sinking deck and played answering phrases to the cornet. That 'little bugler' was Bertie, and his calm cheerfulness helped to make him the toast of the Battalion, after he was rescued himself.

If Bertie is even more upbeat than usual on this evening, there are two reasons. Firstly, it is because he and 'The Smart Set' had performed so well this evening, and to such acclaim.

Secondly, Bertie's best mate, Willie Wootton, had only a few days before successfully transferred to Bertie's Company, so they can serve side by side and fight side by side. As a matter of fact, tonight, they even put their kits down side by side.

True, there is an unpleasantly pungent aroma about – courtesy of the cow dung scattered all around – and it is a warm night, but no-one in the Battalion is complaining, least of all the veterans among them. Compared to the digs in the trenches and open fields that they have been accustomed to over the last few years – from Gallipoli to Pozières to Passchendaele to Villers-Bretonneux – this is comparative luxury.

Late into the evening, Bertie and Willie, lifelong friends, lie in their swags softly talking of home, and particularly of their wives, Ruth and Ina – Willie having married Ina between enlisting in March 1917 and leaving Australia in June. They'd had such a short time together before he'd had to go!

Some 500 yards away, the officers, including Lieutenant Edgar Rule of the 14th Battalion's D Company, are settling down for the night in comfortable tents set up for them by their orderlies.

•

In the German artillery units there is a little excitement, for there is something different on the agenda tonight. Usually, in their nightly shelling, the artillery units are little better than a blind giant swinging wildly in the darkness, hoping to hit something of critical value to the enemy to cause him damage. But, *nicht heute Nacht*, not tonight!

A report has come in from an interrogated prisoner that the village of Allonville is *proppenvoll*, packed with Australian troops. The information is specific enough that the Germans even have the map co-ordinates of some of the barns the troublesome Australians are likely to be staying in. The information is so critical, and so potentially fatal to the enemy, that the Germans are even now putting a plane up to guide their shelling in the soft moonlight, in the hope of hitting the barns with lethal accuracy.

And so now the artillery men load their guns with an 'airburst shell', designed to burst well above the ground and light the way, doing only minor damage. They plan to fire four such shells with slightly different ranges, according to the co-ordinates on the map.

Feuer!

The first of the airburst shells streaks away in the night.

The observer in the plane watches closely.

Nine times the shell bursts near the barns, and after the ninth shot, the observer drops a flare, this time observed by the gunners. That's it. Use that precise range and you will hit the barns.

•

All snug as a bug in a rug, on the Western Front.

At least it is for the men of the 14th Battalion, who have now settled in for the night in their barns, while most of the 13th are in billets in Allonville. Nearing midnight, all that can be heard, apart from the snores of the men, is the odd cluck from chooks, and the mooing of the cows in a paddock – cows who are unhappy to have been displaced from their usual spot in the barns tonight – and the drone of a plane somewhere above, followed by some kind of explosion somewhere in the distance, but most blokes don't even wake up . . .

•

Twelve miles away, at a spot called Bray-sur-Somme, the German naval artillerymen stand along the tracks by their naval railway gun, a 21-centimetre L/45 Feldkanone heavy gun, this time loaded with a high-explosive shell. (And yes, it is an odd circumstance which sees sailors wielding such a gun so far from the coast, but after the sinking of the German heavy cruiser *Blucher*, four spare barrels had been left over in the dockyard at Wilhelmshaven, unsuitable for any other ship. So the engineers had turned them into four railway guns, effectively 'miniature Big Berthas' – making them 'Berthas' for short? – capable of firing shells weighing an extraordinary 254 pounds.) With a range of 14 miles, the barns at Allonville are just inside the outer perimeter of what they can reach.

Following their strict routine, the German officer yells, '*Feeertig!*', as in 'Reeeeady,' and then . . . '*Feuer!*' 'Fire!'

The gun gives an almighty blast, exploding like an angry volcano, and an instant later the first shell – the size of a child – roars forth and soars to the west, lobbing towards the Allied lines and revolving clockwise 100 times a second as it goes.

Of course the German artillery crew don't know exactly where this first shell will land, only that it would be right among those who had been sending exactly the same kind of devastation on them and theirs.

This particular shell, however, reaches its peak perhaps some six miles ahead of where the barn lies, and then begins its descent. Does it have any Australian names on it?

Too early to tell . . .

With every gust of wind and reverberation of air around it, the shell slightly changes its direction of descent – every tiny change making a huge difference as to exactly where it will land and detonate, who will live, and who will die.

Some in the barn at Allonville, some of the men of A Company, can surely hear it. Even over the sound of so many other exploding shells all around – now, can *you* hear it?

It is a screeching, getting louder now, squealing . . . *is this it?* . . . as they grit their teeth, and involuntarily flex their whole bodies and cover their ears, as if that might possibly save them. Yes, they've been in this situation before, and been scared before, but always, without exception, the worst the subsequent shell has done is land near them, not on them. There has been damage done, wounds, and even deaths, but they've never had a shell land right on them before. Surely this shell is not going to be an exception? But still, it's starting to roar like a train coming down the bloody Bulli Pass, coming straight for them, getting louder and louder and louder!

The first shell lands right at the apex of the barn, hitting the very beam that holds the whole roof together. On the instant, all is blown asunder as the shell explodes with 48 pounds of TNT, sending not only the heavy beams tumbling down, not only the shattered shards of the shell scything off in all directions, but, most damaging of all, the razor-thin slates from the roof tumble down like hundreds of guillotine blades onto the Australians below.

A few seconds later, another shell hits a nearby barn, the one occupied by C Company, for a similar result.

•

In his digs in Allonville, Cliff Geddes sleeps on, but from his own uneasy dozing in his tent, just 500 yards from where the shells have hit, Lieutenant Edgar Rule suddenly wakes. It is not the exploding shells that have roused him, and perhaps not even the sound of the falling barn. No, this is something else.

What is it?

There! It is a distant, unearthly shriek. And another. And now *another*.

Telling the others in the tent of his fears, two of his fellow officers laugh at him. But Rule won't be quelled, and once outside the tent he can hear it even more clearly. Somewhere nearby some men are badly hurt and the likelihood is that they are men of the 14th Battalion. Rule scrambles to get his boots on, and is soon running towards the screams. Reaching the farmyard, he runs into some terror-stricken soldiers running from the horror of it all. One look tells him all he needs to know. Rule is soon running himself, back to the tents to get the Battalion doctor, and all the others. We need help, and we need it *now*, for disaster has struck.

Without waiting for the others to get their boots on, Rule races back to where the barns once stood, now just two piles of shattered rubble, from which screams and long, unearthly wails are emanating.

'It was one of the worst smashes I've ever seen,' Rule would chronicle. 'The whole debris had tumbled down on the boys, disembowelling many, cutting off legs and arms as if they were paper.'[20]

So shocked are the survivors that most of them are just standing around with glazed eyes, while half-a-dozen are 'working like fiends',[21] tearing into the rubble like mad things, trying to shift what they can to get to the wounded. A few sharp commands from Rule, however, and nearly all of the survivors snap out of it and join in the rescue efforts. Even as they haul the timbers, and shift the stones, other shells are landing nearby, but there is no time to worry about that now.

Bit by bit, they are able to get to most of the wounded.

'With the aid of a lantern we saw things that we never want to see again . . . I found pieces of legs and bodies under the debris.'[22]

Still, the heroism of some of the men they find would make a brown dog weep.

One bloke, both his legs sheared off below the knees, leaving only bloody stumps, gasps to his would-be rescuers: 'I'm alright, get the badly wounded boys out.'

Yet another, who has been dragged clear, tries to light a ciggie with the one arm he has left. When his mates leap forward to try and light it for him, he waves them away, saying, 'I'll have to learn to do it with one hand . . . may as well begin now.'[23]

The dead are respectfully laid in a row, for burial on the morrow, and, the best the able-bodied can, they put sliced arms, legs and heads with the right torso. But it ain't easy.[24]

And Bertie and Willie?

They grew up together, had served together, and have now died together. All that remains will be to bury them together.

As one of their comrades, Private Clarence Carroll, will note, '[Bertie] and his pal were dead alongside one another in their billet. He was much torn about on the whole of one side of his body . . . His mate Wootten only got shifted from another [company] about a week previously so as to be with Englert and they both died at the same time alongside one another – buried alongside each other.'[25]

Bertie's crushed bugle lies by his side. He has played his last 'Last Post'.

Not for nothing will this tragic episode ever after be known as 'the Allonville Disaster'.

Even though no fewer than 86 of the 500 men in the Battalion had become casualties at Allonville, of whom 18 had been killed, the 14th Battalion were still only four hours late in their deployment in the front-line – on the march by 10 o'clock in the morning – relieving the 54th Battalion.

Yes, a bitter blow, but this is not just any old Battalion. This is, and they are proud of it, the Battalion known to all and sundry in the AIF as 'Jacka's Mob', for their most famous member, the most famous soldier in the whole bloody Australian army, Albert Jacka, VC, MC, who no Turk or German had ever got the best of, and who had only finally been gassed a week earlier and sent home to Australia. Well, Jacka might be gone, and they may have now lost another 86 men, but the Battalion goes on, and it will be for them to hold up their fine reputation. They can hardly wait to have another crack at the Germans.

For their part, the 13th Battalion, while soon made aware of the tragedy, are up at 4.30 am, and on their way by 6 am as planned – halting by the Somme River at 9.30 am under the lovely trees, and staying there throughout the day, before moving forward again at nine this evening, the shadows lengthening in time with their stride, as they eagerly near the end of their journey before midnight.

'We had a very narrow squeak,' Cliff Geddes chronicles their arrival on the line just before midnight. 'Fritz sent some shells over just where my section passed half a minute before. We got against a bank by the sunken road, & more burst 10 yards or so in front of us, just where we had come past. A bit of stone hit me under the left eye, & further along the bank a chap was wounded in the leg by a piece of shell . . .'[26]

Welcome to the Western Front, once more.

•

As Charles Bean's job is to chronicle the derring-do of the Diggers, it is rare indeed that he must actually dig himself. And yet, on this first day of summer, that is what he must do, as he is, after all, a Captain of the AIF and must observe standing orders that all those in tents within range of the German guns in Australian-held territory must be placed 18 inches below ground level to give themselves better protection against any chunks of metal that might be coming their way. Given the disaster at Allonville the previous day, no-one is complaining about taking 'buckoo' precautions, as in beaucoup precautions, against stray shells.

Having decided to set up his tent in the wood next to the Australian Corps HQ at Bertangles Chateau, Bean has just finished the digging and is sitting on a stone seat to rest and embrace his true calling, which is to start writing news in his scrawling long-hand, when one of General Birdwood's key staff officers, Colonel Thomas Dodds, passes by, to . . . suddenly confront him.

'Why,' he asks, in the manner of a man who is both amazed *and* angered, 'did Murdoch and another irresponsible pressman – I don't mean you – interfere and wire to Australia that the force "universally desired Monash to be GOC AIF," and White GOC Australian Corps?

Which is not true. It's a lie. Only one general out of five whom I have consulted wants this.'[27]

Well, then!

It is no small thing to be told by a Colonel that your efforts in the previous weeks doing down the General and Commanding Officer in high places are nothing more than a lie – even if Dodds is not directly accusing him – but still Charles Bean does not back off and even makes it clear that *he* believes what Murdoch believes.

'Monash had, I am sure, worked for this job by all sorts of clever well-hidden subterranean channels; that White had never stirred a finger in his own interest [. . .] [while in contrast] Monash has had friends working for him never doubt.'[28]

That is, Bean might even concede that Colonel Dodds is correct and the Australian Corps is not against General Monash, as he and Murdoch have claimed. But Monash has been using his underground network to push his case, while White has done nothing, as he is too much the gentleman, maybe even too much a Christian gentleman, and that is not fair.

'Dodds, by his face,' Bean at least records in his diary, 'knew that these things were true – and seemed half to assent.'[29]

For his part, Bean remains as firm in his view as the diary entry he had made the previous October when Field Marshal Haig himself had first raised the issue with him.

> But Monash for an Australian Commander in Chief we cannot have. He is not the man. The purity and absence of jealousy and political intrigue in Birdwood's administration is worth anything. There is no 'eyewash' – bluff and humbug and insincerity in it; and there is in Monash's. White would do, but not Monash. Besides we do not want Australia represented by men mainly because of their ability, natural and inborn in Jews, to push themselves [forward].[30]

That's his view, and he is sticking to it, even noting a short time after his conversation with Dodds in a fresh diary entry:

> Monash is a man of very ordinary ideals – lower than ordinary, I should say. He cannot inspire this force with a high chivalrous

patriotic spirit – with his people in charge it would be full of the desire to look and show well – that is the highest. There is no question where the interest of the Australian nation lies. It lies in making White one of its great men and makers.[31]

And he says as much to Murdoch, in a letter where, as one Australian male to another, there is no better metaphor to reach for than a sporting one. In Bean's view, in sending Brudenell White from the Australian Corps to the Fifth Army and mere overseeing of the AIF, the Australian team has dropped its star batsman, left out none other than '[Victor] Trumper', to send to the crease a mere plodder by comparison, 'a Clem Hill or a [Warren] Bardsley'.[32]

He grieves that the decision has been taken.

'I cannot reconcile myself to the loss, so light heartedly, of White to the A.I.F. That the biggest and ablest influence in it, the man who has been far more the father of it than any other, should after four years be suddenly and simply lost to it will always be, in my mind, a big mistake, on the part of the Government. Still, it is done.'[33]

And, as such, he also gives Murdoch fair warning: '[As Monash is] there now and further change would do no good, as things are, I intend to work loyally by him.'[34]

•

Meanwhile, in a curious example of the superiority of biology over physics when it comes to laying mass numbers of men low, a debilitating condition is now taking hold on both sides of the Western Front.

The Australians call it 'dog-fever', as in 'crook as a dog', the Germans the 'Flanders Grippe', the French call it 'la grippe', while the Brits sniff at the 'Spanish flu'. Whatever you call it, as it sweeps both sides of the Western Front in this summer of 1918, it exacts a dreadful toll, taking out whole platoons and even Companies for days at a time.

Your head throbs, your temperature soars, your mates start barking at you as they give you their diagnosis, and far from being able to fight like cats in a sack, you are as weak as a kitten. Reminiscent of sea-sickness, for the first 12 hours you are afraid you are going to die.

For the next 12 hours you are afraid you are not going to die. When it goes for days however, many of those who suffer often *do* end up dying.

All up, there is only one upside, and that is, as one soldier, Gunner Albert Williams would record in his diary, 'Rum issued at intervals was the best cure.'[35]

3 June 1918, London, Monash faces the Murdoch press

Rarely has Keith Murdoch felt so let down.

But there is no getting around it, his great friend Charles Bean appears to have given up on their joint project to get rid of General John Monash as Commander of the Australian Corps.

'I am sorry to say,' Bean has written to him, 'that the changes [in Australian command] seem to have been definitely approved and accomplished [. . .] and there is no chance whatever that they should be altered in the direction which I am sure, if it had been suggested in time, would have been best for Australia. The only course which, so far as I see, we can usefully follow is, as the administration is now I think beyond the possibility of change, to support it, so long as it does its work well . . . Still, it is done. There is no present possibility of undoing it.'[36]

Well, he never.

In response, Murdoch, a formidable force of nature, scheming, irrepressible and entirely untroubled by the fact he is neither elected nor appointed to any official role within the workings of the Australian government – because he *knows* what must be done, just as he had known that Gallipoli had to be evacuated and made it happen – does not back off a jot. He will deal with Bean presently, but for the moment he does two things.

The first is to assure General Monash of his complete loyalty, in a letter he dashes off.

> *Trust me and use me in any humble capacity you can, and always rest*
> *assured that my whole life is devoted to Australia's best interests . . .*
> *I hope to be able to familiarise the Australian public with all your*
> *good work.*[37]

The second is to offer him something awfully close to a bribe.

> *About two months ago I was pressed by a very high authority in*
> *London . . . and I told them that you had our utmost confidence and that*
> *your ability approximated to genius . . . I hold the strongest conviction*
> *that Australian interests demand stronger and independent military*
> *representation here.*[38]

Broadly, if Monash would just give up on commanding the Australian Corps in battle, he, Murdoch, would do everything in his power to get him the job General Birdwood has, running the AIF in effectively the rank of a Cabinet minister, with a full staff, and a much easier life.

'You as a full General with supreme authority,' the 31-year-old journalist attempts to flatter the 52-year-old general, who has not only been around the block, but *built* most of it, 'would be the solution of many of our country's difficulties.'[39]

And you could stay in France, close to the action!

> *The ideal would be a supreme Australian GOC AIF, stationed*
> *probably at GHQ in France in a chateau something like that which*
> *the Canadians maintain here; a man who would answer solely to the*
> *Australian government, who in return are responsible to the Australian*
> *people; a man who would be able to take to the War Office and the*
> *various Ministers here our case, and to fight for it; a man who would,*
> *though removed from actual fighting in the field, be a jealous and*
> *supreme representative of the AIF in all its battles . . .*[40]

Oh, really?

'It is a poor compliment,' Monash would note to Birdwood, 'both for him to imagine that to dangle before me a prospect of promotion would induce me to change my declared views, and for him to disclose that he thinks I would be a suitable appointee to serve his ulterior ends.'[41]

Frankly, Monash can barely stand it, and begins to make reply:

> *You and your friends believe my abilities are mainly administrative, you*
> *probably think that a non-professional soldier is unlikely to be a good*

commander, that in the past I have been a figurehead controlled by [my]
professional staff officers . . .[42]

In the end, however, he simply cannot bear to finish the letter. Acutely
aware of Murdoch's Machiavellian manoeuvres, he has, nevertheless,
far more important things on his mind than to engage in this entirely
undignified exercise, no matter how dangerous it might ultimately be
to ignore it – and so just writes a quick, polite, if starkly brief note,
acknowledging receipt of the letter.

For his part, Keith Murdoch does not back off on his overall plan
for a moment and is quick to tackle Bean when next he sees him, going
for a visit at the AIF HQ at Horseferry Road – universally known to
the Diggers as 'Cowpunt Road' – right by the Thames in Westminster.

'Look here, old chap,' the Melburnian says to Bean, his senior by
six years. 'I'm up to my neck in it [. . .] You're a fine chap to enter
a fight with!'

But Bean will not be moved, and insists on his central point.

'Monash,' he tells his old friend, 'cannot be replaced or removed
without his own consent and wish. It has gone too far for that. It would
destroy confidence among the leaders of the Divisions and Brigades if
such a thing could happen now.'[43]

In some ways Murdoch can see his point, but still resolves to push
on. After all, if he can convince Prime Minister Billy Hughes that he is
right, all things are possible. And there is one thing he really will hold
the line on – the madness of 'Birdwood remaining [General Officer
Commanding the Australian Imperial Force] now that he has gone to
an outside army.'

'I am with you,' Bean replies, 'and will be in opposing it for all it
is worth.'[44]

With Hughes due to arrive in London next week, the best solution, they
decide, is for Bean to leave with Murdoch a missive, pleading their case.

'The ideal to be aimed at,' Bean would note in his diary, 'was Monash
as G.O.C. A.I.F. and White as G.O.C. of the [Australian] Corps. He
will see Hughes on his landing and will give him this and ask him not
to agree to anything until he has read it. There is, I believe, going to
be a big fight over this question.'[45]

Bean is quick to provide the missive.

For Mr W M Hughes

Private
. . . The idea that [General Birdwood], with his immense outside
preoccupations, can in his spare time be responsible for the administration
of the AIF cannot correspond to the idea which would be possessed
by Australians of the immense field of work and responsibility which
would fall upon the G.O.C. of Australia's forces overseas . . .
General Monash is recognised as an organiser of outstanding capacity
and strength; and General White as possessing exceptional brilliance in
the sphere of operations.[46]

In short, Prime Minister, why not switch things around?

6 June, Bertangles Chateau, true blue top brass

Something different . . .

What is it?

As Monash takes his place at the head of the grand conference table
in what used to be the chateau's glorious ballroom, for this, his first
meeting with four of his Divisional commanders at the Australian Corps
HQ, it is General Hobbs of 5th Division who spots it first.

Yes, gentlemen, Generals all, and all your senior staff officers off
your left and right shoulders, please note: for the first time in the
history of Australian warfare, these, the highest echelons of Australian
Army command, are being exclusively manned, at General Monash's
personal insistence, by . . . Australians.

Well, yes, General Sinclair-Maclagan is a Scot, I guess, but this far
down the track winding back – having lived in Australia since 1901,
and having married a Sydney belle in 1902 – he is regarded by Monash
himself as 'whole-heartedly Australian',[47] for the fact that he was a
foundation military instructor at Duntroon, even before the war was
underway – and anyway, even on a bad day, Scots can pass for 'Aussies
with bad accents'.

In any case, from the beginning, General Monash is clear. From now
on these gatherings will be regular, perhaps even fortnightly, and he is

intent that his men are all familiar with each other's work and, most importantly, can exchange ideas. It will be for him to report on the overall strategic situation, what he is hearing from the likes of General Rawlinson and higher about their expectation, what the Germans are likely to do next and so forth. It will be for them to report the state of their troops, their casualty rates, intelligence gained from prisoners, the success of recent raids and the plans for future raids.

Beyond that, Monash also intends to take a collegiate approach when it comes to major actions to be undertaken by the Australian Corps.

A hallmark of Monash's military command to this point has been his insistence on regarding battles as, first and foremost, *logistical* problems, trying to work out exactly what combination of the military resources they have on hand can bring the maximum force to bear on the enemy's most vulnerable point.

As an engineer, building great bridges and the like, he had been used to working in this collegiate manner, calling on experts in different fields to crack different parts of the problem, and bringing everyone together for really thorny problems.

Just as in the building and engineering worlds there are constant innovations, and it is important to be up to date, so too, with warfare. From the first, Monash is eager that the Australian Corps under his command looks to newer, better, ways of doing things.

In all such deliberations, Monash has at his right hand his Chief of Staff, General Thomas Blamey, who he has hand-picked for the task, and plucked from his previous role as Chief of Staff for the 1st Division.

'He possessed a mind cultured far above the average,' Monash would say of his fellow Victorian, 'widely informed, alert and prehensile. He had an infinite capacity for taking pains.'[48] (True, Charles Bean notes Blamey as 'a bad man to cross', with 'few close friends',[49] but Monash can live with that so long as the *detail* of things is attended to.)

Either way, the two make a formidable combination and, from the first, there is a sense that the Australian Corps has a rather dynamic leadership in place, one that stands in strict contrast to the one it has succeeded.

'[Birdwood] was only a mediocre battle commander,' the great Australian historian Geoffrey Serle would note of Monash's predecessor, 'never drew up plans for operations himself, and was unreliable in his frontline observations . . .'[50]

From the first, aware of Birdwood's failings, Monash wishes to prove himself quite the opposite on all counts and, whatever else, brings an *energy* to the task that his English predecessor had never remotely evinced. It is an energy that quickly spreads throughout the top tiers of the Australian Corps.

'Officers of his headquarters staff who set out to work as long a day as [Monash],' the journalist Fred Cutlack would note, 'found themselves committed to the most continuous hard work they had ever done in their lives . . . In his office Monash was always more like a newspaper editor, or the chief of a large engineering construction staff, or the director of a great corporation, than an army leader. He saw everybody; he forgot nothing. He left nothing to chance, which industry and foresight could make certain. He made no plans until he had exhausted the ideas of all staff and subordinate commanding officers; then he would suggest a scheme which embraced the good points of all . . .'[51]

Somehow, he manages it without raising the hackles of those staff he is working so hard.

'The most affectionate and cordial relationship existed between Monash and his staff,' Blamey would recount. 'With the Corps staff he was never happier than when joking and chatting in the mess . . . Probably no commander was surrounded by less formality.'[52]

All up, under Monash, it is quickly clear to most that the Australian Corps has a newly found dynamism, eager to engage in a major action.

Beyond the energy that Monash brings to the cause, the aggressive instincts, if there is a difference for the common soldier it is that they see much less of General Monash than they ever did of General Birdwood. For while 'Birdie' had gone out of his way to mingle with the men and, in the words of General Kitchener, had succeeded with the Australians as he had gone 'among men as a man',[53] General Monash is not so disposed. While he treats all men with humility – and would be regarded by no less than the *Bulletin* as, 'the absolute antithesis of the unapproachable, self-conscious brass-hat'[54] – the truth is that he is far too busy to bother about having cups of tea on the front-lines. He has 166,000 soldiers to look after, two thirds of them Australians – every man-jack of his countrymen volunteers, making them unique – five Major-Generals and 25 Brigadier-Generals to liaise with, and a war to win!

'I spent as much as possible of my whole time at my Headquarters,' General Monash would recount, 'considering reports, planning, organising, and directing, with the result that the Corps at once began to do things . . .'[55]

Which is exactly as it should be, in the view of Field Marshal Haig, and quite a contrast with his predecessor.

'Birdwood,' Haig had written to his wife, Lady Haig, earlier in the year, 'instead of facing the problem, has gone in for the easiest way of saying everything is perfect and making himself as popular as possible.'[56]

Monash doesn't particularly care for being popular, and doesn't bother saying things are perfect. What he really wants, of course, is to do a big thing. It simply remains for him to determine what it will be . . .

•

Not surprisingly, word of Murdoch's activities in London, his whisperings in high places in an effort to deprive Monash of his command of the Australian Corps, continues to get back to the man himself, who is appalled – if still disinclined to confront Murdoch directly with a blistering letter. What Monash cannot understand though, is the vehemence of such opposition to him, particularly from one who sends him letters professing his 'loyalty'.

Here now, though, is one who might have answers.

'Have you seen Murdoch?' General Monash asks the newly returned Charles Bean plaintively, going on to make it clear that he is fully aware of Murdoch's efforts.

At this point, a lesser man than Bean might have thrown down his weapons, and come out with his hands up. Ah, but the long-time correspondent for the *Sydney Morning Herald* is made of sterner stuff.

'I have,' Bean replies evenly, 'and I think Murdoch is right.'

This time it is Monash who reels. The *hide* of them both! Bristling, Monash is quick to fire back: 'I have always been on friendly terms with Murdoch and think it is very cruel that he should attempt to deprive me of the high active command which I have attained in the field. Field Marshal Haig has told me that he has every confidence in me, and gone further, saying that even if the Australian Corps had not been vacant he would have been quite prepared to give me a place anywhere among his Corps Commanders.'[57]

Lest Bean should get the wrong idea, General Monash goes on.

'Mind you [. . .] everything that I do in this I do in a spirit of most complete loyalty to General Birdwood . . .'[58]

The encounter leaves Bean confused, but unbowed.

> What precisely was the meaning or the truth of this last remark
> I cannot quite fathom.

The long and the short of it, however, is dead simple. He simply does not like Monash much.

> [Colonel] Dodds, whom I saw later, struck me as a much more
> loyal genuine man . . .[59]

●

At least the best they can, the Americans of the 131st US Infantry Regiment are settling in to their tents, in the fields just outside the village of Pierregot, some three miles north-east of Bertangles. For a half-dozen of them, including Sergeant Walter Corning, it includes going out on their first shopping trip, which starts with buying bottles of wine from the 1890s for just a few francs! And yes, the Frenchies look at them aghast as, instead of swirling the precious drops around a glass, to properly savour *le* flavour, they just swig it back, neat from the bottle, at which point they get a little untidy, but too bad. We are Yanks. This is the way *we* do it.

Now, what about some eggs, which is what everyone back in the trenches is asking for. The innkeeper directs them to the house of a peasant, just down the road, and they are soon knocking on the old man's door.

'Havey you eggey?' they ask, using their very best French.

'*Que voulez-vous?*' says the peasant.

'Avey vous oofs?' say the American soldiers, a little proud of their grasp of the language.

'*Je ne vous comprends pas, m'sieur,*' says the old Frenchman, completely baffled.

'What did he call us?' demanded one of the party.

'He said he didn't want any company,' replies the interpreter.

'Well, ask him if he's got any eggs.'

'Us wanty plenty erfs,' says the interpreter.

'*Je ne vous comprends pas!*'

'What did he say?'

'He wants to know if you'll be queen of the May,' says the interpreter glibly.

'How about the eggs?' persisted the other one.

'Eggs, oofs, erfs,' says the interpreter, trying to draw a picture of an egg.

The old man shakes his head vaguely and closes the door.

'You're a hell of an interpreter,' says one sergeant.

'Well, you're not so good yourself,' retorts the other.

Half an hour later they do at last manage to get about two dozen eggs direct from the producer, which is not remotely enough for the 250 hungry men back at the billet but it is *something*. And it is with some satisfaction that in the, yes, *oui* hours, just after midnight, they climb over the wall with all their precious 'erfs' indeed in one basket. Concluding that an egg for every ten men would not be well received, their treasure is instead divided between themselves and the officers, with the one bad egg they find being hurled at the guard who it most resembled, the one who'd given them a hard time on their return.

'Thus ended our first shopping tour,' Corning would recount. 'From then on we confined our French to single words like "*cognac*", "*vin blanc*", etc.'[60]

Their experience is, of course, not uncommon.

'It is strange,' an American officer notes at this time, 'that we Americans can understand each other well when we speak our poor French among ourselves; but the Frenchmen make us repeat and repeat, then we write the word and they explain "Ooh, oui, oui". Some French shops have the sign "Speak English; your French is not understood".'[61]

•

A larger than life character is Field Marshal Ferdinand Foch, the Supreme Commander of the Allied forces on the Western Front. Courageous, charismatic, irrepressible, his defining words had come during the First Battle of the Marne, in September 1914.

'My centre is giving way, my right falling back; the situation is excellent,' he famously reported to his Commanding Officer. '*J'attaque.*'[62]

And so he had, beating the Germans back, though at the Marne they had been effectively lapping the shores of Paris, just 35 miles away.

Despite such heroic resistance, however, four years later, once again the Germans are pressing towards the French capital – at the Marne once more – and Foch barely has French troops left with which to attack. What he needs, he tells Sir Douglas Haig, on this same afternoon of 6 June that General Monash is meeting his Divisional Commanders, is for the British forces to prepare to attack the Germans in 'a number of minor actions . . . with tanks, in order to retain enemy force'.

Yes, tanks. Foch not only knows that Britain's brand new Mark V tanks are now arriving in France – no fewer than 144 brand spanking new tanks have just come under the command of General Rawlinson's Fourth Army, for example – but believes they might make all the difference in stopping the Germans, at a time when Allied manpower is so diminished, they need something more than soldiers alone to do it.

'These actions,' Foch says, 'might aim at definite results [and] might be *coups de main* of marked importance with useful consequences.'[63]

That is, he is not demanding full-blown battles, requiring months of preparations, so much as rather more limited attacks that might shock Fritz, make him keep all the German divisions facing the British Expeditionary Force right where they are, rather than use any of them to strengthen the attack on Paris.

In response, GHQ the next day issues a directive for all of Great Britain's five Armies on the Western Front to 'submit at an early date proposals for an offensive action of a nature limited to . . . a few battalions and a number of tanks'.[64]

What Foch most desires, of course, is to get the Americans involved, but in the face of their continued refusal he orders Field Marshal

Douglas Haig to launch attacks along the British front, in the expectation that it will at least force the Germans to divert some of the troops attacking Paris, and put them towards stopping a British breakout.

Underlining the urgency of the situation is that although the Germans' Operation Blucher has, for the moment at least, come to a bloody halt 35 miles outside Paris – grinding to a stand-still on the direct route to the city from the north – on the morning of 9 June they try another route. Probing for another soft spot in the French defences, the Germans launch Operation Gneisenau, attacking at Noyon – 30 miles south of Hamel – with Paris once again the strategic objective. Their early gains of territory are, once again, spectacular, stretching the French line almost to breaking point.

So, yes, it is now more urgent than ever that the Germans are attacked elsewhere, to force them to shift their forces around, and as it happens, Field Marshal Haig has just the Corps in mind to get things underway . . .

For within the Australian Corps there is a minor action ready to roll out – organised and approved in General Birdwood's final days – and on the night of 10 June it is launched.

Just north of the River Somme, at 9.45 pm, the mighty 7th Brigade of General Charles Rosenthal's 2nd Division storms along from Morlancourt Ridge to attack the German lines in a lightning action.

The Brick Beacon attack, as it is known – named for a surveyor's mark, a pile of bricks like a small pyramid on the highest point of ground in these parts – proves to be a great success, with the Australians sustaining only 400 casualties, while the Germans lose no fewer than 1000 soldiers as casualties, 33 machine guns and 600 yards of their territory across a front of 3000 yards. The German 54th Division commander, General Ernst Kabisch, would ruefully record that, 'a complete battalion had been wiped out as if with a sponge'.[65]

Should the 7th Brigade keep pushing east in the days to come?

No. General Rosenthal orders them to stop.

The key reason is that the further the Australian forces push to the east north of the Somme, the more they expose their southern flank to the Germans dug in at Hamel. In fact, the way the situation now stands, Hamel is like a dagger right in the side of the Allied line, as it juts 3000 yards further to the west than where Rosenthal's men have got to with Brick Beacon.

What then of eliminating that dagger by taking back Hamel? It would also answer Haig's order that they take offensive action against the Germans, and at Monash's request, attacking Hamel is one of several potential attacks examined by the Australian Corps' Divisional Commanders over the next two days. On the target of Hamel and, immediately to its south, Vaire Wood,[66] General Ewen Sinclair-Maclagan believes an attack by his 4th Division would be feasible, so long as General Gellibrand's 3rd Division immediately to their south also attacked the German forces before Villers-Bretonneux, making it an enormous operation.

The idea of straightening out the line at Hamel is not new. General Rawlinson had advocated it to Birdwood in late April, and General Monash himself had pushed for it back in early May when his 3rd Division, positioned north of the Somme, had been regularly plastered because German observers had been able to so precisely direct their artillery from atop Wolfsberg, the large hill just behind Hamel.

Back then, however, no move had been made, principally because of the Australian Corps' Chief of Staff, General Brudenell White, who was insistent that – as so few reinforcements were now coming from Australia – they simply could not risk throwing a Division into such an exercise when, at its conclusion, the said Division would likely no longer be able to operate because of heavy losses and no reserves with which to replace them. No, White, in the words of Charles Bean, 'was convinced that the British would need the five Australian divisions as a striking force at some critical stage of the war'.[67] That critical stage, it seems likely, will be in the spring or summer of 1919, so it was important to conserve the forces they had for now.

After convincing both Birdwood and Rawlinson of the virtue of this logic, White had put the same view to Field Marshal Haig upon his visit to the Australian Corps on 17 May, and as a consequence the plan had gone nowhere.

And it goes no further now, for much the same reasons.

The key problem General Sinclair-Maclagan determines is that even if the Allies could take Hamel, there is a real question as to whether they would be able to hold it, with their fighting force so badly depleted. Taking Sinclair-Maclagan's 4th Division as an example, from a nominal strength of 11,000 bayonets, they currently have only 8000 that they can put in the line. For this operation, they would use six Battalions of men, some 4000 soldiers in all, and it is anticipated they might lose as many as 2000 men in casualties.

On the one hand, Monash is still eager to proceed.

'It was high time,' he would later note, 'that some commanders on our side of No Man's Land should begin to "think offensively", and cease to look over their shoulders in order to estimate how far it still was to the coast.'[68]

But on the other hand, it would be madness to launch such a major operation when they would be risking the battle-readiness of the whole Australian Corps by so doing. The anticipated casualty rate is much higher than Monash is willing to accept, and on 13 June, the Australian Corps commander tells General Rawlinson that he has indeed come to much the same conclusion as General Brudenell White had a month before – taking Hamel will likely cost them too much, for whatever ground is gained. If they maintain the low level of operations of the last two months, the Australian Corps can grow by only 1000 men a month and, at that rate, it would still be six months before it could get back to full strength of 90,000 men in the five Australian Divisions. But with the likely loss to the Australians in an operation like this the Australian Corps would become so weak the only solution would be to disband one of its five divisions.

While disappointed, Rawlinson understands only too well the concerns over losing too many men and so losing operational capacity. There is one thing that might help, however. Perhaps the Americans could be persuaded to dig their oars in, to bolster the ranks of the attacking force? It is with this in mind that Rawlinson decides to bring the US 33rd Division, which is now training behind the Australians at Pierregot, closer to the front as a reserve, pitching in with the British III Corps, just to the north of the Australians – 'as long as we can get Pershing to agree to it . . .'[69]

That, he knows, is far from assured. But does it even matter? Nominally, Pershing is subject to the orders of Field Marshal Ferdinand

Foch, the Commander-in-Chief of all the Allied troops on the Western Front.

'There are difficult questions of command ahead,' Rawlinson writes in his diary. 'Is Foch really the *generalissimo* and is he allowed to divide up the armies as he likes, or not? There will be trouble with Pershing . . .'[70]

Ah, General Rawlinson, if only you knew.

•

For most of the Australian soldiers these early weeks of summer remain a pleasant time in their war, with fun in the sun a welcome change from the blood in the mud they have known for most of it. When not directly in the firing line of the Western Front, the Battalions move into reserve, taking their quarters in one of the many abandoned villages that abound all around, where they are able to help themselves to the abandoned larders and cellars to their hearts' content.

Thus, quaffing the finest champagne with their evening meal becomes quite regular, and on a good night they wouldn't call the King their uncle! But need they leave all that great champers behind when they move back to the line? Gunner Albert Williams and his mates of the 53rd Battery don't think so. Instead of abandoning it, they decide to bury it, and simply put a sign saying 'Dead Horse'[71] over the disturbed earth. Returning from the line a few days later to retrieve the cache, they are relieved to see no-one has flogged the dead horse sign, and they simply throw it away, before digging up the champers and moving off to drink it.

'A lot of English troops round about watched the Aussies with curiosity,' Gunner Williams would recount, 'wondering at them digging up a dead horse, but when they saw the bottles unearthed they were astounded. After the Aussies drove away they dug up the ground wherever there was a dead horse notice, but needless to say they only found dead horse.'[72]

•

Extraordinary, how four years of war can change a man. Back at home in Warialda, if some cove had taken a shot at him and the bullet had gone within two coo-ees, or even one bull's roar, of him, Cliff Geddes would have viewed it with some alarm, and no little ill-will towards the said cove.

But not now. The extraordinary truth is, he has become so used to bullets flying about that he and others even have an all but affectionate pet-name for them, as in 'Blighties', the things that will get you back to Old Blighty, England, if you get wounded, just right.

When it comes to shells, however, Cliff is less sanguine.

On this evening, after a *bastard* of a day, digging a six foot trench to lay a cable that would be impervious to being shelled – exhausted, harassed by 'insects sucking blood from our arms, & getting in one's eyes & ears . . . the poor old infantry do all the dirty work & fighting too',[73] – Cliff gets back to his 13th Battalion digs to hear that his mate Freedman had been killed by a shell, and five others wounded.

Freedman! Only a few days ago, Cliff had been chatting to him, a 'picture of health & vigour', who'd had 'a whiff of gas, & was hoping he might get worse & get a Blighty out of it'.[74]

And now, he's *dead*?

So devastated is Cliff, he heads over to A Company dugouts, and, sure enough, there is Freedman's shattered body lying on the stretcher before him, about to be carried off by four devastated mates and a handy 'sky pilot', chaplain, for burial. Good God! Imagine that could be him, or, worse, his brothers Boo or Stanley? How would their family ever recover?

'No language could describe the horror of this cursed war,' Cliff records his thoughts in his diary, '& if God would only end this awful slaughter of good men! A man hasn't a chance, here was Freedman back here at night, & suddenly struck down like a leaf.'[75]

•

Meanwhile, the raids on the German trenches continue, sometimes by way of pure celebration. A case in point occurs on 15 June, when Lieutenant James Minchin of the 16th Battalion mentions to his best mate, Corporal Jack Axford, that he has an idea . . .

An idea? Jack knows what that likely means. The two are both 24 years old, and have fought together for years. Most of James

Minchin's ideas are violent and destructive of the enemy, which is why Minch had risen from Private to Lieutenant in such a short space of time and how he had already earned a Military Cross for his valour at Passchendaele, as well as being Mentioned in Despatches at the Somme in 1916. An idea you say, Minch?

Yes, an idea.

'It's my birthday,' says Minch on this 15th day of June. 'Let's celebrate by sneaking out into No Man's Land and chucking a few bombs in to Fritz's trench.'[76]

And so they do. It sure beats blowing out candles, in terms of having explosive fun – even if, now in high summer, No Man's Land has a stench that is near indescribable.

'Pieces of men were lying around,' one of their fellow soldiers will describe it. 'A lot of them where they had been left when the Tommies retreated. In fact all this place smells like a charnel house. It was here where we stopped the Hun's run.'[77]

CHAPTER THREE

TANKS FOR THE HELP

All possible mechanical devices [should be used] in order to increase the offensive power of our divisions. The only two directions in which such development can be reasonably expected are (1) the increase of machine guns, Lewis Guns and automatic rifles, and (2) the increase of numbers and functions of tanks.[1]

General Sir Henry Rawlinson, Fourth Army HQ,
in directive issued in early June 1918

My dear Bridges,
... When next you see Mr President Wilson you can tell him that if he wants to win the war (and we all know he does) he must replace Pershing [who] is too stupid and obstinate a man ever to win a Titanic struggle like this and the sooner Wilson realises this, the better.[2]

Rawlinson, letter to General George Bridges, 14 June 1918

The Australian high commander was distracted during some of the most vital days of the war. It is perhaps the outstanding case of sheer irresponsibility by pressmen in Australian history.[3]

Geoffrey Serle, Australian historian, 1982, on the involvement of
Charles Bean and Keith Murdoch in trying to remove General Monash as
Commanding Officer of the Australian Corps

18 June 1918, Pont Noyelles, five miles behind the lines, a fall from grace

It does not take long for even new 'reinstoushments' to work out the difference between good planes and bad planes.

The bad planes are often multi-coloured – curse you, Red Baron, lying in your grave just 450 yards from the medieval walls of Bertangles

70

Chateau! – and have the bar cross, *Balkenkreuz,* as the insignia on the wings, enabling them to be identified from above or below. For their part, the Royal Air Force planes have blue, white and red target-like 'roundels', or circles, on the underside and the Australian Flying Corps have the same rounded identifier.

The other way of telling Hun aircraft, of course, is when they start attacking your observation balloons, and this afternoon is a case in point.

Relaxing in rear support trenches west of Villers-Bretonneux, Private Isaac Betteridge of the 23rd Battalion, a 31-year-old farmer from Wondai, Queensland, is just minding his own business gazing at the ponds along the Somme when, suddenly, seemingly out of nowhere, a Hun plane comes screaming out of the clouds, diving straight at one of the many British observation balloons that so gracefully line the Western Front – always with a couple of observers with binoculars taking notes on all German movements they can spy.

Of course the British Ack-Ack guns open up, and bursts of flak are soon puffing all around the Hun in the sun, but it is too late. At least one burst of bullets the Hun has been firing at the balloon has set it on fire and, as Betteridge and his mates watch, appalled but enthralled, the two observers are seen to climb out of their hanging basket and . . . jump!

Before their very eyes, the chute of one of them suddenly blooms like a rose in spring, and he 'sailed away, splendid'.[4]

Alas, the other poor devil's chute won't open!

'He came straight down 1000 feet,' Betteridge would recount. 'He kept kicking and squirming trying to open it.'[5]

The amazing thing?

The bloke hits the top of a large poplar tree, and with every branch breaking his fall a little further on the way down, he not only lives, but walks away with naught but 'a bit of a strained back'.

'The other whom we thought so safe,' Betteridge would recount, 'caught a bullet in the stomach . . .'[6]

•

It is a strange thing.

Sometimes in war, the only thing more disconcerting than an enemy attack is when nothing is happening, and you know, you just *know*, they must be right on the cusp of striking again . . . you just don't know where. But how long can that last?

Surely, the Germans must attack again, soon, as yet more of their Divisions arrive from the newly quiet Russian front? But where?

And yet, as the weeks have gone by, no attack emerges. The diary entry of General Rawlinson, thus, on 21 May 1918, is rather emblematic of the situation:

> The attack [expected] this morning did not come off and I am at
> a loss to know why. All conditions of weather seemed favourable
> yet nothing happened.

And so, a penny for your thoughts, General Rawlinson? Or is that the sound of the penny dropping? Could it be that Fritz is weaker than they think, and actually in no shape to launch another major attack? If so, is the time perfect for us Allies to make a major attack ourselves? After all, just as the first German thrust at Paris, Operation Blucher, which had started in the last days of May, had been halted, so too has their second thrust, Operation Gneisenau, stalled. Evidence is building that the German war machine might indeed be running out of fuel.

General Rawlinson ponders the question, just as fellow Generals do along the Western Front in this period of mid-June. The difference is, with his growing conviction that there is no big German attack coming after all, Rawlinson has a major attack in mind that he has long wanted to pursue and now decides to give it a big push.

20 June 1918, Vaux, 5th Tank Brigade training ground

Meantime, on an open field at Vaux, just 15 miles back from the frontlines and only two miles from Bertangles, on this afternoon, General

Monash and his Chief of Staff, General Thomas Blamey, are present for an interesting demonstration.

General Hugh Elles – the inaugural commander of the newly formed Tank Corps, who had led the most notable tank attack so far, 350 of them at Cambrai in November 1917 – has invited them here with a very specific purpose in mind. A 38-year-old who'd been badly wounded at Ypres in 1915, General Elles, known as 'father of the Tanks Corps', knows only too well the dangers of the battlefield for soldiers, and passionately believes that his tanks can win the war, while reducing casualty rates. Most specifically, he believes in the new Mark V tanks now performing before them – doing turns, firing machine guns and cannons alike – which, he maintains, are 'as superior to the Mark IV as a 1905 motor-car was superior to one of 1895'.[7]

For you must understand, General Monash, the Mark V boasts the very finest of British engineering. This is a next-generation tank, well beyond the ones we used at Bullecourt. To begin with, it has a purpose-built Ricardo engine, delivering an incredible 150 horsepower, with a four-speed gearbox enabling it to get traction even in muddy churned ground. Best thing? It requires just one man to drive it – as opposed to the four needed for the Mark IV – has greater manoeuvrability and a smaller turning circle, yet with a range *twice* that of the IV, being able to go as far as 45 miles, and *much* faster than previous tanks. Yes, as extraordinary as it seems, the Mark V, weighing all of 28 tons, can maintain a speed of as much as five miles per hour!

Now, while the 'male' Mark V has two six-pounder Hotchkiss Guns which can each fire a six-pound shell as far as 7300 yards with devastating effect, the 'females' bristle with no fewer than *six* Hotchkiss Mk 1 machine guns, one mounted at the rear, one at the front and two on each side, meaning that they can be lethal around the whole clock-face of the battle, sending the enemy to eternity wherever he may be found. What is more, both versions have better visibility, and with more tight slots in the armour – large enough to see out of, but unlikely to allow shrapnel in – there is *much* better vision to see the brutes! Even more importantly, the petrol tanks are now armoured, meaning that, unlike the Mark IV, they won't explode even if hit. Yes, with one unlucky hit, you *won't* be automatically burnt to a crisp – the news gets better and better.

All up, Elles is, as one of his tank commanders would recall, 'anxious that they be given a trial run . . .'[8]

What he needs is for an attacking General to *also* believe in them, someone who can throw them into battle.

General Elles is accompanied by Brigadier Anthony Courage of the 5th Tank Brigade, whose tanks are about to be put through their paces, and with a nod from Elles, Courage gets things underway.

For an hour, Monash and Blamey watch with interest that builds into real excitement as several new Mark Vs accelerate, swerve, pirouette and fire both their six-pounder cannons and Hotchkiss machine guns, leaving their targets a mere smoking mish-mash of what they had been, either riddled with holes or completely destroyed. Both men come away quite stunned at the possibilities of such lethal machines, which is exactly the idea . . .

For when General Monash arrives back at the Australian Corps HQ at Bertangles Chateau, sweeping through the now opened gates 'neath an arch that was constructed by skilled French artisans who've been in their graves for the better part of two centuries now, a visitor awaits, none other than General Henry Rawlinson, a man of whom Monash is a little wary, but anyway . . .

From the beginning, Rawlinson had wanted General Brudenell White to get the Australian Corps – 'I am delighted',[9] he had noted in his diary on 12 May last, when erroneously told that White had got it – and had been distinctly underwhelmed when informed it was in fact Monash.

At least in part, Rawlinson's problem is General Monash's Judaism, as he will later blithely refer to another man as 'a clever, slippery, creepy, crawly Jew . . . not unlike Monash'.[10]

Whatever else, however, Rawlinson is professional in his dealings, and on this day the British General is quick to make a proposal to both Monash and the Australian officer commanding the 4th Division in front of Hamel, General Ewen Sinclair-Maclagan, who Rawlinson has also asked to be present. Why not, he asks, launch 'an attack with two battalions of tanks against Hamel village and spur to improve our position east of Villers-Bretonneux?'[11]

On the spot, Sinclair-Maclagan, who had not accompanied General Monash to the tank demonstration, reels.

'It is never difficult,' the most celebrated English comic novelist of this day, P.G. Wodehouse, would famously write, 'to distinguish between a Scotsman with a grievance and a ray of sunshine.'[12]

And here is a case in point.

Rely on *tanks* to overcome the German resistance? The same way the 4th Division had relied on them at the First Battle of Bullecourt in April 1917, only to be torn apart when the 16 tanks were late. All of Sinclair-Maclagan's senior officers and men feel the same way. Remember Bullecourt!

For who can forget Major Percy Black crying out, once the bloody things had not turned up when they were meant to, 'Come on boys, bugger the tanks . . !'[13] only shortly before he was killed. Nearly all of the tanks had broken down, and even of those that had spluttered and stuttered their way forward, none had got as far as the first German trench. Oh yes, they had killed a few soldiers, but they had been Australians, gunned down by mistake! In a day there had been no fewer than 3300 Australian casualties, including 1250 good men captured. A complete bloody disaster, and all because of the fucking tanks!

General Monash, however, is much more receptive.

Two Battalions of those same tanks he has just seen in action? That does sound interesting, and would provide the answer we have been looking for since having had to shelve the planned battle against Hamel the week before, because the casualty cost would be too high. Advances in 'Fighting Machinery'[14] thus are precisely what he is looking for, as he had long ago come to the conclusion that the future of warfare will centre on which side has the best of such fighting machinery, rather than who has, or is prepared to sacrifice, the most men.

And so he listens intently as General Rawlinson takes up where Elles had left off and gives some of the detail of this new type of tank, which has just come off the line and is ready to prove itself in its first battle. And General Rawlinson has no doubt it will.

Gentlemen, the beauty of the whole thing is this. With these tanks, you simply don't need the great artillery barrage, which is not always effective and has the downside of forewarning the enemy that you are coming. No, with these machines of war, you just put the tanks at the front to do the work the artillery did – destroying the wire, crushing the resistance in the trenches with both their tracks and their guns – and keep the infantry tight in behind them to mop up what is left. The beauty of it is that the Germans are very near powerless to stop you! Yes, if they have any artillery close up they are a chance if they get a direct hit, and they've also issued a few anti-tank rifles – singularly heavy and powerful guns, with heavy bullets which can penetrate armour – but our best intelligence is they have very few, as yet.

And Hamel would be *ideal* for the fact that the ground before it slopes only gently, is covered in crops and is relatively firm, not yet torn apart by shell-holes – so getting traction for their tracks would be no problem. Only after taking Hamel and going after Wolfsberg would the tanks meet a steep slope, but even then the tanks should be able to take it!

'Maclagan is not overjoyed at the prospect of tanks,' Rawlinson concedes in his diary that evening, 'but we will get him round when he has had experience of the new type.'[15]

It is arranged that the next day Monash will meet Brigadier Anthony Courage, whose 5th Tank Brigade has been assigned to General Rawlinson's Fourth Army and is to provide the three or four dozen tanks that are mooted.

'Conditional upon being supplied with the assistance of tanks,' General Monash would later recount, 'a small increase in my artillery and an addition to my air resources . . . Lord Rawlinson requested me to submit a concrete proposal in writing . . .'[16]

•

At a much longer meeting the next day at the 5th Tank Brigade's HQ at Vaux, General Monash and Brigadier-General Courage get to know each other a little better, and like each other more with each minute. In part, it is because Courage is exactly Monash's kind of officer, one who relies less on the pips on his shoulder for his authority, and more on the fact that, beyond his rank, he really is a natural born leader.

'General Courage was my General during the whole of my service with the tanks,' one of his officers would later note. 'He was fair in his judgements and gave me a pat on the back when he thought a thing well done. He demanded good work from his officers, and saw that he got it.'[17]

True, it is a tad disconcerting that Brigadier Courage appears to display a permanent smirk, particularly on the left side of his face, but it is not his fault. Earlier in the war, an errant piece of shrapnel had shattered his lower jaw and when all the King's surgeons and all the King's men had put him back together again, it had left him with an expression quite the opposite of the kind of man he is.

Courage is, however, nothing if not *confident* that, if his tanks are used in the right way as part of the Hamel battle plan, they will be able to make a serious breakthrough. Brigadier Courage points out that the tanks can push through into the German rear and create havoc, squash machine-gun nests, and generally so horrify Fritz that he might well run away without a fight!

Together, he and Monash work out a rough plan of how the tanks might be used in the battle, which Courage agrees to refine into a formal memorandum, while Monash begins to assemble other parts of the battle plan. On the basis of their conversation on this afternoon, General Monash makes a note, about what might be possible in attacking Hamel: '36 tanks, bring them up one mile behind our line, wind up engines in early morning then creep up and cross our line at Zero [Hour]. – Consider question of using sledges for tanks to pull up engineer stores . . . All platoon and tank commanders to reconnoitre . . .'[18]

•

Just a little to the south, at this time, an American Sergeant is one of a scattering of his Army who has been placed with Allied armies on the front-line to gather a little experience, and in this case he has been placed with Cliff Geddes' platoon in the 13th Battalion's D Company.

Just to hear him speak makes Cliff want to burst out laughing, as he sounds *exactly* like the blokes who take off the Yanks' ridiculous accent in the various Army stage shows – drinking cups of *cawfee*, firing their *at-tillery* and sometimes being frustrated, *gawsh* darn it!

'We're keen to be right in it,' the Yank tells Cliff. 'We've got a fine lot of young guys.'

'What's the general opinion in America about the war?' Cliff asks.

'The opinion is we'll whip 'em right soon.'[19]

Well, *that's* a relief!

Still, welcome to the trenches, young man. And he really is welcome, not least for the fact that, in the pouring rain on this night, Cliff's platoon is down to just 22 men from its usual strength of 30 and official strength of 44 – flu, 'Blighties', fatalities – so an extra shoulder to the wheel is important, even if it is an inexperienced one. A listening post is set up in No Man's Land to give early warning of any attacks that might be coming, patrols are sent out, the trench is dug deeper, as they hurl ever more mud over the parapet, and it is 3 am when everything is quiet once more. There is no possie for the Yank to sleep in, so he will have to make one himself – no easy task as it continues to piss down rain, and is 'very mucky under foot', but, in this man's army, that is the way it works.

The next morning, Cliff is up early and having a shave, his head momentarily above the top of the parapet, when he steps aside and another cove, Sergeant Peter Dwyer – a tough bricklayer from Thirroul in New South Wales – comes along and stands exactly where he had been, just as there is the crack of a shot in the distance. The German bullet hits Dwyer right in the back of the head, and if not for the fact he was wearing his steel helmet – Cliff had not been – would have killed him.

'What luck, eh, there was I without a hat on, so it would have gone through my skull.'[20]

•

It is a dark and stormy night . . .

And yet, into the wee hours, one dim light continues to shine on the third floor of the Bertangles Chateau, HQ of the Australian Corps. It is, of course, in the study of General John Monash who – ever and always a man for the midnight oil, and beyond – continues to form up his plans for the battle ahead, which he estimates he should be able to unleash in around a fortnight. Though already familiar with the topography of the land around Hamel and its key defences, he is further aided now in framing the attack by examining the many aerial photos spread out on the desk before him, while also using the memo from Brigadier Courage as a key part of the blueprint.

On the far northern end of the attack zone, the hardest nut to crack will be the village of Hamel itself, where the heavily dug in Germans will be able to use the remaining houses and their rubble for protection, not to mention the cellars beneath, many of which are now interconnected by the Germans burrowing through. Behind Hamel is the hill, Wolfsberg, upon which Fritz is also deeply entrenched.

A thousand yards south-west of Hamel, on the lower reaches of the *far* side of a hill that lies before the Australian trenches, the Germans

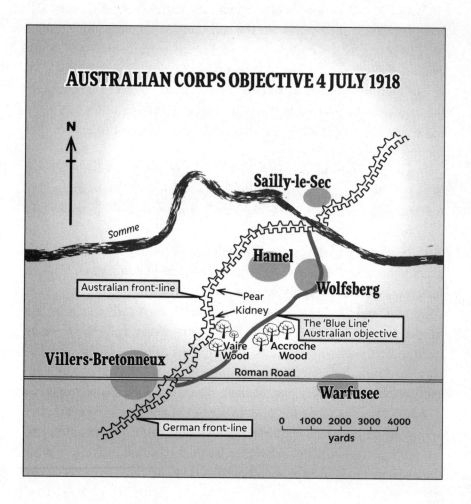

AUSTRALIAN CORPS OBJECTIVE 4 JULY 1918

N

Somme

Sailly-le-Sec

Hamel

Wolfsberg

Australian front-line

Pear
Kidney

The 'Blue Line'
Australian objective

Vaire
Wood

Accroche
Wood

Villers-Bretonneux

Roman Road

Warfusee

German front-line

0   1000 2000 3000 4000
yards

are dug into a trench that curves around. The whole thing is rather in the shape of a pear when you look at it from aerial photographs, hence its sobriquet, 'Pear Trench'. It will be singularly difficult for the Australians to take, for the fact that, as they move forward, they won't be able to *see* the German defenders until they have crested the hill and are right on top of them and under close-range fire.

The next problem will be Vaire Wood, situated just to the south and east again of Pear Trench. The western slope below the wood, the one facing the Australians, boasts a formidable trench stretching for 200 yards, bristling with machine-gun emplacements, and with a support trench behind the first one, the whole lot dubbed 'Kidney Trench', for the fact that its shape on the map looks exactly like that.

Again, it will be a formidable task, as here too the attackers will have to expose themselves on the hill crest to the west, and that is heavily protected by endless rolls of barbed wire, behind which are *dozens* of well-secured machine-gun posts.

Through the plumes of smoke coming from his ever puffing pipe, the engineer's pen flies over page after page – making notes just as he did when building bridges – and again he does his best to ensure that the fog of war will dissipate.

It will later be noted that Monash 'was trying to evolve a science of war which would be as exact as the science of engineering. He wanted to be able to rely on a battle in the same way he could rely on a bridge.'[21]

Perhaps more to the point, Monash brings to building a battle plan exactly the same *methodology* as he once did to building those bridges. As ever, he seeks to apply science to the problems before him, first collecting, and then analysing, a mass of data, then gathering a variety of specialists to consult on particularly thorny issues, and then working out the best way to proceed. The proposed solution is checked and checked again, discussed, refined, and slowly re-refined, ideally with every specialist on every part of the problem working closely together.

And just as the plans for bridges are specific to the sites where they are built, so too does Monash instinctively, minutely, examine the contours of the landscape where his battle is to occur, looking to place the plan on the land in a manner that fits, perfectly.

Whatever else, there is no doubt his timing is good. As the war now moves to a phase where more technology than ever before is being brought to bear in terms of artillery, tanks and aircraft, it *needs* a man with technical expertise to firstly understand the capacities of that technology and properly organise it.

(He is not fazed by trying a combination of methods that have not been tried before, all to the good. He had taken the same approach in championing the virtues of reinforced concrete two decades earlier. In a world of traditional cast iron, wrought iron, brickwork, stonework and ordinary concrete, Monash had recognised that reinforced concrete could do things in building structures that they could not then get close to, and had emerged as *the* Australian leader in the field, completely revolutionising the building world.)

And so it continues into the night, as the famed engineer from Melbourne puts together the bare bones of what he hopes will be the first serious Allied attack on German lines for over seven months.

Though his Chief of Staff, General Thomas Blamey, has been with him through most of the day, discussing various ways of overcoming the German defences, even he has now gone to bed as Monash continues, even as a storm outside passes and the rising moon adds to the illumination of what he is creating.

The broad plan that is forming up is one that has come together over the last 36 hours . . . but has relied on Monash's *lifetime* of experience to bring him to this point. For yes, although on the one hand this is the first time he has been called on to put together such an extraordinarily comprehensive and complicated battle plan, bringing together men, *matériel* and machinery in a manner to overcome determined opposition . . . on the other hand, as an engineer working on major projects, he had brought together those elements in equally complicated plans many times before.

This is, yes, more complicated, and more a matter of immediate life and death than whether a building will stand or fall in the future, but the calculations that pour from his flying pen are based on the same broad principles. In all of his engineering projects, he had relied on tight organisation, thorough consultation between all elements of the enterprise, use of state-of-the-art technology, exploration of all available innovations and enormous intellectual energy, with a fierce commitment to sticking to the plan that evolves. Now, he intends to do exactly the same thing in battle as the hours ebb away and an entire plan forms up beneath his fingertips. And rather than be intimidated by his lack of experience in this particular field of forming up battle plans compared to the many gnarled full-time Army Generals who are his contemporaries, Monash actually believes he is liberated by *not* having their experience. After all, when the long-time professional army men began their careers, warfare was much more a matter of the movement of horses, rifles, and a few cannon. Now, it is about the movement of the *machinery* of war, of technology, and as an engineer this is his precise field. His own background, thus, is 'far more useful for general applications to new problems than the comparatively narrow training of the professional soldier'.[22]

To begin with, while mathematics had never featured large in the studies pursued by most Generals, for Monash the discipline has been the foundation stone of his engineering career, which is as well, because this logistical exercise is an enormous one, as his pen continues to fly. In this case, he must organise 8000 men, 5000 tons of artillery ammunition – borne in 3000 wagon trips – to move together with several dozen tanks and all come together at much the same place, at much the same time, all without the enemy being aware that anything is different from usual.

In many ways, General Monash is now building the very large-scale battle plan – three times bigger than anything he has ever tried before – that he has always wanted to build.

The first, and most important thing, for him, beyond winning the battle, is to be able to do so without the 'inefficiency'[23] of the war to date, which had seen most 'victories', such as they were, built on horrific casualty levels and overwhelming numbers of shells.

No, by relying on the tanks to do the heavy work of crushing the German wire and taking the trenches, it means the Australians could go over the top without first unleashing the usual heavy bombardment lasting several days, a tactic which was not always successful in the first place. Before the opening of the Battle of the Somme, for example, the bombardment of the Germans had gone for an entire *week*, only for the British to have 20,000 soldiers *killed* on just the first day. In fact, Monash is such a believer in the power of the tanks, he decides the troops could even advance without a rolling barrage preceding them, moving forward behind an exploding wall of protective artillery fire that would leap forward by 100 yards every three minutes.

Though 'Zero Hour', the exact time of the attack, and 'Z Day', the day of the attack, are yet to be determined, many other principles and even actions can be determined now, to be fleshed out later.

The second thing General Monash wants is surprise: to make the attack with a massive force assembled close to German lines, without Fritz knowing they are there.

Thirdly, he wants *speed*. When the Allies had taken the windmill above Pozières – the highest point above the Somme – it had taken them six weeks to advance three miles.

Monash thinks Wolfsberg, the hill behind Hamel, can be taken by his men in, let's see . . .

The distance from their current positions to the furthest reaches of the German lines they seek to occupy is 2500 yards, about a mile and a half. Now an unencumbered soldier with no obstacles in front of him, and no resistance, could walk that distance easily in 30 minutes. A fully laden soldier, however, using traditional methods of attack, as at Pozières, might take . . . a *week*, on the off-chance he survived. But in this case, fully encumbered, and with the benefit of massive firepower clearing his way in a lightning, surprise strike, with the pace of the advance timed to the pace of the creeping barrage it should take . . . 90 minutes.

And, if one part of the plan doesn't work, no matter. For, just as he was trained as an engineer to design and build bridges with a liberal safety factor – to allow for unforeseen circumstances, and give a margin for error in his own calculations, or the execution of them by others – so too with this battle plan. If in doubt, provide excess firepower; and always have backup so that, like a bridge, even if one support fails, the other supports will be strong enough to prevent catastrophic collapse.

The two factors Monash now pursues are surprise and *speed*. Hit the enemy not with a succession of blows, but many blows at once coming from so many different and surprising angles, he *must* cede, and retreat!

So, no preliminary bombardment at all, and instead just the tanks roaring forth – on wonderfully firm ground, because it would not have been torn up by the artillery – followed by the infantry.

Now, following Brigadier Courage's idea, and his memo, Monash's plan develops as first and foremost a tank operation, with the tanks on offer attacking over a front of 6500 yards, stretching from the Somme to the Roman Road that runs east from Villers-Bretonneux, and penetrating some 2500 yards in the centre – encompassing, most crucially, Hamel, Wolfsberg and Vaire Wood, while tapering to just a thousand yards or so penetration on the southern edge. At this point the Blue Line – the target line on the map the Australians intend to reach – will rest just before Accroche Wood, a small grove of trees south of Wolfsberg on the same ridgeline that runs north to south. With his ruler and a blue pencil, Monash carefully draws on the map his desired destination. On the north side no tapering is required as there the Australian 42nd Battalion will advance parallel to the Somme, the far bank of which is already in Australian hands.

Time and again, General Monash's eyes are drawn to the memo from Courage, on the desk before him, which had arrived by motorbike courier a few hours earlier:

SECRET & CONFIDENTIAL
H.Q. 5th Tank Bde No. G.26/16.

Lieut-Gen. Dir J MONASH, K.C.B., Commanding Australian Corps With regard to the proposed Attack South of the SOMME ...

Courage envisages an attack led by 48 tanks with the infantry coming on behind.

The way Courage conceives it – based on the density of enemy resistance expected – and Monash agrees, 15 tanks will attack Hamel village, another 15 will be assigned to Vaire Wood, while a dozen should be sufficient to subdue Pear Trench and three to the Villers-Bretonneux flank, leaving three in reserve. The tanks will move forward in three basic waves, with the first wave given the task of crushing the wire and destroying the German machine-gun posts, before wreaking havoc behind their lines, shooting down both fleeing Fritzes and those streaming forward as reinforcements. Just 300 yards behind, the second wave of tanks would come in with the infantry – while the final wave would be 300 yards behind again, ready to mop up remaining resistance and act as support for whatever tanks in the first two waves found themselves in trouble. Now, as well as wiping out any Germans they find, together with the German defensive infrastructure, waves two and three will also act as transport for key supplies for the infantry, such as rolls of barbed wire to establish defensive positions before the newly established trenches, together with ammo, water and rations for the soldiers so they can not only dig in, but sustain themselves in their forward positions.

> Tanks will have to search ground and subdue targets, there cannot
> be any fixed interval between Tanks.[24]

What is more, because it is extremely important that the tanks come as a shocking surprise to Fritz, they will have to be secreted well back from the start line, and only brought up to their Jumping Off Point after darkness falls, finally catching up to the infantry and passing them, just as they reach the first German trenches.

Now, once those tanks pass them, the soldiers will have to do their best to stay in tight behind, 'so that they may at once make good any opportunity the Tanks create and free the Tanks to continue their advance and so keep the battle moving forward by creating a succession of opportunities for the Infantry in rear.'[25]

With one tank for every 120 yards or so, troops will be able to take more of a supporting role, finishing off the Germans who have survived the barrage and the tanks. The troops will then be able to hold the newly won positions, after the tanks have withdrawn.

> The Tanks will leave their Assembly places under cover of darkness
> on night Y.Z., so as to arrive at their Starting Line just before it
> is time to attack.[26]

As to the difficult issue of when Zero Hour should be, the infantry preferred to start while it was still dark, but 'from a Tank point of view [ZERO Hour] should be fixed so as to admit of Tank Crews being able to see their direction'.[27]

Finally, planes will be used for a variety of purposes on the night, but one task is particularly clear: 'If the enemy is bombed it will tend to keep him below ground. This action will help to ensure the attack coming as a surprise to the enemy.'[28]

How many troops?

As few as possible. Obviously, the thicker the attacking formations the greater the losses, and so, concerned to keep infantry casualties to a minimum, Monash's goal is for the 'fighting machinery', the tanks, artillery and aircraft, to do as much of the heavy lifting as possible, so less infantry is needed. Now, to get the balance just right is not easy – as if you have too few infantry the attack fails, too many and it will likely succeed, but at too high a cost – but, as ever, Monash is guided by his instinct, informed by his experience and reaches his final decision based on precise calculations.

All up, General Monash decides, just ten Battalions should do the trick, some 7000 men in all, so in the front-line there will be a man only every four yards.

In the early part of the war, the central idea had been to send so many men forward – as many as five soldiers for every yard of front-line, thicker even than shoulder to shoulder – that even if thousands were shot, there would be enough survivors left to overwhelm the defenders. Using such an approach, at the Battle of Fromelles, 7000 Australians of the 5th Division had rushed towards bristling German bunkers in broad daylight, across a distance of as much as 400 yards with *no cover*, and, not surprisingly, over the next 14 hours, over 5000 had become casualties, of whom 1900 had been killed.

This part of his deliberations is certain – such madness can never occur again, and certainly not in daylight.

One thing that General Monash is sure of, from the beginning, is that this will be a *surprise* night-time attack, in fact in the wee-est of wee hours, when German alertness will be at its lowest ebb for the day.

And while confident that, with the surprise factor, casualties will remain low, either way, he seeks to ensure that what losses there are do not fall on one Division. Thus, while command of the battle will fall to General Ewen Sinclair-Maclagan – whose crack 4th Division is responsible for that part of the German line to be attacked – the ten attacking Battalions will come from four Brigades, of three Divisions. On the far left, 11th Brigade's 42nd, 43rd and 44th Battalions, advancing with the Somme on their left, will take Hamel village and the towering Wolfsberg behind it.

Now, to take on Pear Trench, Kidney Trench and Vaire Wood, positioned right in the middle of the four-mile front that the Australians will be attacking, and the most formidable of the defences – General Monash is quick to choose what he considers some of the finest troops he has available, to accompany the Mark V tanks he has assigned to the task. The 4th Division's own 4th Brigade, three years ago under command of General Monash himself at Gallipoli – composed of the 13th, 14th, 15th and 16th Battalions – will, under the command of General Charles Brand, take on that enormous responsibility.

Finally, out on the right of the whole attack, the 2nd Division's 6th Brigade – with 21st and 23rd Battalions, backed by the 25th Battalion of the 7th Brigade – will be given the task of advancing just 1000 yards to cover the right flank of the 4th and 11th Brigades' main assault.

Helping all three Brigades, from across the Somme River, Brigadier Pompey Elliott's 15th Brigade will launch a series of feint attacks, to confuse the Germans and make them think that the front being attacked stretches all the way up to the Ancre River. The more the German response is diffused, the fewer the forces placed in the way of the actual assault.

•

Finally, the plan is done, and before sending it off to General Rawlinson, General Monash gives it one last read-through, his eyes drawn to the nub of it . . .

Australian Corps.
21st June 1918.

Fourth Army._

HAMEL OFFENSIVE

. . .

(a) The operation will be primarily a Tank operation – at least one and preferably two Battalions of Tanks to be employed [. . .]

(c) The infantry employed will comprise one Division plus a Brigade, i.e., 4 Infantry Brigades, totalling, say, 7,500 bayonets; about one-half of this force to be employed in the advance and the other half to hold our present front defensively taking over the captured territory within 48 hours after Zero.

(d) The action will be designed on lines to permit of the Tanks effecting the capture of the ground; the roles of the Infantry following the Tanks will be:

    (i)   to assist in reducing strong points and localities.

    (ii) to 'mop up.'

    (iii) to consolidate the ground captured.

(e) Apart from neutralizing all enemy artillery likely to engage our troops, our artillery will be employed to keep under fire enemy centres of resistance and selected targets – in front of the advance of the Tanks. Artillery detailed for close targets will work on a prearranged and detailed time-table which will be adjusted to the time-table of the Tank and Infantry advance [. . .]

(h) Contact and counter-attack planes and low-flying bombing planes prior to and during advance must be arranged for.

(i) Artillery and mortar smoke to screen the operations from view of all ground north of the Somme in the SAILLY-LAURETTE locality are required [. . .]

[I]t would seem that this operation cannot take place earlier than the first week in July [. . .]

(Sgd.) JOHN MONASH,
Lieut.-General.
Cmdg. Australian Corps.[29]

How to get the tanks forward without forewarning the Germans?

Monash already has what he thinks is a good idea on that, which he intends to flesh out well before Zero Hour on Z Day. And he also has an idea how to make the Germans even less alert at that hour, less capable of resisting, than they otherwise would be.

General Monash also has an innovative idea about how to get fresh ammunition supplies a long way forward, without risking the lives of the men in the way it has always been done – whole platoons assigned to carry ammunition boxes across the deathly No Man's Land exposed to shot and shell.

It might be a bit tricky, but General Monash has heard tell of just the man who might be of help. Some on his staff had attended Duntroon with a notably inventive officer of the Australian Flying Corps . . .

•

The plan finished, Monash dashes off a note to the Australian Corps' Intelligence Officer:

> *Major Hunn,*
> *Prepare for me a very rough approximate estimate of the number of*
> *enemy likely to be found by us in the area enclosed by our present front*
> *line opposite Hamel–Vaire-Wood and the proposed objective blue line.*
> *J.M.*
> *21/6/18*[30]

Morning, 22 June, Bertangles Chateau, forward on a wing and a prayer

General Monash?

Captain Lawrence Wackett is here to see you.

Of course, show him in.

Now, it isn't every day that a flying officer is summoned to the presence of the Commanding Officer of the entire Australian Corps. But such is the case for Captain Lawrence Wackett, a young pilot from Townsville. Though still only 22 years old, this graduate of the Royal Military College Duntroon has already made a name for himself among his colleagues for his courage and his brilliance. This had included being the first man in the Australian Flying Corps to engage a German aircraft in the war, when taking on a Hun over Beersheba on 11 November 1916. More importantly in terms of his overall influence, however, his creative bent had seen him design a fuse setter to determine at what altitude an aerial bomb would explode, and also invent and construct a bracket to place a Lewis Gun on the top wing of the Royal Aircraft Factory Bleriot Experimental 2c plane he'd been flying through most of 1917. Both innovations had become standard in the Australian Flying Corps. His fame had spread and, sounding like just the man General Monash is looking for, he has been sent for.

Now, though as polite and affable as ever to his junior officers, General Monash does not take long in getting to the central purpose of the meeting. He is a man with a great deal to organise, limited time to do it, and many lives hanging in the balance.

'I am planning offensive operations,' he says crisply, of course omitting to give any specific details, 'and wish to reduce casualties by having ammunition conveyed by air to troops in the front-line during battle . . .'[31]

In short, can you work out a way whereby we can safely and accurately drop ammunition from the air on precisely identified spots?

'I can,' Wackett replies on the spot, 'and will be ready within a few days to give a demonstration.'[32]

No, Captain Wackett does not have an exact solution ready to go right now, but in a few days time he is sure he will be able to come up with something. For, just like General Monash himself, Captain Wackett delights in solving such problems and tends to view the whole field of military aviation as a race between the Allies and the enemy to find the solutions first.

Yes, General, leave it with me.

•

And now what?

Sergeant Walter Corning and his companions from the American 131st Regiment have been sent to gain experience in the trenches in a cushy spot with III British Corps, just north of the Australians.

'Our hearts jumped up to the top of our stomachs,' Corning would recount, 'slid down the sides, and then turned somersaults as we entered the communicating trench. A sign at the entrance of the trench gravely informed us of its name. It was Whiskey Boulevard.'[33]

Making their way down the trenches that lead to the front-line, the Americans are aware of shrapnel flying overhead, even as bullets 'phitted'[34] into sandbags just above, as the men bump and splash their way along Whiskey Boulevard.

'Now and then,' Corning chronicles, 'a *zing-g-g* made us duck as a stray bullet ricocheted. We reached the front line in a light fog with only three minor casualties and felt relieved when we discovered that it was really quiet. Only the intermittent *rat-a-tat-tat* of one Jerry machine gun broke the silence out in front. Our hearts behaved and our knees stopped knocking. All signs of nervousness disappeared into night. The valley below was black and misty. The moon was a solid red ball, making the sky around it a deep purple. Overhead shrapnel flashed constantly in the woods and gas shells landed with a soft thud in the valley . . . the faint odour of gas . . . the gas alarm . . . the shell-torn land between the lines was sprinkled with star shells which lighted up No Man's Land like a carnival. We stood in the mud, leaned against the parapet and waited . . . straining our eyes at every flash, gripping our rifles more tensely . . .'[35]

Gentlemen of America, welcome to the Western Front.

Throughout the long night they continue to keep a goggle-eyed watch, hearing machine guns barking on their left, and artillery roaring in front of them. In the wee hours it grows very damp and cold, and they are relieved to be delivered some stew and coffee, even as the tiniest glimmer of the dawn appears in the east.

'We watched the rising sun drive away the mist in the valley and from the ridges in the distance. The woods grew from black to grey and turned to green as the sun rose higher . . . dancing flashes from bayonets on our right, a complete silence on our left which left little doubt as to its meaning . . . and our first night in the front line came to a close.'[36]

They have arrived.

22 June 1918, Bertangles Chateau, Monash is the man with the plan

It has taken a day and a night, but at last General Monash's nascent plan is complete enough to call in a despatch rider to take his proposal to General Rawlinson to seek his formal approval. Monash is more than pleased with it, as it embodies all of the modern ideas he has been aching to include in a key battle. At base level, the plan is simple: his forces will appear to the Germans to be attacking some 13,000 yards of their lines, but in fact will be designed to capture just 7500 yards, to a maximum depth of 2500 yards and to do the whole thing in 90 minutes.

Beyond that, however, the approach will be highly sophisticated and intricate, with planes, tanks, artillery and infantry cooperating as never before, with the tanks placed to both give, and take, most of the heat – protecting the infantry as they do so.

And yet, despite the modernity, the cardinal and most ancient military principle of the lot – the virtue of surprise – is to be ruthlessly pursued, and enormous efforts made to keep all preparations for the battle hidden from Fritz.

General Rawlinson scans the thrust of the plan quickly, with the practised eyes of a man who has been perusing military plans for the better part of two decades.

> The action will be designed on lines to permit of the Tanks effecting the capture of the ground; the roles of the Infantry will be:
>
> (i)   to assist in reducing strongpoints and localities.
> (ii) to 'mop up.'
> (iii) to consolidate the ground captured.[37]

Rawlinson's first impression is that that 'operation south of the Somme . . . will be good if we can afford the casualties'.[38]

With so few Australian soldiers arriving as reinforcements, he needs to be satisfied that, even if this plan goes wrong, the men of the Australian Corps will not be decimated as a result.

Monash agrees it is an extremely important issue, noting, 'Any substantial Aust loss would precipitate the time when the question of the reduction in the number of Australian divisions would have to be seriously considered.'[39]

But, as you can see, General Rawlinson, with the way this plan is constructed, it is the tanks which are most likely to take the major punishment from the German defences, and hopefully those tanks will themselves be well enough constructed to emerge unscathed.

Satisfied, Rawlinson will shortly send Monash's broad plan on to General Sir Douglas Haig at GHQ, together with information as to the number of fresh recruits the Australian Corps can expect, with a reassuring note that 'If the operation is successful the casualties should not be great, as it is intended to make the operation a surprise tank attack,'[40] and Field Marshal Haig does not tarry long in giving formal approval.

It's on! But when?

It is General Rawlinson who comes up with an interesting idea. As the British now have two American Divisions, the 27th and 33rd, training in their immediate rear – positioned there, as an extra layer of defence, just in case the Germans break through – why not seek Field Marshal Haig's blessing to invite some of them to join in the attack on a very limited basis, evenly scattered among the Australians? (Rawlinson knows that if Monash agrees, his formal request to the Americans will be warmly received, as he has already had a quiet chat with General George Read, who commands the Americans of II Corps who are in training close to the line.)

22 June 1918, Hamelet, George is back

The strongest of the AIF Battalions that General Monash has to call on, whatever happens in the coming struggle, is the mighty 15th Battalion. Having survived some of the toughest battles of the war, including Gallipoli, Pozières and Bullecourt, they have a tough cadre of veterans at the core of their corps, and in recent times these men have been on relatively lighter duties, allowing them to rebuild their strength. In the next week, they are due to receive 87 fresh reinforcements from Australia, to bring them to their highest fighting strength since Gallipoli, with 750 men ready to wield bayonets. All that, and many of their wounded from previous battles are now healed, and making their way back!

On this day, one of those returning is more than usually welcome. For have yers heard? George is back!

Yup, the bloke who used to be Sergeant George Sellars – one of the most highly regarded Sergeants in the Battalion – had been sent to England for officer training, and has now returned to them as, if you please, *Lieutenant* George Sellars. There is much good-natured ribbing as he makes his way along the reserve trenches where the 15th Battalion are positioned, catching up with old mates – some of whom must, hilariously, now *salute* him! – and it feels great to have him back. He's worked hard over the last six months, has passed the officer's training course with flying colours, and now *looks* the part in his notably spick and span uniform – an officer's outfit has a much better cut than that of the other ranks, which are usually baggy and ill-fitting – and even sounds quite authoritative! It's still George, all right, yet a new, smart version!

But, now what? Not long after Lieutenant Sellars' batman – he's got a batman! – drops his kit-bag in a safe dugout on this notably quiet night on the Western Front, the word comes back. Up on the front-lines, some 400 yards to the east, Lieutenant Cyril Drane has developed such a bad ache in one tooth, he must be extracted so it can be. Will Lieutenant Sellars go forward to replace him? He will! It will be his first chance to actually put in action the things he has learnt, take command of a platoon, enforce discipline, make sure weapons are cleaned once a day, see trench hygiene is maintained to a high standard, reposition the Lewis Guns in keeping with the latest thinking . . .

And so it goes, as he goes forward.

No longer than 20 minutes after taking his place, conducting a whole new round of greetings – George is back! Gidday, George, I mean *Lieutenant* George – one of the few German shells on the night lands about 50 yards out in No Man's Land. Really, blokes barely blink. Happens all the time. And yet, out of the darkness, comes a single scything tiny piece of jagged shrapnel which . . . . hits George right in the jugular.

George goes down, his life-blood gushing out of him as if an open tap, and he is dead within a minute – the only casualty that day.

Christ.

Such a man. Such a fate. After six months away.

Not all *is* fair in love and war.

'Sellars' death,' the 15th Battalion history will record, 'cast a deep gloom over the unit.'[41]

One of the men who fights to dispel the gloom, as he fights every obstacle in his way, is a Sergeant from Queensland, christened Henry Dalziel, but known to his men and his mates as 'Two Guns Harry' for the fact that, although it is not regulation, he insists on carrying two revolvers in his belt – a Luger and a Colt – on his reckoning that when it comes to close-quarter fighting, the pistol reigns supreme, well above rifles and bayonets. And, look, maybe Harry does know what he is talking about, you know? The bloke has been around, and survived through some of the toughest parts of the war.

An apprentice locomotive fireman in Cairns when the Great War had begun, he had quickly joined up with some fellow apprentices – telling his beloved mother, 'You'll need to get out the band, when I come back', so certain was he that he would make his mark – and together he and his mates had trained, both in Australia and Egypt, before landing on the shores of Gallipoli. In the thick of it from the first, a man who'd sooner a fight than a feed, he was quickly regarded as a soldier's soldier before an attack on the Turks in August, at the battle of Hill 971, when 850 soldiers of the 15th Battalion had charged forward . . . only to be 'mowed down like a field of wheat, and returned with 250 men'.[42]

Harry had seen his best mate shot beside him, while only narrowly surviving himself, and then an attack of enteric fever saw the Queenslander evacuated to England. Before returning to join his comrades of the 15th Battalion at the Western Front this time, he'd been offered an officer's position, but refused, as he wanted to stay with his friends in the front-line.

'What was good enough for my mates . . .' he wrote to his family, 'was good enough for me.'[43]

He'd gone on to fight at Messines in Belgium, before being wounded at Passchendaele and sent to England to recover once more. And now here he is, again! You couldn't kill Two Guns Harry with an axe, I tell you!

Harry's only frustration right now is that, instead of being put back in the line as a soldier, he is a bloody transport driver, spending his time with wagons and horses! It is not right, and Two Guns Harry is not happy about it, but is hopeful his time will come.

•

In the meantime, however, General, your Chief of Staff, General Thomas Blamey, and the man known as 'Boss Gunner', General Walter Coxen – the latter an English-born streak of misery who at six foot two inches towers over everyone, and is in charge of the Australian Corps' artillery – would like a quiet word.

(Deep inside, Monash groans. Though he is filled with admiration for Blamey, Coxen is another matter. He had been with the Queensland colonial artillery from well before Federation, and wears his experience like a pair of regulation military blinkers. Monash regards him as 'a dour, sour, unsympathetic creature, and difficult to get on with . . .'[44])

Yes, gentlemen?

After having examined in detail General Monash's plan, and having conferred with the Brigadiers concerned, there is some question about which of the officers is the most unhappy with it. It's a close run thing, but 'very unhappy' characterises them all.

For it's about the idea of sending the tanks in *without* a rolling artillery bombardment ahead of the infantry.

Why?

Yes, not using artillery will allow you to put your tanks well out in front of the infantry, but perhaps you might reconsider, so you can have both the tanks *and* the artillery?

Blamey and Coxen make a compelling case, and not just because at a meeting of the Brigadiers at Sinclair-Maclagan's HQ at Bussy-les-Daours on this day, those gentlemen, as Bean would characterise it, 'gave short shrift to the plan of omitting the usual barrage'.[45]

For, as Blamey respectfully points out, while they *know* the artillery will work, 'the tank method would be more of the nature of an experiment'. Surely, a better way will be to modify the plan so the tried and true method of the barrage can reduce the defences, just as they have always done so well? This will mean the tanks will have to go with the infantry, instead of well ahead of them.

'It's a purely limited attack you're making,' Blamey insists. 'We know you can make an absolute certainty of it by relying upon artillery, and you can get the artillery lent you for it – so why not make it a certainty?'[46]

In the end, General Monash is convinced.

Taking his pen up once more, he slashes and burns, scratches out and redraws, and in short order what had been 'primarily a tank operation',[47] which he had conceived while being under the influence of Brigadier Courage, soon reverts to a more orthodox plan, with one rider.

Because the guns firing the barrage will be very close, to get maximum accuracy, the trajectory of their shells will be very low. So low, in fact, that as Blamey and Coxen point out, the arc of a shell coming from just 2000 yards back, heading for a German trench 75 yards in front of the infantry, will pass just a few feet above their heads. A tank, being close to nine feet tall, is likely to be hit by these shells, unless . . .

Yes, unless the tanks pull back, just behind the men, as they go forward – which is not ideal – but there is no other way. In the new plan, the infantry will be marginally to the fore, and the tanks in tightly behind, timing their advance so that they catch up with the infantry just as they are about to hit the German trenches.

And there will be no half-measures. Now that Monash has acceded to the logic of having the big guns involved, he quickly makes plans to have more than 600 British and Australian guns, and a few French ones – 639 in all, 313 heavy and 326 field pieces – which will be used both on the night, and in the intervening nights, as they try to 'soften up' the Germans in an entirely different way.

Now, of the 313 heavy guns, 200 will be specifically targeted on destroying the German artillery with counter-battery fire, while the rest will try to cripple Fritz's capacity to counter-attack by pounding identified HQs, crossroads, and routes by which reserves could be sent forward.

Generals Monash and Coxen agree on a plan for the creeping barrage so precise it amounts to shelling surgery. There will be three distinct belts of fire, of which, of course, the most delicate and precise will be the 200 yard belt that falls just ahead of the tanks and soldiers on the German front-lines. This will be conducted by the 18-pounders, positioned just one or two thousand yards back from the start line, and firing on a very shallow, but very precise, trajectory over the heads of their infantry. Meanwhile the 4.5-inch howitzers will pound a 200 yard band beyond the 18-pounders, and the 6-inch, 8-inch and 9.2-inch howitzers the final band of 200 yards. The barrage will lift 100 yards every three minutes and the instant it lifts from a German trench, the infantry, with tanks helping, will destroy any remaining resistance.

At Zero Hour plus 31 minutes, the first wave of the infantry should reach a 'Halt Line' on the map, a spot to briefly rest, and gird their loins, and allow the second wave, the fresh battalions, to move through them and get ready to push on. For this last part of the advance, until they reach the Blue Line at Zero plus 90 minutes, the barrage will advance 100 yards every four minutes. When the second wave dig in at the Blue Line, a 'Protective Barrage' will keep pounding a band 400 yards further east, and remain for 38 minutes, allowing the infantry to fully establish themselves on that Blue Line. That way, when the Germans strike back and the Australians 'get pie' – as the Diggers call being shelled – they'll be a good chance of surviving, and holding on. There will be a smoke screen along the front to prevent enemy outside the area from seeing targets inside it.

Bit by bit, hour by hour, the plan evolves.

A constant theme of General Monash's is a relentless insistence that his side knows as much about the enemy's strongholds as possible. Intelligence, gentlemen, intelligence. We need to gather as much as possible and analyse it all thoroughly. We need to know the German layout better than they do.

In order, for example, to know the exact position of the German guns to be targeted, Monash is quick to give orders that from now on, No. 3 Squadron of the Australian Flying Corps must increase their reconnaissance flights, taking as many photos as possible in order to determine the precise co-ordinates of the German defences. Come the night of the attack it is important that, beyond the creeping barrage, there also be concentrated counter-battery fire to knock out the German guns that threaten the attacking soldiers and tanks as quickly as possible.

And now, if you'll excuse General Monash, gentlemen, he has another urgent matter to attend to, this very afternoon . . .

For while it has taken some trial and error operations, Captain Lawrence Wackett believes he has the answer. Meeting General Monash and General Sir Henry Rawlinson in the heat of the mid-afternoon at the aerodrome base of the Australian Flying Corps' No. 3 Squadron, the young Queenslander positions the two Generals out in the middle of the field, before he takes off in an RE8 (Reconnaissance Experimental No. 8) Bomber, primed for the occasion, before turning to swoop back in over them at an altitude of some 500 feet.

The RE8 – known to airmen and troops alike in rhyming slang as a 'Harry Tate', after the beloved music hall comedian – is designed to carry four 20-pound Cooper bombs under each wing, but on this occasion it has been modified. Instead of bombs, Captain Wackett is carrying two 40-pound boxes of machine-gun ammunition of 1000 rounds each in the bomb racks, with each box attached by a rope to cloth parachutes 'rolled and stored in half oil drums attached to the aircraft's underside'.[48]

And now, just as Wackett has practised over the last couple of days, the RE8 swoops in a small distance to the right of the two Generals – on the small chance it doesn't work, it *certainly* wouldn't do for them to be hit by the boxes – and when he is still 100 yards back from being level with them reaches out of the right-hand side of the cockpit and pulls a wooden handle, the bomb toggle.

Instantly the crates fall from the wings, the plane surges first higher on the release of the weight and then jerks down a fraction as the ropes from the fuselage pull on the parachutes in the drums and . . . suddenly it happens. The two small dots plummeting earthwards wonderfully sprout big white flowers above, and gracefully float down, landing no more than 200 feet from the watching Generals!

Landing a short time later, and bringing his noisy beast of a plane to a halt outside the hangar, Captain Wackett climbs down from the open cockpit to be met by two beaming Generals, who have walked across the grassy aerodrome to greet him.

'Can you do that on a large scale . . . ?' Rawlinson asks.

'I can,' Wackett replies, 'if given authority, staff and equipment.'

'Go ahead,' replies Rawlinson. 'You can have everything necessary to do the job.'[49]

That problem, at least, appears to have been solved.

Again, it is typical of Monash.

'Those whom he trusted,' one of his officers would recall, 'he trusted fully. When he believed they understood his ideas, his plan, he left to them the carrying out of detail. No use keeping a dog and doing your own barking was a saying of his.'[50]

●

Corning and the Americans of the 131st Regiment in cushy trenches with the Brits?

It is just their luck to have entered a part of the Western Front where the British and Germans have been launching raids on each other and things have been a bit . . . willing. The night before, the Germans had pushed forward, the Tommies had pushed back. And after a quiet day where both sides had licked their wounds, on this evening the Americans are going forward to man a part of the support line themselves, with their route taking them right past where most of the hard fighting has taken place.

But which way? So many shells have hit this area, seeking out Fritz, it has all but obliterated their track, and the guide who had been meant to take them forward has not appeared. Still they push on, trying to get their bearings until . . .

RUN for it!

Fritz sends over some shells of his own, and the Yanks race for cover in a culvert, where they find the remains of dozens of the British dead, blown apart by the shelling of the previous night. Curious, in a ghastly kind of way, to view torn apart bodies for the first time, they go up close to see what had happened to these Tommies – all of them, surely, so much more experienced. And they have been destroyed, so what chance are *we* of surviving? Nearby, they find dead Germans, too, 'covered with a thin layer of slimy wet clay, and looked like broken statues in the moonlight. A few yards farther along a Fritz machine gunner, wearing a Red Cross arm-band, lay against the bank of a gully. His hands still clutched his gun, and his face had an expression of agony. A bayonet had been driven into his breast by a Tommy who was sprawled on the ground, mute evidence of a terrific hand fight.'[51]

The fact that, at this moment, a German star shell suddenly bursts overhead, placing the whole scene in a flaring then fading light, makes it even *more* ghastly . . . which is saying something.

Staggering forth, chilled, they continue looking for the support line they are meant to get to, until an angry voice rings out:

'Wot are you bloody Yanks jolly well up to? . . . Blimey . . . I nearly shot you!'[52]

And so it goes. Through the night they stumble, babes in the woods, trying to find their way, essentially a threat to no-one but themselves, even as now a Fritz scout plane appears to spot them and drops 'hook lights' on them, throwing a light 'like a red-painted sun', which then brings a Fritz bomber to drop bombs that shake the ground and their very souls.

'We were terrified and helpless,' Walter Corning would document. 'My tin hat slipped farther down and I nearly bit my tongue in half when I stumbled . . . another terrifying whistle . . . we flopped down on our bellies as a tremendous bomb landed 50 feet away and tore four buildings to bits and cut a tree like a match . . . the explosion bounced us up in the air . . . raining timbers, twisted iron and tin roofing . . . stifling dust so thick we couldn't see each other . . . a sobbing moan . . . help that poor Tommy over there . . . leg's off . . . he's gone . . . poor devil . . .'[53]

•

While it has long been noted that Australian soldiers tend to amble, rather than march, and most particularly when traversing long distances, German soldiers are not like that. Trained for a much longer period of time, raised in a far more rigid culture, even when tired, they *march*.

So it is with these exhausted German soldiers of the 1st Battalion of the 227th Reserve Infantry Regiment, as on this early evening, they make their way forward to the trenches around Hamel.

Instead of their usual retinue of 700 men, there are just 500 of them illuminated by the setting sun, as around 100 – the cooks, the clerks, the sergeant-armourer and his assistant, the blacksmith, the butcher, the baker and the transport drivers – are all in the rear, or are in hospital with the Flanders Grippe. A part of the problem is that, four years into this cursed war, their powers of resistance are so diminished. The naval blockade which stops ships getting into Germany has been slowly strangling them all. Meat is now only given to the troops nine days in each month, ersatz coffee is made from acorns, and the 18-year-olds now sent to replace the wounded and killed veterans look like little children.

But, what can they do? *Befehl ist Befehl.* Orders *ist* orders, and soldiers must follow them.

In short order, just after dark, the men arrive at their particular part of the front-line trenches, stretching from Hamel to the Ancre River.

Via a series of communication trenches – those trenches that lie perpendicular to the front-line trenches, to allow safe passage back and forth – the troops are finally able to take up their positions, just before midnight. They are due to stay for the better part of a fortnight, and be relieved in the early hours of 4 July.

•

On balance, Rawlinson decides, after two days of consideration of Monash's plan, it . . . *is* worth that risk.

Done, then.

General Rawlinson gives the proposal to launch a surprise dawn attack – using ten battalions, backed by a rolling barrage and with the help of 60 tanks, lasting 90 minutes and penetrating 2500 yards – his approval, and passes it on to Field Marshal Haig at GHQ. The only real change made to the original plan presented is that, upon consideration, Monash has decided, as he writes to Rawlinson that

> although the date of the proposed operation was yesterday tenta-
> tively fixed for July 2nd, I should be glad if you could agree to

July 4th being named as the date. On going more minutely into
the details of preparation with MACLAGAN, COURAGE and
others, I think that, from every point of view, it would be desir-
able to have the two extra days for preparation and training.[54]

After all, surely the Gods of War might smile upon the first battle
fought in this war by the Americans being held on that proudest of
all American days, their Independence Day, 4 July?

Rawlinson agrees.

(So the British General's later claim that 'I selected the date of
Independence Day as it was the first occasion on which American
troops had taken part in an actual attack alongside our own fellows',[55]
is demonstrably not true. It is Monash's idea, not Rawlinson's, and even
then, Independence Day is more in the way of a happy coincidence,
rather than the driving force.)

24 June 1918, US II Corps HQ at Fransu, Rawlinson asks the question

Would that all interactions between senior British and senior American
officers could be so pleasant. While meetings between Field Marshal
Haig and General Pershing can be like an encounter between a lion
and a leopard in a jungle clearing not quite big enough for both of
them – with a lot of circling, sniffing, hissing and very careful grunting
going on – this is not like that at all.

From the moment that General Rawlinson visits the Commander of II
Corps of the American Expeditionary Force, General George W. Read,
at his HQ, just five miles north of Rawlinson's own HQ at Flixecourt,
he finds the American, 'a nice well-spoken old gentleman',[56] who is
warmth and collegiality personified. So much so, in fact, that Rawlinson
is relatively quick to work his way towards the question he has come
to ask. Would General Read provide some of his American troops to
participate in, and he uses the words advisedly, 'a raid of some kind?'[57]

Read has no problems with it, and so advises the relevant officer,
General George Bell of the 33rd Division – which has been training
just behind British lines – accordingly:

> The commanding general of the British IV army has requested
> that certain smaller units of your division be permitted to take
> part in a raid of some kind . . .[58]

For his part, General Rawlinson's report to Field Marshal Haig at
GHQ in June is carefully framed:

> Leave has been obtained from American GHQ through American
> II Corps to employ . . . American infantry.[59]

At a glance, the reference to 'American GHQ' reads as if General
Pershing himself has expressly given permission. Either way, Field
Marshal Haig is impressed, and it plants a seed that will take only a
few days to bloom.

Whatever else, Rawlinson knows it will be easy to sell to General
Monash.

With the Australian reinforcements thin on the ground and many
of the Australian Battalions below strength, General Monash indeed
jumps at the opportunity from the first, and immediately requests
'about 2000 men organized in eight companies'.[60]

Done.

•

The Americans of the 131st Regiment are still here, still trying to get
their bearings, even if by now they have actually found the support
line trench they had been meant to occupy.

Just as the stars start to fade as the barest streak of misty light
appears on the eastern horizon, stretcher-bearers emerge from behind
a low ridge carrying one of their boys, caught in the shelling. And he
really is a boy, a young American who could be no older than 19 at
most. He is hurt, badly, his abdomen torn apart by shrapnel and now
no more than a red mess.

'Sergeant, I got mine – shrapnel . . .' he says weakly to Corning.

And yet, now taking a closer look at the burly sergeant, something
stirs in the lad, and he even half-manages to sit up, muttering something.

Say, what?

'Will you,' he asks Corning plaintively, 'call that Red Cross lady?'

Corning does not even bother looking where the delusional lad is looking, as he knows there is no nurse within 15 miles. A few other American soldiers are nearby and, hearing the conversation, the biggest of them – a huge man – comes over and says with a great deal of sympathy, 'He's out of his head.'

It would seem so, for now the lad turns to the big man, and with just a wisp of a voice, manages to whisper: 'Lady . . . will you do . . . me a . . . favour? You . . . look like . . . my mother. Put your arm . . . under my head . . . and I'll think . . . I'm in . . . her arms.'

Without a word, the big man does as asked, opening his arms wide, as the young lad sinks back into them.

'No mother could have been more tender and loving,' Corning will chronicle, 'no mother could have been more sympathetic, as the big Yank took the boy in his arms and held him there. And he passed away with a smile.'[61]

25 June 1918, Bertangles Chateau, Monash mulls on Murdoch manoeuvres

And *still* it goes on.

No matter that General Monash has been in the role of Commander-in-Chief of the Australian Corps for nigh on a month now, that he clearly has the complete confidence of General Haig, that he is engaged in working 18 hours a day, every day, organising a battle to the best of his abilities, a battle on which hangs perhaps the fate of the Corps itself, and certainly the lives of thousands of men. Still, the word comes to him from London, via a friend in high places, that Murdoch has been agitating against him, getting into the ear of Prime Minister Billy Hughes maintaining that Monash is not fit to run the Australian Corps, not up to organising a battle, should never have been given the post and should lose it.

It is deeply distressing for General Monash, and he does not hide it.

'I have been visiting the Australian Corps today to fix up details of the attack on July 4,' General Rawlinson notes in his diary on 26 June. 'Monash is rather perturbed at what Hughes and Murdoch are doing . . . It may mean that Birdie will have to give up the AIF and Monash be replaced by White.'[62]

At least General Monash knows he is not alone in the struggle.

On a visit to London at this time, his Adjutant General and great friend, Brigadier Thomas Dodds, has even cabled the Australian Defence Minister George Pearce to formally complain of it:

> Organised attempt being made by a small outside clique in London to bring about a change in command of the AIF . . . There is a great feeling of resentment throughout the force here at this apparent attempt of Murdoch to interfere with our administration.[63]

And yes, the loyalty that Monash feels from the likes of Dodds and other senior officers in the Australian Corps – not to mention the soldiers themselves, who generally seem to like him, and at least like being commanded by an Australian – is no little solace against the ongoing intrigues. But, in the end, the Melburnian remains caught between fatigue at Murdoch's persistence, and outrage that it should be occurring at such a time, when he must waste precious energy fighting a rear-guard action against forces within, principally, as he sees it, because he is Jewish.

'It is a great nuisance,' he writes with no little emotion to his wife on this day, 'to have to fight a pogrom[64] of this nature, in the midst of all one's other anxieties . . .'[65]

Expanding, he explains how 'certain people' are attacking his capacity to command the Corps in order to give the job to Brudenell White. But make no mistake.

> I cannot relinquish the corps command until I have made a proven success of it without impairing my prestige . . . I propose therefore to fight them on their own ground and to insist on retaining command of the corps. In this battle I possess of course many strong cards, and some of them are trump cards, among which is my undoubted belief that both Rawlinson and the Chief will see me through.[66]

And if it doesn't see him through, if the Murdoch intrigue actually sees him run through and replaced as Commander-in-Chief of the

Australian Corps, he has made it clear in a missive to Birdwood that he would ask to be sent home. He has no desire to be the pawn, or even Knight, of the realm, moved around at the behest of men who have never commanded so much as a platoon in battle. It is galling, and appalling – and all, as he sees it, because of his race and religion.

Despite the pressure of it all, he does draw strength from such blatant bigotry, later noting that in times of crisis he would always repeat to himself: 'Remember you are a Jew and that if you muck it up our people will be blamed for it.'[67]

For all that, there is no doubt that if the coming battle at Hamel is not a success – achieving its goals with a low casualty rate – the hand of his critics will be strengthened, and his own powers to resist them weakened. His entire career as Commander-in-Chief of the Australian Corps hangs in the balance . . .

CHAPTER FOUR

'JAW-JAW'[1] BEFORE WAR-WAR

A perfected modern battle plan is like nothing so much as a score for an orchestral composition, where the various arms and units are the instruments, and the tasks they perform are their respective musical phrases. Every individual unit must make its entry precisely at the proper moment, and play its phrase in the general harmony.

The whole programme is controlled by an exact time-table, to which every infantryman, every heavy or light gun, every mortar and machine-gun, every tank and aeroplane must respond with punctuality; otherwise there will be discords which will impair the success of the operation, and increase the cost of it.[2]

General Monash

Something had put new life into our enemies, who seemed more confident, more determined. Had they really been reinforced by two million Americans? The Allies hadn't struck yet, but we sensed that they were merely feeling out our weakened position.[3]

Unteroffizier Frederick Meisel, 371st Infantry Regiment

Late arvo, 27 June 1918, Villers-Bocage aerodrome, Wackett wows 'em

It is another busy day for the men of No. 3 Squadron of the Australian Flying Corps, at their aerodrome just 2000 yards north of Bertangles Chateau. Five separate sorties have crossed enemy lines to successfully spot the exact position of German artillery batteries, and then work their wonders from there. Remaining at an altitude just above the enemy's capacity to bring them down with ground fire – about 3000 feet and well out of the path of the shells – the observer in each plane watches precisely where their own Allied shells are landing with reference to the targeted battery, and then sends out messages in Morse back to the battery.

If they are off target, the message will tell the battery how to adjust to get on target.

..- .--. / ..--- ----- ----- --..-- / .- . . . . -. - / .---- ----- ----- (*Up 200, left 100.*)

Or, ideally . . .

--- -. / - .- .-. --. . (*On target.*)

In short, 'You are right on their nasty noggins, now blast those bastards with everything you've got!'

Beyond this, they have been able to take 102 aerial photographs and drop 54 bombs of their own on targets varying from massed German troops to convoys, trenches, and the same artillery batteries that they have been helping the artillery target.

'And here's another bomb for your trouble!'

Alas, the day is not without trouble.

In the early evening, a pilot, Lieutenant Percival Kerr – before the war a grazier from Western Australia – with his faithful observer, a 25-year-old from Victoria, Lieutenant Arthur Brook, take off in their RE8 reconnaissance aircraft, and indeed do fine work in spotting another artillery battery, which they help to destroy by acting as the angels of death from on high, calling in the Allied shelling. On their return, at 9 pm, just as the shadows on the ground are starting to lengthen all the way to the horizon as the night begins to close in, there is a sudden fearful whining from on high, followed by chattering machine-gun fire . . . and bullets start to rip into their fuselage. They have been spotted by the pilot of a German fighter, a Pfalz Scout, whose twin guns are now spitting at them at the rate of eight bullets a second each. In an instant, Lieutenant Kerr takes evasive action, a hard turn as he tries to avoid another spray, but it proves to be touch and go, not least because Kerr has been shot through the head and leg, and is losing blood rapidly. At last Kerr is able to bring his plane in for a forced landing in a field on the Allies' side, near Pont Noyelles . . . only to find poor Brook stone dead in the back.

The plane itself is 'a total wreck'.[4] There remains, however, an important flying mission to fulfil tonight – in fact, the most important of all.

At dusk, just after 10 pm, a squadron of FE2bs – the noisiest Allied plane in captivity – from 101 Squadron take off and buzz over German lines, high enough to escape Ack-Ack fire, but low enough to completely engulf Jerry with noise, something they will keep up for most of the night.

Why?

Well, the pilots and their observers are careful to regularly drop flares, to make it appear as if their mission is to look for signs of a German build-up on their side of the lines. That is, in fact, not the reason at all, but Fritz does not know that, and the truth will only become apparent in, oh, about a week's time?

In similar spirit, at the behest of General Monash, the British artillery starts peppering the German lines with a curious mix of shells – one gas shell to every nine smoke shells – in a practice to be known as 'conditioning firing'.

Again, the reason for this is not immediately apparent to the Germans. They just don't get it.

But they will.

Meanwhile, the precious work of No. 3 Squadron goes on, and they are well on their way to completing this month's allotment of officially recorded work in preparation for the battle ahead: spotting and engaging German guns, taking photographs of the trench system and bombing targets of opportunity, such as a German column of wagons behind the lines or a group of tents. In all, as the report will show:

> The following is a summary of the work done during this month.
> Artillery Patrols: 210
> Successfully observed destructive shoots: 119
> Photographs taken: 613
> Bombs dropped: 1421
> Machine gun rounds fired into trenches: 57,260
> Total hours flown: 1047 hrs. 50 minutes.
> Combats in the air: 14 of which 4 were decisive.[5]

Of all the activities, however, it is those in the realms of intelligence that Monash values most highly, and the photographs are particularly highly prized and earnestly examined for the information they reveal. A complete set of air photos of the Hamel position – now 109 photos in all – has been done by No. 3 Squadron, and it is these which provide the bulk of the information with which the highly detailed trench maps are formed up.

Look here, with the magnifying glass. See? Those are rolls of wire, right in front of Pear Trench, but there appears to be something of a gap – or at least it is less thick, just to the right. And now look at the hollow just behind to the right. The well-worn tracks across the wheat fields coming from a cottage reveals, we think, a Battalion HQ, while 500 yards back on the right, the flash is clearly that of an artillery battery, with the photo taken at the exact moment it was firing. Very useful. Our own artillery has, of course, been given the co-ordinates and, once the battle starts, our big guns will zero in on every dugout, every HQ and certainly every battery we have identified. And look here. That freshly dug ditch – it is not big enough to be a fighting trench – leading from Hamel to the forest has to be a communication trench, leading to this funny looking thing here we think could be a supply dump!

'So thorough was our training and our knowledge gained per medium of the aerial photos . . .' one soldier would note, 'that we knew practically every foot of the ground we had to cover although we had never set foot on it previously.'[6]

•

The word spreads among the men of the 131st Regiment. They are going to take part in some kind of raid, with the Australians!

The response? Well, it is the American version of whatever the opposite of a Gallic shrug is. They make noise. They hoot, they holler. They thrust their fists about. For not only is demonstrable excitement in the American nature, they are genuinely thrilled at such gratifying news. At last, they are going into action, and it is with the *Australians*, who enjoy a very high reputation on the Western Front as very fine soldiers. They can't ask for better than that.

Their equipment is checked, they are issued with spades, picks and extra ammunition, and are soon on their way east, marching wide-eyed through country now cratered from shell-fire.

27 June 1918, Pierregot, the news breaks

Things are moving quickly, rather in the manner of the Commander of the US II Corps, General George Read, who strides about his HQ dictating the order, 'As per Field Order No. 6 the nominated companies are designated for service at the front . . .'[7] The order is soon on its way to the men of the US 33rd Division, billeted in the lines around the small French village of Pierregot, seven miles north-east of Amiens, who are to 'proceed at once to Allonville for training with the 4th Australian Brigade'.[8]

C Company and E Company of the 131st Infantry, fall in!

You are to report immediately to Brigadier James Cannan, commanding 11th Australian Brigade. You will be going into action shortly with them, participating in a small raid.

'There were great manifestations of joy when the order for action with the Australians was received,'[9] Colonel Joseph Sanborn of the 131st US Regiment would chronicle. Nearby, one commander is overheard telling his men, 'You will be fighting along with the lads who always deliver the goods.'[10]

Another gives his men the great news, while adding an exhortation: 'You're going into action with some mighty celebrated troops guaranteed to win and you've got to get up to their level and stay with them.'[11]

Two full Companies of the 132nd Infantry meanwhile, A and G Company, are given similar orders, albeit they are to report to the Commander of 4th Australian Brigade, an 'all states brigade', under Brigadier Charles Brand.

In short order all 1000 American soldiers – 250 in each Company – begin to make their preparations. They must pack up, form up, and get marching . . .

28 June 1918, Bertangles Chateau, a time to dance, a time to chance

In the grand days before the war, this ballroom had hosted many a dance, with the finest ladies and gentlemen, aristocrats all, dancing the Waltz, the Two-Step, the Polka – the overnight sensation of 1844 – all as the orchestra played up a storm.

Now, however, there is a different conductor, a different orchestra, and it is a different kind of storm. And right in the middle of it, sits Captain Lawrence Wackett, agog. Still in school at Townsville Grammar just six short years ago – doing such things as trigonometry, with nothing more riding on it than his own results – he now finds himself in this high council of war. General Monash himself presides at the top of the table in the ballroom of the Bertangles Chateau, holding what he calls a 'Corps Conference', making decisions of life and death, as they really get down to tin tacks, nuts and bolts, bullets and bombs, shells and shrapnel, tanks and timings.

'It was the most remarkable experience for me,' Wackett would recount, 'the youngest and most junior officer present, a captain of 22 years of age, and everyone else a colonel or higher in rank. Sir John Monash presided. He had his divisional commanders, artillery commander, senior staff from army headquarters and the RFC [actually RAF by now] general with our wing commander, and finally myself.'[12]

As each of the aforementioned also has his Chief of Staff with him, and Monash has his own staff, in total, they include the 25 most senior officers involved in this battle and they are here, Monash makes clear, to go over the plan, understand all its moving parts, see what can be refined, and, *yes*, discuss the plan as it stands, and try to work out how it can be done better.

Around the conference table, there is a stirring.

This is not the usual way things are done. Yes, having an all-arms meeting like this has never really been done before, either, but *this*?

No, the usual way is for the Commanding Officer to simply send out very specific written orders, with little reference to others involved in the battle. But now, they are being asked for their *opinion*? Now they are being asked what *innovations* they might add or offer to the broad plan Monash has presented?

Yes, exactly that.

'Very great importance was attached to the holding of conferences,' General Monash would later note, 'at which were assembled every one of the senior commanders and heads of departments concerned in the impending operation. At these I personally explained every detail of the plan, and assured myself that all present applied an identical interpretation to all orders that had been issued . . . Each commander or service had the advantage not only of receiving instructions regarding his own action, but also of hearing in full detail the instructions conveyed to his colleagues . . . he had an opportunity of considering the effect of their action on his own.'[13]

Where has the said plan come from?

Monash makes no pretence that the battle plan is all his.

Later, to a friend, he would note his contribution as 'analogous to that of an inventor who conceives a new scientific idea and who talks it over with his colleagues or friends, who all make suggestions which are discussed, some being adopted and others rejected, so that ultimately the new idea takes a definite form and substance'.[14]

But to the same friend, he would be insistent as to where the basic blueprint started: 'It is undeniable and unchallengeable that the whole conception of the battle . . . rested upon my own unaided efforts . . .'[15]

Either way, the virtues of innovation is a theme that Monash warms to right now. We are not going to go into this battle doing everything the same way we've always done it, just because that is the same way we've always done it. We are looking for *newer*, better ways, and everyone is encouraged to contribute, as they move through the 118 items on the agenda.

All must understand that this is not a matter of throwing Australian infantry at German lines and hoping for the best – as, frankly, had happened for so much of the war to date. No, first and foremost, this is to be a matter of the Allied *mechanical* weapons of war – tanks, guns, planes – all working tightly together in a synchronised dance of death to quell the enemy and *then*, and only then, are the infantry to come into the equation.

And, as much as humanly possible, all moving parts of the war machine they are here constructing have to be aware of what the other parts are doing, and to understand how their own role affected the others. Everyone had to be aware of the big picture, not just the narrow focus of their own tasks.

Some nine decades earlier, the great Prussian military analyst Carl von Clausewitz had delivered an iconic quote: 'War is the realm of uncertainty; three quarters of the factors on which action in war is based are wrapped in a fog of greater or lesser certainty.'[16] The phrase *'Nebel des Krieges'*, or 'fog of war', as it became known, was instantly recognised by military professionals the world over as the most apt description for the inherent confusion commanders in battle frequently experience as conflicting reports come in concerning the strength, position and intentions of the enemy. Much of Monash's effort is now directed at dissipating that fog so that commanders can see exactly what is meant to happen and their own – often, new – role in it.

Always in Monash's reckoning is that his ace in the hole, when it comes to doing things in a new way, is the Australian soldier himself.

'His intellectual gifts and his "handiness",' Monash would later fondly recount of his charges, 'made him an apt pupil . . . He was always mentally alert to adopt new ideas and often to invent them.'[17]

For now, however, Monash, in his serious, educated tones, sets out the broad brush-strokes of the plan.

It will begin in the wee hours of the night, at a time when the Germans will be at their least prepared.

Monash also has an innovative idea of how to get the tanks forward, to do the heavy work of crushing the German defenders, without the Germans becoming aware, which he now puts before the meeting – and meets their general approval.

But the Generals Blamey and Coxen are right, and we will be using heavy artillery as well to get things underway, with a creeping barrage. The tanks will come forward in such a manner that they will be right behind the soldiers until such times as the soldiers get to the first German trench, at which time the officers should be able to locate the key points of Fritz's resistance and allow the tanks to do the rest. As to the planes, while fighters keep the skies over Hamel clear of the enemy, the two-seaters can swarm all over the German trenches, spotting targets for the artillery, dropping bombs of their own, and making observations of enemy strongpoints.

In the spirit of innovation, many new ideas have emerged at the meeting, the best of which have been embraced and are now formal-ised. Instead of having exposed platoons heading out over No Man's Land and then the battlefield, hauling ammunition as far as three miles, why not have specific tanks do the hard hauling? Each can carry the same as 300 men. It is estimated that just four carrier tanks will do the trick, on the reckoning that each one, stripped of most of its weaponry, could contain as much barbed wire, petrol, ammunition, hand grenades etcetera, as 1200 men could carry – and it would take just four soldiers and a corporal in each one to unload them. (The benefits of the innovation will be huge, if it works. In most battles, no fewer than a fifth of a fighting body would be devoted to hauling essentials forward to a newly captured line, and the estimates are that doing it this way might spare as many as 200 casualties. Best of all, the tanks could keep going back and forth every two hours, long after men assigned to the task would have been exhausted – or shot.)

Yes, and when the troops are far advanced, perhaps beyond the range of the tanks, why not use flares to mark out the spots where planes could drop further ammunition by parachute? Again, Monash is more than receptive. These are precisely the kind of innovations that he has been looking for.

Now, about communications between those on the front-lines and those back in HQ, is it not obvious that everything from homing pigeons, to messenger dogs, to runners, is far too precarious, particularly when we now have . . . wireless.

(Wireless is extraordinary when it works – allowing you to telegraph Morse Code, via electromagnetic waves, across long distances. Though the machines are so big and heavy they must be carried on a two-wheeled cart – meaning they're not feasible on the actual battlefield – they will allow General Sinclair-Maclagan at 4th Division HQ at Bussy-les-Daours to be in constant touch with General Monash ten miles away at Australian Corps HQ at Bertangles, keeping him fully informed of developments, as the reports come in.)

Though talking of war, and actions that will take many lives, Monash's tone is intellectual, analytical, almost mathematical.

'It is only necessary,' he would later recount of his approach to breaking the German line, 'to concentrate upon a given front such a density of artillery barrage fire, tank and air-attack, as to make it reasonably certain that it would overwhelm any possible defensive measures . . .'[18]

So now that the front they are to attack is determined and they have a good idea of where the German defences lie, and just how strong they are, the key question is just what resources they must bring to bear to be *sure* of overwhelming them.

'In a well-planned battle of this nature,' Monash continues, 'given a resolute infantry and that the enemy's guns are kept successfully silenced by our own counter-battery artillery, nothing happens, nothing can happen, except the regular progress of the advance according to the plan arranged. The whole battle sweeps relentlessly and methodically across the ground until it reaches the line laid down as the final objective.'[19]

Now, what about confusing the Germans on how long the front of the attack is?

For General Monash is also insistent from the beginning: 'Every effort should be made to mystify and mislead as to the point of the attack and the scope of the operation.'[20]

Of course Fritz will fight back. But the longer he is confused, the more diffused will be his response.

After discussion, it is decided that this task should fall to the obvious candidates, the men of Brigadier Pompey Elliott's 15th Brigade, positioned north of the Somme River. A controlled attack there, up by the Ancre River, matched with much the same artillery bombardment as the real attack – meaning the barrage would stretch all the way from the Roman Road to the Ancre and Pompey's men, 13,000 yards – might just do the trick. (And yes, of course Brigadier Pompey Elliott is ropable that his mighty 15th Brigade will only have a subsidiary role, but that is of little moment. Pompey is ropable at the best of times. All that counts is that General Monash is sure that they will acquit themselves well, in what is an important task.)

Now, with the French, south of the Roman Road, also having agreed to stage something of a fake barrage – mostly sound and fury, signifying nothing – if all goes well, the Germans will think they are under attack there, too, in fact, all the way north to Ville on the Ancre River, over twice the frontage of the *actual* attack. By the time Fritz has understood his blue, he will hopefully have sent some of his reserves to plug the wrong gap, leaving other spots all the more vulnerable.

Of course, Monash is not the only speaker.

'In amazement,' young Wackett will recount, 'I heard each of the commanders recite his part of the battle to the corps commander.'[21]

And of course, often, animated discussion results.

'Oh, I had not thought of that,' General Monash is wont to say when points for or against something are raised. There is a humility in his manner which belies his view of his own superiority of intellect: *he* is *not* the expert on everything, he wishes to tap the expertise of everyone there to work out the best thing to do. But, yes, he remains the ultimate arbiter.

'No,' he would be prone to say, just as quietly, 'we won't do it that way.'[22]

American officers with the 3rd Division when Monash had been in charge had noted his extraordinary capacity 'to say much in a few words',[23] and that is very much his form here.

Item after item on the agenda is ticked off, with Monash, clearly, across every part of the battle down to the tiniest detail, and not for nothing would even Bean note his 'peculiar capacity for organising and training . . . the great care and capacity with which his arrangements were made . . . and at times [the] brilliance [that] flashed through, astonishing those who observed it'.[24]

Now, moving on.

Though they are yet to establish exactly when Zero Hour is, there is still much that can be decided in terms of the structure of the attack.

As it has been established that the best Tank Jumping Off Point is between the first and second trench lines, just under half-a-mile from where the Infantry Starting Line will be positioned, the key question had been, how long would it take the tanks to get up the slight incline that lies between the two lines?

Tests have been done on similar ground at Vaux, and the answer has come back – about eight minutes. That means the tanks will need to start forward at Zero Hour minus eight minutes, to get them to the infantry at exactly the time the barrage falls.

The nightly harassing fire then – shells aimed at crossroads, randomly along the German trench lines and at presumed HQ and the like, to constantly discomfit the enemy, without, yet, an enormous expenditure of shells – must also start at Zero Hour minus eight, which will not only make the Germans think it is a routine night, but also cover much of the sound of the tanks moving forward the final 800 yards.

But make no mistake, for this is a key point from Brigadier Courage himself: 'Tanks should be employed in order to save as many casualties as possible to the Australian Corps.'[25]

After discussion, and typical modification of the original plan, better ways of doing things are worked out and it is decided there will be two basic waves of tanks, rather than three waves as in the original plan.

At Monash's specific and detailed request, it is agreed that Brigadier Anthony Courage will provide more tanks, and there will be 60 in all, with 18 attacking Hamel, 12 attacking Pear Trench and 12 attacking Vaire Wood, with the remainder to help the infantry on the flanks, excepting four tanks, which would be devoted to carrying supplies forward.

In the first wave, 44 tanks will advance tightly behind the attacking infantry, ready to break through to do the heavy work once they hit the front-line German trenches. The second wave, 12 tanks, will provide a strong reserve to enter the fight wherever the first wave has missed or even failed to quell an enemy strongpoint, or has wandered off course, leaving the infantry motherless and fatherless. Finally, the four supply tanks will bring up the rear.

If all goes according to plan, and it must, the troops will reach Pear Trench at 3.17 am, and by 3.28 am the capture of Vaire Wood will be complete. Across the line, the creeping barrage will stop at 3.38 am, for the usual three minutes, but then remain unmoving for still another ten minutes – this special halt is to allow fresh forces to move forward, to prosecute the second phase of the battle, particularly the taking over of Wolfsberg.

At 3.51 am, the barrage will move forward again, and at 4.15 am Hamel village itself is due to fall. By 4.43 am, all troops across the 6500 yard front-line should have reached the Blue Line (where they'll hold a 7500 yard front), and will dig in – protected by the curtain of protective barrage, which will continue to fall 200 yards beyond the Blue Line, preventing the Germans from counter-attacking. That protective barrage will continue for 30 minutes exactly, ceasing at 5.13 am and then, at 6.10 am, the specially modified RE8 planes will swoop in low over the troops and drop them parachuted supplies . . .

Captain Wackett?

Nervously, but soon with growing confidence, the 22-year-old goes over his part of the plan . . .

'I outlined the part the squadron would play,' Wackett will recount, 'its usual role of reconnaissance and artillery observation, together with the new task of supplying ammunition to the newly captured positions. Sir John Monash expressed his satisfaction and said that the time of the attack would be announced at short notice, anytime from now on.'[26]

The good General moves on, now insisting that great emphasis be placed on communications, so at all times 4th Division HQ, which would be the nerve centre for the battle, could have a good picture of the situation, and react accordingly. Beyond, thus, the usual methods of taking field telephones forward with the leading elements, so messages could be sent back, some of the tanks will send messages back with pigeons released through the door, flags to contact the infantry they are to work with, and even different coloured rockets. Particular battalions would be allocated different colours to mean different things, such as a green rocket to mean, 'we have captured the objective', or a white one to mean, 'we have failed to capture the objective'.

A key development from this particular meeting, however, and this is an innovation, is that, as Monash insists: 'The infantry commander on the spot is responsible for the joint action of tanks and infantry. He will give such orders to the Tank Section Commander as the situation demands.'[27]

The tanks, thus, will be under the control of specific infantry commanders, who will be authorised to order them this way and that, take out that machine-gun post, destroy that dugout, crush that wire.

'Each Tank,' General Monash would later characterise it, '[is] for tactical purposes, to be treated as an Infantry weapon; from the moment that it entered the battle until the objective had been gained it was to be under the exclusive orders of the Infantry Commander to whom it had been assigned.'[28]

Beyond verbal communications the men will be issued with Very pistols, so that when they find particularly heavy resistance in a certain spot, they may fire red flares, to call in their tanks to quell it. Yes, the tanks are to do the heavy lifting, but they are to be the tools of the infantry, and not the other way around – and the command structure must reflect that.

(And, typical of Monash, he does not want this to simply be a written order, but an actual integration at a man-on-man level. It is on his instruction that for the last three days before the battle, the tank officers will bunk down and live with the Companies with whom they will be advancing, so these two key players in the battle plan will come to know and trust each other.)

So, yes, it will be for the tanks to sweep in just behind the infantry, following the infantry commander's orders and . . .

And while the officers representing the interests of the 'tankies' reluctantly accept the logic of this, they do express concern that with their machines' eight feet eight inches high profiles, there is a real risk being that close to the barrage that the tanks would be hit by friendly fire.

At Monash's behest, discussion ensues between the artillery officers and the tank officers, with the latter at last reasonably assured that that won't happen.

Again, it is typical Monash.

As one of his officers would recall, it was a frequent occurrence at Monash's meetings for one or other of the participants to protest: '"That can't be done, you can't do it that way." And he'd say "General, I think it can, you know", in his smiling way. He was always so imperturbable and never ruffled, never showed any personal animosity.'[29]

When this particular officer, Colonel Julius Bruche, might come to him with some serious logistical difficulty or other, Monash would say of these problems' grave difficulty: 'Julius, they all yield to treatment.'[30]

And so they would, and so they do!

In this instance it is firmly established that this is no longer a tank operation with infantry support, but quite the reverse.

After moving through all 118 items on the agenda, the meeting finally finishes, four hours after it had begun.

•

Where is a reverse Revere when you need him?

For never was there a moment more perfect for a horseman to charge out the front, shouting to all and sundry, 'The Yanks are coming! The Yanks are coming!'

For their part, Gunner James Armitage of the 8th Australian Artillery Brigade and his mates are at least entertained.

'We amused ourselves,' Armitage would recount, 'watching a lot of very brand-new-looking Yanks arriving with their extraordinary looking equipment.'[31]

Their uniforms, with the odd webbing! Their 1903 Springfield rifles, and their strange-looking French machine guns! No doubt about it, their new cobbers have strange clobber.

'Some of the officers carried leather suitcases and umbrellas and looked more like commercial travellers than soldiers.'[32]

Another is amused when he sees Americans 'coming up the road with bayonets fixed and rifles ready miles away from the front line. They wore their gas masks when there was not a whiff of gas about.'[33]

For their part, the Americans gaze upon the Australians with interest, particularly their curiously tilted slouch hats, which remind one American officer of 'Roosevelt's Rough Riders at San Juan Hill',[34] in reference to President Teddy Roosevelt's famed unit in the Spanish–American war of 1898 and their jauntily tilted hats.

•

Another day, another sortie. Rarely have the pilots and observers of No. 3 Squadron of the Australian Flying Corps – flying their lightly armed Reconnaissance Experimental No. 8 observation planes – been busier than now. Day after day, following the instructions from the Special Intelligence Officer assigned to them by the Australian Corps HQ, they have been flying endless three-hour patrols as low as possible over German territory, looking to locate where the enemy's heavy artillery batteries are – usually two to three miles back from the front-line.

'By the aid of sound ranging devices,' Captain Lawrence Wackett would recount, 'and spotting from the air of gun flashes, and the aerial photographs we took every day, it was possible to locate the positions of a great number of enemy batteries.'[35]

('Sound ranging' required monitors at varying distances and angles from the offending battery. By measuring the different times the sound arrives at each, and cross-referencing, it is possible to get an accurate bearing and distance for each one, the point where the three bearings intersect.)

For the past few weeks, once a battery was located, the spy planes would fly back towards their own artillery, close enough to establish good wireless communication by Morse Code and give the co-ordinates, then head out again to observe the subsequent shelling – ordered on the pilot's flashed signal from the air – before communicating with the artillery again to give more guidance on how close they were. Gradually, the shelling would get closer to its target until, ideally, the heavy German battery would be destroyed.

But, in the last few days, things have changed. Now, the Australians neither want to destroy those batteries, nor even alarm their German commander that they have been spotted. Instead, the Australians want the batteries to stay exactly where they are, so they can all be destroyed on the night of the attack. Thus, for the time being the Aussies simply land, and as their planes are being refuelled, give the co-ordinates to the Special Liaison Officer from the Heavy Artillery Brigade, who attends to 'all arrangements for artillery spotting and the allocation of targets'.[36] And then they take off again, protected by patrols of Royal Air Force Sopwith Camel fighters above, trying to keep them safe from German fighters.

True, sometimes it can be difficult to spot the batteries, as the flashes don't show as much in the daytime, and the guns are under heavy camouflage, but experience teaches the airmen well.

They learn to look for 'the blast erosion on the ground before the muzzle. No one succeeded in preventing these tell-tale marks from occurring after the gun had been in operation for a few days.'[37]

Bit by bit, day by day, the positions of the German artillery batteries are marked on the map, and their co-ordinates spread among Coxen's growing artillery force.

Captain Lawrence Wackett goes on the occasional sortie, but most of his energy is now spent fulfilling General Monash's other request – to organise so that planes may make the supply drops.

With 20 planes under his command, Wackett gets to work. After a dozen sewing machines are located, trucks are sent to retrieve them, together with 'rolls of aeroplane fabric, steel-strip, hoop-iron, bomb rack, and hundreds of boxes of ammunition in belts ready for machine guns'.

A small factory in a hangar is set up, a couple of dozen soldiers put to work around the clock, making parachutes of 12 foot diameter. Ammunition boxes are filled so that each one has exactly 40 pounds worth of bullets. Now, each one has a steel strap fastened to the top, so that it will easily attach to the bomb release on the planes.

'The bomb racks were modified to accommodate the rectangular cases and were fitted with canisters made from cut down oil drums to hold the folded parachutes. All the gear was assembled adjacent to the aeroplanes and covered with tarpaulins.'[38]

Before long, Captain Wackett is able to make the report that General Monash has been waiting for:

> All is ready to drop 200,000 rounds within 24 hours of notice being given to mount the operation.[39]

•

And *ja*, the German soldiers manning the 156 guns that the German *Generalmajor* Viktor Kuhne's XI Corps have to defend their part of the front around Hamel are aware that there recently seem to be a lot of enemy planes flying over, which is a worry. But, against that, it is only one of so many worries that the men have, that it does not particularly stand out.

For they are positioned, as one of their number would recount, on an *'äußerst unruhigen und gefährdeten Front'*,[40] a most uneasy and endangered front. When they have had losses of guns, these have not been fully replaced. When they have lost personnel, these have been replaced by men who are not up to it. In the most recent intake of 90 men, there had been *'kein einziger Artillerist,* not a single artillerist, *und die allermeisten von ihnen hatten in ihrem Leben noch nie eine Kanone gesehen,* and most of them had never seen a cannon in their lives. They were mostly *Armierungssoldaten und alte Familienväter,* armament soldiers and old family fathers. Second Lieutenant Klocke reports that the first one of the arriving men he asked was only *garnisonsverwendungsfähig*: could only be deployed at the garrison due to a fracture, likewise the second, who had *Nachtblindheit*, night blindness, the third was almost *taub*, deaf, the fourth and fifth had similar *gebrechen*, afflictions.'[41]

All this, and they know from Intelligence and a couple of successful raids that they are up against *Die australischen*, which is a *real* worry, *und* no mistake . . . For as they all know, the Australians – against all odds – had somehow managed to stop much superior German forces from breaking through to Amiens three months earlier, and of all soldiers of all the countries the Germans face, the Australians are among the most feared, together with the New Zealanders and Canadians.

•

Occasionally in this exercise, the winds of war blow favourably in your direction.

Just before dawn on a day in late June, for example, some Diggers are idly chatting in the trenches before Hamel, after a very quiet night going out on patrol, and watching with some satisfaction as the darkness slowly gives way to the day, even as, one by one, all the others who had been out on patrol in No Man's Land return to Australian lines in time for brekkie and then a bit of a kip, before resuming duty.

But wait, what's this?

Suddenly, from out of the misty morning, comes a party of half-a-dozen, in massive greatcoats, walking along the front of the wire barricades and clearly looking for an opening to get through. Who the hell are these coves, and how is it that they don't know where the opening is, just back along the way a little?

'That patrol is late,' one Digger notes, curiously, as the stray soldiers finally find the gap and start to file through, 'it should have been in an hour ago.'[42]

At that instant, there is the crack of a rifle and the lead member of the group falls down dead! He has no sooner hit the ground than a Mills grenade explodes among the rest, severely wounding two and knocking the others over.

Half a mo'! What the BLOODY HELL is going on?

As other Diggers rush forth, with rifles and bayonets at high port, the answer soon becomes apparent. This is a *Fritz* patrol, a Corporal and five soldiers who had lost their bearings, not their minds, and simply wandered in to Australian lines by mistake.

'The five were, of course,' one Digger would report, 'taken prisoner and assisted to our headquarters, where valuable identification and information was obtained from them.'[43]

The Australians are up against three German divisions of middling quality, from the Somme to the Roman Road. The best reckoning of Australian intelligence is that the Germans are holding the line that

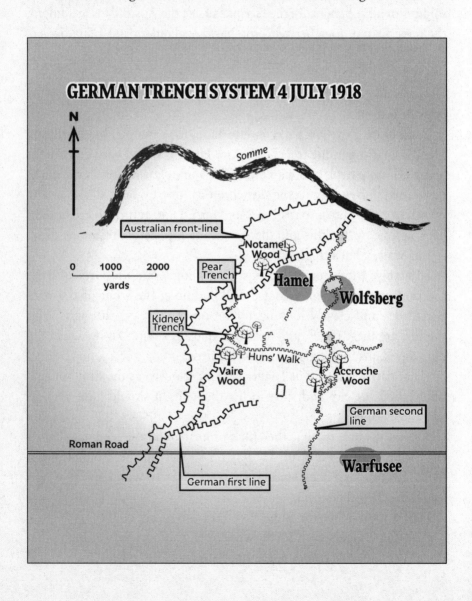

Monash plans to attack with some 2790 soldiers, with a further 2860 in reserve. So there are just over 5600 soldiers this side of the Blue Line, and surely a couple of thousand more Germans beyond it who will counter-attack in an attempt to recover the lost ground.

The reports coming in from the patrols – concerning the state of Fritz's trenches, dugouts, fortified bunkers and the like – are mixed. The good news is that, for the moment, the Germans continue to have few defences of the calibre of what they had at places like Pozières and Fromelles . . .

> During the past few weeks, however, there are increasing indi-cations that [the enemy] intends to develop a complete two line system with the usual saps, dugouts and communication trenches. In certain areas the work is nearing completion and a considerable defence scheme is evidently contemplated, the tendency being to link up the existing chains of rifle pits and incorporate them in the trench lines . . . Mined dugouts have been constructed in numerous places in the forward and battery areas, particularly in the sides of embankments for protection against our artillery fire.[44]

And yet, the German forces actually do have some key strongpoints that will have to be overcome to achieve the goals of the battle. On the western edge of the village of Hamel itself, the Germans are well dug in, for the most part using the rubble and cellars of destroyed houses for their protection, while at Pear Trench they have several troublesome machine-gun posts with built-in protection, concrete dugouts that will withstand even direct hits of the barrage, and a semi-circle of barbed wire around the salient formed by the trench. Further south, Kidney Trench in front of Vaire Wood also prickles with machine-gun posts that will need the concerted attention of the tanks to overcome. It is these four places – Hamel, Pear Trench, Kidney Trench and Vaire Wood – where the greatest difficulties are expected.

•

Oh, the sheer joy of it!

For the likes of the 4th Brigade's 14th Battalion, life continues to be wonderful, here in the farmlands of France, out of the trenches at long last and, in their case, living in billets at Aubigny on the Somme, two miles north-west of Villers-Bretonneux. The sunshine, the greenery, the relative peace, all make for a lovely break in an otherwise muddy and bloody war, and among the favourite activities for people like Lieutenant Edgar Rule is to spend time picking strawberries in the local abandoned patches – and eating them till his nose would bleed. It is such a far cry from the dull rations they have been living on, it is hard to believe.

Another favourite activity is to head for a wash at the baths at the nearby village of Corbie that the AIF has set up in the backyard of a house by the Somme. You can take a hot bath, even as your underclothes and uniform are being washed, and come back fresh as a new pin!

On this day, Rule has sent C Company down to the Corbie baths, only for the Sergeant to come back, beside himself with excitement.

Poking his head into the dugout – just back from the front-line, within shelling range – he asks, 'Do you know there is a big stunt on, and we're in it?'[45]

No, Lieutenant Rule knows nothing about it, but upon investigation, discovers that is clearly the case. In fact, as the Sergeant advises, and Rule soon sees for himself, the back area 'is lousy with guns of all sizes back on the river, and tanks are hidden all over the shop'.[46]

No-one is saying anything, and Rule has received no orders, but they have been through this too many times to be under any illusions. With troops, tanks and supplies flooding forward it is obvious that that there is a stunt coming, and Rule moves quickly.

Gathering his platoon together, he lays down the law for the benefit of the young soldiers who can't be expected to understand the key thing they must now be told: *shut up*. Not a word.

You don't speak of this to each other, you don't talk of it with other soldiers, you don't talk about it to any Froggies you might come across. The danger is that the Hun will capture someone in our front-lines who knows about it and speaks of it, and in that case, they will be waiting for us when we come. From now, *silence*. The men nod, they understand.

Still, for some, the whole thing seems quite unreal.

Here they are in the middle of a Monet painting – 'Everything looked a picture as we came back along the canal,' Cliff Geddes records of his own experience walking back from the baths, 'the green trees & grass & among the grass the yellow flowers & red poppies were lovely'[47] – and they are about to engage in something Dante himself could not have dreamt of.

But, it is as the man said: such is life.

•

Hark!

It is a curious, roughly rhythmical sound, getting closer in the misty moonlight.

Men.

Many men.

Marching!

It is the men of the 131st Regiment, Americans all, now getting closer to the men of the 4th Australian Brigade, positioned just next to the Somme River.

Onwards, they go 'neath the curious moon with the seeming swirl of fireflies at their feet actually the result of their hobnailed boots striking sparks against the cobblestones. And listen now, lean closer, as the metallic beat of those hobnails and horseshoes on cobblestones comes ever closer, together with the shouts of the Sergeants and Corporals along the column keeping the men in time, and on time. Now and then a soldier starts up a marching song, which flares like a lit match in the darkness, flourishes for a short time before slowly fading away, replaced once more by the rattles of gear and swooshing legs and slowly . . . silence once more, as they disappear in the night.

Onwards along the roads, onwards into the night. Exhausted, foot-sore, hungry, it is nigh on midnight before the Lord has mercy. For out of the darkness now come enormous men, 'Or-stralians', with strange, tilted hats, but very friendly manner, who announce they are their guides, come out to steer them to their billets.

At last, at last! So it is that in the early hours of the 29th, most of the Americans arrive at their different destinations.

Whatever else, the American soldiers feel strongly welcomed, with Captain William Masoner of G Company, for example, noting that when he and his men arrive just outside Aubigny to join the men of 15th Battalion, it is to be greeted by the Commander of that Battalion, Colonel Terence McSharry, who personally guides 'us to a Reserve Trench . . . and remained . . . until all men found sleeping places and dugouts'.[48]

29 June 1918, the first tranche arrives west of Villers-Bretonneux

Wake up, Digger. The Yanks are here!

And it's true. When the Diggers of the 42nd and 43rd Battalions wake from their slumbers on this fine morning, it is to find that American soldiers have joined them overnight.

In no insignificant way, the arrival of the Americans makes the Australian Battalions feel *whole* and strong, again. When the 42nd Battalion had arrived in France in early 1916, it had been a thousand strong. But the battles of Messines, Passchendaele and the recent *Kaiserschlacht* have seen its numbers reduced to just over 400 as their losses have not been sufficiently replaced. And now they have another 250 men! The 43rd Battalion is in much the same position. With just 41 officers and 575 soldiers able to fight, they, too, are a long way underweight, and the addition of the Americans lifts their numbers by 250 men.

What remains now is to integrate the new men, acquaint the Americans and Australians with each other, and, as much as possible, have the Australians teach the newcomers what they know about being a front-line soldier. The Yankee infantry prove to be eager pupils, watching carefully how the Australians go about things, and questioning them closely over whatever they don't understand.

Mutual respect quickly grows.

And the Americans, of course, have always made a strong impression of their own.

'We felt today,' Bean had noted when seeing his first lot of Americans, 'as though we had been walking among ghosts. Wherever one goes one is struck more and more by [their] likeness to the men of the old 1st (Aust) Division at Mena Camp and behind the lines in Gallipoli.'[49]

Yes, that's it. Three-and-a-half years ago, when the AIF had just started their own serious training at their camp in Cairo, before Gallipoli, they had looked like this too – they had been big, beefy young men, with a wild-eyed confidence about them. Throw anything at them, they were up for it. Not now.

For one thing, such veterans as there are, have had much of the beef stripped off them by the years of hard living. For another, their youth has gone and instead of wild-eyed confidence, there is a world weariness borne of the horrors they have faced, the mates they have buried, the atrocities they have witnessed and been a part of.

But these Americans are really something else, even if 'they swear a little less, [and] drink coffee rather than tea'.[50] Beyond that, they 'might as well be our own fellows'.[51]

Whatever else, their sheer *size* should intimidate the Germans. Still, one Australian can't resist asking the first American soldier he sees, 'Are you going to win the war for us?'

'Well,' the American soldier replies with some dignity, 'we hope we'll fight like you Australians.'[52]

Generally, the Americans are very well received, and reciprocate the warmth, with Colonel Joseph Sanborn, the commander of 131 Regiment, whose men have been attached to the 42nd and 43rd Battalions, saying 'From the first when our soldiers came in contact with them they mixed well and took kindly to each other.'[53] For his part, Private Harold Shapcott of the 42nd Battalion would report the newly arrived Yanks to be 'very fine chaps, ready and eager to learn and not above taking advice'.[54]

Look, they're wet behind the ears, no doubt about that.

But game? Yes, in their way.

'Many of the Yanks were very funny,' an officer with the 13th Battalion would recall. 'When they came into the line they wanted to know "Is this the front row?" They expected shells and bullets to be whistling overhead all the time and they seemed a little disappointed that it was so quiet in the front row.'[55]

The main thing though is they really do want to learn, and clearly regard the Australian veterans, particularly, with awe.

Let's start with the Lewis Guns. You'll notice they're so light at just 28 pounds, that if it comes to it, just one man can fire it. Go on, lift it up, and have a go. No, not like that – hold it tight and squeeze *gently*, that way you won't spray it everywhere!

These Vickers Guns, on the other hand, weigh more than twice as much, always need their water-cooling system attached, and must be carried disassembled by three men. Ah, but when they're set up, they're so powerful they can, in ideal circumstances, wipe out a company of 150 men in 30 seconds.

The Americans are frequently wide-eyed with wonder at the things they are learning, and are nothing if not enthusiastic.

Their arrival, Edgar Rule of the 14th Battalion would note, 'bucked our lads up wonderfully. Instead of the grim, set faces usually noticeable prior to battle, our men were all smiles and laughter, and determined to show the newcomers what Australians were capable of.'[56]

All up, the arrival of the Americans is so positively received, it is Field Marshal Haig himself who on 29 June proffers a suggestion – though when you are a Field Marshal, mere suggestions can, to be sure, have the clout of Commandments delivered by the Lord Himself. For, in strict contrast to General Pershing's enduring obstinance on this matter, Field Marshal Haig has noted how easily General Read, the Commander of II US Corps, had agreed to lend four American companies. Perhaps, if General Read is asked again, he might do the obvious?

'I suggest,' Haig says to General Read, 'that one American company should be attached to each of [Monash's] attacking battalions.'[57] With *ten* attacking Battalions, that would see ten American Companies in all, some 2500 soldiers, go into battle for the first time, shoulder to shoulder with the Australian veterans. General Read is quick to agree and instructs his divisional commander, General George Bell, to select and send to the Australians an additional six companies. After all, what better way to 'blood' American troops than side by side with brother Australians, who have a long track record of success, in a short battle where casualties should not be heavy – bearing in mind that only those who survived could pass on the lessons learned to the rest of their regiment.[58]

Rawlinson notes in his diary that evening, 'we arranged [to use] 6 [more] companies with the Australians in their attack on July 4. The Yankees will, I am sure, fight like hell.'[59]

•

Cometh the night, cometh the movement.

With his continued insistence that their greatest asset in the battle to come will be to hit the enemy completely unawares, General Monash has imposed a blanket rule that, beyond the normal traffic, there is to be no major movement of men or the machinery of war until after the sun has gone down.

Inevitably, it means that, together with the normal night-time sounds of dogs barking in the distance, owls cooing, cows mooing . . . there is now also the ceaseless tramp of feet, the rumble of groaning trucks edging forward, the grumble of tanks – 60 of them! – clattering as quietly as they can down the country lanes.

'Over the brow of the hill, dimly outlined against the dusk, loomed a herd of strange toad-like monsters,' one account of the movement of such tanks would run. 'The noise of whirring engines and the weird *flap-flap-flap* of the tracks, like the padding of gigantic webbed feet, filled the air. The vast snouts went up and up, and then suddenly dipped down abruptly as the creatures made for home. They made one shiver; they were so repulsive, so inhuman, so full of menace.'[60]

Back in the day, all roads did indeed lead to Rome, but tonight, and for the next few nights, for these men they all lead to that area just west of Hamel where all the pieces are being put into place for the battle to come. They keep going until all are carefully secreted in the orchards and behind the shattered houses around the villages of Fouilloy and Hamelet – the latter so-called as in the French vernacular it is 'little Hamel' – just two and three miles to the west of Hamel itself. Here Brigadier Anthony Courage establishes his advanced HQ in the sturdy stone walls of an old windmill.

The Germans? Despite the fact that they have observers atop Wolfsberg who *'passen auf wie Schießhunde'* are alert like hunting dogs behind Australian lines, they notice nothing out of the ordinary. Bit by bit, Monash is bringing men, machinery and munitions flooding forward, but all is being done in such a way that the element of surprise is preserved at all times.

CHAPTER FIVE

YANKEE DOODLE DANDY

By the way the Yanks shape up they are going to be good fighters, they think the world of the Aussies – we mostly have a few of their N.C.O. in the line with us learning the ropes. They reckon with the Brothers on one side, that's us, and the cousins on the other, that's Canadians ... we will just about win – they are a fine body of men.[1]

Australian soldier, Private Roland Simpson, 9th Battalion, July 1918

The true role of infantry was not to expend itself upon heroic physical effort, not to wither away under merciless machine-gun fire, not to impale itself on hostile bayonets, but on the contrary, to advance under the maximum possible protection of the maximum possible array of mechanical resources, in the form of guns, machine-guns, tanks, mortars and aeroplanes; to advance with as little impediment as possible; to be relieved as far as possible of the obligation to fight their way forward.[2]

General John Monash

30 June 1918, Vaux, eyes right, ranks of Yanks in tanks

Of course it is the Sabbath, the day of the Lord, and there are many in Cliff Geddes' D Company, of the 13th Battalion, for whom it is a sacred day. Ideally, it would be a quiet day of worship. But the war doesn't work like that, and though God might have rested on the seventh day, they have no such luxury.

Straight after breakfast, Private Cliff Geddes and his mates, with parties from each company of each of the four Battalions of the 4th Brigade, first march a mile from their billets around Aubigny and then pile into waiting motor lorries. First they pass through the city of Amiens, before going another few miles to a spot just outside the tiny village of Vaux, 'tucked away in a quiet valley, north-west of Amiens'.[3]

What's it all about?

'There are rumours that we are to be in a big hop over with tanks soon, it looks as if it's right by this – well, a man can only take what comes his way, & trust to Providence,' writes Geddes.[4]

As the men jump off the lorries, the first thing they see are the tanks – big bloody behemoths. Well, the veteran Diggers want none of them. For who can forget bloody Bullecourt? Not them. Fucking things hadn't arrived on time, and even then had broken down when they had been needed most.

(Which is *precisely* the attitude General Monash had expected the men to have. And that is why the tanks are here. 'On the principle of restoring the nerves of the unseated rider by remounting him to continue the hunt,' he would later recount, 'it was especially important to wean the Fourth Division from their prejudices.')[5]

Before the Diggers stands a very pukka English Brigadier who is to explain 'the scheme of attack & the objective'.[6] Not far away, General Rawlinson, accompanied by General George Bell of the American 33rd Division – a handsome 59-year-old with a white goatee beard and bushy white moustache – watches approvingly, as the imposing Brigadier rumbles like thunder . . .

With the help of the Lord Christ Almighty and my beautiful tanks we are going to take Hamel. There will be two waves of my beauties. The first wave of tanks will be with your own leading wave as you hit the Huns in their front-line trenches. The second wave will be right behind, following just a few minutes behind, and will mop up any troublesome nests of Fritzes that the first waves missed. Finally, at the rear we will have four tanks delivering supplies to the newly captured line.

'These tanks,' he explains, 'are now going to be used for the first time in battle and you are to have the honour of trying them out.'[7]

Not that they are impregnable for all that: the Brigadier makes that very clear with a comprehensive lecture on the strengths and weaknesses of these new iron giants. Bear in mind, gentlemen, with a direct hit from a shell, even these can be stopped.

Ah, but the best part is to come. For after all the theory is done, comes the fun. After the tanks are started up with a throaty roar, the troops are invited to climb on board for a ride, both inside and on top!

They don't have to be asked twice, and are soon packed in and on every surface inside and out, bar the turrets of the guns that poke out. The engines roar even louder, the tanks start off with a jerk, and they are on their way. Hold on, you bastards!

The blokes on top love it from the first. For those inside . . . the best they can hope for is that it will prove to be an acquired taste. For with nowhere to stand up, all they can do is squat, or kneel by the roaring engine, and watch as the crew take the tank through its paces.

Still, to begin with, old stagers like Captain Thomas White are impressed to see that, whereas the monsters of 1917, at Bullecourt, required four men just to drive one, these ones can be driven by just one man!

'On the level ground they can go pretty fast,' Geddes records, meanwhile, '[and] look just like huge caterpillars plodding along.'[8]

Coming to a massive shell-hole, Geddes and his mates hang on even more tightly in the hot sunshine as they wait to see what will happen now. To their amazement, the tank driver slows down and the tank moves down the side of the shell-hole, across the bottom, and up the other side! With that sort of capacity, crossing a mere trench will be no problem at all, but what about when the driver straddles the trench and drives along it? Imagine how devastating that would be to any Squareheads if this were a real battle and the tank got among them like that?

And now they come to some trees. Do the tanks stop now?

Not on your Nelly.

I said *hold on,* you bastards!

To the amazement of the troops, the 29-ton tanks just run over the trees as though they are not there!

Soon enough, the makeshift enemy post up ahead *really* isn't there once the six-pounder guns open up on it.

Oh. And the machine-gun nest in that trench over there?

The tanks rumble forward and, after crushing it, execute an aston-ishing manoeuvre.

'This is how we squash Jerry with his gun,'[9] proudly remarks one driver as, with his hand hard down on one side of the steering column, the tank swirls around on the position.

Yes, they actually go 'pirouetting round and round', as Monash would describe it, '[to] blot them out, much as a man's heel would crush a scorpion'.[10]

Oh, how the Diggers cheer! (Even the Commander of the 4th Division had been convinced by such demonstrations a few days earlier, with General Rawlinson having noted in his diary: 'I went out this morning to see the 4th Aust. Div. practice [sic] with the tanks. Maclagan has now got hold of the idea all right. I was afraid that he and Courage would not hit it off, but they are alright now.'[11] Attending on this day, he is even more convinced: 'I think we have now got the Australians to understand and appreciate the tanks.'[12])

Now, let's say that in the battle to come you need to talk to the tank commander, because of some kind of emergency, like a German machine-gun nest 100 yards off to your right that you need help with. How do you get a hold of him? Why, simply 'ring the backdoor bell',[13] the Diggers are told, by tugging on this rope you can see at the back of the tank. A bell rings inside, a slot opens, and the tank commander is all ears.

And now with the fun stuff completed, they get a little more serious, as they engage in some 'set-piece manoeuvre exercises', whereby, again and again, the men practise marching forward in a line, with the tanks just behind. For this is one of two new principles that General Monash is insisting on: 'The deployed line of Tanks [are] to advance . . . pressing close up to the barrage . . .' Yes, there are some tank experts who are insisting that because of their height, nearly twice that of a soldier, it is 'not practicable for Tanks to follow close behind an artillery barrage',[14] but those experts don't have the rank of General Monash, and his insistence counts more.

As to the wire entanglements up ahead, when the soldiers reach them, the tanks go forward and simply crush them, making an easy path for the men. And so it goes, as for the next few hours, the rehearsals continue. As one officer would note, 'the Diggers climbed all over them, inside and out, rode across trenches and over walls and banks, and even drove them'.[15]

Afterwards, the tank commanders and crew emerge and talk with the platoon and company leaders face to face, as they go over what is going to happen, and how they will go about it. For this is not a mere joy-ride for the commanders and soldiers, this is a bonding with the very beasts of battle they will be going to war with.

'Diggers and Tankmen were soon great pals,' Captain Thomas White of the 13th Battalion would note, 'and also treated their tanks as such, the monsters being given pet names, addressed kindly, admired loudly, and, when occasionally scolded, scolded as one would scold a faithful dog.'[16]

At the end of the long day, exhilarated, Geddes and his mates are astonished.

'Provided they get across to the enemy lines alright,' he notes in his diary, 'they'd be grand things in an attack & would put the wind up the enemy infantry, who would be powerless to defend themselves.'[17]

There is of course, one downside, as Geddes also notes:

'But they draw the enemy's artillery fire, & the poor old infantry advancing with them get pie.'[18]

Still, for now, bonza.

'They'll do us,'[19] is the general opinion, as recorded in the 13th Battalion's history. And the men can deal with the pie when it comes, even if there are extra servings for everyone!

Such is the sudden affection the Diggers have for the tanks that they start to refer to each one by the nickname chalked on its sides. ('Havoc', 'Hadrian', 'Harlech', 'Harrier' and 'Hiawatha' are all at Hamel.) To help the troops identify their tank in the battle itself, each one will have the colours of the Australian battalion to which it is attached painted on the side. It will mean that if, for example, a member of the 13th Battalion gets lost in the burly-hurly of battle, all he needs do is spy a tank with the colours of light blue over dark blue and the name of their own tank on the side – 'there is Hiawatha!' and they should be able to get their bearings. Go the way the tank is going! The men of the 43rd Battalion can follow the colours of brown over light blue, while the 25th Battalion soldiers will keep track of the tank with black over light blue.

Now, two other things. As there is some chance that the Germans might counter-attack with *Beutepanzer* – 'booty tanks', as in captured British tanks – each of the Allied tanks thrown into the battle will also have a red, white and blue patch on its front. Any tank coming at the infantry without such a patch must be assumed to be German. Finally, each Allied tank will carry two flags within on four-feet high poles. If you see a red and yellow flag waving from the top of the tank it means 'I am broken down', while a green and white flag means 'Come on!' (If, for example, the tank wipes out a machine-gun nest which has been holding up the infantry who are lying in cover 100 yards back waiting for the tank to finish the job, the waved green and white flag will bring the troops on.)

This is *not* to be another Bullecourt. The tanks will be reliable, and everyone will know what is going on at all times.

'It was invaluable as mere training for battle,' General Monash would later note of the tank displays, 'but the effect upon the spirits of the men was remarkable. The fame of the Tanks, and all the wonderful things they could do, spread rapidly throughout the Corps.'[20]

For his part, Captain Thomas White of the 13th Battalion would exult: 'What a change to the feeling about the tanks of Bullecourt when the very name was anathema. But these Mark V tanks were really marvels and a great advance on the clumsy, imperfect and more weighty monsters of 1917 . . .'[21]

Among the soldiers, heading back to their digs through Amiens once more, the mood is buoyant.

'Amiens is a big city,' Cliff Geddes would record, 'all but a few of the 90 odd thousand people have had to leave there, as Fritz is not far away & shells & bombs it, "but he'll never take it while we're here," say the Aussies'.[22]

•

Beside the sparkling waters of the River Somme, two miles north of Amiens, this little village slumbers in the sun, much as it has for centuries past, with little to distinguish it from dozens of others.

Ah, but on this day, things are different. For look closer now. Of Madame La Grande – who at this time is usually shepherding her children down the main street, home from school, like a glorious mother hen – there is no sign. The village priest? He is long gone. *Le marché*, in the centre of town, where at this time the housewives would usually be buying fresh meat and vegetables for the evening meal . . . is empty.

And now look closer still.

In fact, *all* the villagers have gone, and the new occupants hail from far away. They are soldiers, Australian soldiers of the 14th Battalion, whose own hometowns have strange names like Myrniong, Murrindindi, Macedon and Majorca. Having been billeted in the village for the last six days, helping themselves to the larder, the pantry, the backyard chooks and most particularly . . . the cellar, their mood is generally buoyant. Having spent so much of this war sleeping in muddy trenches, and tents only when they were lucky, dining on tinned rations and drinking muddy water, what a pleasure to live like *men*, sleeping in real beds, dining like kings! (For some lucky Diggers, stretcher-bearers all, who have found a stray cow – which they quickly take into the stable of the abandoned house they are staying at – it includes a constant supply of fresh milk, the only problem being they must guard her against the thieving bastards who might try to nick her!)

Against that, the mood remains a little grim, for there is the knowledge that there is a 'stunt' on, that they will soon have to go over the top once more. Certainly they have faced many stunts before and have always acquitted themselves well. They are good soldiers, the 14th Battalion is a mighty unit – if still badly battered by the disaster at Allonville – and the men are confident they will win, just as they always do. But still, it gives a man pause, to ponder whether, this time, there might be a bullet out there, or a piece of cruel shrapnel, with his name on it, just as had happened to so many of his brethren, and . . .

And what now?

Men, marching into town. Big men. Smiling men. *Eager* men.

Yanks!

These are the men of F Company, 131st Infantry Regiment, from Illinois, the last of the arrivals from the American forces, the second tranche, some 2500 in all. In short order they are divided up, with each Australian Company of 150 men at best, now being bolstered by a Yank platoon of at least 50 men to each ... who generally like what they see.

'These Australians,' an American regimental commander would note, 'appeared to be more akin to our class in that they were an independent, alert, energetic lot of men and splendid fighters.'[23]

For now, however, it is time for a roll call.

'Dwarsakoski?' Present, Sergeant.

'Esser?' Present, Sergeant.

'Ferbstein?' Present, Sergeant.

'Kucklosky?' Present, Sergeant.

'Plsknowlcz?' Present, Sergeant.

'Schwab?'[24] Present, Sergeant.

Lieutenant Rule is amused.

'When their names were called,' he would recount, 'I could hardly keep from laughing, and I felt very grateful to my boys that they had not inflicted such names on my roll book . . .'[25]

In response to the wry grins from the Australians all around, one of the Americans calmly notes, 'You know, I was born in Austria, and my father was a Pole.'[26]

So different from the names of the Australians in Rule's C Company, where 'Smith' and 'Jones' are standard and any moniker ending with either one vowel or three or four consonants would not only be unusual, but, let's face it, *suspicious*.

'They were all men in the prime of their life; and *such* a mixture – one could see among them all the nations under the sun. Yet here they were, citizens of the great republic, with only one idea in their heads.'[27]

They want to attack the Germans.

For their part, the Australians are more than glad to have the Yanks, but are equally eager to give them some basic idea of what they will likely face, and some pointers on how they might survive the experience. Always remember, Yankee, when you are going forward, keep an eye out for whatever cover is right ahead of you – that way, if you come under heavy fire you can throw yourself down behind it. *Don't* get too eager and get too close to the creeping barrage, because it will kill you – stay back at least 75 yards, a bit further than you blokes could throw a baseball, at all times. As you go forward, don't ever bunch up – you present too tempting a target. If you take over a German trench, and want to have a look to see what is out in front, make it a quick look only, for fear of snipers. And if you are going to have a second look, *fer Chrissakes* make sure it is a different part of the trench, or Fritz will blow your bloody head off!

The Americans hang on every word, are very grateful, and ask many questions.

'It was good to see the way they palled up,' Lieutenant Rule would recount. 'The Yanks were out for information and our boys were very willing teachers, and it speaks well for the future to see one set so eager to learn and the other so willing to teach. These Yanks view things just the way we do, and their general trend of ideas was very sensible indeed.'[28]

What they mostly want to do now is fight, to get at the Germans, after all these years of waiting, and *months* of training . . .

And yet, one Australian officer would note a key emotion, when it comes time for the veteran Australians to talk to the Americans of what they will face in battle, the things to look out for, the tips on how to stay alive when the air is alive with a blizzard of bullets and scything shrapnel.

'Company members were appalled at their ignorance and want of perception,'[29] he would record.

Now listen, the Australian troops start to explain. No, *listen*. The shrill sound of that shell? That whistle you can hear? That means it *isn't* coming straight at you. The ones that are going to hurt you are the ones that screech and then rumble like a train, and then *roar* – and then you'll have about a second or two to react. If you're in the front-lines and throw yourself to the ground every time you hear a whistle, you won't do anything else, sport.

Now, when the time comes to go forward, and there's a stink on, make sure you take 'care to follow straight in the footsteps of the man in front, as occasionally he trips over wire or falls in a shell hole which can hardly be seen in the dark, and it puts you right'.[30]

Also, when yer within coo-ee of the front-lines – that means when yers are close, sorry – fer Chrissakes, don't look up as that exposes more of your noggin, your head, to Fritz's bullets. Keeping your melon down means you get more protection from your helmet. And remember, in the dark, you can tell soldiers apart just by the silhouette of their helmets. Fritz has a square helmet so keep yer eyes peeled for Squareheads. If yer see one of the coots, *don't* call out to warn yer mates, no time for that, just shoot! And never *ever* go down a Fritz dugout without first dropping a bomb in there. Oh, and when you 'christen the squirt', that is, use your bayonet for the first time, make sure you put your boot on Fritz's chest, and twist it, as you pull it out, because otherwise the suction can keep it stuck in there. The Yanks listen, agog.

But *keen*?

Hell, yes!

'Their enthusiasm is just great,' a grizzled Australian sergeant would note, 'but of course they are just as we were in early 1915.'[31]

It is a refrain echoed again and again.

'In spite of their extreme rawness,' one lieutenant notes sagely, 'Company officers agreed that they would prove very staunch in action if well led . . . The wide difference between the two parties made thoughtful Company members realise how very far they themselves had travelled since Gallipoli days, and what a vast amount of experience they took for granted, and looked for in troops in France.'[32]

For their part, most of the American soldiers are impressed, with Private Charles D. Ebersole, of Chicago, recording his impression that the Australians are 'very good' and 'very democratic', although 'somewhat undisciplined'.[33]

In short, *exactly* their kind of blokes!

Indeed, an American officer, Lieutenant Kenneth, will describe the Australians as, 'more like ourselves than any of the other allies'.[34]

Extraordinarily, even this close to the front-lines, some of the Australians are able to give their new American pals fresh milk!

30 June, Bertangles Chateau ballroom, Foxtrot, Bravo

'This is my grandfather's axe,' the old line runs. 'My father replaced the handle, and I replaced the blade.'

So too, with Monash's plan, that he had first formed up almost ten days earlier. The plan still looks much like the original, but by now every part of it has been tested, modified, tweaked, polished, replaced, returned, restored, whatever . . . with experts from all fields having had input into it.

And today is to be the biggest meeting of the lot, less to decide issues – bar the few remaining ones – and more to unveil the whole plan to *all* the senior officers of the Australian Corps, the 5th Tank Brigade and the 5th Wing Royal Air Force, including this time, Brigade and Battalion commanders, and those members of the British Army, like their Artillery, who are involved.

'The underlying principle of the conference,' Monash will explain to General Rawlinson, 'was that everyone that mattered was present, and had to explain his plans and proposals; and that where there was any conflict, or doubt or difference of opinion, the final unalterable decision was given there and then, and no subsequent fiddling with the plan was permitted . . .'[35]

(For his part, General Rawlinson will grudgingly note, 'Old Monash talks too much, but [he] is very good at the preliminaries.'[36])

As such, there are no fewer than 250 officers in attendance, and they cover no fewer than 133 items on the agenda for the next four-and-a-half hours, deciding everything from the final timings, to the amount of ammunition to be brought forward by the supply tanks, to how much rum to give the assaulting soldiers as they head out into No Man's Land.

As ever at the top of the table, puffing his pipe, General Monash is broadly guided by the note he'd jotted down in pencil before the meeting, with his surprisingly untidy scrawls, in tiny writing, noting:

> ~~Copy of agenda sheet~~
> ~~Add my notes to do~~
> *Relief model and map to conference*[37] (In the middle of the table
> is the scale model of the ground he'd had made, brought back
> from Sinclair-Maclagan's HQ, where it had been for the last few
> days, so everyone can now see the situation.)

1 *Go over all – settled*
       still to be settled
2 *Each to know what others going to do*
    Each commander states his plans
3 *Try settle each point finally now*
4 *No alterations – only confusion*
5 *Secrecy – prime necessity*

    (a) losing men who will talk
    (b) clumsiness in our preparations[38]

For, just as he has always done – and has already most particularly executed before the Battle of Messines – Monash seeks 'a perfect mutual understanding among all concerned',[39] of precisely what the battle plan consists of.

As the meeting begins, he covers what is settled, and together they go over what is still unsettled, starting off with Zero Hour, one of the first items on the agenda: 'Visibility night [of] 3/4th July'[40] in order to settle Zero Hour.

From the beginning, Monash has always planned for the attack to be in the darker hours, over-ruling the concerns of the 5th Tank Brigade, who feared getting lost in the gloom – particularly as they could only see through a small slot at the front of their machines – and it would therefore be better to attack in the daytime. *Over-ruled*. There will always be pros and cons for any time chosen, and Monash remains convinced that the advantages of darkness, or near darkness, outweigh the disadvantages.

But *when*, precisely? The obvious timing is that it must come after the moon rises at 1.13 am and well before the sun rises at 4.43 am.

More precisely, after long deliberation, it has been decided that it must come at the first lustre of dawn, when not only will the tanks get a little visibility, but the attacking soldiers will have just enough light to see their way pushing east, ideally with the defending German soldiers being silhouetted by the light skies of the coming sun rising behind them. For the Germans, however, the attacking soldiers will be coming out of total darkness.

And what time is the light *precisely* like that?

Monash has had his balloonists check these things, and now consults their report:

Evening twilight lasts from	*8 PM till 9 PM*
Movement can be observed	*9 PM*
Movement cannot be observed	*9.30 PM*
Movement can be observed	*3 – 3.30 AM the following morning*[41]

On that reckoning, it makes sense to send down the barrage at, let's see, yes, 3.10 am . . . when, even if there is cloud cover, the dawn will be guaranteed to be giving just enough light for our soldiers to see. So, we agree, Zero Hour is 3.10 am.

Now, with Zero Hour set, other key timings must work from that as their reference point. What time should the tanks start to move forward, to be at the Jumping Off Point when the barrage starts? After the Blue Line is captured how long will it take to dig in there, because that's how long we'll have to maintain a protective bombardment in front of our newly captured line? Item by item, the questions are resolved and yet more detail is determined within the parameters of Monash's plan.

Monash checks that the build-up of supplies is proceeding as planned, all the while jotting down calculations, checking and re-checking. From half-a-dozen trains arriving at Amiens every night, 900 tons of supplies, equipment and ammunition of all kinds must be brought up eight miles to dumps behind the front-line, and concealed there. Some 160 tons of hay for the 20,000 transport horses, 100 tons of food per day for the men, and most importantly, 5000 tons of artillery shells must be stockpiled by Z Day. That's about 7800 wagonloads per night – no movement can take place in daytime lest Fritz spots it. The wagons, if placed in one column, would take up 15 miles of road. That's more than is available, so a tight timetable ensures there is no congestion. Monash is concerned that the roads won't be able to bear up. He has already stored 6000 tons of gravel along the roads, together with road repair crews. Nor can injured horses or broken wagons be allowed to impede the flow. Wheelsmiths, blacksmiths and veterinarians are also on hand along the main routes. Bridges too must be maintained. Stores of timber and detachments of engineers and carpenters camp by bridges to swing into action if a problem occurs. The whole is under the supervision of traffic police, standing at crossroads ensuring the long columns of wagons proceed at a standard three miles per hour.

Everyone must know not only exactly their own role, but *also* where it fits in the whole plan, on the reckoning that the plan can't run like clockwork unless every cog understands the whole clock.

But make no mistake, Monash makes clear again and again, as per his note to himself: *No alterations – only confusion.* There is to be no altering in this plan. A devotee of the Napoleonic aphorism, 'Order, Counter-order, Disorder',[42] Monash is uncharacteristically loud in his insistence that changes of plan tend to cause confusion and, as much as possible, everyone must *stay* with the plan, most specifically in terms of timing and objectives. Start on time, finish on time.

'The battle plan thus having been crystallised,' he would later note of his own attitude, 'no subsequent alterations were permissible, under any circumstances, however tempting. This fixity of plan engendered confidence throughout the whole command which facilitated the work of every commander and staff officer.'[43]

Such fixity included resisting *all* temptations to go beyond the objective – the Blue Line on the map – that has been set for you, even if you can detect little resistance, and think it might be possible to get among the oh so tempting German artillery beyond Wolfsberg.

'This,' he reiterates, 'is a limited objective we are going for, and no consideration is going to prompt me to allow exploitation beyond the line chosen. On no account will an attempt be made to go chasing after those guns.'[44]

And he also fiercely resists Brigadier Courage's suggestions that they attempt to grab more German territory by pushing the protective barrage out further and letting his tanks mop up all resistance.

No.

Again, it is a firm Monash dictum: 'So long as we hold and retain the initiative, we can in this way inflict the maximum of losses when and where we like. It restores to the offensive the advantages which are natural to the defensive in an unlimited objective.'[45]

Smoothly, Monash continues to tick off item after item on the agenda:

> Precautions to preserve normal activity prior to zero [hour] of
>   Artillery, Machine Guns, Smoke and Gas, Air.[46] Done.
> Precautions to prevent unusual movement.[47] Done.
> Synchronisation of Watches.[48] Done.
> Measures to deceive as to frontage under attack.[49] Done.

Watching how General Monash conducts the meeting – yes, very much like the conductor of a grand orchestra – no few of those attending are amazed at his grasp of even the smallest details of the battle to come.

'[Monash],' General Walter Coxen would recount of this and other meetings, 'with his marvellous mathematical brain, treated it as if it were an abstract mathematical problem, selecting and directing at once his attention to the factors that were of the greatest importance in the solving of the problem. It was a fine education to all who had the privilege of attending conferences held by him at periods prior to any important operation, at which officers of the various arms responsible for carrying out the operation were present. His capabilities of visual-ising and marshalling requirements to the minutest detail, in the proper order of sequence never necessitated his turning back to supplement anything that he had previously said, for nothing had been forgotten.'[50]

What is important now is to keep the day and hour of the attack a secret. For the moment, all the men are told is that the attack will come on a day and an hour to be fixed hereafter.[51]

At the meeting's conclusion, General Blamey sums up those key decisions that have been taken, to be distributed to everyone in the room.

> 1. Movement. The greatest care is to be taken that there is no
>   abnormal movement by day. This particularly refers to the
>   movement of guns, ammunition and transport vehicles.
> 2. Barrage rate. The barrage rate during halt – the full rate of
>   three rounds per minute will be fired by the artillery barrage
>   on the village of Hamel and the portion of [Vaire] wood which
>   is under fire during the halt . . .

3. <u>Enemy CP.</u> In the event of the enemy placing a counter preparation bombardment on our positions just prior to zero, the
   corps heavy artillery will at once undertake intense counter
   battery work.

4. <u>Tanks.</u> [The] infantry commander on the spot is responsible
   for the joint action of tanks and infantry. He will give such
   orders to the tank section commander as the situation demands.
   Tanks will commence to move from their concealed positions
   at 10.30 pm . . .

5. <u>Ammunition.</u> Ammunition carrying planes will start at Zero
   plus three hours.

6. <u>Zero hour.</u> Zero hour will be promulgated from Australian
   Corps Headquarters at 11am on Y day.

T A Blamey
Brigadier General
General Staff
Australian Corps[52]

The plan set in stone on this day is different from Monash's original
concept in two ways. Now there *will* be an artillery barrage, and
it is no longer primarily a tank operation with infantry support.
The Australian infantry will command the tanks, not the other way
round.

•

In these waning days of June, there is growing surprise at how quiet
the Germans are. Not only has there been no big offensive, as had been
expected, but they seem barely to be launching any raids.

What could possibly be going on with them?

Charles Bean records one theory.

'This Spanish Flu – the Dog Disease as they call it in France, is
making extraordinary ravages . . . It is very severe behind the German
lines in France and some people attribute the slowness of their staff in
getting the new offensive launched to this disease.'[53]

(Legs-eleven! In fact, Spanish flu is particularly rife among the
Germans at this very time, with later estimates that each 'German

division [on the Western Front] in June and July [had] 1000–2000 men sick with the influenza pandemic.'[54])

So yes, the German soldiers of the 13th Infantry Regiment in these wee hours of the morning of 1 July are much thinner in numbers than they might be, as so many men have had to pull out with the flu. But, as the first of the 13th IR's Companies begin to enter the line on the 'heights south of Hamel'[55] – to replace the 419th Infantry Regiment, who have been there for the last eight days – they are, generally, pleased and happy to be here. Compared to the trenches they've previously held – in such places as the Somme in 1916, Passchendaele in 1917 and the Hindenburg Line in early 1918 – these ones are so quiet. The tall wheat has not been blasted away by artillery fire – clear evidence that nothing much happens here. The Regiment will be defending 1200 yards, of which the northern half is the stronger, in front of and inside Vaire Wood, and the southern half is in the open country that extends halfway down to the Roman Road, where the 15th Regiment holds the line.

And compared to the scratchy trenches they'd held at the end of their March offensive, these are 'relatively well-developed'[56] while still lacking artillery-proof dugouts, concrete emplacements, and the layered series of trenches they'd known in their first years on the Western Front, many of which had boasted 50 yards of barbed wire in front of them.

These trenches aren't remotely like that, but still they shouldn't be too hard to hold as the whole area appears to be very quiet, and the area in front of their trenches, a 600 to 800 yard deep 'Vorfeld', foreground, has little cover for any enemy which wishes to attack.

Meanwhile, their comrades of the 55th Infantry Regiment, who are taking over positions just to the north of the 13th, are unhappy.

'Unfortunately,' their Regimental History will record, 'the new position was in a poor *Verteidigungszustand*, defence condition. At that time there was everywhere some certain carelessness in the expansion of the newly won front. The short period of the *Bewegungskrieges*, movement war, had sufficed to make people forget the lessons from years of position warfare. The loss of battle-proven old soldiers, their replacement by younger ones, less familiar with the peculiarity of the trench war, might have contributed to this.'[57]

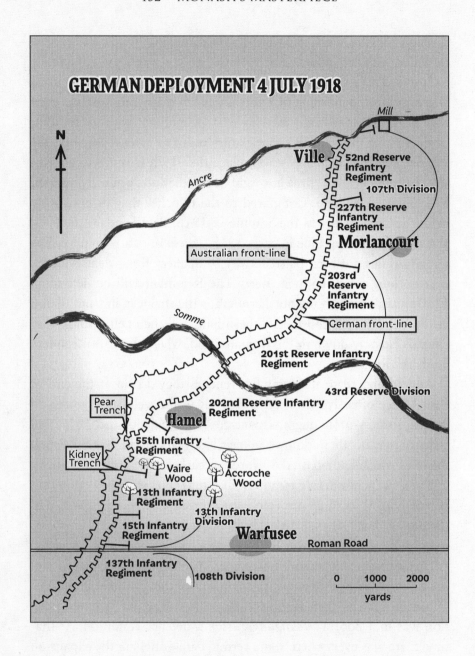

Still, they dig in the best they can.

The Regiment set themselves up catch-as-catch-can, digging the trenches they have inherited much deeper, and consequently their parapets much higher. Their finest troops are put in the key position to hold what they call '*die Nebelmulde*', the Fog Hollow, a curiously shaped trench which makes an outline rather like a pear, and is positioned on their side of the ridge, making it difficult for the enemy artillery to hit them. And yet, while the men are pleased with the defensive aspect of *der Nebelmulde*, the same cannot be said for the rest of their positions.

'The trenches were flat and poorly developed, there were barely any shelters, and the approach paths, especially down to the *Nebelmulde*, were easy to recognise and often could be seen into . . . The foreground troops were in danger of being completely cut off . . . A timely approach of support troops was then almost impossible.'[58]

In short, while this pear-shaped trench is good from the point of view of being shielded from enemy artillery observers, so long as the enemy is on the other side of the hill, its inhabitants will be highly vulnerable should the enemy gain the top of the hill itself – and it will be hell on earth for any reinforcements sent forward to hold it.

Finally, some 5000 yards to their north, Germany's 52nd Reserve Infantry Regiment is moving into the trenches next to the Ancre on the same night, and here things are not so quiet.[59]

They are establishing themselves but, 'constant artillery fire makes the [digging] work in the front line without result . . .'[60]

And since then, 'the enemy bombards us regularly *mit Gasminen und schweren Kalibern*, with gas-mines and heavy calibres. The losses . . . diminish the weak combat-strength *zusehends*, visibly. Enemy planes harass us and prevent any traffic [back and forth from the front line to bring supplies].'[61]

(Brigadier Pompey Elliott and his men of the 15th Brigade may have only been given a minor role in the battle to come, to their chagrin, but they are set on making their presence felt meantime to whoever the unfortunate Germans are who must face them, and it's working.)

•

Not all the British soldiers attached to the Australian Corps had been, at least initially, particularly impressed with the Colonials. One is a 21-year-old English artillery officer with the 5th Field Brigade, Royal Artillery, who had been attached to the Australians for the last three months, Lieutenant Patrick Campbell.

'This was the first time I had seen Australians,' Lieutenant Campbell would recount of his initial impressions. 'They were unlike any of our own divisions, and on this first occasion I was not attracted by them. They were noisy and swaggering, they did not march along the road, they just walked, they seemed to be without any kind of discipline.'[62]

But things had changed, once he had seen them in action, most particularly in the Battle of Dernancourt, three months earlier.

'The German attack had failed. The Australians had shown that their confidence in themselves was justified, and we began to share it.'[63]

It is a confidence that has remained with him and his comrades ever since as they have come to know the Australians better, and they have been excited as the build-up to this battle of Le Hamel has continued.

Just the night before, the 5th Artillery Brigade (one of 42 artillery brigades of the Australian Corps and the British Fourth Army available for Hamel) has moved forward to Sailly-le-Sec, a little north of the Somme, in preparation for plastering the German lines, once the word is given. From his high position in the artillery observation post on the slopes above Sailly, through his telescope, Lieutenant Campbell can not only see Hamel itself, but also the entire German line to be attacked, right up to the Roman Road leading east out of Villers-Bretonneux.

'[I] could see all the world,' Campbell would recount, 'the Somme, a long straight silver line in the middle of the picture, villages and church spires among the trees in the valley; and then mile after mile of rising upland, more villages, and trees on the skyline marking the long straight Roman Road, the road from Villers-Bretonneux . . . behind the German lines, [there were] men digging or walking about, lorries and wagons on the roads, horses in their wagon-line area, even the smoke of a distant train . . .'[64]

All through the day and into the early evening, Lieutenant Campbell stays there, looking for targets, occasionally sending back the co-ordinates to his battery, so they can try their luck shelling them.

The extraordinary thing, however, is how few targets there are, how empty the whole landscape on both sides of the line appears.

'To see so much and to see nothing!' he would recall. 'We might have been the only men left alive, my two signallers and I. And yet I knew there were thousands of hidden men in front of me. Australians on our side of the line, the enemy on his. But no-one moved, everyone was waiting for the safety of darkness.'[65]

Nearby, one of the most formidable Australian officers in the AIF, Colonel Harry Murray VC, DSO & bar, DCM, is setting up the mighty 4th Machine Gun Battalion, which is to deliver the long-range machine-gun barrage from the height this side of the Somme, using water-cooled Vickers machine guns, some from other machine-gun battalions. Each gun can send bullets at a range of over 3000 yards, and spread its bullets in an area the rough size and shape of an Aussie Rules field at home.

With expert eye, Colonel Murray – who had won his VC at Stormy Trench on the old Somme battlefield, ten miles from where he now stands – is setting the guns up so the northern half of 6500 yards of German trenches that are to be attacked will be getting a maximum intensity of fire, with not a yard missed, and the crucial areas, at Hamel and Vaire Wood, will be absolutely plastered.

So dig in here, lads, making sure that you have complete range of movement for your barrels, while also getting maximum protection for whatever Fritz sends back at us – get those parapets thick and high – while also making sure you let the dog see the rabbit, and don't get in the way of the artillery. And haul those ammunition crates forward, and get them secured. With 8000 rounds per gun, we can use three quarters of a million rounds if we need it on the night, which makes no less than 40 tons of ammo that has to be hauled through the night, together with 100 gallons of water to keep the guns cool. And we need endless rolls of telephone wires in place and buried as deep as you can get it, so all of the machine-gunners will be connected to their chain of command.

When Colonel Murray speaks, the men hop to without question because, as noted by one soldier in his diary, 'He is a grand chap, very brave, & very, very few men live to gain the honours he has.'[66]

Now, in addition to the already established machine-gun barrage, Colonel Murray also assigns no fewer than 24 Vickers Guns and their five-man crews to participate in the actual attack, with the task of following up hard behind the leading wave to consolidate the positions once captured.

•

The missive from Field Marshal Foch, directed to his two immediate subordinates, Field Marshal Douglas Haig, Commander-in-Chief of the British Forces, and General Philippe Petain, Commander-in-Chief of the French Army, is typically crisp and to the point:

> Today, 1st July, the enemy is halted
> 18 miles from Dunkirk
> 36 miles from Calais
> 42 miles from Boulogne
> 36 miles from Abbeville
> 36 miles from Paris
> 15 miles from Chalons
>
> An [enemy] advance of 24 miles towards Abbeville [via Villers-Bretonneux and Amiens] would cut the communications with the north of France, and separate the British and French Armies – a result of considerable military importance for the issue of the War. An even smaller advance towards Paris . . . would make a profound effect on public opinion [and] cause the evacuation of the capital . . . Progress of the enemy towards any of the other objectives enumerated above cannot offer him any comparable result . . . It is therefore Paris and [Amiens] before else which we must cover.[67]

Fair enough.

As it happens, Field Marshal Haig is becoming ever more confident that he has the situation of the Germans positioned closest to Amiens well in hand, via the Australians who are about to give them something to think about!

'W Day', 1 July 1918, Bertangles HQ, a visit from 'the chief'
Attennnnnnn-shun!

From the beginning of this war, there have been ongoing problems with the general lassitude of Australian soldiers when it comes to firing off salutes at British officers. At the height of the Battle of Pozières, as a matter of fact, two Australian officers had been conducting an urgent meeting right by a spot known as 'Dead Man's Road', trying to work out how to take a particularly troublesome bunker, when they had been interrupted by an urgent missive, given to them by a breathless runner. The front of the envelope was marked Urgent and Secret, and further inspection revealed it to be from their British Commanding Officer, General Hubert Gough. They'd opened it quickly, knowing it must be very important, only to find something unexpected . . .

> A number of cases have lately occurred of men
> failing to salute the army commander when he is
> passing in his car, in spite of the fact that
> the car carries his flag upon the bonnet. This
> practice must cease.[68]

But there are no such problems, of course, when Field Marshal Sir Douglas Haig himself comes on this day to visit General Monash. For the Commander of the British Expeditionary Force of no fewer than 1,750,000 soldiers, the most powerful Field Marshal of the most powerful British army ever assembled, even the Australians don't mind scrubbing up, and he is greeted by an Australian Corps Headquarters Guard well turned out for the occasion, all steely eyes, flashing bayonets and – unusual in Australian soldiers – bright shining boots.

(The only possible exception is Monash himself. He is the exemplar of Bean's description of the Australian soldier as 'incorrigibly civilian',[69] and it is practically a point of honour with him *not* to be so impeccably turned out it would make the King's Guard at Buckingham Palace blush. As his Chief of Staff, General Thomas Blamey, would recall, as 'a semi-humorous protest against the efforts of his personal staff to have him meticulously correct, [General Monash] invariably wore his spurs upside down'.[70] As to being saluted, he is not particularly fussed for himself, though can insist on it for others, it being recorded that once, noting that a fresh recruit sitting nearby and having a fag had not saluted him, he told him straight: 'I am nothing but a mere brigadier-general, my boy, but one of these days some second-lieutenant is going to come along here and reprimand you severely for your lack of observation.'[71])

Once inside the chateau, and retired to Monash's apartment, the Australian takes his Commanding Officer – or 'the Chief' as everyone called Haig except to his face – through every detail of the plan.

Now, no matter that upon one reckoning the Australian is a babe in the woods in this world. (After all, Monash had planned his first battle only three years earlier at Gallipoli – while Field Marshal Haig has been doing such things for 20 years.) For the truth is, even Haig himself seems to realise the sophistication of Monash's plan, that it is singularly well thought out, and put together by an uncommonly talented commander.

No matter what Haig asks – and their meeting goes for over an hour – General Monash has a ready answer. The Melburnian is clearly intimate with every detail of every part of the action to come, specifically because *he* is the one who has conceived it, designed it, modified it, and ensured that it fits perfectly into every other part of the puzzle that it touches so that it can be relied upon to work properly. Like an engineer building a structure which he knows will only be as strong as its weakest link, Monash has fashioned every link himself, and feels responsible for it all – because he is.

Among other things, Monash confirms how happy he is to have one company of American infantry from the US 33rd Division to be attached to each of the ten Australian Battalions detailed for the attack. It will strengthen the Australian hand, reduce Australian casualties and, perhaps in the tightest of situations, give them just the critical mass they need to triumph.

Haig purrs, which is unlike him. But this is no ordinary occasion, and no ordinary briefing. For the last eight months, the British Expeditionary Force has been spending its energy and its resources in defending. Now, they are about to launch their first heavy attack since the Battle of Cambrai in November of the previous year – and Haig is very pleased to see everything is on track, and in the hands of such a clearly capable commander. (But Haig is not surprised. It is exactly what had happened on the occasion of their first meeting, before the Battle of Messines, in June 1917. Monash, then the Commander of the 3rd Division, had stood in front of a wall of maps and given Haig as comprehensive an overview of all arms of the battle as Haig could possibly hope for, and clearly knew all the detail intimately, because he had personally written it. At the end of the short address Monash had said 'I have the senior officers here from all these commands to tell you anything you may wish to know, Sir,' only for Haig to reply, 'Thank you, but I do not think there is anything that you have left unsaid.'[72]) This is exactly like that, albeit with even more detail, for the much bigger battle. Beyond everything else, such thorough preparation is vindication of Haig's long proclaimed view that Monash was the man to command this most powerful of his 25 Corps, representing ten per cent of the entire British Expeditionary Force.

'As ever,' Monash will shortly write to his wife, 'Sir Douglas was affability, courtesy and consideration personified. He always expresses the very greatest confidence in me.'[73]

Field Marshal Haig does indeed come away, rushing off to a conference of the War Council at Versailles, mightily impressed.

'I spent about an hour with Monash,' he will record in his diary this evening, 'and went into every detail with him of an operation which he is shortly to carry out with the Australian Corps. Monash is a most thorough and capable Commander who thinks out every detail and leaves nothing to chance. I was greatly impressed with his arrangements.'[74]

On paper, there is no doubt Monash's plan does the trick.

The *real* trick, however, is to have it work in the actual battle. Still, Field Marshal Haig takes his leave with something of a spring in his step. This chap Monash may prove to be a splendid find.

For his part, General Rawlinson remains quietly unconvinced, writing in his diary this evening:

> I feel [Hamel] will do well if the Boche does not discover the zero hour – Too much talk is going on . . . We are now using 10 companies of Yanks and 60 tanks.[75]

●

Sergeant Walter Corning and his fellow late arrivals of the 131st Regiment are now settling in with the Australian soldiers of the 43rd Battalion.

'This outfit,' he would chronicle, 'was one of the first in France and had won an enviable name for itself in battle ... We liked the Australians immensely. They were splendid, courageous men.'[76]

Maybe even too courageous?

One Australian soldier, let's just call him 'Mad Danny', shows the Yanks his favourite stunt. Taking a German grenade, he taps the pin on his helmet in the customary way, which means, they all know, there is just FIVE SECONDS before it is to explode!

One ... the Australian doesn't blink.

Two ... he grins like a Cheshire cat.

Three ... he licks his lips like a hungry wolf.

Four ... he hurls it high in the air and away from their trench.

Five ... it explodes, sending a sprinkling of shrapnel falling to earth elsewhere.

'This was dangerous sport,' Corning records, 'and after the first time we preferred to watch him from the shelter of a dugout.'[77]

As well as getting to know the Australians, these newly arrived Yanks are invited by the Aussie to have a closer 'Captain Cook' at their new surroundings, and are quick to notice one extraordinary thing – tanks! Huge ones. There are 15 of them, under green nets with cut branches of trees poking out of the netting to further camouflage them under the trees under which they are parked. Soon enough, the Americans, too, are encouraged to familiarise themselves with these strange beasts.

'It was hot and stuffy inside,' Walter Corning will note. 'The interior was a mask of mechanism and the walls were lined with ammunition. There was hardly room enough for the gun crew to move around, and their places did not look very inviting.'[78]

1 July 1918, Vaux, their Bond is their word

And so the members of the tank crews are briefed. Their primary job in the battle to come is to limit infantry casualties, to have their tanks do the work of taking out the machine-gun posts, crushing the wire, subduing the trenches and letting their own steel and cast-iron shells provide protection when the bullets and shrapnel begin to fly. In these last days leading up to the battle, no small amount of time is spent rehearsing – going up hills, keeping formation with the infantry, going between them, changing directions suddenly, communicating to them what you want them to attack now, and so forth.

And, of course, the boys in the tanks also engage in a little friendly rivalry.

When Sergeant Edwin Bond's tank commander, a relatively young and inexperienced officer, Lieutenant Hadley, finds himself manoeuvred into making a colossal 50 franc bet with another, rather more senior, tank commander officer over who had the more accurate Hotchkiss gunners, Sergeant Bond tells him straight.

'I don't think you need to worry,' says he, 'as the money is as good as won.'[79]

Lieutenant Hadley is relieved. And it's not just the money. It's the prestige!

Sure enough, tin cans are placed on top of targets by the railway embankment west of Villers-Bretonneux, and the two tank gun crews go hard, with a neutral tank captain appointed as judge, and a sergeant as facilitator of the competition.

When both crews are ready, the sergeant shouts: 'Thirty rounds, target to your front . . . in your own time GO ON . . .'

As the Hotchkiss guns roar into life, the shots ring out in rapid succession and the tin cans, sure enough, begin to disintegrate . . . but not in equal number. One team is clearly doing better than the other.

And the winners are . . . Lieutenant Hadley's crew!

The delighted Hadley shares the 50 francs with his victorious crew, and they are more confident than ever that, come the night of the battle, they will acquit themselves well against the Germans.

There is certainly no doubt over the power of the Hotchkiss machine guns.

•

All quiet now.

The now nightly flights of the FE2bs have made their first run over the German lines at dusk, and have returned to their Poulainville aerodrome to refuel. Beyond the odd scattered shell-fire in the distance, a rough kind of quiet has returned to the Allied side of the line, beyond the occasional shouts from various troops, the surprising moo-ing of a cow somewhere near – odd, because, as far as we know, all the animals have been evacuated with the villagers – and the whistle of a lost and lonely freight train in the distance, heading no doubt to the hub of Amiens.

But wait, what's that?

What's what?

That. *Listen*, Dig.

And he's right. At first it is a low rumble, getting louder, and then a strange, exceedingly noisy clattering. What on *earth* can it be?

Oh.

Soon enough, it is obvious. Most of the soldiers standing back to let them through see the obvious: guns. *Big* guns. Some of the more savvy men, however, recognise the specifics of these guns. They are heavy artillery of two types: an Ordnance BL 60, with a 60-pound shell and a 5-inch diameter barrel, and a QF 4.7-inch gun with a 4.7-inch diameter barrel and a 45-pound shell. They are the guns of the first Australian Siege Artillery Brigade, and two brigades of the Royal Garrison Artillery. Behind them now come the 18-pounder field guns – smaller and lighter with barrels just 3.3 inches in diameter, designed to go a lot closer to the line, to do the precise surgical work of the creeping barrage as the Australian Corps move forward under the cover of darkness. The heavy artillery will deploy 6000 to 8000 yards back from the line, west of Villers-Bretonneux. The field artillery, the 18-pounders, will move over the next two nights into their final positions all along the front, carefully camouflaged and no more than 1000 to 2000 yards back from the German front-lines in front of Hamel that they are set to pound. To get the optimal accuracy they need for an effective creeping barrage, they really do need to be that close.

If all goes well, they will move into those positions during the four nights before the battle, with just one artillery brigade of 24 guns to move up on the last evening. Already a few of their guns have gone forward in the last few days to 'register' their guns – that is, fire a few rounds to see if they land where they are expected to land (but only a very few, as we don't want to alert Fritz). Ideally, this will provide the exact co-ordinates for the other guns, when they arrive, so that they can lay down an accurate barrage.

A couple of guns from each battery have also been left in their original positions, to provide the normal harassing fire every night, before moving up on the eve of the battle.

(The Commanding Officers of those artillery crews conducting the harassing fire have one key instruction: *Don't* hit the many German artillery batteries we know of. We want to hit them hard on the night of the attack, and not have them moved meantime. Australians on the ground and in the air – Wackett and No. 3 Squadron – have located 90 per cent of the German artillery batteries, and wish to keep the Germans in ignorance of that until 3.10 am 4 July, when they will be quickly, if a little rudely, informed.)

And now, what is this, clattering along behind the guns? Yes, of course, it is the first tanks of the 5th Tank Brigade heading forward to be corralled around Vaux and Hamelet. In the moonlight they look like menacing metal monsters, coming forward to eat whatever is in their path.

Behind all of them come the heavily laden trucks, filled with rounds of ammunition, grenades, medical supplies, extra rations for thousands of men and tanks of water to fill canteens – in sum, all the *matériel* of war – all to be secreted in fields close enough to the lines to be easily transportable, come the night, and far enough away to be hidden from German observers.

To cope with the extra traffic, a special pontoon bridge has been laid over the Somme, between Vaux and Vaire. Put together at the crack of dusk, it will be gone before the crack of dawn, ready to be set up again tomorrow night when there will be yet more traffic. It works . . . just.

'The traffic jam was terrible . . .' Gunner James Armitage of the 8th Australian Artillery Brigade would scribble in his diary that night. 'We were hopelessly blocked by an English unit's wagon which had got a wheel over the narrow bridge. After a while we could stand it no longer so we unhitched the horses and tipped the wagon and contents into the river. The Tommies took a poor view, but everyone else was pleased.'[80]

By dawn, the tanks will be secure in the woods right by the villages of Hamelet and Fouilloy, covered by freshly cut branches and netting.

Most of these newly minted weapons of war are now no more than 2000 yards back from the line.

In the case of the 5th Field Artillery Brigade's Lieutenant Patrick Campbell, the guns of his own battery are now positioned just 1000 yards back from the line, and his men are given strict instructions not to walk about in the day, as they will be under observation from Wolfsberg.

'The guns were in front of a bank,' he would recall, 'they were covered with branches of trees to make them look like part of the brushwood. We used fresh branches every night, bad camouflage was worse than none at all, it showed you were trying to hide something. We worked through the short summer night, digging shelters, putting away and concealing the ammunition which had come up, covering our tracks with grass. After the night's work we slept.'[81]

Quickly, quietly, the pieces of General Monash's plan are being moved into place, as the conductor prepares to fire up his orchestra as never before.

CHAPTER SIX

AUX ARMES AUSTRALIENS, FORMEZ VOS BATAILLONS!

Since the war I have been told by men whose judgement I value that the only soldier thrown up by the War on the British side who possessed the necessary qualities [for High Command] was a Dominion general. Competent professional soldiers whom I have consulted have all agreed that this man might and probably would have risen to the height of the great occasion. But I knew nothing of this at the time. No report ever reached me . . . which attributed any special merit to this distinguished soldier. The fact that he was a civilian soldier when the War broke out may have had something to do with the tardiness in recognising his exceptional abilities and achievements . . . Professional soldiers could hardly be expected to advertise that the greatest strategist in the army was a civilian when the War began . . .[1]

Lloyd George, British Prime Minister, 1936

Morning, 2 July 1918, Bertangles Chateau, the war waits for no man

'Monash,' General Rawlinson has already noted in his diary, 'is rather perturbed at what Hughes and Murdoch are doing at home.'[2]

Now a week on from that notation, the truth is that General Monash is even more perturbed, having stewed for a week on the outrage that the likes of Murdoch and Bean – neither of whom has ever fired a shot in anger, or led so much as a corporal's guard in battle, let alone been elected to any position – *continue* to manoeuvre against him. And all while he is trying to organise this singularly important battle . . .

Oh, yes, he is aware all right. Despite Murdoch's protestations of personal affection and loyalty – 'Trust me and use me in any humble capacity you can . . .'[3] – it is not possible to have made as much noise as Murdoch has, without the word spreading.

At least, however, the time is drawing near to lance this boil, with Prime Minister Hughes due to arrive today on his whistle-stop battlefield tour, where, at last, Monash will be able to address him directly.

Still, as it is now less than 48 hours before the battle is to begin, Monash is not one to get his priorities mixed up.

'Sir John,' Thomas Blamey would recount, 'would not have the [Prime Ministerial] party at Headquarters lest it interfere with operations and established them in a camp some miles away.'[4]

Instead, he arranges for the Prime Minister and his retinue to meet him at a nearby chateau, and General Monash is indeed waiting – respectfully, but impatiently, as he is eager to get back to his real work – when, in the late morning, the Prime Minister arrives with his Deputy Prime Minister, Joseph Cook. They are accompanied by a large entourage of their staff, together with an escort of the Australian Army Provost Corps, while of course Charles Bean is there covering the whole thing, as is Billy Hughes' shadow, Keith Murdoch, who has accompanied him to France for the trip (the better to get into his ear about the general inadequacies of John Monash).

Aware that General Monash has a battle to organise, and that they will be seeing each other later in the day in any case, Prime Minister Hughes does not keep him long – and the moment the two are alone, General Monash does not tarry long in turn, finally saying to the Australian Prime Minister what he has for the last three weeks been aching to say, man to man, in blunt language.

'I am bound to tell you, quite frankly,' Monash says, 'that any arrangement which would involve my removal from the command of this Corps would be, in the highest degree, distasteful to me, and that I would regard any such removal as a degradation and a humiliation.'

In response, the 'Little Digger' barely blinks.

Putting his hand on Monash's shoulder he says simply, 'You may thoroughly rely upon your wishes in this matter receiving the greatest possible weight.'[5]

And what does that mean precisely?

Exactly. Not much.

But at least General Monash has had his say, and given Hughes fair warning that he will not go quietly.

Of course, when General Birdwood joins them presently, Monash quickly takes both him and the Prime Minister through his battle plan. Both Hughes and General Birdwood are nothing if not impressed with Monash's presentation, albeit for different reasons. Hughes has had many briefings from many Generals and military Commanders in the course of the war but, as he would later recall, Monash 'was the only general with whom I came in close contact who seemed to me to give due weight to the cost of victory. He said "This is what we want to do; this is the way to do it with the least cost in human suffering".'[6]

His every innovation seems designed to protect the lives of Australian soldiers.

'He was no swashbuckler, nor was his plan that of a bull at a gate,' Hughes would observe. 'It was enterprising without being foolhardy, as was to be expected of a man who had been trained as an engineer and had given profound study to the art of war. Monash always understood thoroughly the ground he was to fight on. Maps lived for him.'[7]

For his part, General Birdwood has made many battle plans himself, and experienced even more briefings from other Commanders. But not like this. The detail! The innovation! The way it all meshes together. As battle plans go, he would avow, this one is 'practically perfect'.[8]

Notwithstanding that Monash is calling on no fewer than 300 planning staff to oversee and execute the operation, his personal grasp of even the most minute details of the battle to come is astonishing. For every minute of the barrage, 2700 shells will be fired on the enemy, which he knows because he is the one who did the calculations as to what would be necessary. No less than 18 miles of telephone wire must be transported forward so that secure communications can be established with the front-lines. Visibility? Monash knows the figures intimately, as he has called for a report on it and studied it closely: at 3.10 am, his soldiers will become visible to the Germans at a distance of 20 yards, and from there as the rising sun beyond yonder horizon looms in the gloom visibility will increase six yards per minute until the

Halt Line is reached. He knows how long an RE8 will need to take off and climb to 5000 feet, and that its cruising speed is 90 miles per hour, so in order to arrive over the battlefield for air dropping at 6.10 am, the planes need to take off at 5.35 am. He knows it ALL! This is no General on a distant hill-top with one eye on a telescope and another eye on how history might judge him. This is a General who has built the coming battle from the ground up, and the clouds down, with his own hands, and it doesn't matter what question Hughes throws his way, General Monash has the immediate answer.

And of course, they could have talked on it for many hours, but for now, all three of them have more urgent matters pressing . . .

Afternoon, 2 July 1918, under the trees at Blangy, getting the good oil

The Australian soldiers of the 13th Battalion, and their 200 Americans, are gathered together by Lieutenant Colonel Douglas Marks, the 13th's Commanding Officer – at just 23, the youngest Battalion commander in the AIF – to be told the news.

Cliff Geddes leans in close to soak up every word.

We're going in, men. Sometime over the next three days or so. You will be told with many hours to spare, to prepare. The 13th Battalion will be at the prow, with Geddes' D Company the first to attack, with the specific task of taking the first two trenches, and then securing them.

'A, B, & C Companies are to go on past you. You will have three tanks with you, and aeroplanes will also play a role.'[9]

There is more, much more, with detail about who will do what, and an affirmation as to the importance of the battle.

Oh, and one more thing.

'Prime Minister Billy Hughes will be here later today [to address you].'

All the men laugh to hear it. Fancy old Billy turning up here, this close to the lines! Typical politician, just when there might be a bit of glory about.

'I don't think old Billy Hughes will get much of a reception,'[10] Geddes will note in his diary.

The important thing now is to keep total security on everything.

> It is to be hoped, Fritz doesn't get wind of it, if he spots the extra
> artillery & tanks beforehand, things will be only middling. There is
> a fearful lot of thinking to be done by the heads preparing for it . . .[11]

One of those doing the key thinking, of course, is the 'Old Brig', Brigadier
Charles Brand, Commander of the old hands of the 4th Brigade, who
now rides up to a cheer.

The men like him well, and climbing down from his horse, he gives
them the news.

Cricket. Having just returned from England, he has brought with
him a cricket cup that the Brigade's battalions can compete for, say,
next Sunday?

Cliff Geddes' thought is immediate: '*I guess the lucky ones who
come out, will.*'[12]

On the one hand, the fact that, at such a moment, before such a
battle, their Brigadier has cricket on his mind is encouraging from the
point of view that things can't be *that* serious.

On the other hand . . . 'The old chap didn't say much, seemed pretty
worried, & not his usual hard case self.'[13]

For now, Cliff meets up with his brother Boo, and a couple of their
mates, Privates Alfred Eldridge and Albert Smith, to have tea together
under the trees, discussing the battle to come, even as they share some
of the food that has just come from home, like plum puddings, and
Anzac biscuits, which the veterans had been getting from the days of
Gallipoli on. For Cliff, as ever, it feels good to be with Boo before
battles. They have sworn to their parents, and to each other, to look
after each other, and, this far from home, to be able to talk of normal
things, of family, of friends, is really something.

Returning to his own digs when it starts to get dark, Cliff is just
in time for a meeting of their platoon, gathering around Lieutenant
Smith, who lays out a map, places the lantern before them, and goes
through it all, including the precise timings of harassing fire, tanks
arriving and the creeping barrage. Now, look closer on the map. This
is where we are. This is where Fritz is. This is the ground we have to

cover, and this is where we will find the wire, the machine-gun post, and the heaviest concentration of German soldiers. This line here is their support trench, and this line is the Blue Line, the line we are trying to get to, before digging in.

And who thought that this far into the war, who could know there would be something new under the sun, let alone the moon? They've had briefings before, of course, but never this detailed, never with such precise knowledge of both the defences and the precise mechanics of how the battle should play out, if they all do their part.

Cliff is heartened.

'We are hoping the attack will be very successful, & that few of our good lads may fall.'[14]

Now, pack up men. We move into the front-line trenches, *tonight*, to replace the 50th, who are coming out. You'll be there until the time comes for the battle – we will tell you when.

Right then. There is just time for Cliff to slip away to find Boo, and Smith and Eldridge, to wish them well. As Australian males, of course there is no embracing, just a firm handshake, but all are keenly aware they might be saying goodbye for the last time – and no-one feels it more than the two brothers. Of course there is no mention of the shadow that passes over all soldiers in such times before battle, the fact that they might be *killed*. If there is reference it is only in euphemisms such as 'buying the farm', 'getting a meat ticket', 'got the chop' or 'stopped one'. But even when they make no reference, the spectre of its possibility is there, all right.

Good luck, Boo. Good luck, Cliffy. As ever, they are more worried about the other, than themselves. It is just the way it is.

Christ, the smell of dead horse-flesh is overpowering. But the smell of the horse-flesh left on the battlefield has to compete with that peculiar smell of tension, excitement, nerves and unexpressed fear that emanates from the cold sweat of each soldier preparing to attack. The overall mood of the Australian soldiers on this evening is somewhere between a world-weary sense of 'duty calls', and, in some parts, eagerness to get at the brutes again. No-one doubts they can do it, just as they have done it in recent times. After all, since the beginning of the *Kaiserschlacht*, we Aussies have fought 12 major battles, for 12 victories – and we never gave up an inch of ground.

But, weary and a little depleted?

Yes, across the line, the Australian soldiers are exactly that.

The 4th Brigade, for example – nigh on 3000 men at full bottle – has had just on 12,000 battle casualties since the war began. Each Battalion of 750 or so had lost four times its own strength in three years. In the 13th Battalion, of the current 750, just 143 of them had set foot on Gallipoli, of whom just 40 or so had landed on the first day. Cliff was one of the 40. A good dozen of them have been wounded four times, while 50 have been wounded three times.

You've only been wounded *twice*, you say? Mate, in this man's army that counts as a couple of scratches.

And now they have given us one more call to arms?

Alrighty, then.

At least this time, *we* get to attack *them*.

As it falls completely dark, Cliff Geddes' D Company moves out . . . and slowly up into the line, even as Fritz's shells roar down, just to their left, and just to their right, but never quite on them.

'Just as well he doesn't know the exact spot to put them.'[15]

What's that Digger ditty again?

> *Cannons to the left of us,*
> *Cannons to the right of us,*
> *Volleyed and thundered,*
> *Fritz made an awful fuss,*
> *Missed them and near got us,*
> *Lord, how he blundered.*[16]

•

Even from a distance, the most standout feature of General 'Black Jack' Pershing – named for the fact that, as a young officer in the 1890s, he had fought with enormous distinction in the Spanish–American War and the battles of Kettle Hill and San Juan Hill, commanding the buffalo soldiers of the famous 10th Cavalry Regiment, comprised of 'Negro' Americans – is his shock of white hair.

It had turned that colour, practically overnight, only three years earlier, when he had lost his cherished wife and three daughters in a house-fire at their San Francisco home, while he was serving on the Mexican border. On this afternoon of 2 July, that white hair is shiningly apparent, sprouting 'neath his peaked cap, as he arrives at the II US Corps HQ at Beauval, seven miles north of Bertangles.

'At ten minutes to four,' Captain Will Judy of the US 33rd Division would recount, 'the military police presented arms and the Commander-in-Chief of the American Expeditionary Force, General Pershing, passed by – tall, erect, neither slender nor stout, of quick step, sharp glance, protruding lower jaw, and restless carriage. He was never still; always he was adjusting his clothes, fingering his gloves, looking away in impatience, striking a pose, making those about him ill at ease.'[17]

Despite this, on this occasion, few can be more at ease than the Commander of II US Corps, General George Read, who – a little later, when General Pershing arrives at a field at Allonville to inspect the troops of the 33rd Division – mentions merely in passing that in two days time, over 2000 American troops will be fighting side by side with Australian troops at Hamel, and . . .

And what the *hell* are you talking about General Read?

This is precisely the kind of thing that Pershing has been fighting against – both the desire of the British to put Americans in the line before they are fully trained up, *and* to break them up, scattering them among Allied armies.

Pershing will not have it, and says so in no uncertain terms. Responsible for the fate of a million American soldiers in France, he is not particularly dismayed that 2500 of them were about to go into battle without his express permission, but is greatly relieved to have stopped it in time, and eager to make it clear that no such thing should ever happen again. It is just so terribly typical of the Brits to try this on.

'Regardless of the distinct understanding that our troops behind the British front were there for training,' he would recount, 'and not to be used except in an emergency, the British made constant efforts to get them into their lines.'

This latest is merely the most flagrant example of it. Of course, the Commander of all American Forces in Europe is quick to put a stop to it, telling General Read that this arrangement does 'not meet with my approval, and [therefore] our troops should not participate'.[18]

Quietly, General Pershing is still of the view that 1919 will be the year the war is won, and it is at that point he truly wishes to unleash his massive American Army to do the job.

And *not* before, do you hear?

Yes, General Pershing. General Read promises he will deal with it.

•

It is the military version of 'checking the boundary fences'.

This close to the battle, now just 36 hours away, so much has been put in place, so many crucial decisions taken for better or worse, that the battle preparations have assumed a momentum all their own and there is little that General Rawlinson can do to alter things, even if he wants to.

Still, it feels like the right thing to do, and he does it, to visit the three Australian Brigades charged with the attack – the 4th, 6th and 11th – talk with their Commanders and ensure that all is in as high a state of preparedness as possible.

It is!

'I . . . found everything well ordered and advanced and all in good fighting trim,' he will record in his diary. 'Brand and Cannan who are the two brigadiers chiefly involved are good men and in great heart. They welcome the assistance of the Americans . . .'[19]

No, the problem on the day does not come from the Australians, but from those very Americans. For, returning to his HQ at Flixecourt, Rawlinson receives a message from General George W. Read of the USA's II Corps, the American officer who has given his blessing for the Americans to be involved in this battle, that he needs to urgently see him this evening. Strange. General Rawlinson hopes it does not spell trouble, but it might. For anything simple could be resolved by telephone. The fact that Read is insisting on a face-to-face meeting bodes ill.

•

Taking his leave of Monash, the frail figure of Prime Minister Hughes is still accompanied by his bevy of heavies, including the Divisional commanders, Generals Sinclair-Maclagan, Rosenthal and Hobbs, and led by General Birdwood, who is currently both administrative head of the AIF and commander of Fifth Army. (For the occasion, Birdie is proudly wearing the slouch hat presented to him by senior staff officers of the Australian Corps as a farewell gift.) And the Generals are, in turn, accompanied by their own bevy of 'bum-brushers', the term the Diggers use to describe all the various aides-de-camp, who follow the brass hats everywhere.

Throughout the late morning, Hughes had been taken to visit the troops and their commanders, most particularly the 'attacking Brigades' – the 4th, 6th, and 11th – where he had been able to inspect the troops, get a feel for their state of preparedness, their role in the battle to come, and their general views on the whole situation on the Western Front. At the end of each inspection, Prime Minister Hughes had been careful to take the Commanding Officers aside, where he was able to speak to them in private and – in the Australian manner – ask some frank questions, man to man. He was gratified to receive in turn frank answers, and the hell with the fact that he is the Prime Minister.

Some things on General Monash need to be said, and the Commanding Officers said them, for that was the central question he was asking. In the course of the morning, Hughes managed to speak to three Divisional commanders, and over lunch had a long conversation with a fourth, General J.J. Talbot Hobbs, of 5th Division, on the same subject. The Prime Minister has specifically sought Hobbs' view, because, as related by General Sir Julius Bruche, who is present for their lunch, 'someone in London suggested the Prime Minister should go over to France and consult . . . General Hobbs . . . because he had no axe to grind. So the Prime Minister came to lunch with us and General Hobbs adjourned for their discussion, and General Hobbs strongly recommended Monash, a man with a good record who had done good work . . .'[20]

Indeed, Hobbs himself will describe the conversation as 'a most earnest and confidential talk with Mr Hughes on the question of the higher administration of command of the AIF and I think impressed him with my views . . .'[21]

Hobbs is strongly of the view that, among other virtues, Monash is 'a great judge of men and character, calm and deliberate, resolute and determined',[22] and he has no hesitation in telling the Prime Minister so.

But, hurry now.

The men await.

•

For it is time for Prime Minister Hughes and the Honourable Joseph Cook to make their way to a clearing in a forest just outside Bussy-les-Daours, where 3000 soldiers drawn from all the attacking brigades about to go into battle the following evening are formed up in a tight circle so that their two distinguished visitors can address them. No podium for the visitors, no stage – they are Australians, and a sturdy upturned fruit crate will do, the nearest thing to a soapbox that has come to hand. On this gorgeous summer's day, the gathering of these Australians far from home is lit by the dappled light the forest gently allows through, and the sound of the twittering birds is spoiled only by . . . the boom of artillery in the near distance sending death and destruction to whoever is on the receiving end. So, at least the scene is set for a fire and brimstone speech.

Except . . .

Except, can *this* man really be powerful?

'He hasn't the strength of a child to look at,' Cliff Geddes, up near the front, notes, '[Hughes] is a poor, thin, miserable, misshapen looking chap, & his head is the biggest part of his body.'[23]

Billy Hughes leaps to his feet, with surprising nimbleness for a man in his mid-fifties – let alone one who looks old enough to have been Noah's navigator on the Ark – and climbs atop the fruit crate and prepares to speak.

Watching from a distance, Billy Hughes' 21-year-old soldier son, Ernie – who is driving him while he is in the front-lines – is bemused to note that all the soldiers 'mournfully awaiting . . . carefully rehearsed for the occasion, [now] feebly cheer . . .'[24]

And now a curious Australian soldier moseys past.

'Who's that bounder spouting over there?' he asks.

'Oh, that's only old Billy Hughes,'[25] replies Ernie, easy as you please.

Atop the fruit crate, Hughes is in full cry, taking it as an honour and a privilege to be able to address these men that he admires so much.

Gazing out upon them, with General Monash puffing on his pipe at his feet, he is quite moved at just how impressive they are.

'I can't tell you how splendid they were,' he would write a few days later. 'Words are poor things to describe them but as they stood there thousands of them armed [from head to foot]; helmets, full kit ready for action, their bayonets glistening in the sun; an enemy aeroplane overhead being attacked by our anti-aircraft guns . . . I thought that with a million of such men one could conquer the world.'[26]

But now, time for the Prime Minister to unleash some matching splendid oratory.

And Hughes would, bar one thing.

The very noisy shells continue to scream overhead, and it is all rather distracting.

Turning to the Major beside him, Hughes says, 'This is too noisy, Major; couldn't you let up a little? I won't be long.'

'I'm sorry, sir,' the Major replies very apologetically, 'but I can't do anything about it. That's the other fellow.'[27]

Oh. Very well, then. Fritz? Yes, he can be very uncooperative on such matters.

Nothing for it then, but to carry on. Taking pause now, Hughes clears his throat and, as he is ever wont to do, manages to provide words of eloquence to do justice to this situation and his own strong emotions.

'Your deeds,' he exults in his Welsh accent, 'the history of this war, is the basis upon which the future nation of Australia will be brought up. On the day you landed at Anzac the Australian nation was born. Before that we were New South Welshmen, Queenslanders, Victorians, but . . .'

But somewhere in the near distance, at this moment, oh fie the cannon's roar . . . with an unearthly crack, an artillery shell is sent soaring towards German lines. There is a theatrical pause, just long enough for wee Billy to say, 'Damn that gun',[28] and then he resumes, without even momentarily losing the thread of his speech!

'. . . but, on that day we became Australians. You have fought, and are fighting here to keep our people free – to keep alive in the world the idea which we free nations have of freedom, and more than that – to save our Australia from the Prussian domination, which, if certain things were to happen we would certainly be subjected to. In that cause you have not feared to spend your lives. It is up to us to see that while you are doing that abroad, we shall look after your interests at home. That is the least that we can do; and I pledge my government and the people of Australia to do it.'[29, 30]

Still watching him closely, Corporal Cliff Geddes is now impressed.

'Little Billy made a good speech,' he will record in his diary, noting that, despite his shrivelled appearance, 'his eloquence is there.'[31]

Whatever feeble cheers Hughes might have begun with, he really does receive genuine warm applause at speech's end, whereupon Joseph Cook takes over the fruit crate, warming to the theme of how proud they can be of what they have achieved, the confidence all of Australia has that they will continue to achieve great things, and the 'very fine repatriation scheme ready for them . . .'[32] mixed with a few light asides about how much he is sure they are enjoying the French wines, etc.

Not everyone is impressed. Lieutenant Ulric K. Walsh, of the 17th Battalion, a 23-year-old from Nowra, has heard it all before. 'It was the usual thing,' he will write home to his brother, Austin. '"Australia is proud of you and will not let you down on your return home etc . . ." Matters political and governmental seem petty and almost mean to the boys who have as their motto "Deeds, not words". I don't think that any of our lads give a passing thought to politics these days. Probably if meddling politicians had kept their fingers out of the pie this war would have victoriously ended a long time ago.'[33]

Either way, as Cook continues to speak – or rather shout, as he tries to project his voice to the furthest reaches of the troops – Charles Bean observes closely the actions of Billy Hughes. Yes, he is listening, but he does so lying 'full length on the ground looking into the faces of the soldiers and chewing a stalk of grass'.[34]

What, exactly, is he doing?

Bean thinks he has a fair idea.

'I suppose that he was thinking to himself: "Within thirty-six hours these men will be out there advancing under the bursting shells, going straight into the thresh of the machineguns" . . . and here they are laughing at Joe's old jokes, wrapped up in his speech exactly as if they were on a picnic.'[35]

As a matter of fact, did you hear the one about Cyril, the good Christian? Out the back of his Goondiwindi property, mending fences for a week, he lost his family bible. A month later a kangaroo hops up with the bible in its mouth. Cyril says, 'Thank the Lord, it's a miracle.'

'Not really,' says the roo. 'Your name's written inside the cover . . .'

When the time for the speeches is finally over, the politicians and Generals briefly mingle with the men, and Corporal Geddes is very impressed when Birdie gives him a friendly nod.

'Not that he knows me, but he's not a bit like a general with the boys.'[36]

And now here is Billy Hughes himself, coming along the front two ranks, shaking hands with the men and having a bit of a chat here and there.

Again, Corporal Geddes is impressed this time to be addressed as 'Sir'[37] by the Australian Prime Minister!

For his part, Hughes has been impressed not just by the men, but by the whole show that General Monash has set up here. For inspecting the front-lines and having the position explained to him by General Monash, Billy Hughes is moved by the profound respect that the officers and men clearly feel for Monash. It is the way they look at him, the way they hang on his every word, the way they speak to him, and *about* him when Monash is out of earshot. And all this, *despite* what Charles Bean and Keith Murdoch had been telling him for most of the last month – that Monash enjoyed no respect, that everyone wished Brudenell White had been given the top job!

Bollocks to the lot of it.

On this day, no sooner has Hughes farewelled the soldiers and taken leave of Monash than he whirls on Murdoch, in the presence of Bean, and says, 'Well – I haven't met a single one of them that thinks as you do. They all say the same thing – you tell me there are men who think the other way – where are they?'

Keith Murdoch does his best, telling the Prime Minister that, 'of course the men you have seen all [laud Monash], because it had been arranged that they should be the ones to meet him'.[38]

But making such a claim is a lame nonsense – for Hughes has in fact spoken to all of the key Generals – and all three of them know it.

'Hughes was seriously shaken,'[39] Bean will allow. And now, he is not the only one.

'. . . [W]hen Hughes drove off to Paris [for the forthcoming meeting of the Allied Supreme War Council],' Bean records, 'we all felt pretty blue. I did at any rate.'[40]

For his part, General Monash is just glad to see him go.

'It proved a most highly inconvenient day,' he records in his diary. 'I received a long visit from Mr Hughes . . .'[41]

Too long, in his view.

Back to work.

●

It is a very good thing that Charles Bean's driver, Boddy, has not been given the task of driving the Australian Prime Minister on this day, for they surely would barely have moved. So many vehicles to give way to, so little time!

For indeed, as the Hughes party continues to move back from the front-lines, all around there is a surge forward towards the Allied lines, of men and *matériel*.

Among the troops moving forward now, most prominent are the three attacking Battalions of 11th Brigade, who take over the positions on the left flank near the Somme. These soldiers know that there is something in the wind, that there is a 'big stunt' on, and they are in it – it is just that they don't know precisely when, or any of the details.

The strangest thing is to be marching to a battle on such a splendid summer's evening as this!

'It was a glorious night,' one of the soldiers, Private Harold Shapcott, would recall, 'and the scents of the flowers and the growing crops helped to make the march up seem unreal.'[42]

Evening, 2 July 1918, Fourth Army HQ, Flixecourt, Rawlinson reels

Yes, General Read?

Having returned to his office at his Flixecourt HQ after dinner, General Rawlinson finds General Read indeed waiting for him rather impatiently – with a certain, presumptuous, *where-have-you-been?* in his manner – and the US II Corps Commander is not long in getting to the point. While he had said very clearly, eight days ago, that his troops could be sent into battle with the Australians, things have changed.

'General Pershing has been inspecting the American Divisions in the British area, [has found out about the battle] and has definitely refused to sanction the use of their American troops in the Australian attack.'[43]

General Rawlinson can barely believe it.

But General Read insists.

'General Pershing does not want partially trained troops to participate.'[44]

This close to the battle, and the Americans want to withdraw their soldiers? The commanders are within hours of blowing the whistle to go over the top, and the Americans want to blow the whistle to call the game off? It *can't* be true!

On the instant, Rawlinson decides to try for a compromise.

'I can withdraw the six companies in the rear battalions,' he says, 'but not the four companies which had already gone up into the trenches as we cannot get at them.'[45]

In response, General Read is non-committal. He has been given a direct order by General Pershing. But at least he does not say no. The two agree that the real person to persuade General Pershing will be Field Marshal Haig and, with that in mind, Rawlinson calls Haig's Chief of Staff, General Herbert Alexander Lawrence, and explains the situation.

'Please ask General Pershing,' Rawlinson says, 'to agree to this [compromise] plan.'

Lawrence agrees to at least ask the question, and promises to phone Rawlinson before noon on the morrow.

Rawlinson is happy with that, noting in his diary:

> I cannot just push and I cannot withdraw so am inclined to let
> the thing go on. Read can't get at them to stop them.[46]

(For his part, General George Bell of the 33rd Division, whose men have so unceremoniously been yanked around, is not well pleased, as it is, of course, close to his worst nightmare. As enthusiastic as he is for his men to take part in the battle, it had been his long experience that there was always a risk when those higher up got involved.

'Go ahead and do it,' General Bell had said to one of the key HQ staff the year before. 'Do not ask Washington beforehand. They will find a dozen objections. Let them ask the questions after we've acted.'[47]

This time, sadly, the higher-ups have got wind of it before they had acted.)

•

The central idea of General Monash to hold meetings where full briefings of the whole situation are provided has been filtering down the ranks ever since, and meetings are also held at Brigade and Battalion level, with senior officers from all the other arms of the battle – the artillery, tank, machine gun, Australian Flying Corps and RAF – all in attendance, going through precisely what will be happening and what is expected from each one. Nothing is to be left to chance, everything must be prepared. The battle will substantially be won now, with the work we do to organise it, rather than later during the battle itself, when we will profit from this work, says Monash. Everyone down to the rank of corporal must study the maps and photographs provided, and understand the orders, the objectives and the exact times each of these objectives must be reached. And now at around 6 pm on this quiet evening of 2 July, X Day, the soldiers themselves are gathered together tightly by their Commanding Officers and told the situation.

We are into action, tomorrow night, and will advise you of Zero Hour closer to the time. We are going in with tanks right behind us. Those in the first wave will leave their trenches and get to the Starting Line tape that will be laid out for you in No Man's Land, where you must wait. The first harassing fire is at Zero Hour minus eight minutes, and depending on how far back from the German lines you are at Zero Hour minus four minutes, you must rise from the tape and begin a slow, steady walk, which should place you 75 yards from the German lines when the barrage lifts off it. At Zero Hour plus four minutes exactly, the tanks will reach you – and it is at this point that you and the tanks will attack the first line.

After you take the Germans in the first line, each Battalion must leave one Company there to secure it, and continue forwards. This is the line on the map, from the Somme to the Roman Road, and the time on the dial – Zero Hour plus 28 minutes – divides the first phase of the operation from the second phase. The barrage will stop for the usual three minutes on the Halt Line, and then start again for an extra ten minutes, at the halfway mark in the operation. At Hamel, for example, the Halt Line goes through the far end of the town itself, and after the 43rd has taken most of the town, the 44th will, once the barrage has moved on, pass by them on both sides of Hamel and push on to take Wolfsberg, which towers behind the town. All must then push on to the Blue Line, about 2000 yards forward of where the Germans now lie, and *stop*. There, you must dig in, and prepare for their counter-attack. Whatever happens, do *not* go on beyond the Blue Line, no matter how tempting it might be.

And of course, there are particularities for every Battalion, according to the task set them.

In the case of the 15th Battalion, for example, their task is very specific. The key orders, of course, are written down:

15th Battalion Order No. 45

Task

The 15th Battalion plus G Company of 132nd American Regiment will attack on the north side of . . . [Vaire] wood with their final objective on the blue line as shown on the attached map.

Special Tasks

A Company will co-operate with three tanks for capturing 'Pear shaped' trench, moving on with the rest of the line when this job is complete . . .

Artillery

The artillery will put down normal harassing fire from zero minus 8 minutes . . . to drown noise of approaching tanks which will leave their forming up line 8 minutes before zero. The barrage will come down at zero on the starting line shown on attached map, will remain thereon for 4 minutes then advance by lifts of 100 yards at intervals of three minutes . . . to the Halt Line where there will be a pause of 10 minutes. After the pause the barrage will lift 100 yards at intervals of four minutes up to 400 yards beyond the blue line [the final objective] where it will remain.[48]

The Americans, are, for the most part, hellishly impressed. There is no confirmation yet, but it looks like they will be attacking on the 4th of July and they have personally been promised by the Aussies, 'plenty of fireworks'.[49]

One of the American soldiers present at a briefing by the Commander of the 43rd Battalion, Colonel John Farrell, is at least a little stunned at how it's done, how the Colonel sets things out so lucidly – even allowing for the strange accent of these Australians, who sound as if they've sat on all their vowels before using them. The Colonel points to large maps that make things clear, uses phrases that are easy to understand, and even amuses the men with a joke here and there.

'He explained the entire action clearly and so well,' the soldier would recount, 'that we looked forward to it like a youngster on his first visit to the circus.'[50]

When Colonel Farrell is done, their next orders come quickly, the same ones being given across all ten battalions:

It is time to '*Alley toot sweet*', as in Digger slang for '*allez, tout de suite*', as in, 'Get moving, you bastards', it's time to go and report to the Quartermaster for your extra weaponry and ammunition. So it is that at dumps and dugouts well behind the lines, well away from the prying eyes of German observers, the Diggers and Yanks start loading up.

Each soldier is given a requisite amount of *matériel*, according to the role they will play. Every infantry soldier is issued with two grenades to put in his pockets, and 220 rounds of ammunition to carry in his webbing pouches, together with ground sheets so he can make himself comfortable for the long haul. Every second man is given a small flare, with strict instructions as to when to light them. Listen for the klaxon horn!

'Bombers', those soldiers who specialise in hurling grenades great distances with formidable accuracy – a skill most Australians had developed playing cricket, leaving the Germans for dead, while the best of the Americans were baseballers – are given only 100 rounds, but eight Mills Bomb fragmentation grenades, which weigh one pound and 11 ounces and can be thrown as far as 40 yards!

Ah, and now you Lewis gunners, working in teams of five. The No. 1, of course, must carry the Lewis Gun itself – weighing in at 28 pounds – the No. 2 carries spare parts and specialises in loading the gun, while the other three members of the crew must also haul 18 magazines of 47 rounds each, weighing a collective 81 pounds! It ain't easy, but can be done by slinging webbing pouches over your shoulder.

Oh, and a few more things. All the soldiers are given three empty sandbags to strap around their thighs, which they can fill once they get to the Blue Line, and build their parapet. Many of those going in the first wave are given wire-cutters, officers are given flares to fire off when they reach the Blue Line, and SOS rockets – when fired, they will explode in three red blobs or the like – to call down artillery in case of trouble, ideally just in front of where the SOS is fired, on the heads of the Germans.

In the meantime, there is ongoing concern about the tanks – not just that they will break down and leave the infantry in the lurch, but, in some ways even more horrifically, that tank drivers might run over wounded soldiers that they won't be able to see if they are hidden at the base of some of the three-feet high crops that lie across the battlefield. Therefore, General Monash himself has decreed that each soldier is to be issued with one roll of white linen tape, which is to be used in the case of a fellow soldier going down. Take this tape, and tie it in a rectangle around the soldier, on whatever vegetation is close, or your upturned rifle, and the tank commanders and their guides have been told to look out for them to avoid crushing anyone. (Oh, the horror!)

All up, it makes for a lot for each soldier to carry.

'Lor' knows how we'll go over the top with all this load, a chap won't have the strength to bayonet a plum pudding, let alone a Fritz.'[51]

For their part, the Americans among them are thrilled.

They're going to have the honour of making the first American attack, with the Aussies on the 4th of July! On that day, back in 1776, the United States of America had struck a blow for freedom, declaring herself independent of Great Britain. It will be for her sons, this 4 July, to strike a blow for freedom of their own, and among other things, strike back at the country which had sunk the *Lusitania* and been rampaging through Europe ever since.

•

Advised now of what awaits, the men prepare for battle. Some keep themselves remote from the others, praying, writing letters to loved ones, or simply contemplating what lies ahead.

In 16th Battalion's D Company, Captain Frederick Woods, Second Lieutenant Horace Blee and Company Sergeant Major Harold Blinman stick notably tightly together. There is so much to discuss as they go over their orders one more time, with their primary focus being to work out how best to follow their primary order:

> 16th Battalion will deal with Vaire Wood and on completion
> of these tasks become reserve battalion in the present front line
> [while 13th Battalion goes forward to capture the Blue Line].[52, 53]

It is, and they know it, a tough task. To take Vaire Wood they must first overcome Kidney Trench, where the Germans appear to be well dug in. And they will be doing it at about half-strength, for their Battalion had lost the Americans of Companies G and H of 131st Regiment just yesterday. It means that 14th Battalion – still reeling themselves from the Allonville disaster – who are to follow them in, will likely be bearing a heavy load. Yes, tough across the board. But at least they will be shoulder to shoulder with each other, as the three men are close friends. Certainly, there is a hierarchy in their ranks, roughly observed, but they are intimates, having fought together since the battle of Pozières in early 1916, and through such terrible battles as Passchendaele, where the 25-year-old Blee, an accountant with blue eyes and blond hair, had received a Mention in Despatches for bravery. The men trust and respect each other, particularly when in battle, and know they can count on each other.

(And if the 34-year-old Blinman treasures this friendship more than most it might be because he does not have a happy family to return to, nor a wife right now that he cares to write sweet nothings to. Back in Adelaide, well before the war, his wife had publicly humiliated him by leaving him for another man, and his only revenge had been to refuse to give her a divorce. He had then offered to provide her with a home and 30 shillings a week if she would come back, but her only reply, reported in the papers during legal proceedings – oh, the humiliation – was 'I don't want your home, your money, or yourself.'[54])

'Y Day', morning, 3 July 1918, Pioneer Trench, Hill 104, yanking the Yanks to safety

Yes, true, there have been many times in this man's army that the Diggers have had to make do with a 'Duck's breakfast', a swig of water and a wash, or even a 'Dingo's breakfast', a bit of a scratch, a bit of a fart, a bit of a look around.

But not these days, Digger!

For starters they are in a part of France where fresh food is plentiful, most particularly given that so many of the abandoned houses in the villages have fully stocked larders, not to mention cellars. And when it comes to their normal rations, the AIF is always careful on days like today – the day before the battle – to feed the men up strong.

And so they tuck in heartily, with their newfound Yankee mates, to the whole catastrophe – porridge, eggs, bacon, bread, butter and jam. (Some of the Diggers even have fresh milk. Don't ask.)

Notwithstanding the fact that there is a big stunt on tonight, and a dangerous one at that, the mood among the men of 14th Battalion is particularly strong, as the Diggers and Yanks continue to get to know each other, and talk of the battle to come with eagerness. For the 14th, it will be the first real chance to strike back at Fritz for the horrors of Allonville, and the Yanks for the atrocity of the sinking of the *Lusitania*.

Still, there's eager, and there's too eager.

Now situated in Pioneer Trench on the eastern slope of Hill 104, the 14th and their Americans are in a spot which has an expansive view of the battlefield – if, and only if, you are foolish enough to put your head above the parapet for a gander. And only the Americans are. Time and again the Australians have to pull the Yanks down before they get their bloody heads blown off. It's *not* just for their safety, but also so German observers don't notice any unusual activity in the Allied trenches.

No doubt about it. They have a lot to learn, these Yanks, but they are game all right, and the Australians look forward to going into battle with them.

2 pm to 3 pm, 3 July 1918, Paris, the gall of the Gauls

It is wonderful, what the touch of a woman can do, let alone a French woman. Field Marshal Haig's own quarters are spick and span, of course, and are cleaned and arranged by some of the best orderlies in the British Army.

But they don't look like this. The fact that General Pershing's 23-year-old mistress, Micheline Resco, is a regular visitor to his Parisian apartment at 73 Rue de Varennes makes all the difference. Some flowers here, some lace there, the curtains pulled back *comme ça* – allowing in just the right light, but none of the heat of the French summer – and all of it with a certain feminine French fragrance about the place. Within a stone's throw of Napoleon's Tomb, the apartment with the huge arched black double doors at the entrance bespeaks class and elegance.

(There are many such relationships about. General Monash's own mistress is an old friend of his wife, Vic, the well-off daughter of a Melbourne tobacconist, now living in London, Lizzie Bentwich. Rarely heading to Paris for his leave, Monash nearly always heads to London.)

For her part, Mademoiselle Resco, a small, gorgeous blonde, who the American had first met when the French government had commissioned her to paint his portrait – is as besotted with the 57-year-old general as he is with her.

Field Marshal Haig is in Paris for the 7th session of the Supreme War Council – a gathering of the great and the good from both the Allies' political and military worlds, setting themselves against the mad and the bad of the Axis powers. It began at Versailles on 1 July, and of course Haig takes the opportunity to catch up with the most important American in Europe, the man who, with one quick decision, solves so much of the Allied manpower problem, by unleashing his forces.

As a matter of course, General Pershing offers a salute to Field Marshal Haig, but the fact that Pershing is the Commanding Officer of 1,000,000 Americans, at last about to make their weight felt in this war, and likely make all the difference, escapes neither of them. The Americans will do nothing without Pershing's say-so and that say-so remains dependent on whether Pershing, not Haig, thinks it a good idea.

Hence, the highly skilled *pas de deux* these most senior of British and American officers execute this afternoon. Having come by on a rare visit, Field Marshal Haig is both giving, and receiving, a full briefing, as he and General Pershing exchange information and views. Among other things, the American is not happy that the French are always 'buzzing about',[55] his HQ at Chaumont, almost spying on him and his men, trying to find their state of preparedness for combat operations. *Mais oui*, 14 months after the United States declared war, the French are very curious to learn when the Americans will be ready to do some real fighting.

The Gauls are particularly galling for the fact that General Pershing has always made it clear that America will not be rushed in this matter. The American troops need to be properly trained, properly provisioned and properly ready. As it happens, the fact that both the third and fourth German offensives directed at Paris – Operations Blucher and Gneisenau – appear to have been halted, means that it is slightly less urgent than usual that the Americans become more involved in front-line defences . . .

Yes, well, on that subject, inevitably, the conversation turns to the forthcoming action by American troops, the first attack they *will* have been a part of, as 2000 of them are due to accompany the Australians in their attack on the German lines at Hamel.

On this subject, Pershing is suddenly adamant.

'I think them insufficiently trained and I told Rawlinson yesterday that I do not wish them used.'

After all, under the agreement signed between the British and American governments, the terms of engagement, it had been made clear that only in an emergency would the Americans be taking foreign orders, and this is *not* an emergency.

'Do you wish me to interfere in the matter?' Haig asks.

'No,' General Pershing replies calmly, 'that has all been settled between me and Rawlinson . . .'[56]

•

And now the news breaks on this late afternoon of 3 July. A messenger has just arrived from Battalion HQ.

There has been a change of plans. An American general has decided the Yanks are *not* to take their place with the Australians after all.

'Those with my platoon had to withdraw,' Edgar Rule would recount, 'and I never saw such disgust and disappointment in my life. Our boys were just as disappointed as they were, and amid many goodbyes they moved to the rear.'[57]

A similar message is going out to other Americans across the line, including those with the 44th and 16th Battalions. But in many cases the bond between the Americans and the Australians, so quickly established, cannot be torn asunder by a mere order – most particularly when so many of the Yanks are so eager to get amongst it. A few of them simply refuse to go, deciding to insist afterwards that they never received such orders. In another case, two attached Americans simply take off their American uniforms and don borrowed AIF kit. Who will know the difference, over the next couple of days? The 44th Battalion Official History will record, proudly, 'To the credit of the Yanks a good number heard the order with deaf ears and took part as arranged. Some of their officers shed their American uniforms and entered the scrap as diggers.'[58]

That afternoon, the photographer Hubert Wilkins is coming out of the line when he comes across some of the American troops who've just got the word.

'They were most depressed,' Bean will record Wilkins' impressions. 'It is said that there are probably a fair number of Americans who will refuse to hear that order – I have no doubt about it.'[59]

Most of the Americans, of course, dutifully obey the order, with the lucky ones, like Sergeant Walter Corning, placed in reserve close enough that they will at least be able to watch the forthcoming attack go in. Those Americans in the four companies who remain feel extra privileged because of it, as soldiers like the US 131st Regiment's Corporal Henry Zyburt from Chicago – attached to the 43rd Battalion – pack their battle kit, and start to move forward with the Australians.

For his part, General Monash is deeply aggrieved to be losing so many of the Americans at this late juncture, when there is simply no time to replace them.

There is no way around it, it weakens the punch they are about to throw. In the 16th Battalion alone, due to attack Vaire Wood, the fighting force goes down from 1050 soldiers to just 500 – yes, more than half their manpower gone, just like that! Overall, the numbers of 4th Brigade drop from roughly 3400 to 2100. The 11th Brigade is hit nearly as hard, with the men they have to throw into the line going from 3000 to 2200.

'Strongly averse, as I was, to embarrassing the infantry plan of General Maclagan,' General Monash would recount, 'to whom I had entrusted the conduct of the actual assault, it was not then too late to rearrange the distribution [of Americans]. The United States troops who had to be withdrawn were loud in their lamentations.'[60]

How on earth can General Monash make good the numbers of soldiers suddenly lost from front-line positions, when the plans are so advanced, when everything has been calculated down to the last bayonet-wielding soldier, and hundreds of them have now gone?

Only a short time afterwards, late that morning, 'Two Guns' Dalziel is sleeping under his wagon after another long night hauling forward what the French call *matériel* – and the Diggers call 'bloody shitloads of stuff' – when an officer from 15th Battalion HQ calls him and fellow drivers together.

A little flustered, like a man who has just received bad news, the officer gets to the point very quickly.

They are looking for volunteers to join the big stunt on *tonight*. As you might know, some of the Americans have had to pull out, and we need to replace them as best we can. As the hard work of much of the transport men is done, getting everyone forward, would some of you like to join in the actual battle?

Two Guns Dalziel's hand shoots up as fast as a flare, maybe as fast as *two* flares. Yes, he is keen!

Within minutes, Dalziel is reporting to the Quartermaster and being issued with ammunition, Mills grenades and all the rest, and 15 minutes later again, he is taking his place with the other volunteers from the transport section of the 15th Battalion, as the No. 2 on a Lewis Gun team, feeding the ammo in, a genuine front-line soldier again, if you please! Now no longer a non-combatant, Dalziel is one of Monash's '7500 bayonets',[61] going into battle. In the case of his 15th Battalion, they start their move forward on this late morning of 3 July.

•

Cliff Geddes and his 13th Battalion are now equally informed. Their job, he knows by now, is to swing past the southern end of Vaire Wood and make for the Blue Line.

The best he can, Geddes sneaks a peek at the ground they will have to cover in the night, noting, 'It is a long way across to the ridge & wood where Fritz's trenches start, [and] he is sure to have isolated machine gun pozzies in the open that will trouble us . . .'[62]

The first part of their advance will be through thigh-high crops, mainly wheat, though the coves out to the right will have to go through some clover fields as well. The wheat will provide good cover for those lying out on the Starting Line, but anyone who goes down will, of course, risk being run over and killed by the tanks.

The good news is that everything appears so 'quiet today . . . there are no signs that he [Jerry] has any idea of what is to happen. I don't feel the slightest bit excited now, but when the starting moment arrives, & our hopes rest on the tanks working without any hitch, it will be more sensational.'[63]

For now, Cliff and many of his mates grab some sleep, in preparation for the big night ahead.

•

Strictly speaking, no French civilian is now allowed within 12 miles of the Western Front on the Allied side of the line. It is a regulation imposed by Field Marshal Haig's GHQ, partly for the safety of the residents, and partly to lessen the chances of spies getting close to Allied lines, reporting the things they see back to their German masters.

There are a few exceptions allowed, however, and a case in point is an 'old peasant and his middle aged daughter',[64] who have been allowed to stay living and working their fields, right by the spot where the artillery has positioned itself. On this late afternoon, as they walk past the guns with as much interest as if they were blocks of stone that had been there for decades, Gunner James Armitage and the brigade interpreter engage them in conversation.

'Are you not afraid of being so close to the line,' the French interpreter asks, 'and are you not afraid of being overrun by the Germans?'

'There is no need to worry about the Germans getting through,' the old man replies simply, 'when we have Australian infantry in front of us. I know in my heart they will never cross this ground again.'

Three months earlier, he recounted, when the Germans had controlled this area, they had a German cavalry officer billeted with them.

Just before the second Battle of Villers-Bretonneux, the officer laughingly told them that two battalions of Australians were marching through Amiens to drive back the whole German Imperial Army.

'We buried him that afternoon,' the old man finishes, 'while the Germans were being driven back through Villers-Bretonneux.'[65]

He really does believe that *les Australiens* will sort things out, and that he and his daughter are safe.

CHAPTER SEVEN

'Y DAY'

*With fondest love to you and all the children and hope to
see you all again soon if we can keep the Germans on the
run the war will not last long but it is tough work and the
people look to the Aussies to do the hardest fighting and they
make sure to put us in the battles knowing we can beat the
best German troops.*[1]

Private Sydney Huntingdon, 4th Machine Gun Company

Morning, 3 July 1918, before Hamel, before the fall

Now if it's true that in the tension of it all, quite a few blokes
appear to have aged overnight – as they have barely slept a wink,
wondering if they are on the edge of the eternal sleep – yet there is
one bloke in the 16th Battalion who can definitely be forgiven for
looking like he's 60. That's because he is 64! Yup, Charlie Hubbard,
from the town of Northam, about 60 miles north-east of Perth, a
former miner, a single man, had joined up in March 1917, to do his
bit. And yes, perhaps the recruitment officer had suspected that the
then 63-year-old was not the 44 years he had claimed in his papers,
and was a good 18 years over the 45-year age limit, but on the
other hand, with the times so grim, why be picky? Charlie wanted
to fight, let him fight! In the time since, he has earned the respect
of men nearly half-a-century younger, and through such battles as
Bullecourt and Passchendaele, has proven himself a capable, if not
necessarily very energetic, soldier.

And so on this day, Charlie gets himself ready with all the rest.

•

In the meantime, there is much to be done. Those officers with luminous compasses are seen to take them out and expose the open face to the sun. All else being equal, they will need those compasses to be glowing all night long tonight, as it would be an unimaginable horror to be out in No Man's Land without any idea which direction to head in.

•

Far to the south, in Versailles, there is rising excitement, and activity, as a particularly important meeting of the Supreme War Council is due to take place on the morrow – with all Dominion Prime Ministers present for the first time. There will be important decisions to be made, and an enormous number of agenda items to tick off.

On this late morning British Prime Minister Lloyd George's Cabinet Secretary, Maurice Hankey, is working away in his room at Villa Romaine, just a few doors down from Lloyd George himself, when, as he would recount, 'just at the very moment I was off for a walk, [Prime Minister Billy] Hughes turned up unexpectedly, and I had to look after him. He demanded tea (which could not be got) and declined coffee, wine, or whisky and grumbled a good deal, but at last I got some tea and he was quite nice.'[2]

Prime Minister Hughes seems a little troubled by something, though precisely what it is remains unclear.

3.30 pm, 3 July 1918, 73 Rue de Varennes, Pershing doubles up to decimate

Reflecting on his conversation with Field Marshal Haig an hour or two ago – General Pershing decides to make doubly sure, *Goddammit*, and phones the Commander of II Corps, General George Read again – *put me through!* – to give 'further and positive instructions that our troops should be withdrawn . . .'[3]

Things begin to move quickly.

For no sooner has General Read put the phone down than he is calling Lawrence, Haig's Chief of Staff, saying that now *all* US troops must be withdrawn, that is, the remaining four Companies as well.

Good Lord.

Soon this is confirmed by British GHQ when Rawlinson receives, as noted in his diary, 'formal orders from Lawrence that no Americans were to take part . . .'⁴

Rawlinson is quickly on to General Monash at 4 pm, who . . .

Who explodes.

Good Lord!

Within the bounds of military respect and propriety, the Australian makes clear his disbelief that such an order could come through so late in the piece. Already, at enormous inconvenience they are in the process of withdrawing six of the ten American companies – and now the final four must be pulled out, too? It defies belief.

Perhaps, Monash suggests icily, General Rawlinson would like to come over to the 4th Division HQ of General Sinclair-Maclagan at Bussy-les-Daours where he is, right now, sending his troops forth to fight for their lives, *and depending on the Americans to be at their shoulders, right by them, as has been locked in now for several days.* There, at 5 pm, all three of them together can talk over the situation.

In the meantime, *good Lord!*

•

Time to move.

Behind the lines, the 2000 men who are to be in the second wave prepare to move forward. Their sergeants ensure that each man has all of his regulation weaponry and ammunition with him, together with extra water, rations for two days, and basic medical kit as well as his gas mask, in case he gets a whiff of that tell-tale odour of 'fried steak & onions cooking and another sort smells like pineapples'.⁵ Also, and this is crucial, the men check their identity discs – or 'dead meat tickets', as the men call them – in case they don't survive. Meantime, they have already put aside those things they don't wish to take with them, and tagged them, to put into storage to be collected when they come back. *If* they come back.

Time now. As one, the men of Cliff Geddes' D Company form up, and, with growing nerves, start marching along the country lanes to where their part of the front-line lies. And so they go, their faces regularly lit by the flare of explosions ahead and, soon enough, explosions on either side, as the Germans – perhaps aware that *da liegt Ärger in der Luft*, there is trouble afoot in the air – are sending out shots in the dark, a blind man groping with sharp fingers for the eyes of the enemy. If the Germans see them, they will 'draw the crabs', attract a real pounding from the German guns, but for the moment, they have the most crucial thing of all on their side . . .

> There is a lot of luck in this game alright, on the road up, Fritz was dropping shells both on the right & left of the road, but none of it luckily where we were going along, also lots of limbers going to & from the line. Just as well he doesn't know the exact spot to put them.[6]

Finally they make it, and take their place in the trenches that lie before Vaire Wood, which they are due to attack in the otherwise silent watch of the night.

•

On the Villers-Bocage aerodrome of the Australian Flying Corps' No. 3 Squadron, the pilots are being briefed by Captain Lawrence Wackett on their missions for tonight. Zero Hour, they are advised, is 3.10 am. The pilots of No. 3 Squadron are assigned to their regular work, counter-attack contact, and counter-battery patrols, while the 20 pilots here from the RAF's No. 9 Squadron will – led by Wackett himself – be dropping ammunition boxes via parachute, just as they have been practising. (If it all works out the way they have planned, each sortie will take off from Villers-Bocage, drop their precious cargo over Hamel, just 13 miles south-east, and be back on the ground, ready to load up again, all within 30 minutes!)

Outside, by the grass airstrip, as the briefing goes on, the ground crew are carefully wheeling their fully laden carts from the fuel store – built hundreds of yards away from the huts, hangars and planes against the possibility of being hit by a bomb – towards the RE8s, which must do the work tonight. Each of the two-wheel carts – carrying a 44-gallon drum filled with fuel, a hose and a small pump – is pushed to the foot of a plane. And now one of the 'erks', the nickname given to the squadron's ground crew of mechanics, riggers *et al*, climbs into the cockpit and, standing, feeds the hose into the fuel tank that lies between the pilot's seat and the engine, while one of the mechanics below starts thrashing the hand-pump.

(Meantime, if one of those ground crew seems to have remarkably good-looking boots, you are right. A little over two months earlier, when the Red Baron had been shot down, one of the mates of Corporal Mechanic Joe Porter of No. 3 Squadron Australian Flying Corps had stood guard over the body in a hangar at Bertangles Aerodrome through the night. Of course Joe's mate had let him in for a gander – 'He looked very insignificant lying there in his plain stained overalls,'[7] Joe would note – but Joe had also noticed Von Richthofen's very fine boots, hand-made, of the finest leather and . . . about Joe's size! The spring in his step a few minutes later was for very good reason. He was walking in the footsteps of a legend, while the Red Baron would be resting for eternity in the boots of Joe Porter, of Morningside, Brisbane.)

On the far side of the 1000-yard square flat grass field that is Villers-Bocage aerodrome, No. 9 Squadron RAF is also at work. Ammunition boxes are being secured to the bomb racks, with particular care being given to the ropes attached to the parachutes – if they don't open, or if the parachute becomes tangled in the plane's wing or undercarriage, disaster would be a strong possibility.

•

On the northern side of the Somme, opposite Hamel, no fewer than 88 Vickers machine-gun crews spread across the hill behind Sailly-le-Sec – as placed by their redoubtable Commanding Officer, Colonel Harry Murray – are getting their sightings on the relevant sections of German trench. For the guns of the Australian Corps artillery, two miles back from the German line, the last of the shells are being hauled forward, ready for explosive action in the wee hours to come. Some of the men are getting a little kip, on the reckoning there is a long night ahead.

•

At Vaux and Hamelet, the last of the tanks are being given their final 'tank-fill',[8] as it is called. Each 'female' Mark V has been topped up with '60 gallons of petrol, 10 gallons of oil, 20 gallons of water, 10lb

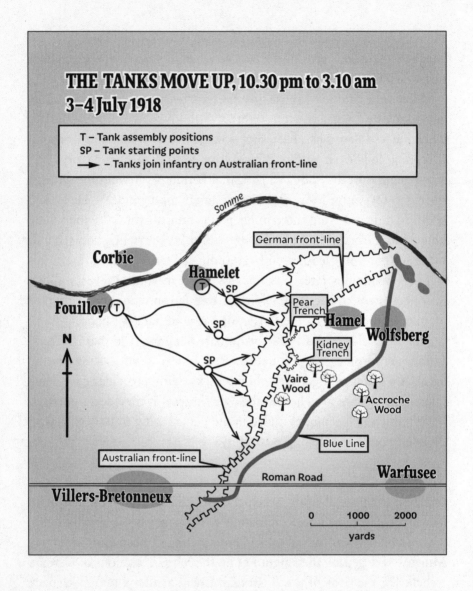

of grease, 10,000 rounds of S.A. ammunition for a female tank.' Each male tank gets the same amount of petrol, oil and water, but also, 'has 200 rounds of 6lb ammunition for the guns and 6,000 rounds [for] the machine guns, in addition to food supplies and drinking water'. Oh, and not to forget, 'a "medicinal" bottle of whisky locked in the officers' foot-locker inside the tank'.[9]

A glorious chateau, it ain't.

While it's all right for the likes of Generals Haig, Rawlinson and Monash to reside in their quasi-palatial residences, General Sinclair-Maclagan's 4th Division HQ is rather more on the rustic – read, rough-and-ready – side of things.

Not only is it closer to the coal-face of battle, but it could almost be a camp for coal-miners: with higgledy-piggledy huts scattered in a quarry just outside the village of Bussy-les-Daours, some five miles back from Hamel.

In one of those huts now a singularly important meeting is about to take place: Rawlinson arrives in a slightly undignified rush just after 5 pm. Half-a-dozen grim-faced officers stride hither and thither, while one or two orderlies glide about with cups of tea and the like. The air is thick with the smoke from endless nervous cigarettes. And yet, truly? Despite the extreme tension of the moment, the fact that this is the nerve centre for an operation which will shortly see 8000 soldiers, 60 tanks, 200 planes and 600 guns attack German lines in perhaps the most intricately planned battle in history, no-one – bar one – is flustered. This is not ad hoc, this is *planned* down to the last tiny detail. And right now, at 1700 hours, everything is going according to plan, so the tension is good tension – the tension needed to stay tightly focused, to ensure that there is no deviation from the plan.

And yet Rawlinson has good reason to be so flustered, as it turns out. After trying to contact Field Marshal Haig to have him resolve the impasse, he has been told that the Commander of the British Expeditionary Forces is in his convoy of Rolls-Royces *en route* to his HQ at the Chateau de Beaurepaire just outside Montreuil, and will be unavailable until 6.30 pm at the earliest. Rawlinson's only real hope, thus, to avoid what will likely be a major confrontation, is to convince General Monash to pull the remaining Americans out . . .

Good luck with that.

For when he arrives just a few minutes later, Monash makes no bones about how appalled and outraged he is by even the idea of pulling the Americans out. For you *must* understand, General Rawlinson. We have obliged General Pershing by withdrawing six American companies, but it's too late to take out the rest.

The clock is ticking! Men are on the move! Tanks are moving into position, and planes fuelled. Our artillery is, right now, 'in the act of dissolving its defensive organization with a view to moving forward into its battle emplacements as soon as dusk should fall'.[10]

The whole attack is going to be fully launched in just ten hours.

Monash's language is strong. He is still respectful, 'for even a Corps Commander must use circumspection when presuming to argue with an Army Commander',[11] but only just.

'I resolved,' Monash would recount, 'to . . . press my views as strongly as I dared.'[12]

And he feels it strongly. To even *try* to remove 1000 soldiers from the frame, when all the carefully calibrated plans are predicated on those soldiers being in place, is now problematic, and dangerous for all concerned. All the troops are in their forward positions, ready to go, with all of their Americans equally forward and assigned their own tasks! (Among them Captain John Moran with a French flag on a staff . . . but we'll get to that.) At this late stage, you want to try and unscramble the egg and remove the Americans?

By withdrawing the Americans now, you place at risk the lives of those attacking.

'Even had I been ready to risk the success of the battle by going ahead without them,' General Monash would recount, 'I could not afford to take the further risk of the occurrence of something in the nature of an "international incident" between the troops concerned, whose respective points of view about the resulting situation could be readily surmised.'[13]

And yes, I appreciate, General Rawlinson, that this is an order from Field Marshal Haig himself, and he is currently unavailable until at least 6.30 pm. But in giving that order he cannot have realised that executing it, and withdrawing all the Americans, would see abandonment of the whole battle. You are here, the Army Commander *in situ*, you now understand the whole situation, that the hour is too advanced to pull out the Americans in safety, and therefore you have the discretion to nominally disobey the order.

Truly? It *is* still possible to pull them out, and for the battle to go ahead as planned. The Americans had been a bonus to the battle plan, never a foundation stone. And, as it is only just after 5 pm, no-one has actually yet moved into No Man's Land. To pull them out now would entail Battalion commanders changing their plans to allow for the loss of the Americans. But – Sinclair-Maclagan assures Monash – it could be done, if the order is given before 7 pm. After that it really would be too late.

And yet Monash's instinct, as ever, is to bring maximum force to bear on the enemy's weakest point, and so break them – and the Americans are a part of that maximum force. More importantly, pulling them out now would fly in the face of one of Monash's cardinal principles: 'order, counter-order, disorder'. From their last meeting on 30 June, Monash had forbidden any changes to the plan, to honour this very principle, and now his superiors want to pull out the Americans with just hours to go? *Not on your Nelly, at least not without a fight.*

In fact, bluffing, General Monash tells General Rawlinson outright:

'The whole of the Infantry destined for the assault at dawn next morning, including those very Americans, [is] already well on its way to its battle stations.'[14]

Thus . . .

'It is already too late to carry out that order. If the Americans do not take part, the attack must be cancelled. I therefore propose to go on, with them participating, unless you expressly order me not to do so. Unless such an order arrives by 6.30 pm, it will find the infantry and artillery already on the move to their battle stations and starting tapes.'[15]

And let the aggrieved General Monash be absolutely clear here. If the Americans are pulled out at this last minute, then, 'No Australian [will] ever fight beside an American again.'[16]

(And, in fact, it is not *all* bluff. 'I well knew,' Monash would later frankly recount, 'that even if orders could still with certainty reach the battalions concerned, the withdrawal of those Americans would result in untold confusion and in dangerous gaps in our lines of battle . . .'[17])

With the stakes now this high, just as Monash has intended, it is clear that General Rawlinson must go back to Field Marshal Haig one last time, to let him know that if the orders to pull all the Americans go through, then the Australians will pull out, too, and the whole battle aborted!

Shaken by the Australian's fury – caught between Monash's unalterable logic and the simple fact that the Commanding Officer of the Americans, possibly soon to be backed by the Commanding Officer of the British forces, wants the Americans withdrawn, and has given orders to that effect – the British officer is momentarily blindsided.

'But you don't realise what it means,' Rawlinson expostulates. 'Do you want me to run the risk of being sent back to England – do you mean it is worth that?'

'Yes, I do,' Monash replies flatly, a lot more strongly than he would have been if Sinclair-Maclagan were with them, as in company it would be even more humiliating for Rawlinson than it is now. 'It is more important to keep the confidence of Australians and Americans in each other than to preserve even an army commander [such as you].'[18]

Goodness!

'But orders are orders,' Rawlinson argues.

'Haig would not have given such an order,' Monash replies, 'if he had known that it meant the abandonment of the battle.'[19]

Does he have the English general cornered? Monash thinks so, but follows up for good measure, pointing out that a 'commander on the spot [may] act in the light of the situation as known to him, even to the extent of disobeying an order'.[20]

A more authoritarian leader than Rawlinson might well have simply said, 'General Monash, I am *ordering* you to remove the Americans from your battle plan. What you decide to do with the battle is for you, and with any Americans thereafter, a matter for your government.'

But such high-handedness is quite beyond Rawlinson, most particularly when General Monash makes sense, *and* it is important that the Australians go through with the attack. These men from the far south have not failed in the last eight months, since their final attack at Passchendaele, and even then it had not been their fault. These are crack troops, under a strong commander. It would be a terrible pity, and something of a blemish on Rawlinson's own reputation, if the attack was aborted at this late stage. (And there is also the fact that Rawlinson knows that both Haig *and* the King regard General Monash very highly. He is, very likely, the best connected of all the Corps' Commanders, and pushing him around may well provide Rawlinson with more than a spot of bother, later.)

Beyond all that, however, this is essentially a dispute between nations, and therefore the proper place to settle it is at the top. Let Field Marshal Haig decide!

So for now – while keenly aware, as he will later recount, that, 'If things had gone wrong I suppose I should have been sent home in disgrace'[21] – Rawlinson simply tells Monash that he will again try to get through to Field Marshal Haig, but for the moment the battle plan may proceed.

For their part, the only concession offered by Generals Monash and Sinclair-Maclagan is that they agree to give General Rawlinson just a little more time, until 7 pm, to try to reach Field Marshal Haig to explain the position and receive guidance from him. But if they haven't heard by that time, they will proceed exactly as planned.

'That,' General Sinclair-Maclagan says, 'is the latest hour at which an order could issue if it was to reach [all] of my outposts.'[22]

Exit General Rawlinson, with an urgent phone call to make.

General Monash is very pleased, in a grimly satisfied kind of way. Having done his own calculations, he has placed a time limit on altering the orders just outside when Haig will be able to do it, even if he wants to.

•

It's always like this before a big battle, Lieutenant Edgar Rule knows. As the sun starts to sink, you inevitably wonder if it is the last you will ever see. And if not you, which of your mates – most of whom are like brothers, now – will bite the big one in the battle tonight. Every man is thinking the same. It makes for a tight, tense atmosphere, with many men writing letters home, some quietly praying, a few playing cards to take their minds off it, or doing such things as checking their weaponry and ammunition to make sure all is in order.

For his part, Lieutenant Rule checks in with D Company HQ, in Pioneer Trench, Hill 104, to go over the final detail of their orders one last time. He finds most of his fellow officers there, talking of the battle tonight, and notes all of them already in their battle clothes – it is now standard to dress down like a private, to deny snipers any chance of identifying them as officers, making them superb targets – with the exception of one man, Lieutenant Ramsay Wood, a rather flamboyant journalist before the war.

Instead of dressing down, Ramsay looks like a ship of the realm, under full sail, with all the trimmings – resplendent in his best dress uniform, with open-necked tunic, collar and tie complete with a magnificent non-regulation pair of riding breeches.

'Aren't you going to change your togs, Ramsay?' Rule asks.

'Not on your life, my boy. I would not go about like you fellows for all the rice in China.'

'Well,' says another officer, 'we are not in for a beauty competition. Anyone would be excused if they mistook you for Gladys Cooper.'

'Listen to me, Ramsay,' says the cheery CO, Colonel Stanley Perry, 'those lavender pants would draw the "crabs" on you anywhere.'

But Ramsay will *not* be dissuaded. He is an officer, proud to be so, and is not going to hide that fact for some ruddy Germans.

'Very well, gentlemen,' he says simply, 'I'm going in just as you see me, and, if I'm going to get it, well . . .'

And with that, he shrugs his shoulders.[23]

•

For his part, General Monash must now make time for a quick briefing of the war correspondents, giving them broad information of what is about to happen so that what they are about to see, albeit from a distance, may make sense. If the battle goes as well as he hopes it will, their informed reports may help lift recruitment rates in Australia.

For a good 30 minutes, in the ballroom at Bertangles Chateau, General Monash ticks off the essential points, detailing just how the tanks, infantry, planes, artillery and signal systems will integrate to overcome the German resistance . . . and is nothing if not impressive.

'You can interview any of the great British Generals, including Field Marshal Haig,' a British correspondent once noted, 'and not feel any great trepidation; but immediately you come before General Monash you know you are in the presence of a great man.'[24]

In truth, despite their despair at his selection as Commander of the Australian Corps, even the likes of Fred Cutlack and Keith Murdoch (who has returned for the battle, just a few hours before Charles Bean), cannot help but be impressed. Yes, they had insisted that Monash would not be up to the task of organising a major battle, but, as they will tell Bean, who dutifully records it in his diary, at least his depth of preparation is demonstrably nothing less than extraordinary:

> There is no question that the old man gave us, as always, a very able discourse indeed. Very few men could have done it. He stood up at his desk there so as to get at the map, and gave it to us without a note – names of battalions and everything . . . The thing has been planned with a thoroughness like that which went before Messines – every particle of the plan, down to the action of companies, being known to the commander of the corps.[25]

His command is such that he effortlessly enunciates what is expected of even individual platoons, their task intimately known to the highest officer commanding the attacking force.

And there is no doubt that he is being honest with the correspondents, even telling them something of the misunderstanding with the American brass-hats over the Yank soldiers, and the fact that it has been agreed that if Field Marshal Haig does not get back to them before 7 pm, everything will proceed as planned.

Which sounds, desperate. However . . .

'Field Marshal Haig,' Monash says with a grim smile, 'is in a motor car between Paris and GHQ and is unlikely to be back before 7 pm . . .'[26]

•

The drive from Paris has been quicker than expected for Field Marshal Haig.

Just before 7 pm, two majestic Rolls-Royces sweep into the driveway of General Headquarters at Montreuil, both fluttering Union Jacks from the bonnet. Which one contains Haig? Not even the duty guard knows until both doors open and the great man emerges from one. On this evening, as he arrives, as ever, there is a slew of important messages waiting for him, one of which is brought to his attention as being particularly urgent.

General, there has been some kind of misunderstanding over the issue of the American soldiers participating in tonight's battle with the Australians. General Rawlinson informs us that Monash is insisting that if the Americans are withdrawn the battle must be postponed.

'Some six companies have already been withdrawn,' he is told, 'but about four could not be withdrawn. Is the operation to be stopped in order to do so?'[27]

Field Marshal Haig pauses only a moment. One does not rise as far up the military chain of command as he has without being able to make quick decisions, nor for having an instinctive feel for what the correct decision is.

'No. The first essential is to improve our position east of Amiens as soon as possible. The attack must therefore be launched as prepared even if a few American detachments cannot be got out before Zero hour.'[28]

General Pershing may well be upset, particularly if the affair goes badly. But, firstly, having closely examined Monash's plan, Haig is confident that it will go well. And secondly, it is high time that the Americans became involved in this war and now is as good a time as any. To cancel a whole attack at this late stage, when it was already effectively underway, just because of the sensitivities of the Americans, is unthinkable.

This attack is *underway*.

For his part, General Rawlinson – now back at his Flixecourt HQ – receives a message from Haig just after 7 pm that 'the operation is to continue and if you cannot withdraw the Yankees they must take part'.[29]

Very well then.

As Rawlinson writes in his diary on the night of 3 July:

> I have therefore changed nothing and trust to the attack being a success. If Pershing goes on like this we will never win the war.[30]

•

At their digs in a house at Querrieu, Charles Bean is dining this evening with Keith Murdoch and wire correspondent Gordon Gilmour, finishing in time so that in the long twilight to 9 pm they will be able to make their way forward to find a secure spot that will enable them to watch the battle unfold.

For his part, back at Bertangles Chateau, General Monash does that rarest of all things for him: he goes to bed early. Everything that can be done, has been done. Later, when the battle begins, it will be important that he be at his most alert, so the best use of his time now will be to actually get some rest.

•

Dark at last.

Across the entire front to be attacked, the preliminaries to the battle proper can now be put into place, along precisely the lines prescribed – and, as a matter of fact, those very lines must now be laid out. Crawling out of their trenches into No Man's Land, each Battalion sends some of its best men forward under the supervision of the Battalion intelligence officer. In their haversacks they have rolls of lightly luminescent white tape which they must lay out as the Starting Line for the assault troops, so that, come the time, they can send all their men out into No Man's Land, to a common Starting Line, ready to assault the German lines once the barrage starts.

Among those crawling forward is Corporal Jack Axford, a bloke as hard and tough as the Flinders Ranges in which he was born. As a labourer in Kalgoorlie – where he'd been the champion boxer of the goldfields, and keen member of the unlikely named 'Kalgoorlie Swimming Club' – Jack had joined up shortly after the landing at Gallipoli, and has since fought in all of Mouquet Farm, Passchendaele and Hébuterne, where he was awarded the Military Medal for a particularly brave act.

Yes, despite his boyish face and rather stick-out ears, he's a tough one, is Jack, and calm under pressure, which is why he has been given this task. Just one mistake by one of these blokes, and it is possible that the whole fate of the battle might be put at risk. For just let the Germans know that even one bloke is out there with starting tape, and they would have to figure that 'shits is trumps' at Hamel, and start plastering No Man's Land accordingly.

But, on this night, all goes well. When Jack gets to the designated position, about 300 yards out and 200 yards from the German lines, he stakes one end in, and then crawls off to his right for 400 yards or so, where he is able to join it up to the tape laid out by the adjoining Battalion. In short order, with just one zig and one zag, the tape stretches 6000 yards, from the Somme to the Roman Road.

(If all goes well, the creeping barrage will begin 200 yards forward from the outline of that tape, broadly parallel to it, in a band that itself will go for a width of 600 yards.)

And even now, however, he is not done, as Jack has also been ordered to stay out there, on special patrol, 'to ensure that no inquisitive German should enquire too closely into what was happening in our lines; or that, at any rate, such a one should not return with his news'.[31]

•

Having reached their hill on the north side of the Somme, Charles Bean and his companions, Keith Murdoch and Gordon Gilmour, find a spot to give themselves an uninterrupted view for what should be a very interesting night – the whole tight battlefield is before them like an open book, history's page, at every stage, just waiting to be written.

Peering across the soft, moonlit landscape, they can just faintly make out the lagoons, the dark trees, the sleepy Somme River winding its way through the valley before them, and on the other side, the shattered village of Hamel, with the menacing bulk of Wolfsberg behind it, and over to the right, 'the dark outline of the plateau by Villers Bretonneux against the misty grey sky'.[32]

Mostly it is astonishingly quiet and normal-looking, when for a sure and certain fact the journalists *know* that on the Australian side of the line at least 8000 men, 60 tanks and over 600 guns are even now moving into position, if they are not already there, primed to go. And yet there are at least *some* signs that this really is the Western Front, after all.

'Every now and then a flare shot like a low rocket out of the woods or fields on the opposite hillside, sailed by brilliantly to earth, and lay there dying faintly on the ground. Occasionally the swift whine and bang of a German whizz-bang, pecking into the other side of the valley – you could see the little shell flash before you began to hear the noise.'[33]

Just as happens every night at around this time, an Allied plane flies up the valley, just above the range of the German Ack-Ack guns, and drops a flare on their noggins, looking for a juicy target to bomb or shoot at.

Bean and his comrades watch, as the flare falls 'through the clouds, and descended slowly through them like some strange misty moon'.[34]

And now, having clearly spotted something, the plane lazily turns, and opens first with its machine gun, which looks to Bean and his companions as 'a swift series of white sparks, most deadly, straight and swift'.[35]

The four German searchlights that wildly started to scan across the clouds look 'like the eyes of a frightened snail'.[36]

Everything is as it should be. This is *nearly* standard for this time of the evening, at this time of year, at this stage of the war.

'It was one of the quietest nights one had ever seen on the front. Now and then a machine-gun chattered a few halting sentences.'[37]

But, as Bean knows, the German snail is about to have a whole lot more to be more frightened about, in very short order.

•

Across a front eight miles wide, extending from the Roman Road heading eastward from Villers-Bretonneux, south-west of Le Hamel, to Ville on the Ancre River, the Australian artillery crews are getting ready. Following their strict routine, the gunners working the 639 guns – a quarter of the guns and crews borrowed from the British Army – carefully place shells a safe distance to the rear of their pieces.

Beyond the creeping barrage, the heavy guns – one third of the whole – now have the precise co-ordinates on the map for specific targets that have been worked out over the last fortnight, as they attempt to destroy the most sensitive installations of the German defences, their artillery batteries and ammunition dumps being the most important, as by crippling them, the advancing soldiers will be protected. German Battalion HQs are also targeted, to prevent a co-ordinated response from Fritz.

Just some 1000 yards back from the Australian front-lines, Lieutenant Patrick Campbell and his comrades of the 5th Artillery Brigade are positioned close to the 88 Vickers machine guns positioned on high ground above Sailly-le-Sec on the north side of the river, ready to do their bit.

•

In the village of Hamel on this night, all is relatively quiet. Though German sentries man their posts, gazing out into the darkness of No Man's Land, most of the soldiers are asleep, either in the rough dugouts that are dotted along the trenches, or in the village itself, in the battered houses or their cellars. The luckier ones are sleeping the sleep of the dead, the dead exhausted, and the dead drunk – having been able to help themselves to some of the remaining contents of those cellars. It is, at this stage, as the Official History of the 202nd Reserve Infantry Regiment, records 'a quiet night',[38] no more, no less.

To their south, their *Kamerads* of Pear Trench, the brave if equally tired soldiers of the 55th Infantry Regiment, have been finding it a little less calm, 'as the hitherto quiet opponent began to stir. Then in the evening hours of 3 July increasing *Artillerie- und Fliegertätigkeit*, artillery and aviation activity . . .'[39]

Still, there is no cause for undue unease. They are seasoned soldiers, and they are manning the best armed, most built-up trenches in the area, with ten machine guns spread out across their 200 yards of front. Their defences are bolstered further still by half-a-dozen *Minenwerfer*, trench mortars, that have been brought forward, which can lob mortar bombs onto the enemy from as far away as 350 yards.

Those Companies of the 55th Regiment holding Kidney Trench just to the south again, are in much the same position. There is a little disquiet at what seems to be increased *englische* activity, but they are dug in, well-armed, and ready for Tommy – a term they use for all those fighting for the British Empire – if he comes.

In the German lines north of the Somme, opposite Brigadier Pompey Elliott's 15th Brigade, things are very quiet, as the 1st Battalion of the 227th Infantry Regiment is just completing their relief by the 2nd Battalion, after the 1st has spent 12 days in the line. Tramping back through the darkness, the exhausted soldiers of the 1st, thus, are just trying to settle down to sleep in their relatively calm billets at Cerisy for what little is left of the night. A couple of hours rest, in peace, before dawn, is that really too much to ask? *Bitte lasst uns schlafen,* please let us sleep!

•

And now it is time.

At 10 pm, precisely as planned, four FE2bs from No. 101 Squadron, Royal Air Force, roar in low over the German lines around Hamel, and for the sake of form, at least, first drop parachute flares to illuminate the German enemy trenches, and then drop the first batch of what will be no fewer than 350 25-pound bombs on to their German noggins in 'selected enemy billeting areas'.[40]

Of course, in their standard response, the Squareheads send their searchlights to the heavens trying to seek their enemy out, followed by Ack-Ack fire, but it is rather in the manner that a hand brushes away flies on a summer's day – it is a reaction only, and there is no real expectation of a kill. As it happens, nor are the pilots of the planes themselves particularly interested in doing real damage.

For what the planes seek to deliver to the German soldiers is not explosives, but *noise*. Yes, they want to so engulf Jerry with the noise of the twin roaring Beardmore six-cylinder engines that all other noises from near (soldiers moving forward) and far (tanks moving forward) will be blocked out . . .

And, of course, by the time the planes are at full throttle, and their noise at full bottle, just over the German lines, they are in time for what is occurring back from those lines.

10.30 pm, Fouilloy and Hamelet, give thanks for the tanks

All up, they amount to nearly 200 big bruisers of soldiers, holding between them 60 oddly shaped pieces of metal, as across an expanse of one mile, stretching from Fouilloy to Hamelet, they squat with ominous purpose. Squatting at the back of each tank, three or four of them grab the crank at the rear of the six-cylinder inline Ricardo engine, and again and again, 'and once more!' shouts the corporal . . .

heave for their lives until suddenly there is a gurgle, a cough and now a throaty roar as the engines burst into life!

Ah. But one more thing, before they start off up the hill, each tank takes on board a guest . . .

For yet one more strand of General Monash's plan to integrate the tanks and the infantry – to make them one cohesive unit instead of two separate, distrusting parts – has been to insist that each tank must carry an Australian soldier familiar with the ground to be covered, who can act partly as guide, and partly as a 'liaison . . . between [the tanks and] the battalions who were to make the attack'.[41]

Some of the soldiers get in the tanks more willingly than others.

The red-headed Digger, for example, who now climbs into the tank of Captain Peter Batten, MC, of the 5th Tank Brigade, introduces himself as, yes, 'Bluey', but actually looks green around the gills from the beginning, clearly dubious about the wisdom of getting into one of these flamin' tin cans. He seems unhappier still, once inside, to find he is with eight men, packed around the now roaring, hot engine, as it lurches up the hill, in this first part of the journey pushing its way through shoulder-high corn. (Yes, the Ricardo engine is far more powerful than the Daimler-Foster one carried by the Mark IV tank, but so too is it much noisier, hotter and prone to pumping out much more deadly fumes.)

More comfortable, in another 5th Tank Brigade beast, is the 13th Battalion's Private Thomas Parrish, a quietly spoken 20-year-old bloke from Boolaroo, a peaceful burgh up Lake Macquarie way, who had reported in to Captain William Edwards, and, after discussion, had decided his own best place would be high in the new spotting tower – another innovative feature of the Mark V – as 'I have been in No Man's Land every night for the last month as a scout.'[42] Fair enough then, and Captain Edwards agrees.

Another crew member, Private Percy Jarvis, would recount:

> We'd been resting up under the trees. We moved out separately in the evening to our starting point . . . At the time the tanks were getting into position the planes were over . . . this allowed the line-up to be done quite secretly.[43]

Indeed, with their engines now producing just enough power to get them moving, the Mark V tanks start to move forward, passing the Battle HQ of the 4th Brigade as they do so, secreted in a quarry just outside Hamelet, and continue to their designated 'point of assembly' areas, just half a mile behind the front-lines.

Through the two small shutter slots at the front of Captain Peter Batten's tank, both he and the driver keep a close eye on their designated officer, who has come back to retrieve them, and specifically the glow of the cigarette he carries for a very unusual purpose. (Bluey, their Australian liaison, says nuttin' and does nothing, bar watching them all with a gimlet eye that would have done justice to a dead fish. He looks distinctly uncomfortable.)

The glow of the cigarette keeps swinging in the darkness. This close to him, all Captain Batten and the driver need to do is keep track of that rhythmically swinging firefly and they know they will be steered right. For his part, the officer with the cigarette just has to follow the 'white tape, about two inches wide with a black line along the centre, which had been laid along the whole distance',[44] by the scouts earlier in the evening. All the tank men must do is to move in a manner that the tanks do not rip up the tape as it will likely be useful later in the night, too, when reserves come forward and, perhaps, if badly damaged tanks must make their way back and . . .

And wait! Suddenly, one of the flares dropped by 101 Squadron over German lines gets caught by a stray gust of wind that brings it over the precise area where the tanks are moving, illuminating the brooding beasts for an agonising two minutes, as they make their way up the slope.

Time hangs suspended . . . as all wonder . . . . . . whether German shells are about to come crashing down upon them, but . . . but, presently the flare impotently lands, and all falls dark once more without incident. Up ahead, at the front-line trenches, parties of Allied soldiers begin to cut paths through their own barbed wire defences so that when the time comes, shortly, to leave those trenches and head out into No Man's Land, there will be an easy way through.

•

Of course Private Isaac Betteridge and the rest of the 23rd Battalion's D Company know there is a big stunt on. But only now, nearing midnight, do they learn the precise details.

They gather around their Captain, in the darkness, out on the far right of the Australian lines, near the Roman Road, and he gives them the good oil.

At 2.30 am precisely, you will leave these trenches and go out very quietly to the start line tape, where you will wait for the stunt to begin. A scattered barrage will start just after 3 am. At 3.10 am the heavy barrage will go for four minutes, and you must rise at 3.12 am, and walk slowly forward so that you will be 75 yards off the German lines at the moment the barrage lifts, getting ready to go hard at their hopefully shattered trenches.

With similar briefings across the line, the Americans are impressed. So this is how it is done?

'When they put on a stunt,' one of them will later note, 'it was timed to the second . . .'[45]

1 am, 'Z Day', 4 July, St Quentin, bombs away

Like a flock of hungry nighthawks, a dozen aircraft circle the skies at 6000 feet, above the city of St Quentin, 30 miles east of Hamel, looking for the railway station. They are from No. 207 Squadron RAF, Handley Page 0/400 heavy bombers known as the 'bloody paralysers' – with the 720 horsepower of each plane's two Rolls-Royce Eagle engines easily lifting its four-man crew, almost a ton of bombs and five machine guns . . . seven tons in all. Their task is to destroy the rail-yards through which German reinforcements would come towards Hamel once the battle begins.[46] West of St Quentin and not so far behind the German line at Hamel, where it has previously been reckoned the Germans' immediate reserves are most likely to be quartered, the RAF's 5th Wing's two-seater Airco DH4s also patrol, like sharks beyond the breakers, just on the other side of the German lines, looking for targets of opportunity such as ammunition dumps and bivouac areas.

Midnight to 1.45 am, to the west of Hamel, movement at the station

Floating phantoms of the night. Flitting figures in the darkness. Men born and raised beneath the Southern Cross now find their way forward 'neath foreign constellations, with France's fabled *étoile polaire*, North Star, out to their left.

Precisely as scheduled, the Australian soldiers, with a sprinkling of Americans, begin to make their way forward in the moonlight. Cliff Geddes and the men of the 13th Battalion have left the Pioneer Trench atop Hill 104 and are, even now, quietly moving forward to get to their start line tape a mile north of the Roman Road. The orders are clear: no talking, no smoking, no clanking of metal on metal. In fact, a sergeant has already checked the less experienced soldiers to ensure that all of their equipment is tightly secured, that no spade is positioned so it might hit your rifle or rim of your helmet, and that all rifles are unloaded to prevent any chance of an accidental discharge.

Also coming from Hill 104, Edgar Rule's 14th Battalion are doing exactly the same thing, albeit just starting a little later. As both Battalions are moving in single file, 1400 soldiers in total, the first of the 13th Battalion are arriving in the front-line, just as the last of the soldiers of the 14th are leaving Hill 104.

Everything has been worked out to the minute, so that all the pieces of General Monash's battle plan slot smoothly into place, still without alerting the Germans of what is going on, and all will be in readiness for Zero Hour.

•

Behold, the softly roaring monster in the mist. This particular one is the tank of Captain William Edwards, slowly pushing forward to get to its Starting Line, 1000 yards back from the soldiers of the 13th Battalion, lying on their own Starting Line before Vaire Wood. But it ain't easy. With the moon mostly behind the clouds, the darkness is oppressive, and on unfamiliar ground the only way to proceed is slowly and carefully. If it is like this *before* the barrage stirs up the dust and sends billowing smoke into the air, what will it be like afterwards? For now, all they can do is nudge the tank along. Finally finding their designated spot in a small orchard, their tank has no sooner lurched to a stop than one of the tank crew members bursts through the hatch, anxious to answer a call of nature.

Squatting with his bottom facing the German lines, just on principle, it just so happens that at the very moment he squats a stray German shell is heading his way.

Getting closer now . . . closer still . . . closer *still* . . . there is a *screeeechinggggggg* . . . and the shell hits . . . . the ground 'slap between the chap's legs as he squatted in a crouched position',[47] and . . . doesn't explode. 'Except for a large hole neatly drilled in the ground he was no worse.'[48]

Under the circumstances, the chap's excretions are completed with remarkable rapidity and volume after the shell lands, and, shaken, he gets back into the tank.

All is moving into place.

In short order, not only are all the tanks in position, but no fewer than 7000 Australian soldiers and 1000 American soldiers are in position, ready to move when the word comes.

Those in the front-line trenches who can sleep, do so. Those who can't, cradle their rifles while constantly fingering their ammunition pouches laden with 200 rounds, and their two grenades, each capable of killing everyone in a German machine-gun nest. Every now and then they look at their luminescent watches, as each tick on the countdown brings them closer to the carefully calibrated climax to come.

From a little after midnight onwards the word is hissed along the line, as the first of the Battalions due to take their place in the first wave stir themselves.

As opposed to so many other attacks they have undertaken in this war, it is now less time to 'hop the bags', to use the Diggers' expression, as to silently steal across them as quickly as they can – indeed many of the men have their boots wrapped in empty sandbags to silence their footfall.

Once out of the safety of their trenches, and in single file – following a guide who knows the lie of the land even in this infernal gloom – the men make their way forward. If the Germans are aware they are coming, and have set an ambush, it means they are about to be met with a deadly fusillade of bullets. But, slowly, surely . . . softly, softly . . . all remains quiet. With a little more confidence thus, they continue forward into No Man's Land until, about 100 yards forward of the front trench, and still some 100 to 300 yards back from the German lines – depending on which part they are attacking – in the gloom, they can just make out the lightly luminescent tape previously laid out, at which point they fan out along it, guided to their allotted spot, and fall to their bellies. (In some ways it is like organising a thousands strong audience to make their way into the very wide front row of a theatre, where everyone must be shown to their seats, and the whole process will take well over two hours.)

For many, most particularly the Americans, who have never done this kind of thing before, it is a dreamy, unreal kind of experience to leave the warm and comforting embrace of Mother Earth – the warm smell of the trench walls, the physical closeness to each other – and to climb the ladders up into the open air, vulnerable to any stray bullet that comes, and walk to their allocated spot along the tape, with a casualness that belies the fact they are carrying M1903 Springfield rifles, as well as French-made Chauchat light machine guns and hand grenades.

But it has to be done.

The Americans are now with them all the way, their hearts in their mouths that they have at last 'hopped the top',[49] as they coin it, and are now on their way to their first serious battle.

Meantime, look at what the Germans have put on, just for them! Occasionally, flares rise lazily from the German lines, just as they do every night so there is no cause for undue alarm, soaring skywards and throwing out an ethereal flickering light, against the possibility of precisely what is happening now. Just one eagle-eyed sentry, they all know, and it will be over as far as surprise goes. And so, as Lieutenant Keith Lode of the 43rd Battalion would recount of the experience of him and his men as they move slowly towards Hamel, 'all would stand still – ghostly forms on a ghostly job – with the expectancy of the rattle of a machine gun or the "ping" of a bullet as we were observed by Fritz'.[50]

Not all of them, however, are so petrified.

'I was just tickled to death to see them fireworks,'[51] one of the American soldiers would later note. It is, after all, the 4th of July, Independence Day. Could there ever be a better day, to have the honour, to be the first of your nation to take revenge on the Germans?

Either way, the job is done, and they all move into position, 'neath *the rockets' red glare, the bombs bursting in air*, without incident.

'As we were lined up with our bayonets fixed we all felt nervous,' Captain Fred Rinkliff, an American of the 131st Regiment with the 43rd Australian Battalion would recall, 'but when we reached our position [at the tape], we took our places, lay down and . . . we were soon asleep.'[52]

Awake or asleep they all simply must wait there – hopefully unseen, or they will be slaughtered – until '*beaucoup* barraging' begins.

At least most of them have been given a good stew before heading out, warming their tummies and their souls alike. (Strange, how comforting such a simple thing as a hot meal can be at such an otherwise tense time.)

Once complete, the 6000 soldiers in the first wave are stretched out along a front some 6500 yards wide, with another, much smaller wave of 2000 men behind, readying to move forward.

For the veterans, this is different from the usual way of things. At Pozières, they had been so thickly packed together that there had been five times as many of them per yard of front, meaning that any fusillade in their general direction would exact a terrible cost. Here, however, their lines are much thinner, and a bullet sent their way has at least as much chance of passing between the men, as *through* the men. At Fromelles, a helmet thrown above the trenches just before they went over the top was blown back by the fusillade of bullets the Germans were keeping concentrated on their positions, in expectation of the attack to come.

But here, all remains quiet.

•

It is 2 am, and not only has most of the work been done, but the time is nigh, requiring just a few last-minute things to be attended to.

For Gunner James Armitage and his comrades of the 30th Battery, 8th Artillery Brigade, 3rd Australian Division – positioned near the village of Hamelet – the barrels of their guns have been laboriously cleaned, by plunging huge wooden poles with wet sponges attached down them. The shells that they are to fire have been moved forward from their buried dump, some 200 yards back. (In all, across the whole line of artillery, no fewer than 200,000 shells have been brought forward, ready to fire in this battle.)

And now the gunners must set the progressive fuses on the first of the shells they are about to fire, which will determine – according to how long the fuse is set – exactly how long after the shell is fired that it will explode. Of course, as the creeping barrage creeps forward the fuse must be set a little longer. At least with these modern shells it can all be done quite easily by moving a marker at the head of the shell to the desired position.

Quietly, carefully, they continue with their final preparations.

•

For the soldiers on the tape, it is extraordinary.

> Not a sound broke the stillness, and an awe seemed to be over the whole landscape . . .[53]

(Well, there are a few mutterings of 'Here you go, Dig', as each soldier is passed a tot of rum to take a small swig to warm their souls and soothe their nerves as Zero Hour approaches.)

In the second wave, some 400 yards back from the first, Lieutenant Edgar Rule of the 14th is quietly leading his platoon out forward to the support line that lies some 200 yards back from the front-line.

'The old Hun was very quiet as we moved up,' Rule would recall, 'only an odd shell came over and a few machine gun bullets kept flying around.'[54]

In the gloom, sure enough, they presently come to the support line where they are to await the barrage proper to begin before charging the Germans.

So far, so good, but still Rule, like all of his comrades, is beset by questions.

Does the Hun know we are going to attack?
Does he know the time?
Is he waiting?
What sort of barrage will be put down on us in retaliation?
If it's big, can we get beyond it before it falls?
Are my last minutes on earth approaching?

Out on the far right, near the Roman Road, Private Betteridge is asking himself all these questions and more, noting too, 'Everything most weirdly quiet.'[55]

When all is settled and there is no further movement from behind, meaning there is nothing to do but wait, many an eye once again goes to the luminous faces of their watches, synchronised at 9 pm.

Still 40 minutes to Zero Hour at 3.10 am.

Christ.

•

Getting time, now.

The two Lieutenants walking in the darkness to their slender craft at No. 3 Squadron air base at Villers-Bocage – pilot Francis Lock and his observer Bob Barrett – carry themselves with careful purpose. They are heading out on counter-attack patrol, looking for any sign of enemy reserves moving up to counter-attack, whereupon their task will be to bomb them and strafe them before calling up their own artillery to bombard them. The two have been up for the last two hours, eating a big meal of bacon and eggs in the mess, washed down by cups of tea, and going over the plan with the other pilots and observers – though Lock and Barrett are scheduled to be the first to take off. And here is their Harry Tate, their RE8, their Reconnaissance Experimental No. 8, which awaits. The mechanics have already started and warmed the engine. A nod of thanks to them as they stand by, and Lock and Barrett climb into the cockpit, their flying helmets firmly fastened, their gloves on.

Following procedure, Lock waggles his joystick to ensure that all is as it should be, and is satisfied when the ailerons on the wings react to his touch. He pushes down first with his right foot, and then his left, on the rudder bar, to ensure that the rudder at the back of the plane swivels to the right and left, to push the nose of the plane right and left.

He nods to the hovering mechanic, who now comes forth and grips the huge, two-bladed wooden propeller.

'Switches off,' the mechanic calls.

'Switches off,' Lock affirms.

'Petrol on,' the mechanic calls.

'Petrol on,' Lock affirms.

The mechanic pulls the propeller backwards a few turns, to suck petrol vapour into the combustion chamber.

'Contact!'

'Contact!'

With one mighty effort, the mechanic starts the propeller lurching to the right, whereupon it coughs like an old man, gurgles like a baby and suddenly . . . roars like a lion going in for the kill, even as it blows angry blue-white smoke out of its nostrils. Quickly now, being very careful to stay well clear of the blades flashing in the moonlight, the mechanic removes the chocks holding the plane back and it starts to move. Under Lock's expert hand, the lion trundles at first, then starts to bound down the big grassy field that serves as a runway, accelerating all the while. Just 20 seconds later comes that magic moment of lift-off that never fails to thrill him, as the shuddering, juddering of the wheels on the rough field stops, and he is airborne! The Lion is taking its leap, and all that remains is to find out what it will pounce on.

•

'One of our planes began to drone up the valley,' Bean recounted, describing the scene before him. 'The night was like the page of an open book. We lay on our backs listening to the drone of this plane, his wanderings and his return. Presently from the sky opposite there now shot up a flare. He [the plane] was searching for his target . . . Four German searchlights began to feel the low clouds for him, moving restlessly in the night . . .'[56]

Things seem to be warming up?

Yes indeed.

'Dull red explosions on the plateau opposite,' Private Sydney Huntingdon of the 4th Machine Gun Company noted, like Bean observing eveything from the heights on the other side of the Somme. 'Must have been his bombs.'[57]

•

Right on cue . . . It is 2.50 am.

In their trenches, stretching from *der Römerstraße*, Roman Road, to *die Ancre*, the River Ancre, the German soldiers suddenly become aware of *many* planes roaring overhead, followed shortly afterwards by bombs exploding along their lines.

Out to the far right of the area the Australians like Private Isaac Betteridge and Lieutenant Lionel Short are to attack, Germany's 15th Infantry Regiment – some 1600 soldiers strong – takes pause.

Was ist los? What is going on?

Why all the *Feuerüberfälle*, fire-attacks?

'It was peculiar,' their Regimental history will note, 'that during the night English planes flew across the position at very low altitude and, in the light of dropped *Leuchtkörper*, flares, shot at the trenches with M.G.'[58]

And yet, 'peculiar', they can live with. It makes them a little nervous, but no more than that.

The planes, of course, keep going.

At an altitude of just 2000 feet, the 18 Farman Experimental 2b planes of 101 Squadron RAF are making the first of what will be three sorties over the German lines, dropping the first of what will be no less than four tons of Cooper bombs in the course of the night's proceedings. And *that* should keep their bloody Squareheads down, while we get things organised up front.

Much of the bombing is focused specifically on Hamel itself – which the pilot and his observer can just pick out in the dark – where the Germans are most heavily dug in. As 101 Squadron continues to roar overhead, the tanks, now on their own start lines 1000 yards back from the Australian front-lines, again have their engines cranked to a start at 2.59 am. Their commanders just keep them with their engines ticking over, knowing what is to come.

Portrait photo of Sir John Monash, c. 1918. (AWM A02697)

Sir Henry Rawlinson, commander of the British Fourth Army in July 1918. (AWM H08865)

Monash's Chief of Staff, General Thomas Blamey, photo portrait, 1919. (AWM E05006)

General John 'Black Jack' Pershing, Commander of the American Expeditionary Force. (AWM A03490)

The theatre of the 'Smart Set' concert party of the 4th Division at Allonville after being hit by a German shell in the early hours of 31 May 1918. The barn had been used as a soldiers' billet, and the two direct hits at 2 am caused 87 casualties, including 27 killed. All the casualties were from the 14th Australian Infantry Battalion. (AWM E02462)

Australian Prime Minister Billy Hughes, standing on an impromptu podium – in this case, four ammunition boxes – addresses Australian troops near Amiens on 2 July 1918. (AWM E02533)

A view of Pear Trench and the slope over which the Australians and Americans advanced on the morning of 4 July 1918. The enemy machine-gunner, seen dead in the centre just behind the trench, caused many casualties to the attacking troops as they came over the horizon on the right. (AWM E02709)

5 July 1918. Australian soldiers and British tank crewmen stand beside one of the three tanks which were put out of action in the fight for Hamel. The houses are those of Hamel village and the French flag on the roof is the one placed by Captain John Moran of the 43rd Australian Infantry Battalion. (AWM E03843)

The Australian barrage on enemy territory to assist the attack on Hamel, 4 July 1918. The photo was taken from the high ground above Sailly-le-Sec. (AWM E02632)

A British observation balloon behind the lines from which the movements of the retreating enemy were closely watched. (AWM E03055)

Crew of an RAF RE8 reconnaissance aircraft – the same aircraft as those used at Hamel – preparing for a night bombing operation. (AWM E01178)

A scene during the battle of Hamel showing American and Australian stretcher-bearers working together in the front-line area, after the infantry had passed. (AWM E02691)

Wounded Australians and Americans on stretchers awaiting ambulances during the battle. (AWM E02715)

The village of Hamel and the country in the direction of Corbie, seen from the trenches held by the Germans until the battle. The enemy front-line on the morning of 4 July was on the crest of the hill in the middle distance but the trench in which the men are seen is on the western slope of the Wolfsberg hill and was occupied by the supports some 200 yards behind the new front-line. (AWM E02844A)

Private Henry (Harry) Dalziel
VC, 15th Battalion – an
informal portrait taken in 1918.
(AWM P02939.031)

View of the ruined village of Hamel on 5 July 1918, after the battle. The tank in the
street assisted in the 'mopping up' of the village. (AWM E02864)

Studio portrait of Corporal Thomas Leslie Axford VC MM, 16th Battalion, 1918.
(AWM P02939.030)

Men of the 15th Battalion on the day of the battle, worn out and asleep under a camouflage which was found covering a German trench mortar in Pear Trench.
(AWM E02664)

Charles Bean, Australian Official War Correspondent (left), Prime Minister Billy Hughes (centre) and Brigadier General H.A. Goddard DSO (right), observing operations two months after the battle of Hamel, during the battle of Mont St Quentin, 15 September 1918. (AWM E03292)

His Majesty King George V congratulating John Monash after his investiture as a KCB, on the steps of Bertangles Chateau, HQ of the Australian Corps, 12 August 1918. (AWM A03316)

•

3 am. Two minutes to go till the harassing fire is due to begin and ten minutes to Zero Hour. Across the starting tape, the officers continue to look at their luminescent watches, while answering the same endless question from their men: 'What's the time?'

'The intense subdued excitement,' Lieutenant Lionel Short, would recall, 'seemed to radiate through the air.'[59]

In his office at Bertangles Chateau, the man everyone knows as 'Boss Gunner', the commander of all the artillery of the Australian Corps – some 400 guns in all – General Walter Coxen, sits by the telephone. Every minute it *doesn't* ring is a good sign, because when it rings this close before a barrage, it is almost always a problem. Still he remains as tense as a cat on a curtain.

And what is that?

Glancing out of the window, indeed 'twixt the ancient gracious pulled-back curtains of the chateau, he can suddenly see in the dim moonlight the outlines of a man slowly pacing up and down the gravel drive that lies in front of the chateau. General Coxen instantly recognises him: the powerful shoulders, the aquiline nose, the steady, methodical way he paces . . .

'The figure was that of [General Monash],' he would recount. 'The stage was set, he was awaiting the rise of the curtain. Every now and again he would pause and look at his watch, awaiting zero hour.'[60]

Yes, the rising of the curtain is now just minutes away, and the conductor readies to unleash his orchestra.

CHAPTER EIGHT

THE STUNT BEGINS

In relation to the machines at his disposal, Monash's tank-infantry
tactics have rarely been equalled, and probably never surpassed . . .
to read his orders for [Hamel] is to discover once more the strange
little thrill which comes from lifting up the edge of the curtain
of war and looking at the future.[1]

Douglas Orgill, historian, 1970

4 July 1918, Hamel, strike up the orchestra, starting with the big drums

A beautiful night for a battle?

Yes. But also just a beautiful summer's night, with bursts of soft moonlight illuminating the barest wisps of mist floating up from the Somme, and the slight rustle of a breeze wafting those wisps away – even as the odd cloud passes across the face of the moon.

Precisely as Monash and his senior officers had counted on and expected – because the fact that it is like this nine nights out of ten at this time of year has been carefully researched – the light breeze is blowing from west to east, coming from behind the attacking forces. This means that whatever clouds of dust are generated by the shell explosions to come on the dry soil of summer, mixed with the smoke screens, will inevitably drift towards the Germans, making it difficult for Fritz to see the men and tanks who will soon be charging towards them through that genuine 'fog of war'.

But, all up, right now, it is very pleasant, if just a little darker than expected because of the drifting cloud cover.

For the grizzled veterans among the Australians – the Americans, of course, have no-one answering that description – it is an extraordinary contrast to the way it had been in battles past.

224

Back at Pozières, for example, the Germans had known the Australians were there and sent out such scything blasts of machine-gun fire that, as one Digger would recall, 'We could see [them] cutting off the poppies almost against our heads.'[2]

But this is not like that at all. For the 6000 men lying out behind the Starting Line in No Man's Land, due to attack in the first wave, all is calm and quiet, apart from the odd plane overhead, and the odd explosion of a bomb dropping somewhere over German lines.

The main thing is the Germans do *not* yet know their enemy is here, meaning that the soldiers on the tape actually have time and space to contemplate what lies ahead. It seems extraordinary to think that just ten minutes from now, all hell is going to break loose 100 to 200 yards up ahead, and that they will then be in for the fight of their lives, but there it is. And some blokes will get knocked, but, as Lieutenant Lance Horniman blithely notes, 'That's all in the game.'[3]

In the northern section of the attack zone, in the flat fields by the Somme, Private Vivian Brahms, with the 42nd Battalion, is lying quietly with his mates, remaining as silent as possible, their only real activity being to roll cigarettes – though of course they are careful not to light them. This close to Fritz, as absurd as it may seem, just a lit match or the glow of a fag could prove fatal.

Some 500 yards to their right, facing the German trenches that defend the nearby village of Hamel 1000 yards ahead of them, the 43rd Battalion are also keeping their heads down, bearing in mind that as Hamel is on the high ground, they are even more at risk of being spotted. Trying to be quiet comes more easily to some, and to no-one more than Corporal Frank Shaw of C Company, the notably silent son of a Methodist minister from Hobart, who is more aware than most that he may be about to meet his Lord and Saviour Jesus Christ, and is even now in silent prayerful communion with Him.

A further 500 yards to the right again, Two Guns Harry Dalziel, with the 15th Battalion, *does* struggle to stay quiet, and still. As excited as he has ever been in his life, he is aware that his dearest wish – to once more take part in an actual battle – is about to take place. And there is little doubt that it is going to be a tough one, with his battalion charged

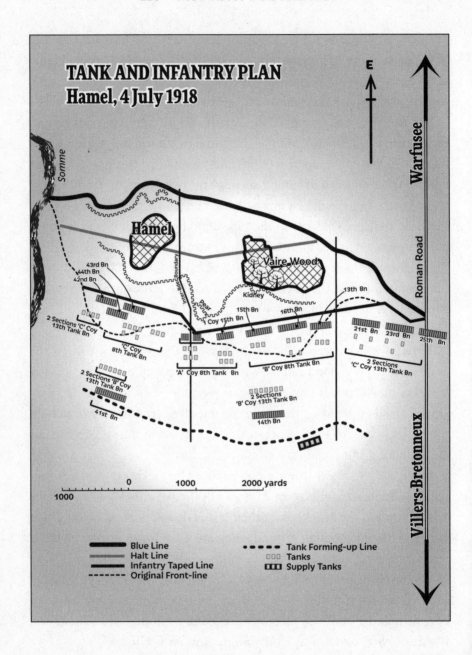

with taking the bristling Pear Trench. As the men of the 15th Battalion peer into the gloom to their right, along the hill crest, they can see their brother battalion, the 16th, also by the tape, ready to attack Kidney Trench and after that get to grips with Vaire Wood.

Among the soldiers of the 16th is Corporal Jack Axford, the unassuming Kalgoorlie labourer, while some 1000 yards behind the 16th is 'Jacka's mob', the 14th Battalion, which includes Lieutenant Edgar Rule and his mates.

Still further to the right of the 16th is the 13th Battalion, with Privates Cliff Geddes and his brother Aubrey 'Boo' Geddes, set to push past the south side of Vaire Wood, and on to the Blue Line. Cliff is feeling . . . all right, all things considered. The hot stew is still warm in his belly, and he and his platoon have managed to get through their own wire, and crawl to the tape without incident. (He is not sure what is about to happen, only that he must do his duty.)

And finally, to the right of the 13th, the three final battalions – the 21st, 23rd and 25th Battalions – are in position and ready to go. Private Isaac Betteridge and Lieutenant Lionel Short, an *Argus* reporter before the war, from Melbourne, are in the thick of the 23rd Battalion. Their task is to quickly push along the north side of the Roman Road, behind the smoke screen that will be laid down for them, and dig in, protecting the southern flank of the main assault against German attack.

•

In Pear Trench – the key German stronghold of the Australians' planned battlefront – all is quiet among the soldiers of the 55th Regiment.

So quiet, in fact, that when one of the officers hears a strange sound out in No Man's Land, he takes pause.

Da drüben! Over there!

Kannst Du es hören? Can you hear it?

Was ist das? What is that?

To his ears it seems to be 'the sound of men moving in [*Niemandsland*, No Man's Land].'[4]

Or is it a party of enemy soldiers setting up defensive rolls of wire in front of their own trenches, and the sound is carrying?

Whatever it is, it is going on, and he is quick to tell his men of his suspicions: A raid is very likely being prepared and they must stand to arms, grabbing their rifles, standing by their machine guns and getting ready for anything. Fortunately for the Australian and American soldiers of the 15th Battalion lying silent, 200 yards away in the tall wheat, he does not report his suspicions to his superiors, and he remains one of the few with a clue on what is going to happen . . .

•

For the most part, all the Australians and Americans out in No Man's Land can do now is wait, and wait – extraordinary how the day has raced by to this point, but from now on the seconds crawl past like dying slugs on a dead frog. Beyond the rolling of cigarettes, they check their ammunition belts for the umpteenth time, even while assessing the virtues of using the butts of their rifles as clubs.

At last however, right on cue, at 3.02 am, the first of it starts, with the crash of artillery coming from behind them, followed by explosions in front of them, the boom rolling over them one way, the dull roars of the exploding shells rolling back the other way.

It does not worry the Germans unduly. Just as happens every morning at this time, with the first distant glow of dawn, the artillery batteries of the German and Allied forces send their best wishes to the other side.

By way of saying 'Gidday', the Australians fire a few shells upon the German lines, which is responded to – *und* here's '*Guten Morgen*' to you – by a few rounds of their own.

So it's just that *Die Australischen,* the Australians, are starting a little earlier than usual on this day.

Ah, but there really is a difference this time, Fritz. For instead of just the normal 'harassing fire', as the Allies know it, after the first cheery exchange, 'some guns quickened step for a few seconds . . .'[5]

•

The engines of the tanks are a little louder now, as they push their way up the hill, closing in on where the first wave of soldiers is lying in a line along the white tape, as they all ready themselves for Zero Hour.

Because of the planes and the harassing fire generating noise, there is now less need for the tanks to just rumble lightly, and they are able to open their throttles just a little as they move from their assembly point, 1000 yards in the rear, towards the point of attack.

Not that it is easy for all that, and it is not just the pressing darkness leavened by the odd burst of moonlight that is the trouble. It is the unfamiliar and sometimes treacherous ground.

As the tank of Sergeant Edwin Bond lurches forward to support the 16th Battalion, so they can attack Kidney Trench, 'our tank went straight down a ten foot bank which in the dark the driver could not see and the back of his driver's seat hit him in the middle of his back making him *hors-de-combat*'.[6]

All they can do is lie him down at the back of the tank while another crew member takes over, and they push on, the best they can – particularly as they know the fall of the major barrage must be just seconds away.

•

In the heights of Sailly-le-Sec, Lieutenant Patrick Campbell and his comrades of the 5th Field Artillery Brigade stand by their 18-pounder field gun, knowing what is coming.

5 . . . 4 . . . 3 . . . 2 . . . 1 . . . go.

On the tick of 3.10 am, the shout goes up from the battery commander. 'Fire!'

In an instant there is an almighty blast as the gun roars into life, the barrel recoils 26 inches and the 18-pound shell, carrying four pounds of explosive, streaks skywards at 530 yards per second, due to land on the German noggins four seconds from now.

In another instant, all other guns across the line – deployed in camouflaged positions anything from 1000 to 5000 yards back from the German lines – erupt like angry volcanos, their shells disappearing as searing, soaring streaks of flame into the darkness, hurtling towards the German lines.

And now the five-man gun crews are going at it like navvies, on the seemingly endless line of powerful 18-pounder field guns spaced ten yards apart across the slope. And load! And . . . fire! And ignore the puff of acrid smoke that blows into your face every time a breech is opened to eject the shell casing and insert another shell. All across the front another 50 batteries – each one with six guns – just like Campbell's, are doing the same.

At this 'sustained' rate of a shell fired every 20 seconds, it is exhausting work, but the gunners never waver, following exactly the commands of each gun battery commander, standing 20 yards to the rear of his battery with a loud-hailer.

'The earth shook and the mind boggled at the concussion . . .' Gunner James Armitage would chronicle. 'Thick smoke settled into a fog and we had difficulty seeing our aiming lights.'[7]

•

And of course, the boom of the guns rolls all the way in the other direction, too, to Bertangles Chateau, some 12 miles to the north-west. Still watching through the windows at Bertangles, General Walter Coxen observes the man of the moment, General Monash, outside in the dark, still walking up and down the pebble driveway, the crunching echoes making it sound as though he is several men, instead of just one.

'[Sir John,]' General Coxen would recount, 'stopped for a moment, looking in the direction of the battlefront, his anxiety relieved, he turned and slowly mounting the steps of the chateau . . . went to his office. The curtain had risen, the first act was in full swing.'[8]

And the big bass drums of his orchestra are booming, as never before.

•

Watching from their part of the hillside nearby, Bean and his comrades know exactly what to expect from the first, given that they know that the initial shells rammed down Fritz's throat are *not* the high explosive and shrapnel shells to come shortly.

'Smoke shells,' Bean describes the scene, 'explode as if some young cumulus cloud had suddenly lifted itself upon the ground and turned slowly over in glowing brilliant firelight before fading again. Well, there were smoke shells thrown all across the enemy's front in that bombardment, and into the air also.'[9]

The preponderance of smoke shells falling along both flanks of the intended battlefield, however, provide the left and right frames of the military masterpiece about to take place.

•

In their own front-lines the German soldiers first groan as the acrid whiff of smoke assaults their nostrils. This has been happening every night about this time for the last ten days. And of course, once they smell the smoke they have learnt what to do. As poison gas is likely to be with it, the men of 202 RIR in the village, 55th IR in Pear and Kidney Trenches, and 13th IR and 15th IR south of them, know they have no choice. And so now – desperately trying not to breathe in – their hands fly to their gas masks, and their fingers fumble furiously to get the masks over their faces in time.

True, such gas masks are very uncomfortable and severely reduce the wearer's ability to see, smell, speak, hear and fight . . . but the alternative is much worse. Just one lungful of the enemy gas and you risked, within minutes, being a wheezing, vomiting, dying mess and . . .

And, now that you mention it, this fire does seem to be heavier than usual, as are the planes going overhead lower and thicker than usual. In short order, there seems no way around it, as the Official History of the 55th Infantry Regiment, now defending Pear Trench, will document, their officers come 'to the conclusion that the enemy's *Angriffsabsichten*, intentions to attack, were imminent'.[10]

There is equal alarm, across the whole German line, not least among the troops in the trenches just south of the Ancre River, where it would be recorded '. . . *eine trommelfeuerartige Beschießung unserer Linien*, a drum-like bombardment of our lines announces an imminent attack . . . *Artillerie und Minenwerfer schießen Sperrfeuer*; artillery and mine-throwers fire barrages'.[11]

The German soldiers steel themselves, look down the sights of their machine-gun and rifle barrels – at least the best they can through their heavy gas masks and the smoke – and get ready.

The fact that *Schwärme von Fliegern*, swarms of planes, continue overhead, dropping bombs, is an indication that this really might be a *major* attack . . .

Korrekt!

For now come the high explosive and shrapnel shells, roaring, soaring, whistling down and . . . *exploding* with staggering ferocity.

For those Allies lying by the tapes in No Man's Land, their world is instantly turned turvy-topsy. At first there are angry flashes, like sheets of lightning coming from behind and momentarily lighting the ground in front and now . . .

And now geysers of red flame suddenly erupt right in front of them as the ground beneath them shakes, and various bits of the ground ahead of them start to fall upon them, all while their ears are battered by explosive roars!

Good God, talk about 'Pie'! They've never seen anything like it, at least not up close.

'The place seemed transformed to an inferno,' Isaac Betteridge, over on the far right of the Australian attack, would recount. 'The air full of the shocks of bursting violence . . . Hell couldn't be as bad, and the line of men dropping and lying still, staggering back wounded or lurching drunkenly forward into shell holes. Falling over wire, buffeted by explosions till they looked like devils in their proper element.'[12]

Flying over the lines at this time, in their slender craft from No. 3 Squadron air base at Villers-Bocage – pilot Francis Lock and his observer Bob Barrett are delighted to see an entire line of flashing guns on one side, and just to the east the resulting conflagration. 'They lit up our machine,' Barrett would recount, 'and when we flew over the guns it was almost like day, although the first glimmers of dawn hadn't appeared.'[13]

And now, billowing up from that conflagration come stabs of flames bursting forth from rolling balls of dust and smoke, with waves of percussion and heat that start to buffet their planes.

Good God, if it is like that up here, what must it be like *down there*?

•

Mein Gott! The hideousness of their situation is indescribable. For the Germans in the front-line trenches, most of whom had been asleep just ten minutes earlier, their whole world is now one of shells bursting all around, screams, sobs, explosions, billowing flames, scything shrapnel, trench walls collapsing, severed heads, disembowelled comrades, more screams, and sheer unending terror. And there is no way out, they must stay here as shell after shell keeps pounding into them – ten to 20 a minute – tearing flesh, shearing off limbs, disfiguring, burning to a crisp, and leaving many a man as a quivering mess of blubbering wreck. And if they can survive all that? The German soldiers know only too well that an attack of this magnitude must mean that either Tommy is doing a short barrage, in which case he'll be here in 15 minutes – hurling grenades, shooting them and stabbing them with bayonets – or he's doing one of those week-long day and night preparatory bombardments which drive men mad in their dugouts, where food cannot be got in and wounded can't be evacuated.

Either way, it is *nicht gut*, but if ever there is a time to '*nehmt die Arschbacken zusammen, als wenn ihr eine kleenen Zwanziger dazwischen hieltet*, pull the arse cheeks together as if you held a small coin',[14] it is now, and they set to with a will!

Their key hope, of course, is to get help from their own artillery.

'The German flares spouted at once,' Private Sydney Huntingdon of the 4th Machine Gun Battalion would recount. Not far away from Bean and his colleagues on the hill, Huntingdon keeps firing at the Germans, as ordered, but still can't help but be fascinated by the scene before them, including the urgent signals that keep sprouting up from the German lines, calling on their own artillery for protection. Perhaps calling on his background as a Tassie florist of 20 years standing, he is careful in his description. 'Double reds, double greens, once or twice golden clusters, but they soon died out, all except an isolated flare from one of the woods where some brave chap must have died at his post . . .'[15]

(What the Germans don't expect is what happens next. Some of the Australian soldiers are armed with SOS red rockets of their own, and now send them up. If, perchance, the German Battalion commander has sent up two SOS rockets to signal 'enemy now in No Man's Land', the fact that the artillery will now see three or four such rockets will mean something else entirely. Ideally, back at German HQ, there will be a confusion of different signals coming back to them.)

'The whole sky,' one soldier would report, 'was a blaze of light as the gunners pumped it into old Fritz.'

'You felt a great pity for the men underneath that fire,' another would comment, 'yet knew it was your salvation.'[16]

Even for those further back in the second wave, like Lieutenant Edgar Rule, in 14th Battalion's C Company – all of them now stirring in readiness – the results are shattering, as the barrage comes down 'with the most terrifying crash I've ever heard. Not a bit of use to try and get the men to double, for in the roar of the guns and of the shells bursting ahead it was impossible to hear your own shouts.'[17]

With their eyes streaming, their temperaments steaming, the Australian and American soldiers know that the time is nigh . . .

•

True, it is a tad odd to draw so much comfort from the conflagration of furious explosions coming just 1000 yards or so to the east, but comfort it is that the tank commanders draw as they see it.

With calculated synchronicity, the 8th and 13th Tank Battalions of the 5th Tank Brigade – totalling five Companies of 12 tanks, making 60 tanks in all, and 480 crew members – now start to *roar* forward. No need to purr any more, they can give it the full throaty roar, and do so.

•

From across the other side of the Somme River, in the heights of Sailly-le-Sec, Lieutenant George Mitchell is watching closely with his comrades of the 48th Battalion. They had known to expect a bombardment to the south, but somehow had not calculated on it being *this* big.

'Flares shot up all along the enemy lines,' Lieutenant Mitchell would describe it. 'The light of them playing on the billows of smoke from within which rose constantly renewed fountains of flame. The noise saturated air beat on us. The ground rocked unceasingly.'[18]

Not far away, from the heights of the Morlancourt ridge, 88 Vickers Guns send a criss-cross of lethal fire right at the German trenches, drawing – as every fourth round is a tracer – extraordinary spider web patterns in the sky, even as they unleash an enfilade for the ages on the most dangerous of the German trenches.

On the instant, a 'mad elation' takes possession of Mitchell. Grabbing a rifle, he starts blazing away at the German parapet, some 1000 yards away, his target lit by the flash of exploding shells. Hearing the firing, Sergeant Tommy Halliday from Nymagee, New South Wales, quickly comes up from the 48th's dugout, concerned that Mitchell is firing at an approaching enemy.

'See anything?'

'No, Serg, just shooting to keep happy.'

Now, a different Sergeant, in a different situation, might have just wandered off. But Halliday is the kind of man, and this is the kind of situation, that he, too, can't help himself.

Seized by exactly the same kind of elation, he grabs his own rifle, and unleashes volley after volley at the German noggins.

Attracted by the noise, others from the platoon come up, wondering what the *hell* is going on?

Mitchell's mate, Tom Davis, answers for them: 'They're just fillin' in cracks in the barrage.'[19]

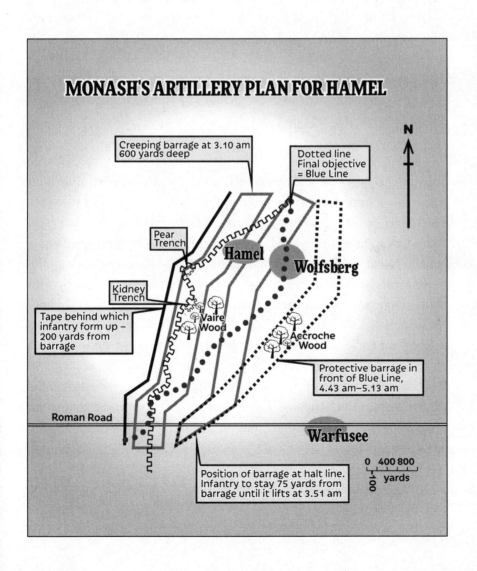

MONASH'S ARTILLERY PLAN FOR HAMEL

•

In truth, there are few cracks. For while the barrage focused on the forward trenches is essentially a straight line, with just one zig and one zag, Pear Trench is, of course, curved.

But for the German soldiers at the apex of Pear Trench, it is extraordinary. At 3.10 am when, clearly, *die Hölle bricht los*, all hell is breaking loose, all around them, they are substantially untouched, as most of the shells in their area are landing some 50 yards in front of them, which is to say, nearer the summit of the hill.

Grimly, they stick to their machine guns, and wait for the soldiers who they know must shortly appear coming over the top of the hill, before descending down towards them. In the meantime they check their ammunition, say their prayers and steel themselves for what's coming – surely they will soon face a wave of Tommies and they intend to be ready for it.

•

Still by the tapes of their Starting Line, the 8000 Australian and American infantry await their time, mostly with their heads down. The heavens continue to roar, the ground just ahead continues to erupt, and what appears to be a solid sheet of billowing blasts appears as a wall all along the line of German trenches.

And still the tanks roar forward, to catch the soldiers . . . albeit with mixed success. Some are struggling, and none more than the 8th Tank Battalion's No. 1 Section of A Company, led by Captain Cyril Scott. In the lead tank of three, he has orders, 'To support infantry with attack on Pear Shaped Trench and Blue Line',[20] in his pocket, and he has been trying to do just that. Alas, in all the dark, the smoke, the dust and confusion, the tanks have lost contact with their guide and, proceeding on dead reckoning and the natural lie of the land, the pod has veered to the north of Pear Trench.

Christ.

A little to the south, at least Captain Peter Batten's tank is on course to assist the soldiers of 15th Battalion as they push towards the German trenches between Pear and Kidney, but one of them inside the tank is struggling. As the engine roars, the fumes belch, and the tank lurches from side to side and back and forth, the Australian liaison soldier, Bluey, appears more grey than anything else, with all the colour drained from his face. As the tank keeps roaring forth towards the German line, things get worse, as the engine gets hotter, and those fumes inside the metal box get thicker. But there is no time to worry about Bluey, and they must just keep pressing on.

•

With so many Allied guns firing under battle conditions and in the dark, it is perhaps inevitable that there are errors. One factor is that 'barrel wear' affects the distance a projectile will go – the older the barrel, the more worn from firing, the less distance it will send the shell – and while that is supposed to be factored into the calculation, in a couple of the guns the barrels are more worn than has been noticed by those who inspect them, so the shells from those one or two guns drop short.

To forestall this very possibility, at the last instant the 43rd Battalion's C Company, together with their Yanks from Company E of the 131st Battalion, had been ordered to move their Starting Line back by 50 yards . . . just to be on the safe side. It is for this reason that, just minutes after the advance begins, they are lagging just a little behind the lines on either side when there is suddenly a screeching overhead, getting louder, roaring now, squealing . . . *is this it?* . . . getting louder still . . . And louder . . .

And louder still . . . Shrieking now, even over the sounds of battle all around.

Get down! The dirty drop-short explodes on the right-hand side of the advancing line, causing 20 casualties. Right next to them, Two Guns Dalziel and his mates of 15th Battalion are about to attack the crucial Pear Trench when the drop-shorts hit them, too, and they have 12 men killed – Lieutenant William Spencer, 31, a clerk of Cooma, whose person took the full hit of the shell, is blown to bits – and more than 30 men wounded in A Company.

Screams fill the night, with calls for 'Stretcher-bearers!'

Christ, Jesus, Holy Father, Mother Mary . . . *help* me.

As tragic as the deaths of the men by drop-shorts is, in many ways what is worse is that the inaccuracies of the artillery on Pear Trench leaves the German machine-gunners, waiting for their attackers there, substantially unhurt. And so they stay, crouched behind their heavy *Maschinengewehr* 08, MG 08s, capable of spitting out 500 bullets a minute. As most of them have 10,000 rounds on hand, it means there is a *lot* of firepower left in those trenches.

But for the Australians and Americans about to hit Pear Trench it is worse still. For their *bloody* tanks have not arrived, *Goddammit*. In all the smoke and confusion, the tanks appear to have gotten lost, and there is no time to find them. Is this to be bloody Bullecourt all over again? Again, all they can do is ready themselves to rise, regardless, and hope the tanks will catch up. But curse the wicked Gods of War, which can see one Battalion head off to take a well-armed trench, only to have three things go wrong at once – drop-shorts, intact German defences and no bloody tanks!

Still there remains a minute or two to go, so there remains a chance the tanks will suddenly appear.

•

As devastating as the odd drop-short is on the attacking troops, far more devastating are the Allies' accurately targeted shells of the 200 big guns, the 9.2-inch howitzers which are now laying waste to Fritz's Battalion command posts and the German artillery batteries whose locations have been so carefully worked out over the last fortnight.

'A heavy bombardment of the regiment command post began,' the Official History of the 232nd Regiment records. 'About 250 rounds, only heavy 24-cm calibres, including about 50 *Stollenquetscher* tunnel-squashers, whizzed onto the command post and in its immediate vicinity. They were *schlimme Stunden*, horrible hours . . . Nearby *ein furchtbares Trümmerfeld*, a terrible field of debris arose: all was shot to pieces . . . The nearby 5th Field Artillery Regiment, the 213th, had a gun knocked out, nine dead and seven wounded.'[21]

Across the German lines now, battery after battery is wiped out as the Allied shells crash into them. And those soldiers who are still alive in their dugouts dare not venture out into the storm of shrapnel to man the guns that do remain. It all means that, for the attacking troops, the return artillery fire on them is vastly diminished. Adding to the German agony is the night bombers of No. 101 Squadron Royal Air Force – the FE2bs, with their roaring 160-horsepower Beardmore engines – now at work dropping no less than three tons of bombs on the German batteries and reserve trenches, together with roads and camps in the German rear.

So effective is the targeted shelling and bombing on the German batteries that, from the heights of Sailly-le-Sec, Bean notes that while just about no flashes of German artillery are coming from north of the Roman Road, which is where the attack is going in, over the 6500 yard front, 'the German guns further south [are] busy . . . for we could see the flashes of them, playing like fingers on a piano up and down the skyline of the plateau'.[22]

Even more satisfying are the red flares he can see going up 'all along line by Warfusee',[23] in the forward trenches held by the Germans 1000 yards south of the Roman Road, where Bean knows, no attack is going in!

What it means is that the panicky German soldiers south of the road are calling in artillery to stop an attack which, for them, is non-existent. It is a good sign that Monash's painstaking plan to confuse the Germans about where the actual attack is going in is working.

•

For the German soldiers of the 13th Infantry Regiment, defending Kidney Trench in front of Vaire Wood – facing the Australian 13th Battalion – it had started with 'setzte schlagartig Trommelfeuer ein, sudden drumfire', and continued when 'hinter einer starken Feuerwalze, behind a strong rolling-barrage, in breiter Front, wide along the front, the attack followed, which was executed by numerous tanks with the infantry following them'.

Oh, but it gets worse still.

'The attack,' their Official History recounts, 'was supported by Schwärme von Fliegern, swarms of planes, which interfered with M.G. fire and dropping bombs in the ground battle . . .'[24]

Shells! A lethal lattice work of machine-gun bullets! Gas! Smoke! Rifle-fire! Advancing soldiers! Tanks just behind them!

So many things are happening at once, and everything so *fast* – so many blows falling upon them at the same time – that the Germans are not sure what to do next, how to react, how to counter. And still they have not faced the worst monsters of all . . .

•

With the AIF's 13th Battalion about to attack the trenches south of Vaire Wood, Cliff Geddes looks behind him, and is 'pleased to see the tanks moving forward, they had arrived to time without mishap'.[25]

Not all the Battalions about to get to grips with the Germans are so fortunate. Both the soldiers of the 43rd Battalion about to hit Hamel, and the soldiers of the 15th readying to go at Pear Trench, continue to look behind them in the gloom for the reassuring menace of those metal monsters moseying forward, but they are still not there.

For the moment, the men may have to do without. Their officers continue to look at their watches. There are surely only seconds to go . . .

And . . . now.

Across the line, from about 3.12 am on – depending how far back from the German trenches the white line is – the battle commanders give their orders.

Rise, my children! Go forth, towards the German lines being pounded up ahead, until you are about 75 yards off, ready to charge, when the barrage lifts at 3.14 am!

Now, it takes no small amount of courage to stand up before such carnage, but so they do. Slowly at first, once again fearing a fusillade of German bullets will cut them to pieces, and now with more confidence as no fusillade hits, the first wave of men rise and slowly but steadily walk towards their objective. This is not a mad dash. This is a calculated advance towards the closest edge of the barrage which, as they start, is 200 yards from them, and the furthest edge 800 yards away.

In the 42nd Battalion, by the Somme, Private Vivian Brahms and his comrades have been waiting for this moment.

'Immediately the order to advance was given,' Brahms would record, 'matches were struck, cigarettes were puffed, as the troops went forward courageously and unperturbed . . .'[26]

And so it is, across the line . . .

'We moved forward slowly,' Cliff Geddes would recount 'one would think the awful crash of artillery & bursting shells would deafen or drive you crazy, but your blood is warm, & really, I felt as cool as could be, just slightly "Keen", I'll admit. We moved to within [coo-ee] of our barrage, & one felt he could go through to Berlin under it.'[27]

The 6000 soldiers in the first wave, well spread out and several lines deep – spaced out, so that one burst of machine-gun fire can't take out 20 men at a time – continue to walk towards the German trenches.

'We were up and off,' Private Betteridge of the 23rd Battalion, out on the far right, would recount. 'The noise and din were indescribable. Our own [targeted trench] just in front . . . burst in great sheets of fire 30 feet across and looked like golden rain.'[28]

The commander of C Company of the 131st Regiment, attached to 42nd Battalion, is Captain Carroll Gale, and as he marches forward with his men from Illinois, he is mesmerised by the 'most wonderful' curtain of catastrophe that lies before them. It goes all the way to the Somme on his left, and as far to his right as he can see, and the whole thing is 'laid down so perfectly that we were able to approach it [to] about seventy-five yards as ordered, without receiving any casualties from it'.[29]

Across much of the line, with Pear Trench being a notable exception, the tanks now move smoothly through the soldiers and get to the shattered German trenches first . . .

•

The heat! The noise! The acrid smoke! The smell of gunpowder. The cordite fumes!

And that is just inside Captain Batten's tank. *Gawd* knows what it must be like outside. But the agonised expression on the face of the Digger Bluey says it couldn't possibly be any worse than this. With every firing of the Hotchkiss Gun it sounds exactly as if your own tank must have been hit, as the whole tank rocks backward, and as they continue to make their way through German territory – in this case doing devastating work on the German line in front of Vaire Wood, which starts with flattening a tank-width path through the rolls of barbed wire for the rampaging infantry to follow – there is no doubt they really are being hit by shrapnel and bullets. Mercifully, to actually stop the tank it will take a direct hit from an artillery shell, but, so far, so good, they are able to keep going, even as the temperature inside gets to 120 degrees Fahrenheit . . .

Bluey hates it.

But Captain Cyril Longmore of the 44th Battalion watches the work of the tanks ahead of him with enormous approval.

'The tanks did wonderful work,' he would recount. 'Cruising between the moving barrage and the advancing infantry. They shelled strong-points with their 6-pounders, caused havoc with their machine guns, put the wind up Fritz and gave much moral support to the attackers.'[30]

•

The smoke! The dust! The noise!

But, mostly the dust. Because the ground in these parts is so chalky, every shell that lands throws enormous plumes of white dust skywards – much of which, as predicted, starts to drift over German lines, pushed along by the prevailing westerly breeze. For the attackers heading into it, however, there remains so much dust that it not only stings their eyes, but starts to cover their face in a sweaty sheen of mud, and falls down the back of their shirts to become a greasy slime.

•

With the battle now begun, there is no doubt that most of the Americans are keener than ever.

'They went forward with fixed bayonets shouting the word "*Lusitania!*" as a battle-cry,' British war correspondent Philip Gibbs would chronicle. 'Again and again Australians heard that word on American lips, as though there were something in the sound of it strengthening to their souls and terrifying to the enemy. They might well have been terrified, any German who heard that name, for to American soldiers it is a call to vengeance.'[31]

Onwards the soldiers press, with every firing of the field guns behind them causing shells to streak forth on such a shallow arc, that as they pass over the lead soldiers – sounding like a roaring train – they are no higher than ten feet over their heads, and explode 75 yards in front of them!

It takes guts to head towards such a destructive barrage when it is not moving, purely on that promise that it will move away ahead of you, but, sure enough, when the first wave gets within 75 yards of it, at exactly 3.13 am, the barrage – *some 1000 to 2000 yards back, the battery commander on his bull-horn shouts, 'Up 100!' meaning the No. 3 man on the crew turns the small wheel on the gun one notch to adjust the angle of the barrel* – indeed starts to creep forward away from them.

The shattering geysers of flame subside, there is a pause for just the barest second and then the barrage smoke starts to blow back . . . before fresh geysers of flame go up, 100 yards or so back.

One last time, the Diggers of 15th Battalion, A Company, closing in to within 75 yards of Pear Trench, look behind them, hoping to see the tanks looming, but there is nothing. *Where are the fucking tanks? Are we to be let down, again?*

Alas, the three tanks that had been meant to push forward to do precisely this kind of work, trampling the wire and getting to grips with enemy machine-gun posts – are still lost in all the confusion. And the men cannot wait for them! For, as the survivors of A Company, who have already lost 30 men to a drop-short, are keenly aware, the other Companies of 15th Battalion are now pressing forward to their own German lines, and if A Company doesn't take out the machine-gun posts at the apex of Pear Trench *now*, it will be a simple matter for Fritz to bring devastating enfilade fire right into the flanks of the other Companies.

Steeling themselves, the Australians and Americans charge, their bayonets to the fore, flashing fire from the receding barrage . . .

•

At least out to the far right of the Australian battlefront, things are proceeding exactly as planned, as the 23rd Battalion, with the 21st on their left and 25th on their right, and the six tanks in tightly behind them, push forward with the Roman Road on their right flank.

With the 23rd Battalion, Private Isaac Betteridge is part impressed, part horrified. 'Talk about a hell,' he would recount.

'The earth fairly rocked and the air was full of explosions. I don't believe a straw could have went through it but it was a big surprise for [Fritz] anyway.'[32]

And ain't that the truth?

'The gunfire lit the whole scene as on a moonlit night,' one of Betteridge's 23rd Battalion officers, Lieutenant Lionel Short would note, 'and the men [went] as you have seen a crowd from a cricket

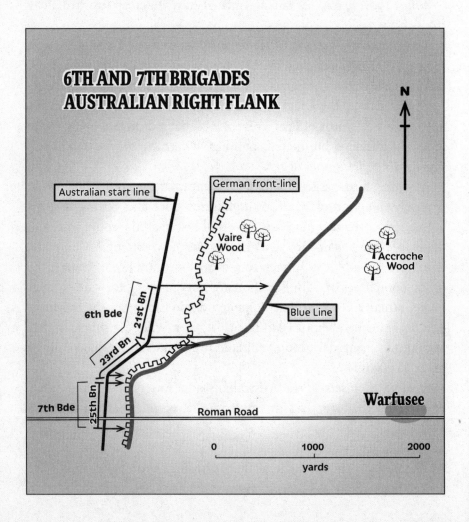

match when the crush has lessened and all are spreading out. They moved in batches with gaps of stray ones. The excitement of the wait was gone. There was no feeling of fear . . . We could hear each other only by shouting . . .'[33]

As Short, Betteridge and the rest of the 23rd Battalion move towards the German trenches, it is to see only a few brave souls remaining there, ready to fight.

'Most of his troops ran for it . . .' Betteridge would recount. 'I shot at 2, the first was aiming a machine gun. The other threw a bomb that I got a few splinters off. It was good while it lasted. You could see them running 1½ miles away.'[34]

But careful! There is some fight in the Germans still standing and Betteridge, side by side with his mates – many of whom are 'swearing in a sort of strangled undertone' – go for them. While keeping his mouth tightly closed to avoid breathing too deeply the acid and acrid fumes of the shell explosions, Betteridge hurls a couple of Mills grenades.

'Don't think they went into the trench,' he would recount, 'but the bang of them going off made me feel good, so I run up and rolled a couple more in underhand to make sure they got there.'[35]

They do, and explode!

Now peering over the top, he catches the barest glimpse of a Hun with a machine gun, pointing it right at him. Betteridge fires from the hip like a flash, as do some of his mates.

'Who got him I dunno, anyway he fell . . .'

Another Hun now hurls a grenade, which mercifully goes over Betteridge's head.

'I fired on him, he also went down . . . Just then a party of ours came up the trench. They had entered it lower down.'[36]

In fact, all across this section of the German trenches, members of the 23rd Battalion are storming.

'When we reached the front line,' Lieutenant Short records, 'every live Hun was out in a state of terror, like rabbits frightened to death. They wore no equipment and carried no rifles or gas helmets. They must have been sleeping or chatting when the barrage fell on them . . .'[37]

The 23rd Battalion has taken the trench!

Similar scenes are occurring all along the front.

'I saw a Fritz with his hands up surrendering to some of our boys,' Cliff Geddes will recount of the experiences of the 13th Battalion tackling the trenches south of Vaire Wood. 'They fired into other dugouts, in case there were some hiding in there before we moved on.'[38]

Alas, the situation of the Australian soldiers to their left, trying to crack the toughest nut of the lot, Pear Trench, remains . . . troubled.

•

The German soldiers at the apex of Pear Trench can barely believe it. For while the first barrage had been landing about 50 yards in front of them, even as further down their trench both ways, their fellow German soldiers are screaming and dying, now that the straight line of catastrophe has moved forward, it is landing 50 yards *behind* them, further down the hill. They are still alive!

And now, peering through their gas masks, the Germans in Pear Trench can just see the first of the attackers, as the shout goes up.

Tommy kommt! Here comes Tommy!

•

Because the artillery barrage has substantially missed the trench and its surrounds, it has left the barbed-wire defences before Pear Trench intact. And with still no tanks joining the 15th, the only way through is to use wire-cutters. To give the men tackling the wire a chance, the Lewis Gun teams must push their way forward, with the No. 1 man on the gun firing from the hip, while the No. 2 carries the round magazines, ready to slap on a new one as required.

One of those No. 2s, Sergeant Harry Dalziel, has his dander up. The 15th Battalion is going to have to fight like hell to make up for the drop-shorts, the lack of tanks, the fact that the wire is still intact and Fritz seems unaffected by the barrage, but Two Guns feels like he is the man for the job. And so it is that Two Guns Harry and his No. 1, like a couple of wildly stumbling Jack-in-the-boxes, keep running forward the best they can, doubled over to make as small a target as possible, with Dalziel in the lead to shield the sight of the Lewis Gun No. 1 man from snipers as the Lewis man regularly falls to the ground to fire a burst at the Huns, before getting up once more and charging forth again. And the other Lewis gunners are doing the same.

Down on your bellies! Up and run! Down! Up! Down! In extreme situations like this, the whole process of reloading takes no more than four seconds, meaning the bursts of bullets from the Lewis Guns tearing into the Germans are all but constant. And by alternating which Lewis Gun team goes down, they are able to provide each other, and the rest of the Company, crucial cover.

But it is tough going for all of the 15th all right. Beyond their loss of men from the drop-shorts, they had also been delayed by the catastrophe, so they have not been able to keep close to the barrage, and suffered accordingly – and the German resistance has been strong and they have lost even more men. Dalziel's A Company are copping the brunt of it, with two machine guns at the apex of the German strongpoint in Pear Trench sending out such withering fire they cannot get close to it. Three other machine guns along the 400-yard length of the trench are also still active, and . . .

And now what?

Out of the smoke of battle suddenly emerge wreaking wraiths of vengeance, German soldiers hurling stick grenades, creating more havoc!

At 'em lads! Stung into action, several men of A Company, with a couple of Americans, charge straight back at the bombers, firing from the hip. And yes, those Germans who are not cut down quickly retreat, which is satisfying, but when the Diggers try to follow up hard, it is only to get further caught in the wire entanglements ahead of the trench which have not yet been cut through.

It requires action, and A Company is up for it. The word is passed along the line.

And *now*.

As one, across the line, all of A Company's Lewis gunners – some eight in all – suddenly leap to their feet and start firing from the hip, over the tops of the corn stalks, bringing their own devastating fire upon Pear Trench, at which point 30 Diggers rush forward, eager to throw their own grenades and get to grips with the Germans manning the guns.

And yet, while for the moment it seems those two guns have been quelled, suddenly a third gun, previously silent, now opens up on them at short range with 'murderous fire'.[39]

The section around Two Guns Dalziel is under particularly heavy attack, as the rhythmic *thud-thud-thud* of the German MG08s keeps coming from 'our left, about 100 yards distant',[40] as men start falling – sometimes with a soft gurgle of death, sometimes with a groan or scream – all around.

In such extreme moments of life or death, but mostly death, no-one knows just how they will react. Will you be a blithering mess, or will you rise to the occasion?

Two Guns Dalziel does neither; with all the others he goes down hard on his belly so as to get out of the line of fire . . . but he does not tarry long. What is clear to him is that if they are to complete their mission, and take Pear Trench, as ordered, then that machine gun is going to have to be taken out, and in the absence of anyone else making a move that leaves . . . the eldest son of James and Eliza Dalziel, born in a shack at a tin mine called Ragged Camp, south of Cairns, 25 years before and raised to be a fireman, not a soldier, but to at least have a go, you know? For Harry always wanted to be a soldier. Fascinated by the Boer War from the age of six onwards, he learned off by heart the song 'Soldiers of the Queen', would sing it to anyone who asked, and was quick to join the school cadets, so he could learn how to handle firearms. He had dreamed of a moment like this presenting itself, and in many ways had prepared himself.

On this occasion, 'Two Guns' Harry should have been called 'Four Guns [Harry]', for the fact he has 'a revolver in each hand, two in his belt and a dagger in his boot'.[41]

So yes, this might be the moment he's dreamt of.

Just up ahead in the darkness, Two Guns can see the angry flashes coming from the muzzles of the German MG08s and MG15s guns. Bringing both pistols to bear, he chooses his moment, waiting until, in the gloom, he can actually see a figure to fire at.

And now operating more in the realms of furious instinct than conscious thought, Dalziel first fires a quick burst of blasts from his hurriedly grabbed Lewis Gun, which, sure enough, instantly silences one distant German machine gun ... before another opens up! This time Two Guns decides to charge at it, 'balls out', as the Diggers refer to a flat-out sprint, which means dropping the heavy Lewis Gun and again relying on only his revolvers. It will be for his mate to give covering fire, to fire burst after burst right at Pear Trench to keep their blasted Squareheads down.

Ready?

Ready.

NOW!

Just a second after the rapid thudding of the Lewis Gun breaks out right beside him, Two Guns Harry is up on his feet once more, this time with his favourite German Luger pistol in his right hand, and his Colt in his left. A flitting cold-eyed killer of the night, he flies across the broken ground, looping out to his right, out of the lines of fire between the two machine guns, and now starts to narrow in once more, coming back to his left.

'First thing I saw through the smother,' one of Dalziel's fellow soldiers would recount, 'was [Two Guns] Harry rushing straight at death ... It seemed suicide and how he escaped that hurricane of lead no one on this earth will ever tell me.'[42]

And *still* he keeps going.

There!

And there!

And there is one now, a goggle-eyed monster, just up ahead, a Fritz with a gas mask on, which is clearly one reason he has not been shooting straight ...

Fritz, this is how it is done.

Dalziel fires, and the German soldier firing the machine gun goes down hard, causing the gun to stop. His *kamerad*, who has been loading the gun, tries to get away, but Dalziel fires at him, too, and he also falls.

Just as that gun ceases however, another German gun opens up on the right. Again, the fact that Dalziel can bring his pistols to bear quicker than the Germans can manoeuvre their heavy guns gives him a crucial advantage at close quarters, as he swivels, fires, twists and fires again, as 'single-handed he sailed into the Germans'[43] and German after German goes down, seven killed in all and . . .

And seemingly from nowhere, a German soldier rises up, lunges at him with his bayonet and succeeds in wounding Two Guns Harry in the hand, before the Australian jumps on the 'German blood-hound'.[44] In such close quarters as this, Dalziel reaches for the German dagger he keeps in his boot and drives it hard into the German, 'catching him right over the heart. His dying cry upset me and I shivered.'[45]

And now *another* German soldier, a young one – instead of running away like many of the others had – brings his own gun to bear and fires off a volley of shots. Miraculously, only one of them hits Dalziel, and even then it is only his trigger finger. Again, Dalziel closes on him quickly, and soon has the young German on the ground, at his mercy, and could easily kill him, too, by plunging the dagger down once more, but . . .

But he decides to spare him, 'because the youngster fought so well'.[46] Instead, he captures the man, keeping his pistol trained upon him.

'Come on lads, we've got 'em guessing!'[47] he shouts to the men behind him.

And he's right.

Two Guns has opened the door to Pear Trench and the Aussies pour in, fighting their way down the trench in both directions.

All around Dalziel, the hand-to-hand fighting is soon raging as the soldiers of the 15th Battalion get amongst the remaining Germans, wielding their bayonets with great effect.

'The *Boche*,' Captain William Masoner, commanding G Company of the 132nd Infantry with the 15th Battalion, would recall, 'came running from their positions with their hands on their heads calling "*Kamerad!*"'[48]

Not all those trying to surrender succeed, as the problem is that the Germans who don't surrender start firing upon the Australians attempting to take prisoners. Those Germans do not last long, with yet more well-placed grenades solving the problem.

As the 15th Battalion continues their rout, more and more Germans throw their hands into the air and surrender, sometimes even being organised by their own sergeants to do so.

'With the *Mute der Verzweiflung*, courage of despair,' the Official History of the 55th IR will sadly document, '*die erschöpften deutschen Truppen*, the exhausted German troops defended themselves, but in the long run they could not cope with the onslaught of an opponent far superior in numbers as well as in *Kampfmitteln*, weaponry.'[49]

Coming forward, some of the German soldiers surrendering across the line don't even bother to hide their naked relief that they will now be in the care of the Allies, meaning that in all likelihood they will finish the war alive – something they had barely thought credible only 30 minutes earlier when they had been hit in quick succession by a devastating barrage, scything machine guns, gas, marauding soldiers and rampaging tanks.

Going up to one German, one Digger says, almost by way of making conversation, '*Finis le Guerre.*'

'Yes,' the German laughs in reply, in what amounts to a broad Australian accent with a Teutonic flavour, 'my bloody oath.'[50]

Turns out the bloke had been an emigrant to Australia before the war, finding work in the Boulder mines in Western Australia, before heading home in 1914, once the war had broken out. He has done his duty by the Fatherland, fought the good fight, but can ask no better than to be among Australians again.

(The Germans themselves will judge the defence they offered of Pear Trench admirable, and its loss understandable, with the Official History of the 13th Regiment noting: 'The *sich tapfer wehrenden*, bravely-defending-themselves front-line companies – its *Mannschaftsbestand*, manpower, greatly diminished by the *Grippe*, influenza, which had been prevalent for a few days – were *von der Übermacht nach heftigem Kampfe überrannt*, overrun by the superior strength after a violent battle.'[51])

With this key part of the battle over, and Pear Trench secured – now protecting the flanks of their brethren out to the right – Dalziel is warmly congratulated by his surviving officer, Lieutenant Jack Hynes, for his astonishing bravery. As Hynes has known Dalziel since Cairns days, he is not surprised at his feat, but with one look at the blood pouring from the stub of his finger, the Lieutenant is quick to order Two Guns to go to the rear to seek medical attention.

Those who secure Pear Trench, particularly the Americans who have not seen war close up before, are amazed by what they see.

'A great many Germans were killed at this point,' Captain George Mallon of the 132nd Infantry, would recount. 'I counted forty in a very small sector.'[52]

Indeed, Private James Shearer, an Australian stretcher-bearer, arrives soon afterwards, and cannot help but be horrified at 'Pear Trench, where the white chalk trenches were stained with blood'.[53]

Quickly, he gets to work, doing what he can to help the doctors save as many soldiers as they can, including Germans. Some, of course, are beyond help, and among the dead Shearer recognises fine men such as 'Potts, Elliot and Williams, and other Queenslanders whom we had reason to admire and respect, [who] had fallen in action and were laid to rest on the battlefield where the poppies had bloomed this morning . . .'[54]

But what now?

Two of the Army doctors are having a dispute, with the senior man, the Australian Doctor Major Basil Kennedy – a 28-year-old former Resident Medical Officer at Sydney Hospital, who'd learnt battle medicine at no less than Gallipoli – glancing down to see, amid all the carnage, the blood and guts, the American doctor, Lieutenant Schramm, busily jotting down notes with a very fine fountain pen.

'What the hell are you doing with that bloody pen?' Dr Kennedy bellows to the American medico.

'Guess I'm making out my diagnosis chart!' drawls the well-trained Schramm, who had been taught to do exactly that by his Director of Medical Services, back in Chicago, noting down all casualties and their wounds in his casebook.

'Chuck the bloody book away,' snaps Kennedy.

'So,' the 15th Battalion History will read, 'Schramm scrapped it and set to work to give immediate attention to the wounded, minus the red tape.'[55]

In this man's Army, it is not just the soldiers who are learning how the war works.

(And in this particular trench, the relationship between the Australians and Americans can be a little fraught. As the 15th Battalion History records, the distinguishing feature of stretcher-bearers is white armlets, and when a hard-worked stretcher-bearer by the name of Private Edward Moles – a hard-bitten miner from Tassie, already decorated with the Military Medal for his bravery at Pozières, for rescuing the wounded under fire – spies a fellow stretcher-bearer doing three-fifths and maybe four-fifths of bugger all bar wandering around uselessly, despite the carnage all around, he asks him for some help. When he is ignored, Moles bursts into 'a stream of blasphemy' that would peel paint, if there were any. 'Then Moles discovered the American was not a stretcher-bearer but an officer with a wounded arm whose white band was a bandage staying haemorrhage.'[56]

(Oh. Oh, dear. Yes, Sir. Sorry, Sir. As you were, Sir. Three bags full, Sir.)

In the meantime, one fellow who takes Private Shearer's attention, as Doc Kennedy treats him, is a brave young fellow, bearing two pistols, who is bleeding badly from one hand – and who the stretcher-bearer recognises from the last big scrap the Battalion had been in – it is Two Guns!

'A young lad of our company,' he would recount, 'who we had carried in at Passchendaele seven months before with a fractured leg, and who had just rejoined the unit . . . is worthy of comment . . . Although badly wounded in the hand at Pear Trench he would not go back [to safety] after it had been dressed, but gallantly carried on.'[57]

For yes, although Two Guns Harry has appeared to obey orders and momentarily disappeared from the Captain's sight, only shortly afterwards he resumes his position as No. 2 on the Lewis Gun, with his mate, his only concession to sanity being to have a rag tied around the dressing Doc Kennedy had applied to his hand, in a further attempt to stem the flow.

'I'm proud to be a comrade of Harry Dalziel,' one soldier would later say, 'one of the best and bravest in H.M's uniform.'[58]

And of course Two Guns is soon back in it with the best of them, intent on carrying on, as he and the others prepare to push forward . . .

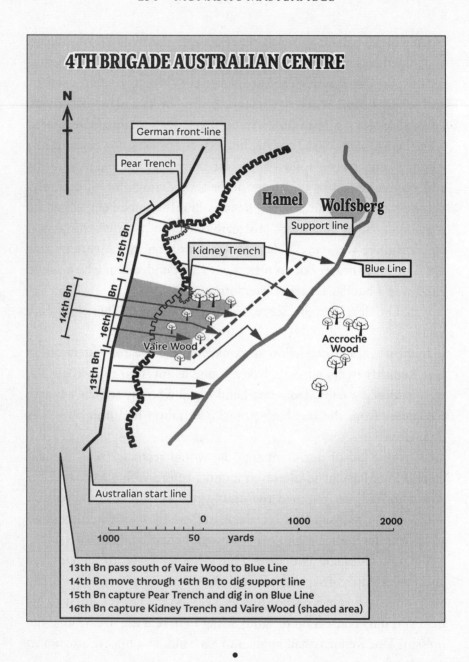

4TH BRIGADE AUSTRALIAN CENTRE

N

German front-line

Pear Trench

Hamel

Wolfsberg

Support line

Kidney Trench

Blue Line

15th Bn

14th Bn

Bn

16th

Vaire Wood

Accroche
Wood

13th Bn

Australian start line

0   1000   2000

1000   50   yards

13th Bn pass south of Vaire Wood to Blue Line
14th Bn move through 16th Bn to dig support line
15th Bn capture Pear Trench and dig in on Blue Line
16th Bn capture Kidney Trench and Vaire Wood (shaded area)

•

Over to the right, some 500 yards to the south and at much the same time as Two Guns has been performing his heroics, the 16th Battalion – despite still also lacking their tanks – are making their own good progress behind the creeping barrage towards Kidney Trench, while dealing with problems of their own. For, here, too, the creeping barrage has left the enemy wire substantially intact, and the only way through is to send scouts forward to cut it under covering fire. This accomplished, more or less, they go forward – when it happens.

Some 50 yards to their front, a heavy machine gun, positioned somewhere in Kidney Trench, suddenly opens up, cutting a swathe right through them, killing the commander of D Company, Captain Frederick Woods, and his Company Sergeant, Major Harold Blinman, outright, mortally wounding Second Lieutenant Horace Blee, and wiping out an entire Lewis Gun team in its first salvo, before all those behind immediately throw themselves to ground to seek cover.

In fact, it is only *nearly* all those behind who seek cover.

For Corporal Jack Axford is just one of those blokes . . .

Line up 20 soldiers and pick one who is going do a bit of derring-do that would turn your hair? No-one would pick Jack – with the possible exception of his best mate and platoon commander, Lieutenant James Minchin, who has seen him in action before. Generally, Jack is quiet. He is just an average bloke, of average strength, and average size. Unlike Two Guns, he is never the centre of attention, never the one in the corner telling war stories, never one you particularly notice at all . . . until the stink starts. And *then* watch Jack go!

He's been doing this caper since the brutal days of Pozières onwards, and has already a Military Medal to his credit for bravery under fire in the 16th Battalion action which had stopped the German offensive at Hébuterne, three months earlier. He always fires up when under fire, and here is a case in point. For no sooner has Captain Woods gone down, than Corporal Axford is up, and *running*, heading off on an act that one of his fellow soldiers will describe as 'the bravest thing I ever saw any man do'.[59]

Running fast, dodging, weaving, up and down, making himself as difficult a target as he can, lest the next lethal burst from Kidney Trench cut him in two. And seeing him go, it's not that his mates join him in his suicidal rush, but they at least bring their weapons to bear, trying to keep fire on Kidney Trench that won't also take Jack down.

Fifty yards to go now, 40 yards . . . in range!

Reaching into his pockets, Jack Axford takes a grenade in hand, removes the pin, and hurls it forth, straight in over the stumps, straight where the German machine-gun crew can be found. For good measure he keeps going, 'flinging bomb after bomb in front of him as he ran'.[60] There are explosions, and screams, and cries for mercy of '*Kamerad!*' but by now Jack Axford is a whirling dervish of bayonet blades, slashing, thrusting, twisting, again and again and again, and, as described once more by his fellow soldier, though there are 16 Squareheads in the trench, 'the Germans for all their numbers could not kill this mad Australian'.[61]

Some 50 yards to the rear, the platoon remains, shocked at how quickly everything has happened. They have seen Jack run, heard the explosions and heard the screams. And there is no doubt the machine gun has stopped firing. But what now?

Suddenly, up and over the parapet, comes two Maxim machine guns, Jack's indisputable signal that it is now safe, followed by 'a helmet of a familiar shape'[62] coming up over the parapet, and his voice calling for them to 'Come on!'[63] and 'The Germans are all dead!'[64] And so they do, come on, tentatively at first, and then with more confidence.

By the time they look over the top of Kidney Trench, there is Jack all right, with no fewer than ten dead German soldiers, together with half-a-dozen terrified prisoners – scarcely believing they can still be alive, and infinitely relieved to be released from this *verrückten Mörder*, murderous madman.

For his part Jack Axford simply rejoins the platoon, and proceeds with the rest of the operation, as if nothing has happened.

(It is, in fact, an event he will rarely speak of afterwards, allowing only that, 'I must have been mad.'[65])

Meanwhile, not far away from Axford at the time of his heroics, his mate, Private Charlie Hubbard – the much admired oldest man in the Battalion, at 64 – takes two bullets, one to the back, and one to the neck, and goes down hard. He is still alive, but only just . . .

•

The very instant the defenders of the Eureka Stockade realised they were under attack from the British Red-coats, the first action from the rebels' leader Peter Lalor was to roar, 'California Rangers to the front!'[66] It was a call for the few battle-hardened men among them, about 20 Americans who had fought in the Mexican War of 1848, to lead the way.

Now, some 70 years later, things have changed.

This time the Australians and Americans are on the same side of the battle as the British, and it is the Americans who are looking to the battle-hardened Australians to take the lead. Ah, but the Americans will not be far behind for all that, and even then, not for long.

The situation of the 43rd Battalion, with the survivors of its American attachment of Company E of the 131st Regiment, which had been hit by drop-shorts, is a case in point. With the aid of their Americans and their tanks – who have at last arrived – A Company are overcoming some determined resistance to take Notamel Wood, the small wood just on the northern edge of Hamel. At first, in the darkness and heavy smoke, it had been difficult to even see the woods, but soon enough the flashes from the exploding shells had illuminated the tops of the trees, and they had pushed on from there, quickly coming under heavy fire from the German defenders, and returning it in kind. In this sort of battle, the tanks, as it turns out, are worth their weight in gold – no small thing, given that they weigh no less than 29 tons!

At one point, when a German machine gun off to the right, on the edge of the village, opens up on them, an A Company Sergeant is quick to scramble towards the rear of a tank and, yes, pull the rope at the back, which rings the bell.

'Yes?'

A tiny hatch at the back of the tank opens.

The Sergeant points to the machine gun, and asks them to deal with it. And, sure enough, before their very eyes, the hatch closes, the tank engine roars as it turns on its tracks, and charges at an extraordinary five miles per hour straight towards the troublesome gun, as the men cheer!

For, as one contemporary account would note, the tank 'went straight over and rubbed it out'.[67] The woods are soon theirs!

With that mission accomplished, A Company now sends patrols south into Hamel itself, to meet up with the men of B Company as it moves through, down the main street from the west. In the meantime C Company, which has been without tanks, is now, nevertheless, moving into Hamel from the south, eager in turn to join up with A and B Companies – who are working hard to dislodge those Germans dug into deep cellars, having the benefit of the shattered homes for shelter.

As C Company make their way across the fields to the now burning village of Hamel, it is to the accompaniment of the continuing roar of the barrage now moving to the east, the chatter of machine guns, the explosions of grenades – and the billowing smoke coming from the many burning buildings the barrage has left behind makes breathing difficult. The situation is more than dangerous, as they are still without tanks, and there is still no time for Harry to tarry, let alone Tom or Dick to stick around. Still, whatever happens, it has been drilled into them, they must keep to the schedule – and so they push on.

And now it happens. C Company suddenly come under heavy machine-gun fire, with Lieutenant Frank Brook killed instantly, and many other men badly hit. Everyone throws themselves to the ground, but two men don't stay longer than a few seconds.

At this point, the Tasmanian Lewis gunner of the 43rd Battalion's C Company, Corporal Frank Shaw, and the US 131st Regiment's Corporal Henry Zyburt from Chicago don't know each other at all, and have been propelled to be together at this place and this time by entirely different forces. Frank is quiet and softly spoken, a devout Christian who believes it is *duty* to fight for his country and his God against the forces of evil. Henry just *likes* fighting, always has, and has joined up because there'll clearly, in his lifetime, never be a bigger fight than this one.

As the German machine gun keeps chattering, Shaw is aware that the whole mission to take Hamel hangs in the balance. They need to shut down that machine gun and quickly, or fail. And with no tanks, they will have to do it themselves.

So where is it?

Scanning the ground ahead in the still dim light of dawn, Frank suddenly sees flashes – like angry fireflies – about 200 yards away, and a set of dim figures just barely silhouetted behind it. *There they are.* They are a dozen Germans, firing from just atop a bank upon the advancing lines of Australians and Americans.

Moving fast with a Lewis Gun on your hip is not easy, but needs must, and the Australian is up to the task. As Charles Bean will later note in his personal diary, 'Shaw went straight at it.'[68]

For he is up with the gun in a moment, and running hard, followed just an instant later by Henry Zyburt. Either man advancing on his own would likely have been slaughtered, as all fire would be directed on just one of them. But as Zyburt is careful to move away from the line of fire on Shaw – just as he had been advised – it means the fusillade on both men is cut by half. And when, within 100 yards of the Germans, Shaw opens fire with his Lewis Gun, all the Germans take cover, even as Zyburt races close enough to start hurling grenades.

So lost in the moment is Shaw, so powerful, he is able to keep up a relatively steady stream of fire, changing magazines several times until one bullet actually hits the Hun machine gun and destroys its firing mechanism.

The silence of this 'shot' German machine gun allows the charging Zyburt to rush past Frank, jumping into the trench to get at the remaining Germans and using his bayonet in a frenzy of fury to slash and stab the three Squareheads who are too petrified to run away. An instant later Frank Shaw is there too, spraying the Germans with his Lewis Gun.

The whole thing has happened so fast, the odds against survival, let alone success, so staggering, no-one can quite believe it, but when the rest of the platoon gets to the silenced machine gun it is to find the Australian and American, real brothers in arms, surrounded by the dead and dying.

An astonished American officer, Captain Carroll Gale, reports, 'The enemy gun was found with bullet holes through the casing'[69] and Corporal Frank Shaw has 'proved the value of a Lewis Gun in the hands of a brave and determined man'.[70]

Thanks to Corporal Shaw and Corporal Zyburt – not forgetting Mr Lewis – there are six Germans dead at the machine-gun post, two are dead just in front of it and four have fled.

'My God!' Zyburt says to the latecomers, 'I've just bayonetted three men!'[71]

Later Lieutenant James Luke, Zyburt's platoon commander, would note, 'Our men were timid at first in using the bayonet, but after they once drew blood it did not bother them in the least.'[72]

•

And so it goes. Behind the creeping barrage, lifting 100 yards every three minutes, the Australians and Americans continue to push forward across the line. Meanwhile, the billowing smoke from the exploding shells, and the dust kicked up, combines to cover the entire battlefield in a 'fog of war' that not even Clausewitz could have conceived. While Charles Bean notices the black cloud spreading, from which bursts of fire emerge – rather like an upside-down storm-cloud emitting lightning and thunder – for those in the middle of it, visibility is down to just ten yards or so, with the barrage line appearing at first as a throbbing glow, and then nothing, as the fog gets thicker still! Still the men press on, the best they can, judging where the barrage line is both by the sound of the explosions, and from where they can see the shrapnel shells bursting above the fog. Into chaos, led by the memory and hope of a master plan.

CHAPTER NINE

FRITZ FLEES

The greatest individual fighter in the war was the Australian.[1]

Marshal Foch, in 1919

The success of the [Hamel] operation was due to the fine leadership of platoon commanders and the superb dash and daring of the men themselves who dealt with any situation that presented itself on their own initiative. The gallantry displayed both individually and collectively was quite up to the Australian standard.[2]

Colonel Terence Patrick McSharry,
Commanding Officer 15th Battalion AIF

As individual fighters they [the Australians] were superb. Their initiative, vigour and bodily strength enabled them to surprise, wear out, or overpower the foe in almost every encounter.[3]

Un-named American officer, after the Battle of Hamel

North of the Somme, the German soldiers of the 227th Regiment's 1st Battalion – opposite Brigadier Pompey Elliott's forces just south of the Ancre River – are as alarmed as they are exhausted, which is no small thing. For only just after settling down to sleep, as their Official History will record, 'a strong *Trommelfeuer*, drumfire broke out towards the morning'.[4]

Their brother regiments flanking them, the 52nd and 203rd Reserve Infantry Regiments are in the same position. Obviously, they are under some kind of attack, but in their positions here north of the Somme, it is only unclear what kind of attack it is. Artillery only? A raid? Or a full-blown assault? Gripping their Mauser rifles, their *Maschinengewehr*

08 machine guns, they peer into the darkness, towards the Australian lines, straining to see something, anything, to give them a clue.

•

For these specially designated Australian soldiers of the 15th Brigade, it is time.

Exactly as planned, 25 soldiers of the 55th Battalion, under the command of Lieutenant William Campbell – a 30-year-old one-time stockman from north of Tamworth – dug into their trenches at Sailly-Laurette, first start showing bayonets above their trenches, and then they start shouting orders and blowing whistles before . . .

Before they start waving about the 15 *papier-mâché* dummies they have been making over the last few days. Each dummy is dressed in an Australian uniform, has a rifle slung over its shoulder and a helmet cocked a little to the side, just as the Aussies are oft wont to do. And now look!

For the Germans opposite, straining to see in the darkness, there is now no doubt: *Der Tommy greift an!* Tommy is attacking!

From the Australian point of view, the response is wonderful. For no more than ten seconds after Campbell and his men start shaking their dummies and shouting, a furious fusillade of German machine-gun fire coming from the opposite trenches completely *riddles* their dummies, in horrifying manner. No matter, once a particular dummy has been hit they take it down, run to another part of the trench and hold it up again, whereupon the same thing happens. On the German side, in the gloom, it looks as though they are mowing down dozens of *den Australiern*.

Obviously, to the Germans north of the Somme, the soldiers of the 201st Reserve Infantry Regiment, this is no ordinary trench raid, but a major attack and they urgently despatch a messenger to their Divisional Commander, *Generalmajor* Wilhelm Theodor Knoch at 43rd Division HQ at Bray-Sur-Somme, so advising. It is uncertain if the messenger will get through, but they must try, and there is no other way – as has happened all along the line, the Allied artillery has torn up their cables.

North of the bullet-riddled dummies, near Brick Beacon, a second feint has been organised. Captain Ken Wyllie leads 200 men of the 55th

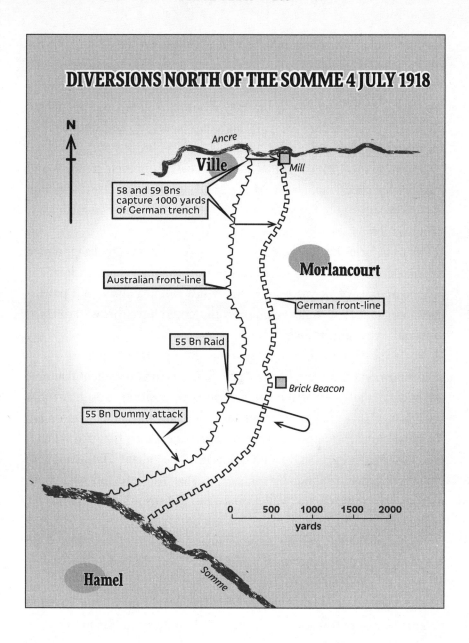

on a raid into the German trenches. Capturing three Germans and two machine guns, they return to the Australian line.

To the left of the 55th Battalion, right tight by the Ancre River, an *actual* attack – using just 400 men drawn from three Companies of the 58th and 59th Battalions – readies itself. First up, though they have no tanks, the traditional barrage – calling on the 72 guns of the whole 5th Division, bolstered by 24 guns from the Australian Corps – unleash brief hell on 1300 yards of the German outposts held by the 52nd and 227th Reserve Infantry Regiments. It is a barrage which the 227th would note, saw, 'Gas, high explosive, fire and smoke shells completely covering the position.'[5]

And now the 400 Australian soldiers burst from their trenches and 'rush with a cheer'[6] across No Man's Land, where they blast to oblivion those few still dazed Squareheads who do *not* surrender immediately, or have already escaped.

For as Charles Bean would recount, the Australians are disappointed to see a good part of 'the Germans ran off through the tall crops'.[7]

'The number of Germans I personally saw running away,' one participant, Sergeant P. W. Eales, would recall, 'could have thrown stones at my small crew and routed them.'[8]

Not a lot of fight from the Germans in this part of the line.

It is only on the far left, by the Ancre River, as the Australians continue advancing, that they strike some serious opposition. For, nearing a mill, some 500 yards forward of their Starting Line, Lieutenants Ivo Thomson and Herbert Willis are bringing their men forward when a German machine gun in the mill opens up. The gallant Thomson, with Corporal Edwin Skinner by his side, rushes forward, only for both men to be cut down and killed. Enraged, Thomson's men charge the mill as one, and a furious melee breaks out.

North of the Ancre, the Australians of the 57th Battalion – who have not been called on for this battle at all – realise what is going on and swim the waters to join in!

Together, thus, with a great deal of bayoneting of the German defenders, the mill is soon in Australian hands, a significant advance.

Lieutenant Willis calls a halt, as the mill had been the obvious limit of their ambitions and it will be for the AIF Companies to their right, the 57th and 58th, to take the trench that leads south from this structure. It does not take those Companies long, and as Captain Arthur Ellis would recount, 'by 3.30 am consolidation [all along the line of the feint] was progressing well'.[9]

Success! No-one is more pleased than Pompey Elliott, who had had carriage of the whole affair from the Australian side.

'My Brigade had only a small part,' Brigadier Elliott would write proudly to his sister-in-law, 'but what they had to do they did magnificently.'[10]

And who can doubt it? Beyond, hopefully, confusing the Germans about where the real point of the Australian spear is directed, pushing the Germans back in this spot protects the northern flank of the real attack, keeping the Germans there so occupied trying to hold them back, they won't be able to attack into the Australian flanks, south of the Somme.

'The boys were splendid, particularly the 58th boys from Geelong under Captain Forbes Dawson,' Brigadier Elliott would write to his wife, Kate. 'We did not know there were three times as many *Boche* in their trenches as we had, but notwithstanding that we hunted them out and killed about 120 of them, captured 17 machine guns and 64 prisoners, whilst the rest bolted like rabbits.'[11]

In fact, some of the said 'rabbits' keep running all the way back to 107th Divisional HQ, where, with eyeballs rolling, they report the horror of what they have faced and that the Australians have launched a major attack just south of the Ancre.

•

Meanwhile the Germans in the support line of the 13th Division, behind Pear Trench, have been unnerved. What is going on, in front of them? Is their own line holding, or are the Tommies coming on? And now they hear it.

'Powerful infantry-fire coming from the front.'[12]

Clearly, the Tommies are in the trenches! But can we hold?

And now, the worst . . .

Not far behind them, Australian infantry '*sichtbar wurde*, became visible, and the combat troop commander knew that his forward companies were overrun'.[13]

Urgently, the commander gives the order for '*Sperrfeuers*, barrage fire!' to come down on the advancing Australians, but there is too little, too late. Most of the German batteries had been destroyed by the Allied artillery, and even those soldiers who have survived had been 'in the process of the change-over'.[14]

Well, if they cannot rely on artillery to stop Tommy, they will have to do it themselves.

And so it is that some 1000 yards back from the now lost Pear Trench – taking shelter in the incomplete support trench that lies there – a German counter-attack is organised from the reserve companies of the 55th Infantry Regiment to try to retake what has been lost.

'On the orders of the *Kampftruppenführer*, Battle-Troop Commander, Captain von Busse, the reserve battalion's two companies, which were subordinated to him, were immediately deployed . . .'[15]

Some 150 men in all, they set off once more to the west, towards Tommy, knowing that what awaits them is bound to be fierce . . .

Under the circumstances, it is an extraordinary thing that there is no revolt from the shattered German soldiers at the very idea of even trying to take back Pear Trench against an enemy that is now surely well dug in, further protected by tanks, but the survivors of the 55th are nothing if not disciplined and the man leading them, *Leutnant* Ball, is no ordinary officer. He has been given an order, he follows it without question and, as is ever his way, he leads from the front.

Which is precisely where *Leutnant* Ball is when the Diggers of the 15th Battalion, to their amazement, see grey-clad figures coming towards them from out of the smoke. In the brief clash that results, the counter-attacking Germans even manage to regain some of the most eastern parts of Pear Trench, before the fire brought upon them is simply overwhelming.

Still undaunted however, *Leutnant* Ball takes matters into his own hands.

'*Der tapfere Führer*, the brave leader, himself,' the 55th Infantry Regiment records, 'found the hero's death when he, *ein leichtes Maschinengewehr ergreifend*, seizing a light machine gun, *seinen Leuten voranstürmte*, stormed ahead of his men.'[16]

Without him, the remaining German soldiers no longer have the stomach for this mad attempt, and retire.

Pear Trench is now firmly in the hands of the 15th Battalion. And yet, leaving just enough men behind to secure it, they must now swarm forward, straining to get to the Halt Line by 3.38 am, where they can reassess as they take stock, before pushing on to the Blue Line, to dig in, by 4.40 am.

For now, still the air is filled with thick, acrid smoke, endless explosions, screams, whistling shrapnel and seemingly unending machine-gun fire.

In it with the best of them, of course, is Two Guns Dalziel, firing, hurling grenades and only ever pausing when, such as now, he and his mates come to nests of Germans – in this case a deep concrete dugout, which proves to hold half a company of German soldiers, about 40 or 50 of them, who, it seems, have had all the fight knocked out of them. For no sooner has Dalziel's No. 1 gunner held his Lewis Gun on his hip and fired down the steps of the concrete dugout, than the Germans troop up, with their hands in the air, shouting in their guttural accents, '*Merci Kamerad*'.[17]

As ever, the Australians strip them of their valuables – hauling in so many beautiful watches that Harry would confess to feeling 'like a war lord',[18] as he piles together his loot and he and the others send their prisoners back under guard, before moving on. Soon enough, the sheer devastation wrought by the barrage in this area back from the German front-lines is apparent, as they find, 'Huns dead in all directions, up in trees, under duck boards, in shell holes . . . everywhere.'[19]

They move on.

•

Out to the left, the retaking of the western half of Hamel village goes on, as the Australian and American soldiers move from house to house, street to street, finding and quelling German resistance – even as the eastern half of the village continues to be pulverised by the barrage. They will get to the surviving Germans there, in due course, after completing this task, and then pausing at the Halt Line.

For now, they keep going . . . with a minimum of ceremony, and a maximum of violence.

For you see, Fritz, this ain't *der milkman* calling.

There is no ringing of any bells, or knocking on any doors. Working their way steadily eastward, instead of knocking, the Australians and

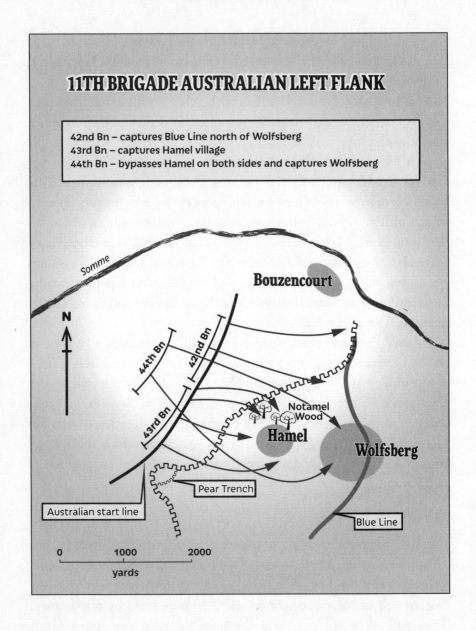

11TH BRIGADE AUSTRALIAN LEFT FLANK

42nd Bn – captures Blue Line north of Wolfsberg
43rd Bn – captures Hamel village
44th Bn – bypasses Hamel on both sides and captures Wolfsberg

Somme

Bouzencourt

N

44th Bn

42nd Bn

43rd Bn

Notamel
Wood

Hamel

Wolfsberg

Pear Trench

Australian start line

Blue Line

0   1000   2000
yards

Americans throw a grenade through the window and then burst through the door and hunt room to room, before looking for the door to the cellar, which, after a swinging boot bursts the door open, cops another grenade bouncing down the stairs.

And now to the next house!

With any signs of resistance, as in a machine gun opening up on them from one of the houses, the most popular member of the platoon, 'Mr Lewis', is sent forward to do some extremely rapid door-knocking, as the soldiers first plaster the door with bursts from their Lewis Gun, then follow this by spraying every window, and throwing in a couple of grenades to ensure that any crazy German bastard inside who still wants to resist will be met with a blizzard of bullets, a storm of splinters and flying glass. Meantime, other members of the platoon charge around the back to throw bombs through the windows there. Such is the Diggers' version of *Guten Morgen*.

Often, extraordinarily, they come across dazed German soldiers still in their gas masks who, deep in their dugouts, had not even realised they were under attack until grenades had blown down their cellar doors. Whatever else, it is clear that General Monash's plan of doing everything to keep the Germans in the dark had worked, and the 43rd Battalion history will note 'surprise' as 'the most outstanding feature'[20] of the attack.

Still, there remains a great deal of dangerous work to do, as the Australians keep moving from street to street, quelling resistance as they go. Few soldiers are more in the thick of the action than 'Mad Danny', the one who'd delighted in frightening the Yanks by tossing grenades high in the air, just an instant before they were to explode. Now that the real battle is on, he seems an unstoppable force, hurling his grenades, firing his rifle and slashing with his bayonet to such effect that he 'managed to capture three machine guns single handed',[21] only to prove stoppable after all, as he falls, finally, fatally wounded at the hands of a German soldier.

One particular American platoon, under the command of Lieutenant Ivor Symons, formerly a high school teacher of Trewville, South Australia, boasting 40 Americans of the 131st Regiment, is also in the thick of it, from the first, with the men of the 43rd's B Company.

In a part of the village where the farmland laps right to the shores of *les habitations* and has spilled a little over the side, a flare suddenly rises from a spot behind a large pile of beets, and bursts over the approaching 'Crow-Eaters' of South Australia, even as a withering fusillade of German fire is sent their way. Hurling themselves to the ground, the B Company men can clearly see the forms of the German soldiers silhouetted by the flames of the burning village behind them. Because they are just beyond the range of even the Australians' longest grenade throwers, Lieutenant Symons comes up with another solution.

Indicating to the Americans to follow him, he charges away to his right, on a long loop, designed to bring them in on the German flank. The Americans eagerly follow, flitting forms of fury in declining darkness, knowing only that the Australian Lieutenant seems to know what he is doing and their own baptism of battle is truly about to begin and . . .

And *now!* The Germans never know what hit them. One moment they are firing on soldiers they think they have pinned down to the west. The next, they are engulfed by a posse of soldiers from the south, firing from the hip and hurling grenades their way, which exact a devastating toll.

Lieutenant Symons and his American platoon soon kill 15 Germans while capturing another 40 . . . before Symons, a married father of two . . . falls . . . gravely wounded.

Who can take command of the platoon, with the inexperienced Americans needing leadership now more than ever? There is no time for any ceremony.

But the man suddenly shouting orders – *Stretcher-bearers! Attend to Lieutenant Symons. Corporal, lay your section down here and give me covering fire when I go down that street. Sergeant, follow me with those two sections!* – is Private David Anderson, a one-time labourer of Broken Hill, just 21 years old, who up until a minute ago had been simply the runner for Lieutenant Symons, charging back and forth with messages. With Symons now out of action, it is Anderson who takes over, and leads the Americans, including men well above him in rank.

It is the Australian way. No matter that he has not been to a fine school, or a military college – Anderson knows for a fact that many privates like him have gone on to be fine officers. Most importantly the battle-wise veteran knows what needs to be done now, so starts giving orders, and the American soldiers, and officers, follow him!

Together they continue to move from house to house up the main street of Hamel, Rue de Villers-Bretonneux, clearing them of Fritzes, door by door, cellar by cellar.

Inevitably they take some casualties, but don't stop, aware that they are just about to reach the Halt Line, and must pause from 3.38 am to 3.51 am.

'By his gallantry,' Private Anderson's later bravery commendation will read, 'he saved a critical situation, and set an excellent example to his American comrades who were under fire for the first time.'[22]

•

With Lance Corporal Jack Axford having knocked out the machine guns of Kidney Trench, his C Company are quick to fan out to secure it and take ever more prisoners. Private Henry Richardson is particularly outstanding with his bag of Mills grenades. A good cricketer, with a notably long and accurate throw, time and again he hurls his grenades at every bit of German resistance he can find, pauses for a moment to allow for the explosion, and times his rush so that he will be there with his bayonet flashing and slashing an instant after he can't be killed by his own grenade. (Bravo, Private Richardson, though the official 16th Battalion History would be firm in its own summation: 'At Kidney Trench, where the Germans fought stoutly, Lance Corporal T. L. Axford's bravery and initiative were responsible for its final capture.'[23])

With that secured, 16th Battalion is able to enter Vaire Wood, pressing forward against the scattered resistance they find there, noting with satisfaction that the German soldiers they encounter are mostly wearing gas masks, which limits their abilities to both aim their rifles and fight with vigour. Clearly, General Monash's ploy to fire a mixture of gas and smoke shells in the fortnight before the battle, to 'train' the Germans into wearing gas masks on this night, has worked here, too.

At the forefront of this sweep through the woods is Lieutenant James Minchin, the great friend of Corporal Jack Axford, who Charles Bean would note is 'formerly a private and once a company cook, but now one of the outstanding leaders of an outstanding battalion'.[24]

And never more outstanding as on this occasion, Minchin – having effectively taken the baton from Axford – leads the 16th Battalion forward through the wood, using the trees for cover, while the tanks, of course, are restricted to advancing along the one useable trail that goes through it alongside a trench, known to them as the 'Huns' Walk'. No, this is a job where the infantry truly come into their own, under Lieutenant Minchin.

'Practically the whole line, riflemen and Lewis gunners,' Bean would chronicle, 'fired from the hip as it advanced [through the wood] driving the fleeing enemy into the barrage.'[25]

In short order, a green flare is seen rising from Vaire Wood – the signal that it has been cleared of Germans. The attacking force has advanced a total of 800 yards from Kidney Trench, which they had so forcefully taken from Fritz.

•

Out to the right, pushing on south of Vaire Wood, the 13th Battalion are going well, and according to plan. As day starts to break, D Company's Cliff Geddes finds himself with some tanks, and some Yanks in the ranks – as, during the attack, they had all got mixed up with each other – continuing to move forward, subduing whatever German resistance they find. Some of that resistance, alas, is all too apparent. For now that the Germans in front are a little better organised, they have even been able to bring some artillery fire to bear, and, as Geddes would recount, 'I then saw the tank in front of me hit with a shell.'[26]

It is the tank of Captain William Edwards, and it has indeed taken a direct hit, smashing into the weakest part of the tank, the spotting tower, where the Australian liaison soldier is peering out.

'Out, out,' Captain Edwards roars, 'everyone out!'[27]

And so they tumble forth, coughing, shaking, spluttering, infinitely relieved to still be alive, after no less than 11 pounds of explosive and metal has detonated just inches from their heads.

All make it out except one – Private Tom Parrish, in the tower, trying to guide the tank forward, has been killed instantly, and will not be returning to Boolaroo, the peaceful burgh up Lake Macquarie way.

Shortly afterwards, another issue arises with one of the tanks, when, as Geddes will describe it, 'a tank came along, & a chap was pulled out of it dead drunk, a tank officer came along with a revolver, & was almost going to shoot him; the officer in charge of the tank this corporal came out of, said "he's not drunk, he's delirious from the shell fumes", but one whiff of his breath told me he was drunk too'.[28]

What to do with a drunk tank crew member in the middle of a battle – particularly when he is now struggling violently and babbling – if *not* shoot him?

Exactly.

Geddes is ordered to 'tie his hands behind his back, and put him in a shell hole'.

This works okay, for the moment, as the difficult and drunken bastard soon falls into a sozzled slumber, but what will happen when he wakes is what worries Geddes.

'We tried to put 3 Fritz prisoners on carrying him back, but he was so heavy & limp from booze the young Fritzies couldn't.'[29]

And so he is left there, as the battle rages on, with the shells screaming, the bullets flying and the aeroplanes flying just 200 feet over their heads to attack enemy infantry, guns and transport.

The 13th Battalion continues to move forward behind the creeping barrage, the Australians and Americans working generally well in tandem, though some Yanks, it must be said, are so eager to get at the Germans, so determined to show that they are every bit as good as the 'Ossies', as they call the Aussies, that in certain cases – amid the dust, and confusion – they actually risk getting too close.

When it happens within coo-ee of Corporal Mick Roach, and he sees the accompanying Americans of Company A of the 132nd Regiment getting too far ahead of themselves, the 22-year-old labourer from the mines up Inverell way bolts forward and risks his life to go out after them, rounding them up like a concerned barking sheepdog, saving a flock that would otherwise be lambs to the slaughter, and bringing them back . . . It is for good reason that Roach is known to everyone as 'one of the gamest of soldiers [in the Battalion]'.[30]

Alas, having succeeded in turning them around, it is only for a shell to explode nearby and engulf him with cruel splinters that catch him all over, but most particularly his back, abdomen, left leg and head.

A stretcher-bearer risks his own life to get to Roach, to find him 'conscious and in a bad way . . .'[31]

But, effectively, Roach waves him away.

'There is no use worrying over me,' he says simply. 'I reckon I'm done.'[32]

The stretcher-bearer ignores his pleas to be left alone, and has him carried back to the Regimental Aid Post regardless . . .

•

And now what?

High atop the ruined remains of one of the tallest houses in Hamel, an Australian officer and decorated veteran of the Boer War, the Commander of D Company of the 43rd Battalion, Captain John Moran, totally ignores the strong possibility of German snipers atop Wolfsberg to precariously climb out on to the skeleton of the shattered house, onto the bare rafters, holding something in his right hand that is trailing behind him.

What on *earth* is he doing?

Bugger me! Look what he has with him!

The thing that he is trailing is a French flag – about a yard by a yard – and in short order he has tied it to 'the ridge pole of the highest house'[33] in the village, to allow it to lightly flap in the dawn breeze.

Let the word go forth. This part of Hamel at least, this side of the Halt Line, is no longer German territory, but *French*!

(Oh. And the South Australian has also won a bet with a mate, made the previous afternoon, saying he would never be able to do it.)

Meantime, one soldier of the 43rd Battalion, Corporal Boyce Schulz, a 25-year-old farmer from Willowie in South Australia, pursues a hunch. In previous days he has been earnestly examining the aerial photos of Hamel and, by comparing earlier photos with more recent ones, had noted what appeared to be a very recently dug, very narrow trench, quickly filled in, leading from Hamel to a spot just outside the village, to its immediate north near a small grove of trees.

Could that be what he thinks it is?

Now finding on the ground what he had previously seen only in photos, he takes two Americans with him who can speak German and carefully follows the trail of freshly turned over dirt to, yes, a 'mole-hole', a dugout! Unless Schulz misses his guess, this will be the dugout for the Battalion HQ of those defending Hamel.

After the Americans shout down the stairs in German, advising that Hamel has fallen, their comrades have surrendered and those downstairs better do the same – *Schnell! Schnell! Schnell!* – or have grenades thrown down upon them, it does not take long. In short order, a German Major comes up the stairs, his hands in the air, immediately followed by three other officers and 23 soldiers of other ranks. Schulz keeps his revolver trained on them all, the best he can, and starts to take them back to behind Allied lines.

SCHNELL! Once they have been taken in hand by other Australian soldiers, Schulz returns to the Battalion HQ, to search for documents that might give further clues as to German plans, and strengths.

All up, no fewer than 350 prisoners are taken from Hamel alone, together with no fewer than 25 machine guns.

A little further to the left, the men of 42nd Battalion continue to push between the southern banks of the Somme and the village of Hamel, as the tanks wreak havoc on the German defences, and the infantry mop up effectively.

Out to the far right, meantime, back on the newly advanced Australian front-line by the Roman Road, the most urgent task for the men of the 23rd Battalion is to make sure there remain no pockets of resistance further down the German trench they have just taken. Private Betteridge carefully makes his way along the trench with the others.

'The trench we were in was a regular shambles,' he chronicles. 'The sides in dozens of places splattered with wet blood. Dead men lying everywhere.'[34]

Inevitably, there are also some Huns who are not so dead. Yet.

For now, in a dugout, they find a shattered German soldier, 'a poor scared creature that whined and cried like a kiddie afraid of the dark. Our officer called for him to come out. The whining continued, to be cut short by a shot. Hope his conscience don't worry him later.'[35]

No time for that now. With the trench now theirs they must continue to move forward to capture more ground, until they can establish themselves on the Blue Line.

•

Just a few hundred yards to the east of the 23rd Battalion, the 1st Battalion of Germany's 15th Reserve Infantry Regiment have been standing by in their support trenches right by the *Römerstraße*, Roman Road.

They had been awoken by the barrage, been appalled by the sheets of flame and explosions landing on the front-line, where their brothers of the 2nd Battalion 15 RIR lay, and steeled themselves as the creeping barrage had approached and then passed over them, like a thunderstorm from hell. Those who have survived now brace themselves, knowing only too well that Tommy cannot be far away.

•

It is 3.38 am – for the next 13 minutes the creeping barrage will pause, pounding its current band only, allowing the troops to get to their Halt Line and the second wave to move through them.

Charles Bean is watching closely.

'Hamel burning very brightly,' he scrawls in his notebook, '+ we cd see the Germs in the light of it.'[36]

•

Along the line now, most of the attacking forces reach the Halt Line on time at 3.38 am and pause, as the creeping barrage stops creeping and simply drops an unmoving curtain of hell to protect them from any counter-attacks.

On cue, at 3.51 am, the barrage once again moves forward. Monash's machinery of war starts rolling again, with the second wave passing through the first, ready to take it from here. In the case of the 44th Battalion, their job is to do much the same as, three months earlier, the 13th and 15th Brigades had done when they had been instrumental in taking back Villers-Bretonneux from the Germans by splitting to either side of the village and meeting beyond it on the Roman Road. In this case the 44th Battalion splits in two to skirt either side of Hamel village, with the intention of meeting at the foot of Wolfsberg on the far side.

So too, with Lieutenant Edgar Rule and his men of 14th Battalion, part of the second wave, who now begin to move into position to take over.

It had been, and no doubt about it, a bit *how's-your-father* getting across what had been No Man's Land when the still mostly intact German artillery had been plastering it. But through the explosions, the smoke, the whistling of shells, the scything shrapnel and the distant screams, the men of Rule's platoon had charged forward to reach the safety of the old German line, and tumble into it, breathless but relieved – and certainly in better shape than the many dead and dying German soldiers all around, who have been devastated by first the barrage and then the ministrations of the first wave. The main thing is, the Australians had made it through No Man's Land.

Lifting his head above the parapet, Rule glances ahead to see a world completely lit by 'bursting shell, and phosphorus smoke shells, like the sun shining through a thunder cloud, which lit up places like day, and across these bright patches could be seen our tanks waddling along, keeping up to the barrage . . . We could see our boys in the front wave, and it was a very weird sight.'[37]

Steeling themselves to leave the safety of their trench, Rule and his men were soon up and moving once more, settling to a line about 60 yards behind the first wave. The best he can, Rule keeps his men spread out and they continue, passing through the 16th. Their task is to keep moving forward to a point 300 yards short of the Blue Line dealing with any stray nests of Germans as they go, and then *dig in*, Diggers. To their right, their immediate south, Cliff Geddes and D Company of the 13th are doing much the same. They also must dig a support line behind A, B and C Companies of their Battalion, who are going all the way to the Blue Line.

Cliff looks out for his brother Boo, knowing he must be with B Company somewhere up ahead, but can't spot him. If only, if only he could go forward with them, he would be a much better chance of being there and could do his bit to make sure Boo is okay, but there is nothing for it. He remains, as ordered, well back from the Halt Line, suddenly sick at heart.

•

Not far away, but obscured by the smoke, and the sheer numbers of his comrades, Aubrey 'Boo' Geddes pushes on with the rest of B Company, eager to get to the Blue Line, which lies just 300 yards short of Accroche Wood, which is still reckoned to be held by the Germans.

Sure enough, they are not quite yet to their ordered destination, when they come under heavy fire from at least three machine guns. One of the guns is taken out by an heroic charge by A Company's Captain George Marper, while the other two are more problematic, as they are in a trench that had been so well camouflaged, and protected, that not only had it survived the barrage, but previous aerial reconnaissance had missed it, meaning no-one in the 13th Battalion had had any idea it was there.

It is time for one of the 13th's magnificent tanks to come to the fore, and so it does, aided now by the irrepressible Captain Marper, who risks his life to run in front of the tank to show exactly where the machine guns are – receiving two bullets for his trouble, one through the chest and the other through the arm. He is dragged out of the way, and the tank takes full revenge and wipes out the offending machine gun by crushing its operators, prompting the crew of the second one to surrender.

Still, Captain Marper, partially recovered, keeps going, and guides the rest of the 13th Battalion to the Blue Line, where they – with Boo Geddes among them – are able to dig in, as planned, across a front of 1200 yards, with the 15th Battalion on their left, and the 21st Battalion on their right.

•

At the Cappy-on-the-Somme HQ of the German XI Corps on this night, things had started out normally for those whose task it is to monitor the situation on the front-lines, just ten miles to the west. As ever, *die Englände* had done some bombing just after dusk, without doing any real damage, and that bombing had continued throughout the night.

Then, *auch wie gewöhnlich*, also as per usual, harassing fire had begun at around 3 am, and shortly thereafter, there were scattered reports of a barrage coming down on them, across a front of 13,000 yards – from the Ancre River in the north to south of the Roman Road. And then, nothing. Either this was because the barrage was so powerful it had destroyed all the communication cables, or there was some other technical reason – as sometimes happened – but what could they do meantime? They had to wait for some word to get through from the front-lines before they could react.

And now, *guter Gott*, while there remains a black-out of communication from some areas, from a few other areas some rather more urgent reports are flooding in.

With the telephone lines from their front to the rear all shattered by the barrage, the German 13th Division – holding the line from the Roman Road to south of Hamel village – have sent runners back, saying they are under major attack. The 43rd Division, which is defending Hamel village and to the Somme and then 1000 yards the other side, reports the same, via equally terrified runners counting themselves lucky to have made it back alive through all the explosions.

Finally, the 107th Division, defending from the crest of Morlancourt ridge north down to the bogs beside the Ancre, reports similar attacks. Of course there is no *detail*, just a general alarm that they are under attack across a wide front.

But how wide? The Commander of XI Corps, *Generalmajor* Viktor Kuhne, processes all the reports and makes his way to a decision. Put together with the just received accounts of another terrifying attack, launched at Sailly-Laurette and this time mercifully stopped by the brave German soldiers, it looks very grim indeed.

Clearly, they are under attack, all the way from the Roman Road at Villers-Bretonneux, across the Somme to the Ancre! Such reserves as are available, thus, must be sent forward across that span of 13,000 yards under presumed attack (rather than the 6500 yards under *actual* attack).

If Kuhne's moves at this time are not his most sage, there is good reason for it. Nothing if not experienced at 61 years old – an accomplished graduate of the Prussian Military Academy, a highly regarded artillery specialist and worthy leader of the 13th, 43rd and

107th Divisions making up his Corps – in the last two hours he has suffered the unprecedented and calamitous indignity of having all but his entire Corps' artillery knocked out. Somehow, the enemy has not only managed to move his own heavy artillery forward without anyone on the German side being aware of it, but has also been able to pinpoint where their heavy batteries were, and knock them out all at once! Kuhne has never seen anything like it, never felt so militarily impotent with much to do but nothing to do it *with*.

Close to the front-lines, of course – in the German support lines, just 500 yards back from the front-lines – there is even more confusion, and alarm.

One sign of how appalling the situation must be is that no-one is coming back from the front-lines to tell HQ what has happened – no fleeing soldiers, no runners, no nothing. And even when they send patrols forward to find out, the patrols don't come back.

Worse still? A curtain of death is heading their way, as the creeping barrage inexorably approaches, a thunderstorm of hell, 6000 yards wide, that will take a good 30 minutes to pass over – not that all of them will be alive to experience it, let alone steel themselves for the wild infantry assault that must inevitably follow it.

•

Back at Sinclair-Maclagan's 4th Division HQ at Bussy-les-Daours, their own reports come in, in a much more controlled and certainly less panicked manner. For this battle General Monash has insisted that communications be a top priority and, as such, beyond the usual telephone cables that have been snaking forward with the front-line troops, there have also been radios, together with runners and rocket signals indicating position and – in a wonderful example of a harnessing of the natural world to aid with state-of-the-art modernity – slots have regularly been opening in the side of the tanks to release pigeons, which have small messages tied to their legs. Meanwhile, other signallers are, even now – exactly as planned – making their way forward with telephone wires, laying them out in newly captured territory, so that, as soon as possible, instant communications will be available to those in the front-lines.

•

As soon as the Diggers of the 43rd Battalion and their accompanying Yanks see the barrage underway again, as the 'curtain of death' moves off the eastern half of Hamel, they move forward to clear the rest of the village. Alas, it becomes apparent, that the fact that the barrage has been resting on recalcitrant Germans for no less than 13 minutes has done nothing to take the fight out of Fritz.

Many of the German soldiers have stayed secure in their cellars – with the shells doing little more than bouncing the rubble above – one German machine gun, in particular, is soon firing heavily on the advancing 43rd.

Once again, astonishingly, it is Corporal Frank Shaw who sees it first and charges. Once lucky. Why not twice? For the second time Shaw fires from the hip with his Lewis Gun and when his last magazine is spent, he throws the Lewis Gun down, and *still* keeps firing, this time with his revolver.

The Germans watch him coming, stunned.

Who is this madman, and how can he be stopped? A brave German officer attempts to answer the second question by leaping out himself and running towards Frank, firing with his own revolver but . . . missing. With his sixth and final shot, Frank Shaw kills the German officer, only to see a German soldier just behind him. No matter, Shaw turns his revolver into a hammer by gripping it by the barrel, swinging his arm up and uses it to club the advancing soldier in the throat. 'Shaw . . .' as Bean will note in his diary, 'hit him over the head with the butt end of the revolver [and] then shot him.'[38] Eight Germans are found dead in the trench around the machine gun. All shot dead by Frank. It is the second incredible feat that Frank Shaw has managed in one day, or rather in one half-hour. It is simply amazing.

•

At last!

At last, right in the middle of the Australian attack, as the 15th Battalion moves forward from Pear Trench – after resting for 13 minutes on the Halt Line – they are joined by the tanks! Gawd knows where they've been for the last 40 minutes or so, but the main thing is they are here now.

Truly, Captain Cyril Scott with the three tanks of the 8th Tank Battalion's A Company is likely nearly as relieved as the soldiers are, having endured a nightmare hour of being lost, having veered left, gone too far, and then, after realising his error, doubling back to find the Battalion again. More than eager to make up for lost time, he and his tank, at least, set to with a will, helping the 15th Battalion move towards the Blue Line.

'One tank was put out of action,' the 15th Battalion War Diary records, 'and another was not very keen, but the third tank made up for the other two and was gallantly handled which saved us a great number of casualties . . .'[39]

For now, look at Captain Scott's tank go! It sallies forth, it fires, it swerves to take out a pod of German soldiers in a trench, it swings out to the right, where a German machine gun is firing from an outpost, which it crushes and then pirouettes on for good measure, and then it moves on!

With its help, the men of the 15th are not long in coming to the spot on the landscape that marks the Blue Line on their map, and begin to dig in, with Two Guns Dalziel still among them, quickly setting up, by filling the empty sandbags he had strapped around his legs with dirt, and setting them up as a wall in front of his carefully positioned Lewis Gun before settling down to fire short bursts at every German soldier he can. They are about 300 yards away, running from one broken-down trench into another, and he is able to bring many of them down, until . . . his ammunition runs out.[40]

Recalling the pile of ammo that had been dropped by one of the tanks some 250 yards back, Dalziel heads back to get more magazines, and though at one point he has to crawl on his hands and knees to escape German fire that is sweeping the ground he is covering, he makes it, grabs the first box he sees and starts to make his way back. It is, for all that, hell on earth as shells start to explode all around. The shells include a massive 'whizz-bang', so-called by the Diggers because they announce their arrival with a *whizzz*, followed by, yes, a bang. Even more troubling is when a '5.9', an even bigger shell, explodes, sending some shrapnel close to Dalziel's groin, but mercifully – *thank you, Lord!* – doing no damage.

And it is even no matter that one of the explosions knocks him off his feet and into a shell-hole full of water. They make 'em tough in Ragged Camp, and Dalziel is soon underway once more, crawling forward while dragging the ammunition box with his belt! He keeps going until, exhausted, he finally arrives back at the machine gun and collapses.

•

It is extraordinary. Marvellous. *Inspiring!*

For those soldiers far enough back – like the 11th Brigade Reserve, the 41st Battalion, the receding barrage allows them their first clear view of the battlefield, even as the first true light of day starts to reveal it.

'It was a truly wonderful sight,' the 41st Battalion history will record, 'watching the tanks creeping over the ground through the grey mists of dawn, and the long line of flashing shell-bursts as the barrage lifted and lengthened, while the colossal din of the whole titanic combat smote upon the ears and set the heart palpitating with awe and tense excitement.'[41]

•

In that growing light, Charles Bean also begins to see more and more things starting to emerge from the gloom, even in the shadow of death in the valley below, shapes appearing, forms appearing.

'We could see the dark trees around Hamel and the Bois de Vaire up the hill slope south of it,' he would report to Australian newspaper readers. 'A house in Hamel was burning fiercely, the black frameworks of rafters against the flares. Then the skyline began to grow clear. It was not the real skyline. But the smoke shell in the valley beyond our advance so obliterated the rest of the scenery that every onlooker thought it was.'[42]

With Hamel now back in Allied hands, the task for the 44th is to take Wolfsberg, the hill directly behind Hamel which has proven so troublesome. It is 4.15 am.

•

As the 23rd Battalion breaks free from their own Halt Line out on the far right, it is with Monash's 'machinery of war' in full play, helping them.

In the increasing light now, the men of the 23rd take joy in watching 'a tank out front like a rhinoceros in a fit, cleaning out posts. The planes swooping down to 10 feet off the ground firing on masses of Huns in retreat . . . Prisoners kept coming in from the front . . .'[43]

Ahead of them, the men of Germany's 1st Battalion 15th Regiment, positioned in the support line, are appalled, as things go from bad to worse to terrifying: 'Tanks appeared on the *Römerstraße*, Roman Road, and in the terrain north of it.'[44]

It can only mean that those in the German first line, their own 2nd Battalion, have been, indeed, overrun. And now the enemy soldiers are coming for them! What can save them?

Certainly not their own big guns . . .

'Our own artillery shot, despite the order of the *Sperrfeuers*, barrage fire, extremely little because it was just in the process of replacement.'

(Like many other German formations in these trenches, the 15th Infantry Regiment has moved in and settled before their artillery has managed to do the same, and now the Battalion is paying the price for it.)

What to do?

Back at the crossroads, near Warfusee, *Rittmeister Freiherr* von Preuschen is at the centre of a worried knot of officers, together with '*Meldern, Burschen und Nachrichtenpersonal,* messengers, orderlies and communication staff', as he tries to work out what to do.[45]

Yes, it has come to that. With so many soldiers killed, wounded or missing, the orders have gone out for anyone who can hold a gun – pen-pushers at HQ, chief cooks and bottle-washers – to come forward and hold the line. For *Rittmeister Freiherr* von Preuschen, they just might do it. Other officers can be '*Flohfotzen*',[46] flea c—ts, when the bullets start to fly, but not him. He is courageous, well-liked and a natural leader of men. No-one wants to let him down.

Worried, but resolute, these ring-ins now stand shoulder to shoulder with what few soldiers that can be mustered, and man the trenches on the western edge of Accroche Wood, but . . .

But what is that roaring?

For suddenly, from *behind* them, an enemy tank appears! Clearly, it has broken through on their left, and now doubled back to terrorise them.

Mercifully, as their Official History records, '[The] battalion drummer, Vice-Sergeant Schumicki, *kaltblütig, wie er stets war*, cold-blooded, as he always was, let him approach to 30 meters and shot at him with a *Tankgewehr*, tank rifle, whereupon he disappeared.'

For the Germans it is the rough equivalent of having satisfactorily scared off one lion in the jungle, while remaining staked to a post, surrounded by fresh meat.

Still, heartened, the German soldiers of 3rd Company and 1st Company 'jumped onto the embankment', bringing their rifles to bear and taking on the oncoming enemy, '*mit wohlgezieltem Feuer*, with well-aimed fire. Tommy then disappeared in shell holes in the high wheat fields. Also the M.G. nests of the *1. Maschinengewehrkompanie* (*M.G.K.*), 1st Machine-gun Company, had a substantial part in stopping the enemy advance.'[47]

It is *gut*, for the moment, but very likely a mere delaying of disaster.

'Again the English planes, which flew at very low altitude along the *Pionier-Mulde*, Pioneer Hollow, and shot at our positions with M.G., were sensed as *besonders unangenehm*, particularly unpleasant, during the defence.'[48]

Still, valiantly, *Rittmeister Freiherr* von Preuschen and his knot of messengers, orderlies and staff, continue to hold the line, in desperation, against the marauding Tommies, to do everything possible, to defend their position 'and to stop the advance of the Englishmen'.[49]

A long day, it seems very likely, lies ahead.

•

A long day, it seems very likely, lies ahead.

As a veteran of four years standing, Cliff Geddes is more aware than most that his best chance of surviving is not only to dig in, but to dig in *deep*, tearing at the chalky soil as he and his men dig the support trench some 1000 yards back from the Blue Line.

Cliff Geddes is so engaged when he looks up to see a bloke from the 13th Battalion's B Company, who he'd got to know on the troopship the *Euripides* on the way over.

His news is simply expressed. '[Boo's] been hit.'

What????

'When? Where?'

'He's . . . lying in a shell hole . . .'[50]

Boo, *hit*?

Instantly, Cliff is on his way. If his platoon officer and sergeant had been around he may possibly have asked for permission, but, as it is, both of them are wounded so there is no-one to ask. Come to think of it, he doesn't give a hang anyway.

Boo, hit!

All this time, he had been 'wishing . . . I was with the lot pushing ahead whacking the Hun'.[51]

But no, he'd had to stay back, and now Boo, who had gone forward with A Company, has been hit!

•

While the 44th Battalion move along both flanks of Hamel Village, suddenly the 43rd Battalion, finishing off the last of the German resistance in the village itself, come under heavy fire once more, as there proves to be a heavy concentration of German soldiers with three active machine guns dug into the town's quarry.

Once again, it is Corporal Frank Shaw who comes to the fore. While organising for one of the tanks to go after two of the machine guns, he arranges to take out the other one. Ready, men? Firing from the hip, Shaw advances, shooting with such accuracy that the German machine-gunner dare not lift his head until the burst is over. Using that time, Shaw's men are able to complete a looping run of their own, and fall upon the gunner and his crew before they can get firing once more. All up, the Australians are able to capture the gun, and take one German officer and 20 soldiers prisoner.

'Throughout the operation,' the commendation from his superior officer will read, 'Private Shaw showed conspicuous gallantry, dash, and initiative. His coolness and prompt action saved the platoon on three occasions and enabled the advance to be carried out. He showed an utter disregard for personal safety.'[52]

•

Exactly as planned, even as the 42nd on the left and the 15th on the right are approaching the Blue Line, the 44th move up to fill the gap between them. With the sounds of shots, exploding grenades and screams from behind – as the 43rd Battalion close in to mop up the remaining resistance in the village – the 600 men of the 44th, following the tanks, start up Wolfsberg. (Their numbers, of course, include several American soldiers, who are now dressed in the uniforms of Diggers of the 44th, just so they can take part.) If all goes well, the 44th will take the summit, some 800 yards upwards, and then storm down the other side, to dig in on the Blue Line, 200 yards away, the furthest advance for the morning of around 2500 yards.

CHAPTER TEN

HOLDING THE THIN BLUE LINE

The [Germans] fled incontinently . . .[1]

Captain John Hassett, 8th Tank Battalion officer

The battle once commenced went according to plan. The excellent cooperation between all units, the complete surprise of the enemy, the care and skill regarding all details by the staffs, the effective counter-battery work and barrage, and lastly the skill and dash and fine fighting spirit of the infantry and tanks, resulted in a success unparalleled in the history of the Australian infantry or the tank corps.[2]

Captain John Hassett, 8th Tank Battalion officer
[his underlining]

4.30 am, western slopes of Wolfsberg, over to the Western Australians

By now, of course, all element of surprise has gone and the Germans of the 3rd Battalion of the 202nd Reserve Infantry Regiment – dug into what had been the well-constructed trenches of the old Amiens Defence Line, built by the Allies near the top of Wolfsberg – have a clear view of all those coming at them from below in the growing light, allowing them to bring withering fire down the hill.

Under normal circumstances, the men of the 44th Battalion, pinned down and taking terrible punishment, would have no chance. But these are not normal circumstances! They have TANKS, a *dozen* of them. And it is now these tanks that come to the fore, rumbling forth, dodging their own men and taking the lead.

Still watching from the slope above Sailly-le-Sec, Charles Bean, with Keith Murdoch and Gordon Gilmour by his side, is gazing earnestly at where he knows Hamel lies, though despite the growing light he can see little as the valley is covered in a thick shroud caused by the smoke shell. What is going on down there?

And now he sees it. Look there!

It is a thrilling vision.

Above the cloud of smoke, far on yonder hill, Wolfsberg . . .

'It was the very moment when our men should be nearing that hill-top,' Bean would recount. 'There was moving along the top of it a low, grey monster . . . It moved slowly along the crest sideways, like some legless insect – perhaps a wood-louse would be the most resembling. There was another and another to right and left of it, and crowds of infantry between them. They moved up towards that skyline along its whole length.'[3]

Hurrah!

From his own high position at Sailly-le-Sec, Lieutenant Patrick Campbell of the 5th Field Artillery Brigade is watching the same thing. 'Through the smoke and semi-darkness I saw a line of tanks ascending the hill, and infantry following. I could see the red flash of our own shells bursting along the ridge beyond the tanks, beyond the village of Hamel, which seemed already to have been captured. I saw no Germans . . . Only a few shells came back at us. All the signs were that the attack was succeeding.'[4]

The attack is succeeding, and then some.

Up close, those 12 tanks are now able to bring their own withering fire on the German machine-gun posts ahead – punctuated by regular bursts from their six-pounder cannon – even as the soldiers of the 44th advance with them, firing from the hip at any Squarehead brave enough to lift his head above the parapet, which is not many of them.

Inside the tanks, all is a super-heated hell of roaring engines, choking fumes, and constant firing as, time and again, the six-pounder gunner squeezes the pistol-grip trigger that fires the Hotchkiss cannon, whereupon there is a roar, the six-pounder recoils, and a shell bursts forth, hurtling at 500 yards a second, with one pound of tightly packed explosive in its head, complete with six pounds of metal to tear apart whatever it hits . . .

Inside the tank, the gunner tugs on the breech and the shell casing ejects to the floor of the tank, while the Lewis gunner, also trained as a loader, slams another shell in the breech, with the gunner pausing for just a second so the Lewis gunner can get his fingers out of the way before slamming the breech shut once more. After some more whirling of the wheels, and another check that the gun is on target – German soldiers in the trench, just up ahead – the six-pounder gunner fires once more, for another shudder of the entire tank. Now is their time, and for the moment they risk little as there is half an inch of metal between them and whatever Fritz wants to throw back at them.

And now, as the tanks reach the German trenches, having steered straight for the strongpoints, they do it exactly as Monash had described it – 'pirouetting round and round [to] blot them out, much as a man's heel would crush a scorpion'.[5]

In short order the scorpions are no more.

'One entire line of dugouts was crushed by a single tank,' Colonel Joseph B. Sanborn of the 131st would note in his official report to General Bell. 'They appeared to be a great surprise to the enemy and prisoners taken were very frightened of them.'[6]

Finally, on the lower slopes of Morlancourt Ridge looking south towards Hamel, Lieutenant George Mitchell – who had been so eager to add to the barrage a couple of hours earlier he had taken his rifle and blasted away – will never forget the vision that greets him as the day rises and the smoke clears.

'There, on the far slope of the river,' he would recount, 'was the beautiful and terrible panorama of war. A fire was burning furiously in Vaire Wood. The death-hedge of our barrage was a long way into Germany. The squat dark shapes of tanks could be seen crawling over the terrain. Lines of our men were advancing steadily. Occasional shells burst among them. Overhead were our planes in swarms, holding unquestioned mastery of the air.'[7]

Most impressively, his compatriots are *still* advancing!

As Mitchell peers closely, he focuses on one tank at the prow of the attack, now closing in on a German stronghold from which an ever more urgent stream of red flares is streaking skywards, clearly calling on the surviving German artillery batteries to *MACH WAS, do something*, to stop this tank.

Inside that stronghold, Mitchell realises, 'some gallant enemy soldier was keeping his rendezvous with death'. Around and about him, in all likelihood his comrades are either slaughtered, or already fled, but still he is remaining at his post, doing what he can to stop these iron monsters.

'The last red flare went up when the tank was only a few feet away. There were no more flares from that place.'[8]

As dugout after dugout falls, whole sections of the German trenches fall to the attacker, allowing the Australian soldiers to rush forward to get to grips with the survivors and stream left and right along this former line of resistance, quickly overwhelming the German soldiers of the 202nd Regiment who remain.

Continuing over the crest, they get to the Blue Line, some 200 yards down the other side, killing whatever Germans they find, and then begin digging in to the old German trenches, making them deeper and more defensible.

The advance stops cold, exactly as planned. The 41st Battalion are in position on the left flank by the Somme, the 44th are digging in atop Wolfsberg, while the 15th to the right of them and the other battalions further south, are all at their allotted stations. Now they all must continue to dig in, roll out their barbed wire, consolidate and hold through guts and gumption what has been so brilliantly gained. From Wolfsberg the men of the 44th Battalion are suddenly able to look out upon the spectacular vista before them, the rich mosaic of farms and villages, not to mention the Somme itself winding away to the east . . . But, far more importantly, they can also see the German rear positions, supply dumps, their trucks, a train in the distance and, yes, their surviving *artillery batteries*. Look at all those beautiful targets! It is nothing less than nirvana for an artilleryman. If the mouths of the Allied artillery observers – even now struggling up the hill behind the 44th with binoculars round their necks and telephone wires trailing out behind – are starting to water, it is understandable . . .

•

At last, Cliff Geddes recognises the blokes just up ahead, digging in on the Blue Line, as B Company men, Boo's men! And all around he sees dead Germans, dead Australians, some of whom he knows – *Jesus Christ!* – severed body parts, and oceans of blood.

His primary thought: 'The men who brought this war on the world ought to be tortured to death.'[9]

Where is Boo?, he asks, fearing the worst.

Over yonder, in the shell-hole.

Cliff breathes again, but what is he about to find?

Racing over, not knowing what to expect, he gets to the shell-hole and finds Boo . . . alive!

He is 'pale but conscious, his right thigh bandaged & all blood, but a smile on his face as he spoke'.[10]

He looks like he's going to be all right! All he has are three nasty flesh wounds, and there might even be cause for celebration because, together, they might be the perfect 'Blighty'.

All around Boo, however, things are grim and getting grimmer.

'Cruel sights, dead Australians & Yanks, & men groaning with awful wounds.'[11]

Boo is glad to see him and explains what had happened.

'We were moving too fast behind the barrage,' he says simply. 'One shell burst near, and while Eldridge dived into a deep hole, I jumped into a very shallow one, and as I tried to get in a deeper one, another shell burst and blew me into a hole. I landed on my rifle. Just then a young German looked over the edge, and, though wounded in the leg, I made an attempt to point my rifle at the young Fritz & told him to surrender. Fritz put up his hands, and said "*Kamerad*".'[12]

The German could have taken him easily, but made no attempt. Maybe the barrage had knocked the fight clean out of him. Boo and all the other wounded blokes are waiting in the comparative shelter of the shell-hole until the stretcher-bearers can get to them. Speaking of which . . .

In this still-early morning, their bloodied uniforms now wet with dew, all of the wounded men are shivering – a cold compounded for many by the fact that they have lost so much blood, which lowers their body temperature still further. Some of them are in a very bad way indeed, and one of the worst hit, a Yank, manages to rasp the words out to Cliff, 'I'm shot to pieces, are the stretcher-bearers coming?'

Mercifully, the 13th Battalion stretcher-bearers answer the call quickly and, after assuring himself that Boo will be okay for the moment, Cliff Geddes is soon one of four men carrying the very big Yank back to the dressing station, as he is the one in most urgent need.

'Lor' it was hard work, talk about heavy, I was done when we reached the dressing station, & how these grand stretcher bearers make trip after trip down with the wounded, Goodness only knows.'[13]

Boo arrives shortly afterwards, carried by four stretcher-bearers, and Cliff stays with him until yet more stretcher-bearers arrive to carry him back to 4th Field Ambulance, where trucks await to get him and other wounded to hospital.

'He was very bright, smoked his pipe . . .' a thankful Cliff will note. 'I'm relieved he is safely out of the cursed business (for a while anyhow).'[14]

Cliff heads back to his trench, vastly buoyed and yet, after talking to an artillery officer about how successful the whole battle has been, how many prisoners have been taken and so on, has cause to soon reflect: 'Of course it will look very nice in the papers. "Gallant advance by Australians," but the people who write it, & delight in reading it, don't know the horror of it all.'[15]

At least in the middle of such horror, so many deaths, so much gore, so many missing, humanity is present.

'The thing that was grand to see was the way our chaps bandaged wounded Huns, & carried them back to the dressing station, with just the same care as our own men, & Australians, Yanks & Fritzes lay side by side on stretchers.'[16]

•

Meanwhile, Lieutenant Edgar Rule and his men of the 14th Battalion now come to the south end of Vaire Wood, where their orders are to dump the ammunition and water they have been carrying for the use of the 4th Brigade if the Germans counter-attack, before again moving forward to where they are ordered to dig in a support trench, some 300 yards back from where the Blue Line is marked on the map Rule carries. Reaching the trench, a spot just beside a road, Rule and his platoon are soon digging for dear life, just as the sun fully unveils their current weakness. It is going to be a splendid summer's day, but they are unlikely to see much of it unless they can quickly get their trenches dug and solid earth between themselves and the German snipers, who are *bound* to be taking aim shortly.

In the meantime Lieutenant Edgar Rule and his men are feeling just that little bit . . . lonely.

•

To their front, on the Blue Line, about 300 yards away, some other members of the 4th Brigade are digging in too, but as yet there is no one on their left and right and their own line remains thin. The simple fact is that, with their cut in manpower just before the battle, the 14th has not been able to move forward as a solid line and there have been many gaps. For the moment they are protected from a serious German counter-attack by the barrage falling some 500 yards in front, and Rule knows that it will continue to do so for another half an hour or so, but what then?

Unless more men arrive soon, and in force, they will have no chance of holding the ground they have won. Compounding his worry is that somewhere out in front, some Germans, unnoticed by the first wave which had passed through the area, are clearly drawing a bead on them in the growing light as bullets start to fly around them.

There! No more than a hundred yards forward of where Lieutenant Rule and his men have dug in, Rule sees half-a-dozen helmets bobbing up from a trench.

And they have . . . Squareheads!

Rule calls forward a tank, which obliges, but it doesn't work the way Rule plans.

'[The tank] waddled all around it and came back and said he could see no-one there.'[17]

And yet, no sooner has the tank commander reported it than a white flag goes up, from precisely where Rule had seen the Germans. Clearly, they are surrendering. Rule takes half-a-dozen men forward to capture them, only . . . only for the villains to open fire. It had all been a ruse! Calling for the tank once more, the grim-faced Rule and his men are soon advancing again, intent on taking *no* prisoners this time.

As bad luck would have it, alas, when they are within just 30 yards of the German trench, a piece of shrapnel, a stray shell from their own artillery, a drop-short, fatally wounds one of their men . . . just before a precisely aimed bullet instantly kills another. And still they keep going.

Getting close now, the instant a German head pops up, Rule snaps off a shot:

'Bang, and down he went.'[18]

Charging into the trench, however, they find it abandoned, as the Germans have clearly fled along the trench the other way, but Rule and his four survivors do find a couple of dugouts and there is some movement down there!

Shouting for the Germans to come out, he does not have long to wait.

'Out came two hands with a loaf of black bread in each, and presently a pair of terrified eyes took a glimpse at me. They must have been reassured by my look, because the Huns came out at once, and when I sized them up all thoughts of revenge vanished. We could not kill children, and these looked to be barely that. If any of us had been asked how old they were, most of us would have said between fourteen and fifteen, and that was giving them every day of their age. We knew these babes had not worked the white flag on us – they were too terrified for that; and, with a boot to help them along, they ran with their hands above their heads back to our lines.'[19]

It is at this point that the best-dressed man among them, Lieutenant Ramsay Wood, arrives and just as they are looking along the trench to find the rest of the Huns, a single shot rings out and . . . down goes Wood, killed by a bullet through his temple.

'He had his officer's tunic on,' Lieutenant Rule would sadly note, 'and I'm positive that tunic was what "drew the crabs" on him.'[20]

•

The bastard of it for Two Guns Dalziel? Having hauled his ammunition box all the way forward to where the 15th Battalion is now digging in on their Blue Line, he finds the box is full of hand grenades, not the rounds he needs for the Lewis!

Worse, the situation is now even more urgent, as the light and lethal German grenades Fritz is hoiking his way right now are plentiful and coming from *enormous* distances . . .

(Fritz had played a little cricket or baseball? Who *knew*?)

For Dalziel, still bleeding heavily from his trigger finger, there is only one thing for it.

Giving the grenades to his mates, he heads back, moving more quickly this time as he knows the route and has already worked out the safest way to reach the ammunition. Once back, he sets up and starts firing immediately, just in the nick of time, as something of a counter-attack appears to be underway.

Dalziel and his mates are fighting for their lives when suddenly, from out of nowhere, the Queenslander sees a German soldier near at hand. He is about to blow him apart – and at this distance the Lewis Gun really would cut him in two – when his finger pauses on the trigger, as he takes a closer look. Why, it is only a boy, 15 years old, at best!

Allowing him to surrender, the young lad rushes towards him with his hands in the air, crying '*Merci Kamerad, Merci*', only for two burly Americans to rush forward clearly intending to bayonet him.

'Stop!' Dalziel cries out in turn, raising his two totally empty revolvers at them. 'Don't move or I will blow your bloody heads off!'

The Yanks don't move, allowing Dalziel to say, 'Take this little German back to the Captain. Possibly, he may get some information from him.'[21]

Dalziel settles down and keeps firing the Lewis Gun until he must once again head back for more ammo. This time, he passes a newly established dressing station, where wounded soldiers are being treated by Doc Kennedy and a quite frazzled American doctor, with their most urgent cases, including a German soldier who has had his foot blown away, being worked on by a couple of AIF doctors. Hovering right by him is the 'little German' Dalziel had seen earlier, still being guarded by the two Yanks.

One of the Yanks comes over and says, 'This German soldier wants to speak to you.'

Bemused, Dalziel goes over to the man with the blown-off foot to be told something extraordinary by the German.

'Comrade,' says he, reaching out to shake Two Guns' hand, 'you have saved my son.'[22] The 'little German' is indeed just a boy, a young son fighting alongside the now footless father. Two Guns has no time to tarry, as though he has indeed spared the lad as it had never been a fair fight, he does have plans to kill more of the boys' countrymen. His immediate task remains urgent, and he is quick to get back to the ammunition dump, where, this time, he makes damn sure he secures a box filled with bullets not grenades, and after crawling, hauling, huffing and puffing, falling into shell-holes but never stalling, he makes his way back to his mighty Lewis Gun, loads it and begins firing once more. The only difference is that this time he has to shift his 'cocking handle' – the knob on the gun that cocks the gun before firing – 'over to the left side because my right hand was getting stiff'.[23]

Beyond that, his feet are sore, and his head aches so much it feels like he has two or three heads on his shoulder. And though the Germans have backed off a bit, their snipers haven't.

Hugging his gun more tightly than ever, and the ground, trying to get ever lower, Two Guns is aware that the snipers are getting closer, as bullets start slamming into his sandbags, causing rivulets of sand – from the hourglass of eternity? – to start pouring from many spots at once.

Bugger them!

A lesser man at this point might crawl away, if not run away, but not Two Guns. Putting another magazine on, he starts firing once more, even as the sniper's bullets get closer and closer to his melon, ever more apparent in the growing morning light.

•

With the key hill of Wolfsberg seemingly secured, Bean's attention turns to other fields of battle now plainly visible.

'Far south, on the plateau in front of Villers Bretonneux,' he would recount, 'were other men, moving, standing easily and talking, and working at some business hard to make out, as men are always soon after having reached their objective.'[24]

And yet while it is one thing for the fastest of the attacking forces to have reached the Blue Line, it may well be quite another for them to hold it – as well as continue to mop up the pockets of resistance that have been left behind, such as those pods of German soldiers still holding on in the cellars of Hamel. Whatever else, however, it seems likely that those in the forward position will not be lacking for the *matériel* of war. For one of those men that Bean can perhaps see, from so far, is 23-year-old Colonel Douglas Marks of the 13th Battalion, who is looking for the spot which, on his map, is marked as the place that his Battalion must establish its forward dump of ammunition and supplies. Ah yes, here is the spot, by the track, and . . .

And, hang on, what's this? On the very spot where his dump is to be placed, there is *already* a dump of stores!

'Why, what's this?' he asks rhetorically to the Lieutenant with him.

On the instant, a Digger appears from behind the said pile and tells him, 'It's from our tank, sir.'[25]

Be buggered! To the Colonel's stupefaction, one of the four carrier tanks assigned to the task has been ferrying back and forth throughout the battle and has managed to bring forward no fewer than 150 trench-mortar bombs, 10,000 rounds of ammunition, 20 boxes of grenades, 134 coils of barbed wire to establish impenetrable barricades in front of the newly dug trenches, 45 sheets of corrugated iron to build rough dugouts, and 50 petrol tins of water, among other things! Busy as worker ants, the carrier tanks have been, and will be, dropping dumps like these all along the strip just 400 yards back from the Blue Line.

'Never,' Charles Bean would be obliged to conclude, 'had supplies reached the front with the swiftness with which they were delivered that day.'[26]

Not long after the Colonel finds the supply dump, Australian soldiers could be seen marking out huge Vs. (V, of course, stands for Vickers' ammunition – the boxes of .303 bullets needed to feed the 24 Vickers Guns that have been brought forward to the Blue Line after it had been established. Though the Lewis Guns use the same ammunition, their crews have carried their own ammunition forward in panniers.

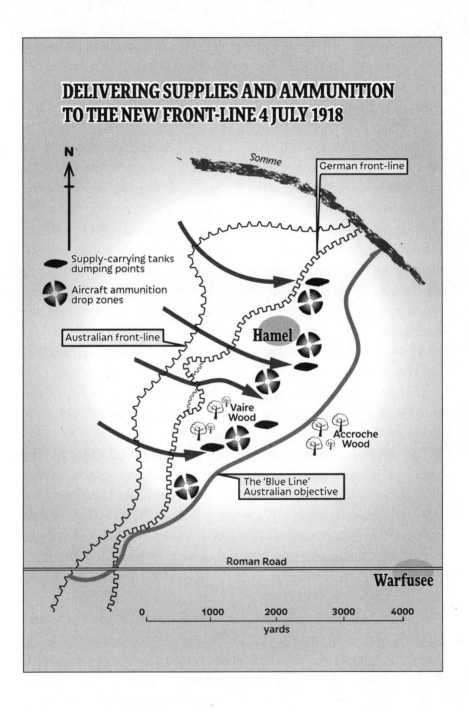

DELIVERING SUPPLIES AND AMMUNITION TO THE NEW FRONT-LINE 4 JULY 1918

N

Supply-carrying tanks
dumping points

Aircraft ammunition
drop zones

Australian front-line

Somme

German front-line

Hamel

Vaire
Wood

Accroche
Wood

The 'Blue Line'
Australian objective

Roman Road

Warfusee

0   1000   2000   3000   4000

yards

•

In the meantime, though it is rare indeed for a Brigadier and his troops to be pleased to find themselves under major attack, that is indeed the case, when, just after 4 am, German shells start pouring down onto Australian positions between the Somme and the Ancre Rivers.

Rah!

Their feint has worked. For, of course, every shell that falls on Pompey Elliott's men of the 15th Brigade is one that is not falling to their south, where the 4th, 6th, 7th and 11th Brigades are doing the *real* work of the attack.

They can only hope their mates are reaching their objectives, without suffering too many casualties. Responding to the deception plan of attack from the 55th Battalion near Brick Beacon, exactly as intended, the German defenders, 203rd Infantry Regiment, send back a panicked report that they have repulsed a full-scale attack on their lines, but need reinforcements to be sure of holding it.

And yet it is not as if the Germans are without the strength to fight back.

That much is clear by their counter-attack on the far left of the Australian positions, by the Mill on the Ancre where Lieutenant Thomson was killed.

'Two sections *zurückgewonnen*, won back [some of the trench],' the Official History of the 52nd Reserve Infantry Regiment records, 'but with the weak forces and the soon-to-come *Mangel an Handgranaten*, lack of hand grenades, it is not possible to hold the won-back part of the trench, which is then occupied by the enemy again. At the right section, too, the opponent at first is thrown back by a counter-attack, but penetrates again from the left . . . to clear the trench. A counter-attack . . . remains unsuccessful.'

Among the Germans, no-one is more heroic than Second-Lieutenant Schulze, who, with the 6th Company, actually manages to throw the Australians out of the mill on the Ancre, only to fall, fatally wounded, as the enormous Australians *counter*-counter-attack.

'Only the day before,' the Official History sadly records, '[Schulze] had returned from his *Hochzeitsurlaub*, honeymoon.'[27]

•

With the result of the battle no longer in doubt, and many Germans who have managed to hold on unnoticed in pockets in their own forward positions now finding themselves totally isolated, there are inevitably more and more surrenders. The results are not always pretty . . .

'In the taking of German prisoners,' Captain Gale would delicately note, 'a tendency was noted on the part of Australian troops to an entire disregard for the personal property rights of prisoners of war; they strip them as a rule of anything of personal value.'[28]

They do indeed.

'What a harvest for our boys,' Lieutenant Rule would recount. 'Talk about "ratting". As each Hun advanced with his hands above his head, several of our lads would dive at him, and, before the astonished Hun knew what was happening, hands were in every pocket, and he was fleeced of everything but his name and his clothes . . .'[29]

Right by the body of Ramsay Woods, with his head half blown away, one of the more recent arrivals to the 14th Battalion is furiously frisking a Hun, and filling his own pockets with – what are these? – cigars, when Rule yells at him.

'Are you not aware of the order that all loot has to be handed to an officer to be sent back to headquarters?'[30]

Shamefacedly the soldier hands over all the cigars, only for Rule to light the first of what will be many cigars this day, as the rest of the platoon falls about laughing, enjoying seeing the loot looted.

•

Six miles into 'Hunland', as they know it, Lieutenants Lock and Barrett, up in the air in their valiant little Harry Tate, are feeling vulnerable . . . but committed. Never before have they come this far over to the other side, but their orders are clear and they are to follow through: they are to look for anything German, particularly anything which looks like reinforcements heading to Hamel, and destroy it.

It is, Barrett will explain, 'an almost unheard of distance for the machines we fly', and they feel 'very lonely', the more so because the smoke from the barrage is so thick and wide they can't even see their own territory anymore.

But to work. Following orders, they now turn their guns and bombs onto whatever targets present themselves, which starts by strafing a train so comprehensively that it stops in its tracks, and continues by dropping bombs on some Germans resting by a road. Ah, look at all those grey-clad ants below, scurrying hither and thither! And now, what is this?

It is a pair of German field guns being pulled by some horses in the rough direction of Le Hamel. There could be no juicier target and, after turning, the plane roars towards them, towards the battlefront.

'We shot the horses of one and it overturned and the other seemed in difficulties.'[31]

Of course, in an effort to stop them, German machine guns are opening up from all quarters – Lieutenant Barrett counts no fewer than 14 streams of tracer bullets coming for them, trying to drag them from the sky – but they are mercifully just beyond the Germans' reach.

In any case, the flyers have now done the first part of their work and they are getting low on fuel, so it is time to return to Villers-Bocage. By the time they land it is to note that another eight No. 3 Squadron planes have taken off and are now, hopefully, wreaking their own havoc on the German side of the lines. At least five of them are. Three of the planes have a special mission ...

For what is this now?

Some RE8s from No. 3 Squadron are roaring back and forth over Australian lines, signalling, as one soldier would describe it, with the 'deep *ur ur* blurting of their klaxons'.[32]

Ur-Ur-Ur!

Ur-Ur-Ur!

Ur-Ur-Ur!

It made him think of a 'particularly large masculine bird in pain from indigestion'.[33]

The forward Australians know what to do. From the shelter of their trenches or shell-holes they light red flares. From the air, thus, visible only to the Allied aircraft, a zig-zagging line of red dots appears in the gloom, marking the exact contours of the Australian advance.

The positions are carefully marked on maps, by these 'Strike a Light' patrols, as the Diggers call them, photos are taken, with all plates then rushed to the airstrip closest to the HQ of General Sinclair-Maclagan at 4th Division HQ, in the village of Bussy-les-Daours, five miles from the front-line. At that HQ, the photographs are quickly developed and analysed. And the information they reveal is good.

The line of flares on the photograph matches exactly the Blue Line on the map! It means all positions have been secured, exactly as planned.

In any case, at 4.43 am the artillery batteries lay down their protective barrage, a curtain of fire some 200 yards beyond the Blue Line, which will forestall any immediate counter-attacks by the Germans.

(Inevitably, the insistence by the Australian officers that their men observe General Monash's order that they go no *further* than the Blue Line will see German commanders claim credit for their men that does not properly belong to them. Similar to the example above, the Commander of the 107th Infantry Division defending from the Ancre river southward, facing Pompey's 15th Brigade sector, *Generalmajor* Otto Havenstein, will faithfully report to his own superiors: 'The fact that the Englishman did not come any further, despite great superiority and initial success, once again puts *die zähe Tapferkeit und die schneidige Führung*, the tenacious bravery and the dashing leadership *der 52er*, of the men of the 52nd, and the excellent artillery *ins hellste Licht*, into the brightest light, [and it] means a new *Lorbeerblatt*, laurel-leaf, in the history of both the men of the 52nd and the artillery and honours the whole 107th Infantry Division.'[34])

All up, however, the course of the battle thus far has established that in just 93 minutes, the attacking force of Australians and Americans, sustaining only a minimum number of casualties, has moved the Western Front forward by 2500 yards on a front of 7500 yards, with six square miles of France recaptured, an astonishing achievement, particularly bearing in mind that on 19 July 1916, at the Battle of Fromelles, Australia had sent a force of 8000 soldiers forward, at a cost of 5500 casualties, including 1900 men killed, without gaining *any* ground at all.

In short, in just over an hour and a half, Monash's forces have accomplished what a force ten times as large would have taken weeks to do in 1916, with 20 times the casualties. Monash's methodology is not only vindicated, it is now the exemplar of how it can, and *must*, be done, from here on in, the state-of-the-art model.

The only question now is, can they hold their winnings?

That remains to be seen but, for now, General Monash, the architect of such a remarkable plan, such an extraordinary victory, is . . . drawing. He has been passing the time doing a sketch of one of the French drivers assigned to the Australian Corps, then dashes off a quick note to his wife, Vic, explaining how doing such a sketch at the height of a battle has helped keep him calm.

> *When once a commander's orders are issued, there is little left*
> *for him to do but to wait and watch, and to do a little sketch*
> *like this keeps one's nerves cool and steady.*[35]

After the dawn, 4 July 1918, lining the Blue Line, with force

The full flood of day reveals the Australians and Americans furiously continuing to dig into the Blue Line, while they have the luxury of the protective barrage falling 200 yards to the east to prevent any chance of a major German counter-attack.

With the bulk of their work now done, the majority of the tanks return to where they began, most carrying wounded soldiers, though several tanks stay back to ensure that the last of Fritz's resistance in the ground taken really is mopped up. Over on the far right, in the area taken by the 6th Brigade, when a nest of 50 Germans is discovered, *still* holding on, the infantry simply summon a tank and – having seen from a distance what awaits them if they don't surrender – 50 prisoners are soon on their way to the rear.

Oh, those beautiful tanks!

'With my runner I sat on the grass,' Lieutenant Short, of the 23rd Battalion, records, 'and watched a tank . . . make for a strongpoint that worried our men with machine gun fire. It was soon mopped up. Our men were out for souvenirs. Their blood had not been roused to kill and they treated prisoners well.'[36]

(Particularly if they behave when they are being 'ratted'.)

Another couple of tanks, just behind the Blue Line, rove threateningly, looking for any German counter-attack that might materialise, and are all the more vigilant when, just as planned, at 5.13 am, all falls relatively quiet, as the protective barrage dies away, and, for the first time in just over two hours, there is no curtain of artillery between the attackers and defenders.

6 am, 4 July 1918, in the skies over Hamel, a flight to remember

For Captain Lawrence Wackett – on this morning in charge of no fewer than 20 RE8s from No. 3 Squadron AFC and No. 9 Squadron RAF – now comes the *real* test. It is one thing, of course, for his invention to have worked in trials, but quite another for it to work in battle conditions, dodging Ack-Ack flak, Mac. But at least they are off to a good start, because, sure enough, up ahead, over the smoky battlefield, the fire still raging in Hamel, the ant-like soldiers from both sides gazing up at them, he can see huge white 'V's laid out.

A waggle of the wings, an easing forward of the joystick – this is it, we are going in.

Bringing his RE8 down to 1000 feet, Captain Wackett judges his moment and, just as they have practised, at approximately 300 yards before the target, reaches out of the cockpit to pull back on the bomb toggle. In an instant, his plane bucks higher with the release of the weight! Again, a great start, but it is only when Wackett looks back to see a parachute mushrooming beneath and behind him that the relief surges through him. Wonderfully, along the line, the other planes have succeeded in doing the same and now box, after box, after box, after *box* – the first lot of 93 in all – are floating down, each one carrying 1200 rounds of ammunition.

Captain Wackett's wacky idea works!

At least, nearly always . . .

In one plane, there is a mishap, which will need a miracle to save the pilot and his observer. For no sooner has the pilot, Lieutenant Harry Reikie – a happy-go-lucky 22-year-old Londoner – reached out of the right-hand side of his cockpit and pulled the bomb toggle on the fuselage than the parachute gets caught on the left wing, creating a fearful drag. Within seconds, the plane is tilting dangerously.

With extraordinary courage, Reikie climbs out of his cockpit and now, without a prayer on a wing, tries to clear the chute, while the observer, Lieutenant Knowles, wrestles with the auxiliary joystick in his own cockpit, trying to keep the Harry Tate level.

Mesmerised, the men of the 43rd Battalion, still mopping up the last German holdouts in the village of Hamel, watch the drama unfold just above them.

Just 100 feet above the ground, Reikie . . . succeeds in detaching the chute, and it flutters away . . . . only for the plane to suddenly nosedive and hit Wolfsberg. Both Lieutenants Reikie and Knowles are killed.

That disaster notwithstanding, from the heavens themselves now – sent by the Gods of War, and borne on the wings of the angels of death – or at least by those blessed parachutes – the many boxes of machine-gun ammunition keep gracefully descending to land with a series of thumps across the landscape, but mostly clustered around the big white 'V's. Excitedly racing forward to gather them in, the Australian and American troops greedily grab any boxes they can, take a side each on the rope handles provided and haul them to where they are needed.

The boxes keep coming, and the soldiers keep scurrying to get them. But look there . . . One soldier, surely, looks familiar?

The pistols in both belts?

The dagger in his boots?

The bloody rag around his right hand?

Of course, it is Two Guns Dalziel!

Despite having been ordered to retire nearly three hours earlier, he is *still* going, *still* pushing hard, *still* doing what needs to be done, and then some.

Such a man deserves, surely, for the Gods of War to smile upon him?

And yet, and yet, somewhere a couple of hundred yards to the east of Dalziel as he hauls an ammunition box to his Lewis Gun and starts loading, a German soldier – likely surrounded by his own dead and dying *Kameraden* – bearing arms against a sea of troubles, takes random aim at one of the shadowy figures he can see in the distance and squeezes the trigger.

In all the cacophony of catastrophe going on around him, Two Guns does not even hear this particular shot being fired. It is just one among many.

Ah, but no. Not actually . . .

For this steel bullet really does have his name on it, and, flying through the smoke at a speed of 600 miles per hour, heads straight for his noggin and . . . takes a chunk off the left side of his skull. With a soft sigh, the man christened Harry Dalziel, beloved son of James and Eliza, of Irvinebank, North Queensland, dearly beloved eldest brother of Victor, James and William sinks to the ground.

Shocked, horrified, devastated – *not* Harry, not *Two Guns Harry!* – his mates are quickly to him, but there is no hope. There is no movement, and a big bloody hole in the side of his head you could stick your fingers into. No-one bothers putting white tape around Two Guns, to stop the tanks from running over him, because he is obviously dead.

In any case, sadly, two men are assigned to carry his body back to the nearest row of corpses, for later burial.

In the meantime, the surviving soldiers must rush, grab the boxes they can and get back into their newly dug trenches, to prepare for what is coming. Clearly, today, the 4th of July, is going to be about consolidating the territory they have grabbed, working out how to hold on to it, and how to counter the counter-attack which is surely to come. And the fact that they now have supplies of ammunition in forward positions really *is* a good start.

Still, for the most part those holding the Blue Line will have to do it without the tanks, as with the exception of a dozen of the behemoths secreted behind Vaire Wood – against emergency – they are being withdrawn on the reckoning they would be too obvious a target for German artillery.

So it is that, rumbling their way back from the front-lines now are most of the tanks, laden with cheering Diggers and Yanks – some of them wounded, but many of them cheering still.

Those tanks! Those bloody beauties!

'The boys much appreciate the tanks on their Hun-routing excursions,' the 21st Battalion newspaper will later record the warm views of the soldiers when it comes to this extraordinary addition to Australian and Allied battle plans. 'Their ugly appearance and ungainly movement are in themselves sufficient to put the "wind up", but when their "for'ard" belches into flame of spitting slaughter, our sympathies should be with the enemy.'[37]

Even as one of those tanks lurches past near Hamelet, however, it suddenly halts and one of the side doors bursts open. Out gets Bluey, now a very shaky Digger indeed. Forget liaising with his own troops on the ground – throughout the entire battle he has not said a *single* word. No, he has just got progressively greener, and grimmer in countenance, near suffocated by the fumes, and dying from the heat of the engine. But now, *now* is the time of his delivery. The instant his feet are back on solid soil, and he can take a huge breath of precious fresh air, he has the strength to say what he has been aching to say for all of the last two hours, not quite the equivalent of Shakespeare's famous line from *Hamlet*, 'Something is rotten in the state of Denmark', but certainly his own version of it. 'Thanks, Digger,' he calls back through the side door to Captain Batten, 'but if they ever get me inside one of them flamin' things again, my name's not "Bluey"!'[38]

(*Exit, Bluey, stage left.*)

And yet, whatever Bluey and his fellow Australian liaisons inside the tanks might think of them, those in the 5th Tank Brigade leave the battle with an exceedingly high opinion of the soldiers they have been fighting alongside.

'One final word, written not in flattery, but as fact,' Captain Batten would note many years later. 'I can safely assert that there isn't a member of the original Royal Tank Corps who will not bear me out when I say that we were all agreed that if we had to choose troops to take into action, we'd prefer the Australians every time. They possessed that little extra "something" that some others hadn't got. And I am still hoping that one day I'll again meet that "Digger" I took into action at Hamel . . .'[39]

Not bloody likely.

And yet Bluey will be one of the very few not thrilled with the performance of the tanks. Sixty of them had gone forward, and no fewer than 55 of them had returned, intact, only two knocked out and three had broken down. They had run over none of the wounded, and only 18 of their own crew members had been wounded (five wounded so slightly they remained on duty), with just one man, poor Private Thomas Parrish, killed. They have been a resounding success.

•

For the American reserves pulled out at the last minute, it has been a frustrating, nervous time. They have so desperately wanted to take part, only to be denied at the death, and yet as envious as they are of their comrades in the 131st and 132nd Regiments, so too had they feared for them. Would they acquit themselves well? Would they survive? Would they *win*?

The semi-darkness had offered just about no clues, beyond 'red and yellow flashes from the artillery' puncturing the gloom, and the fact that the flashes from the German side seemed to have diminished every few minutes. But that had been it.

So it is that as full light starts to flood the whole scene on what is proving to be a glorious morning, those like Sergeant Walter Corning who have been lucky enough to be placed in reserve close enough to see the battlefield, gaze earnestly to the east looking for a sign.

And what a sight now meets their eyes!

'When the sun came out,' Corning would recount, 'the diamond-like sparkle from bayonets, through a haze of smoke, spelled success in a code that was distinctly original. The waves of Australian infantry, in perfect liaison, stretched as far as we could see, and mingled here and there with the dark grey uniform of the German army.'[40]

Before long, the first of their comrades arrive, coming back from the line in various manners.

'A line of ambulances crept along slowly. Then came the walking wounded, smiling through cigarette smoke. Next came [a] column of silent prisoners with downcast eyes, a lone Aussie grimly leading the way on horseback, with a buddy bringing up in the rear.'

Most of the victorious soldiers are carrying 'souvenirs', and their haul includes everything from German helmets and bayonets to Regimental insignia, tassels, and belts with '*GOTT MIT UNS*' on the buckle, together with Luger pistols and field glasses.

'A brisk business in Iron Crosses was established.'[41]

Souvenirs, like you cannot *imagine*!

On that very subject . . .

'I guess we're shark troops now,' one of the Americans remarks.

Shark? *Shark?* He must be referring, the men of the 13th Battalion presume, to the rapacious gathering of 'souvenirs' of the German prisoners. Oh, the *presumption*.

A still wet-behind-the-ears Yank thinking he is better at that caper than veteran Australians?

To put him in his place, the man known to the 13th Battalion as the 'Souvenir King' takes from his coat a whole pile of German watches, coins, photos, revolvers and daggers, and proudly retorted, 'You'll have to be Some Shark Troops to beat that little heap, I guess, Guy.'

'I wasn't referring to souvenirs, Aussie,' the American replies. 'I said I guess after that battle we'll be regarded as shark troops like you Australians. Shark Troops – SHARK Troops like you.'

As the Australians are clearly still perplexed, the American spells it out: 'S . . . H . . . O . . . C . . . K . . . *shark* troops.'[42]

All that aside, however, the Americans have done well, and not only do they know it, but so do the Australian officers who have had the honour of commanding them in battle. One Australian colonel tries to muster the words to say this, beginning in formal fashion, before blurting out, 'Yanks, you're fighting fools, but I'm for you.'[43]

The Americans feel much the same.

'Well, guy,' one American soldier is heard to say to a comrade, 'these Aussies will do us; they've plenty of guts.'[44]

•

It is about this time that Great Britain's Official War Correspondent Philip Gibbs, having heard a major action has taken place overnight, arrives in the back areas of the Australian lines to notice something more than passing strange . . .

'It was difficult to believe an attack had taken place,' he would recount, 'for there were none of the usual scenes which follow a battle, however successful, showing the price which must nearly always be paid for a victory. There was no great traffic of ambulances on the roads. I passed several casualty clearing stations above which Red Cross flags waved, but their tents were empty and there was nothing doing at that hour of the morning. There was no long trail of lightly wounded men . . . The truth is the enemy were so utterly surprised and the Australians so perfectly successful that the whole thing was completed within an hour and a half of the start. Hundreds of prisoners had been sent down under escort and the record of this brilliant little victory was already being written.'[45] Continuing on, he soon comes across some Australian officers who have taken part and, again, finds them unaccountably merry and bright.

'The joy of the thing,' one of them tells him, 'is that we have taken the initiative again, and that is much better than waiting for an attack. It is better for us and worse for the enemy. Our men have their tails waving over their heads and the Germans are very down today.'[46]

•

Indeed they are.

In the bright light of the mid-morning, quite at odds with the *sturm und drang* coming from afar, 500 odd soldiers still capable of fighting with the 1st Battalion of Germany's 202nd Reserve Infantry Regiment are having a rest three miles to the rear at Mericourt when, *mit Entsetzen*, with great dread, they notice a messenger from Regimental HQ turning up with a great sense of urgency about him.

Surely, the worst is not about to happen?

It is. They are to go back into the inferno, to the *Vallée d'Abancourt*, which lies at the eastern base of Wolfsberg, and prepare to take back the hill.

On the other side of the Somme – where, because of Pompey's feint, the German commanders are convinced they face a major attack – the same thing happens to the soldiers of the 1st Battalion of 227th RIR.

'Major von Rode [has decided] *schweren Herzens*, with a heavy heart, to deploy the just relieved and severely exhausted 1st Battalion again.'[47] Despite the fact they have just completed 12 days in the front-lines – and only been pulled out hours before – meaning they not only deserve, but *need* rest, they have been ordered to go back to counter-attack.

Scheiße!

•

Back on the battlefield, the mopping-up operation continues, wiping out whatever pockets of German resistance have been left behind as the Australians and Americans have swept over them and, just as a green flare going up over Vaire Woods at 6 am had indicated it was clear of Germans, so too, another green flare going up over Hamel at 7 am indicates the same.

Behind the newly established front-lines, it is time for the Australians and Americans to devote their full attention to looking after their wounded and burying their fallen.

'I saw some pals lying dead,' Cliff Geddes will sorrowfully confide to his diary, 'also Yanks, Aussies & Huns, a hellish, cruel business war is.'[48]

The coming of bright sunshine and the ebb of the battle's roar reveals many of the dead, scattered across the battlefield, already beginning their eternity, with only the spot they must spend it to be decided. Many of the corpses are missing limbs, some are missing heads, lots of them are disembowelled, with flies now buzzing around their entrails. Still others look entirely unharmed, and lie there exactly as if they are just having a bit of a kip after the night's heavy work.

The key now is to gather them in, lay them out, row on row, and get them identified and buried as quickly as possible – as one of the lessons of this war so far is the danger of disease from putrid bodies. (And nothing saps morale quicker than that sickly sweet stench of death that makes a man gag just to whiff it.)

Not that it is always possible, for all that.

Having hauled the bodies back here – sometimes just a head, other times just an arm or a leg – it is now also the job of the exhausted stretcher-bearers to start to arrange them. For scattered body parts, they carry hessian bags and, ideally, put the body parts from the one body, in the one bag, and hopefully with the right head, if they can find it. In one spot, inevitably, a small pile grows of body parts that don't seem to belong to anyone. In another spot are relatively intact corpses with, alas, no identification. Ultimately they will be buried separately in graves simply marked with the words 'an unknown Australian soldier'. One of those soldiers, so gathered now, likely has an extraordinary postscript to his tragic story . . . but we will get to that.

For now, the work goes on, even as the sun starts to heat the day and the flies begin to buzz.

You know the blokes who've done this before by the fact they are not regularly vomiting, but just have a glazed look at the horror of it all.

For, of all the foul jobs in this war, this, this is perhaps the foulest. To gather in the shattered corpses of comrades, to pick up with your own hands the severed limbs, the disgorged entrails of men once held dear is the worst of the worst.

Sadly, silently, they go through their protocol, arranging the body parts just so, and even more importantly searching for identity discs – 'meat tickets' – or, failing that, other marks which might identify the man they're about to bury. The two identification discs hang around their necks. The round one is for you, the octagonal one remains with the corpse, against the possibility that the body will be exhumed and placed in a cemetery.

All too often, you have to feel around for the disc among gore, bits of bone and shattered flesh. Such as this bloke, missing such a big chunk out of his left temple, you can actually see his *brain* . . .

What's his name? Using his finger to wipe away the gore on the disc, the Private can read the name now.

So it is a H. Dalziel, from the 15th Battalion, of the Australian Infantry, and he is of the Church of England. Poor bastard. The private is just turning to go when he hears a moan . . .

From where?

There!

From *that* corpse?

Dalziel?

He's alive?

He's ALIVE!

Stretcher-bearers! This man is still alive! Get him to the Regimental Aid Post, yonder, immediately!

•

For the Germans, it has been an even more bitter harvest, even though it is far too early to know the overall numbers. The men of the 15th Infantry Regiment, for example, who had been defending their trenches by the Roman Road, note that while six are dead and 27 wounded, no fewer than 199 are missing.

'The 4th of July,' their Official History will record, 'meant *eine starke Einbuße an Gefechtskraft*, a severe loss of combat power . . . *Es erlag der Übermacht der angreifenden Australier und ihrer Tanks und Flugzeuge*; it succumbed to the superiority of the attacking Australians and their tanks and planes.'[49]

•

Still at their position on the heights across the Somme at Sailly-le-Sec, Charles Bean and his colleagues continue to closely watch the battle-field as a glorious summer's day allows them a full, distant view of what is going on.

By this point in the early morning it is obvious that Fritz has at last roused himself to react, as 'the German artillery for the first time that day began to crash into the village of Hamel and into the woods. Long columns of red and yellow dust streaked from those woods across the sky.'[50]

Unfortunately for those dug into the newly established front-lines this is less an angry sally than a sustained pasting.

'From now onwards,' Bean will recount, 'the Germans began to strafe the right battlefield. He had found out where the attack really was.'[51]

Ah, but he is not having it all his own way. Only shortly after Bean gets word that the Germans are pulling some of their big guns back from what are now their highly vulnerable positions – courtesy of the artillery observers atop Wolfsberg – they are thrilled to see 'our planes just over him, diving and diving like young sea-hawks over a shoal of fish'.[52]

•

Ah, how the men in the Blue Line cheer to see the pilots of the Royal Air Force and Australian Flying Corps roar overhead and go straight at Fritz!

To keep the Germans off-balance in whatever counter-attacks they have planned, three RAF squadrons – 23, 41 and 209 – are despatched to drop bombs on any juicy German targets they can see, particularly those that might be forming up to have a go, as well as a little light strafing between friends. They are joined by several planes from the Australian Flying Corps' No. 3 Squadron. All up, in the course of this day, the RAF and the AFC will carry out 199 offensive patrols, and take part in 57 combats to destroy ten enemy aircraft. 'During the night,' their official report will read, '26 machines dropped 9 × 112 lb bombs and 350 × 25 lb bombs on various woods, etc east of Villers Bretonneux. During the day 1,358 × 25 lb bombs were dropped on favourable ground targets east of Hamel.'[53]

Among those who now suffer from their attention are the German soldiers of 202nd RIR 1st Battalion and 227th RIR 1st Battalion, who are among the many reserves now being pushed forward to ready themselves for a counter-attack on the new Allied lines. Again and again the Allied planes swoop on them, strafe them and bomb them, meaning that again and again they must dive for cover.

Gott im Himmel, when will this stop?

The best they can, the Germans continue to push to the west, set on their mission to counter-attack and remove Tommy from his newly won positions, but it is heavy going.

And yet, for those Australians and Americans newly dug in, things are far from easy.

In his own newly dug trench, Cliff Geddes is just trying to hold on with his mates, as the German artillery zeroes in on their positions.

'We & the Yanks,' he would describe it, 'were huddled up in the bottom like chickens, & didn't know which way to turn to get away from them. It's an awful feeling, so helpless, under shell fire. It's a fine day, & our planes are up in crowds trying to detect the *Boche's* next move. I was mighty hungry, & had a feed of bread, butter & jam at noon, while Fritz's shells were dropping uncomfortably near.'[54]

To pass the time, even while knowing that the next shell might have his name on it, written in capital letters, Cliff goes through a 'Fritz pocket book' he has found, filled with 'post cards, letters, German little printed books, photos . . . & c'.[55] The letters and postcards, he notes, are just a week old, sent on 26 and 27 June from Essen and Mulheim.

Somewhere, in Germany, there is a family who love this soldier. Who is it? Cliff has a look. 'Wilhelm Kulka., 4 Komp. Inftr. Regt. 13'.[56]

There is no way of knowing if he is still alive, but the Australian soldier committed to doing his best to kill other German soldiers, particularly if they make a move to counter-attack to take this newly won territory from them, hopes so.

In the meantime, one of Cliff's mates, Charlie Mann, arrives – in charge of one of the ration-carrying parties, ensuring that all those in the front-line trenches are able to keep their strength up. It gives Cliff a little lift to see that this one of his mates, at least, is still alive and kicking.

'I am glad you are still alright,'[57] he tells Charlie with some feeling.

•

And what now?

In their RE8, the pilot, Lieutenant Arthur Grigson, and his observer, Lieutenant Harry James, are a mile over German lines, about 2000 feet above Accroche Wood, when James sees them. Two German fighters – they are Pfalz D.IIIas, the sleekest planes of the war, with the white nose and black stripes of their unit, Jasta 58 – diving on them!

Bashing Grigson on the shoulder as if this is a matter of life and death – because it is – James points and yells in his ear: 'Left! Left! Left!'

A cool character, the 22-year-old Grigson – a Cunnamulla station hand before the war, who'd *gone to Queensland droving, and we don't know where he are*, and is now a long way from home – pushes the joystick left and instantly kicks the left rudder bar so their plane swerves away from any fusillade of bullets that might be coming their way. James, meantime, does his own swivel, bringing his Lewis Gun to bear on the first of the diving planes. At their speed, diving, the Pfalz D.IIIas – powered by a Mercedes DIIIa six-cylinder engine, delivering 180 horsepower – have a momentum all their own which makes it difficult for them to suddenly alter course, meaning that if he times it right . . . steady . . . steady . . . *steady* . . . NOW!

Lieutenant James squeezes the trigger and in a stuttering six-second burst, sends a full magazine, 47 rounds, straight into the fuselage of the enemy scout. It judders, shudders, suddenly starts blowing smoke and is observed by the cheering of the 78th Brigade of the Royal Garrison Artillery, in the heights of Sailly-le-Sec, 'to fall out of control' until it indeed hits the ground, a confirmed kill that the 78th Brigade RGA will soon officially report to No. 3 Squadron.

One down, one to go. But where is it?

Not surprisingly, the other German fighter has withdrawn, and with things getting a little hot in these parts even for two Australian lads trying their luck, Lieutenant Grigson turns their kite for home, only to suddenly come under attack from *three* German fighters.

It is enough to make a man glad he has done his time on the target range, and Lieutenant James – not so long ago a humble baker from Muswellbrook, New South Wales – feels exactly that as he swivels his Lewis Gun once more and fires off another smooth burst.

Again, one enemy plane is observed to dive away east out of control.[58]

Grigson and James would have followed to confirm the kill, but, owing to the other two machines persisting in the attack, the first one could not be followed down to the ground.[59]

Ah, yes, the other two machines. At this point things would likely have been a bit on the grim side, bar one thing.

In their own RE8, two mates of Grigson and James, Lieutenants David Dimsey and Frank Mart, have seen that Artie and Harry are in trouble, and have immediately flown to their rescue.

As it turns out, Lieutenant Mart is a dab hand with a Lewis Gun himself, and after he squeezes off a magazine full at a distance of 100 yards, one of the enemy aircraft, a Pfalz D.IIIa, is seen to go down . . .[60]

The final German aircraft scarpers, and both planes of No. 3 Squadron are more than happy to head for home as, from the east, it is clear that a whole swarm of German aircraft is heading their way. It is always good to get back over your own lines, and today it is particularly good.

As to Lieutenants Grigson and James, the No. 3 Squadron war diary will be uncharacteristically lavish in its praise: 'This was a very fine performance on the part of the Pilot and Observer concerned.'[61]

Elsewhere the RAF and AFC planes continue to create havoc, most particularly among German troops trying to come forward to counter-attack.

Time and again throughout the morning, *Generalmajor* Rudolph von Borries has been trying to move his 202nd Reserve Infantry Regiment into position, but it proves impossible as they continue to be strafed and bombed from on high by *feindlichen Luftgeschwader*, enemy air squadrons.

In desperation, the Germans send forth their own planes from Second Army's *Jagdgruppe VII*, led by 30-victory ace Captain Emil Thuy, to try to control the skies once more, and it works . . . for a while.

The enemy swarm coming their way seen by Lieutenants Grigson and Dimsey arrives over Hamel from 9.30 am and is able to exact at least some revenge when another *Jagdgruppe VII* ace, *Leutnant* Martin Dehmisch, of Jasta 58, is able to shoot down another of the RAF's No. 9 Squadron RE8s that had been doing the parachute drops, killing Lieutenant Sydney Harris and wounding Donald Bell. It's his fourth victory. Others of the RAF and AFC planes are able to get away.

•

After the German fighters have gone, Bean and his comrades are filled with admiration as, 'the observation planes took up their ceaseless patrol . . . Observation buses kept the air, doing every sort of menial service – watching, reporting, carrying.'[62]

Whatever the Germans do in the way of counter-attack, 4th Division HQ is going to know about it, as are the artillery batteries which, time and again, are able to bring lethal salvos down on any Fritz troops seen to be moving forward.

•

Back at the Australian Corps HQ at Bertangles, the delighted General Sir John Monash remains where he has been since the wee hours, in his office overlooking the front of the chateau, going over all the reports, gazing at the maps, working out not only where all his forces are – that part is relatively easy, for they have all made the Blue Line – but just what their strength is, and what the likely contours of the German counter-attack will be.

The most crucial thing now, of course, is going to be to hold on when it comes, and he gives orders accordingly, moving troops and artillery forward into the newly won positions.

Though busy, he does make time to dash off the script for one quick telegram to the man who had not long ago actually been contemplating relieving him of his position, because of the agitation of two journalists who had never led so much as a platoon in battle.

> Prime Minister of Australia
>
> Versailles.
> Today's operations brilliantly successful. All objectives captured. More than 1000 prisoners taken and many more coming in. Our casualties believed very light.
>
> General Monash
> Australian Corps
> ADC 18
> 9.55AM
> 4/7/18 [63]

Ah, vindication be thy name . . .

CHAPTER ELEVEN

THE AFTERMATH

A Yankee who could speak German asked a German prisoner did he think they were winning the war, he replied: 'Yes, God is with us.'

The Yankee replied: 'That's nothing, the Australians are with us.'[1]

Diary of Private Sydney Young of Campsie

11.30 am, 4 July 1918, Salle de bal, La Grande Palace de Trianon

Welcome to the seventh session of the Supreme War Council in the one-time ballroom of the Trianon Palace Hotel, Versailles, and by the bright morning light coming through the heavy curtains, gaze around the table at these political and military heavyweights of the Allied cause, as we see such major figures as British Prime Minister Lloyd George, British Foreign Secretary Arthur Balfour, Italian Prime Minister Vittorio Emanuele Orlando, General John Pershing, Field Marshal Ferdinand Foch, Sir Henry Wilson and Field Marshal Douglas Haig, together with Australia's Prime Minister Billy Hughes, and the Prime Ministers of New Zealand, Canada and Newfoundland.

And now lean in, as the French Prime Minister Georges Clemenceau – whose favourite meeting opener is *'L'ordre du jour est le travail. Travaillons!'*[2] – stands to welcome on this morning the Prime Ministers of the Dominions, who are joining them for the first time.

You, *Messieurs les Premiers Ministres*, 'who have travelled so many thousands of miles to reach Versailles . . . assembled together in league against a common foe'[3] are *le bienvenue*, most welcome, and . . .

And what now?

An aide-de-camp comes in, bearing news.

Clemenceau beams just to hear it, and soon exults to the wider gathering.

There has been a victory, an important breakthrough of quite inspirational stature. It is *les Australiens*, with *les Americains* by their side. Together, they have attacked the German lines at Le Hamel, and advanced almost *two* miles!

Billy Hughes and General Black Jack Pershing are, of course, the two present who are most warmly congratulated, the American doing his best to hide his gobsmacked surprise that his troops had been there in the first place, when he had given *specific* instructions for them to be withdrawn. Under the circumstances, of course, now is not the time to hoot and holler, nor to say that the Americans had been there *against* his orders and he had known nothing about it.

Another small parenthesis here. Even later, in his public remarks, General Pershing will be measured. 'It was . . .' he would only allow, 'somewhat of a surprise to learn on the following day that four companies of 33rd Division had taken part in the attack.'[4] Privately, however, he is ropable, and the recriminations will go on for some time, with Rawlinson noting in his diary five days later, 'I visited Bell . . . Bell says Pershing and Read are still fighting over American troops being employed on 4 July.'[5]

And Pershing has taken the slight to heart.

'The incident, though relatively unimportant in itself,' he would note, 'showed clearly the disposition of the British to assume control of our units, the very thing which I had made such strong efforts and had imposed so many conditions to prevent. Its immediate effect was to cause me to make the instructions so positive that nothing of the kind could occur again.'[6] From now on, the protocol will be that all requests to use American troops in battles must be passed by him personally.

Close parenthesis.

In the here and now, however, on receipt of the wonderful news, a motion is immediately passed to send congratulations to the Australian Corps, while, for his part, Georges Clemenceau asks his secretary to cable his personal congratulations, before thinking better of it.

'No,' he says, 'I'll go and see them and congratulate them myself.'[7]

For his part, Billy Hughes is beyond thrilled, so proud he can barely raise spit – 'Excellent! Capital!'[8] – though he will soon exclaim to his redoubtable son Ernie, 'In my opinion, it was certainly my very inspiring speech that was responsible for the victory!'[9]

•

Back at Hamel, the day begins to settle as both sides lick their wounds from the battle of the night before, and gird their loins for the battle to come.

'From the morning onward,' Bean would note, 'one could see small parties moving towards the line, both from our side and the German. As they neared the line, they usually spread out. Now and then a man who had been walking would start to run, and you saw spurts of dust flicked up near his heels. Sometimes he would fling himself flat for a minute and then get up and do another bolt. Those were the cases in which the snipers were after them. Then, far beyond the German line, there moved down through the crops at a fast pace three or four wagons. They may have been ambulances . . .'

And what now?

'A small number of men – perhaps twenty – immediately came from the place where they stopped, and moved in two parties towards the back of Accroche Wood. They seemed to get into some trench or sunken road before they reached it. Later, those three wagons went back again. A Red Cross flag was flying in front of another wood . . . Parties of men were moving up most of the distant roads. Probably it was the German building up a new line to face us, for his line in front of us was certainly gone.'[10]

•

Yes, it is exactly that.

While some of the German units are preparing to counter-attack, others are doing their best to recover some semblance of order amidst the carnage. At least, now, mercifully, the 55th Infantry Regiment, which had been defending the pear-shaped trench – where things had been in fact *going* a little pear-shaped – are no longer being actively pursued by the enemy soldiers and they have been able to dig in once more, with such machine guns as they still have, manned by their brave surviving soldiers.

'Though the enemy could not be thrown back, stopping his further advance was successful finally . . . The new line ran about 1 km further back than the previous line. The enemy had planned a considerably farther advance . . .'[11]

•

The planes drop bombs, the artillery fires shells, and even snipers manage to pick targets off. As the wretched morning wears on, the German soldiers of 202nd RIR 1st Battalion continue to push to the west.

'*Wie gehetztes Wild*, like hunted game,' one of their number, Second *Leutnant* Pyritz, 1st MG Company, will recount, 'we often seek shelter in holes and entries of tunnels as the *Brisanzgranaten*, high-explosive shells, are *ganz abscheulich*, truly abominable. We call them *Glaskisten*, glass boxes. The splinters fly close to the ground up to about 100 metres from the explosion. A very special surprise awaits us, however, when we finally reach the *Taillenschlucht*, our reserve position. An English railroad-gun bombards us with 24-cm shells. *Wie schwere Eisenkoffer*, like heavy iron-suitcases, the *Höllenbiester*, hellish beasts, turn up, and *mit gehirnzerdröhnendem Krachen bersten sie*, with a brain-bursting crash, they burst. In a few moments the entire gorge is wrapped in dense dust and smoke. This is meant to be our period of rest! Thank God, Tommy can afford this pleasure only a few times a day.'[12]

As they move forward despite it all, '*Feindliches Luftgeschwader*, an enemy air squadron with up to 80 aircraft circulated continuously at low altitude above the position and made any traffic impossible. Every individual man was attacked with M.G. and bombs.'

At noon, at last, a strong squadron of German planes appears to chase the Allied planes away, but no sooner has the German squadron gone off to refuel, than the enemy planes reappear '*in großer Überzahl*, in great excess, and soon had unrestricted air control again'.[13]

It seems the enemy has been expecting them to do exactly this, and has prepared for it. Everything they have done for the last 12 hours, the enemy has already thought of it! There is no way around it, as the Official History of 202 RIR records: 'Under these circumstances the approach of the 1st Battalion was *sehr zeitraubend und verlustreich*, very time-consuming and high in losses.'[14]

All they can do is keep pressing on, using all the cover available, first along the banks of the Somme, and then into the *Vallée d'Abancourt*, a gully that leads from there to the base of Wolfsberg. After such a journey, weakened in numbers all the way, are they *really* to attack the enemy on high, in broad daylight, as they have been ordered?

The Battalion has come forward to get into position, where, for the whole morning '*feindliches Sperrfeuer*, enemy barrage-fire of the heaviest calibre [*zerstampfte*, stomped] the battlefield, especially the *Anmarschwege*, approach-routes through the Somme Valley . . .'[15].

All the signs point to an horrific battle ahead. Mercifully, at least a little sanity prevails, as in the early afternoon their commanders tell them they may find shelter the best they can, in many of the old dugouts to be found in the gully at the eastern foot of Wolfsberg, and then wait till it's dark – which gives them at least a few more hours to live.

That is, unless you are unlucky . . .

•

The Australians on the Blue Line, nevertheless, are not without troubles of their own, as the German winged observers on high combine with their artillery to direct extraordinarily accurate fire – most of it seeming to concentrate on those on Wolfsberg, while also plastering the new occupiers of Hamel. In the meantime, there is also a little more stiffness in the sinew of the German soldiers facing the Blue Line, as they have clearly brought their snipers forward with instructions to shoot anything that moves. In front of the 6th Brigade on the far right, the snipers exact such a toll that, for a short time, the new tenants cease to do the wiring in front of their newly dug trenches.

Nevertheless, by late morning the work is resumed and completed, and across the front now, the Blue Line is not only occupied, but relatively well dug in and wired. *Now* let the Germans try to counter-attack – something that will be even more difficult for them now, as the Australians' own artillery is organising rapidly. Observers atop Wolfsberg with binoculars are connected by field telephone to their artillery brigades a mile back and, first at 11 o'clock and then at noon, they are able to bring down withering fire upon the Germans clearly congregating in the *Vallée d'Abancourt*, which lies before the hilltop and is the obvious place to launch a counter-attack on Wolfsberg.

•

The day wears on, and both sides of the line carefully, oh so carefully, rearrange their forces, to attack, counter-attack and even *counter*-counter-attack.

In the HQ of Germany's 201st Reserve Infantry Regiment, it has taken some doing, and many messengers heading back and forth, but finally *Oberst* Kuczkowski has come to a decision. It seems that the reported attack by Tommy at Sailly-Laurette (where, still unbeknownst to the Germans, the Australians had used *papier-mâché* dummies) was not an attack at all, but more likely, a mere feint.

This means that, in the first instance, they will not send their reserve Battalion, the 1/201, that has just 'arrived at the Buchhain-Mulde, to be at the disposal of the regiment', forward to Sailly-Laurette.

Where to, instead?

They will send the men to the other attack, just south of the Ancre River (where Pompey Elliott's 58th and 59th Battalions had launched a more aggressive feint, capturing 1000 yards of German trench using just 400 men). Yes, when it falls dark, the reserve battalion, 'together with three companies and one heavy M.G. each, moved into defensive position on the *Dewitz-Höhe*, Dewitz Height . . . The height was to be held against enemy attacks.'[16]

And yet, are they right to have thought Sailly-Laurette was a feint? 201st RIR HQ is not sure. Just to be on the safe side, 'in the late afternoon, the regiment received also III/448 as battle troops',[17] as in another fresh reserve battalion, who are moved into position at Sailly-Laurette.

In short, the best part of a day after the attack, the feint on the Australian left flank is working better than even Monash could possibly have hoped for, as it continues to confuse the Germans about how best they should defend against further thrusts, and so diffuses their response on where the actual attack has occurred.

•

Atop Wolfsberg, however, the Australians in the newly won trenches are in little doubt that a counter-attack on their positions is building.

'The Germans are shelling the trench and we have to keep very low,' Private Charles Manners of the 44th would recount, 'the beggars have the range to a "tee".'[18]

Sure enough, from 4 pm onwards they can even see the Germans starting to gather lower down in the *Vallée d'Abancourt*. The brutes will be coming all right.

'Everyone is on the alert, awaiting anxiously for the next move. We are short of bombs. Their fire is very heavy about 6.00 pm and about an hour later A Coy on our left fire their SOS and are seen retiring to a shallow trench about 30 yards behind the frontline.'[19]

Things are grim and getting grimmer – and come the night, their attack will almost certainly be unleashed with full force.

•

In the meantime, various postscripts of the battle just gone are still being written in the blood trailed on the rich French soil.

'At 6 o'clock in the afternoon,' the history of Germany's 55th Infantry Regiment, which had been so bravely trying to hold, and then retake, Pear Trench – records, 'the brave officer and his loyal men [*Rittmeister Freiherr* von Preuschen and his messengers, orderlies and communication staff] managed to get back to our lines *mit Abständen einzeln kriechend*, crawling, one-by-one. Apart from the battalion staff, only one officer and 20 men have returned from the front line to the regiment.'[20]

Devastation! Of the 500 men of the Battalion who'd been holding the line and the reserve line the previous evening, this appears to be all that is left.

And of course, on the Australian side of the line the burying goes on, as does the process of getting the merely wounded evacuated to receive better medical treatment well behind the lines.

In the front-lines, the Australian soldiers are holding on.

Having withstood the German artillery barrage all day, Cliff Geddes also feels that, with the onset of the near darkness, it must be at last okay to rise a little and move around their half-dug trench – not least to organise an evening meal – and so stands up . . .

In the gloom, a German machine-gunner is sure he has seen movement, and fires off a burst.

Straight and true, one of the bullets heads straight to Cliff's head and – there is no sergeant to take his spot after shaving – this time hits him in the back of the skull.

Fortunately, this time, Cliff is not shaving, and has his helmet on.

'It dented the hat making a big hollow, but didn't pierce it, & I was unharmed, only the weight of the blow on the steel hat making my head ache.'[21]

It is a great headache to have, under the circumstances.

For all that, 'the chap near me got a nice "Blighty" a hit in the shoulder, the stretcher bearers took him away, lucky dog'.[22]

The rest of them must hold on.

'At dusk,' Bean would recount, 'we left that scene almost as peaceful as the earth before man was made.'[23]

Up close, it is not quite as it first appears, as the darkness will shortly be bringing movement . . .

For among those waiting on the German side, for that very going down of the sun, are the soldiers of the 1st Battalion, of the 202 RIR, who know that their time is nigh to take back Wolfsberg.

•

At his Fourth Army HQ in Flixecourt on this evening, General Rawlinson writes with some satisfaction in his diary:

> It has been a good day. The Australians with 4 [Companies] of Americans attacked and gained all their objectives including Hamel and Vaire wood . . . I visited the wounded in hospital and found them all very cheery. I fancy the Boche will put in a heavy counterattack tonight. We are ready for him if he does . . . I saw Bell and Monash later [in the] PM and congratulated them on

their success. This attack . . . will upset the Boche plans. What a mercy it was not postponed!!![24]

•

Some 100 miles north-east of Rawlinson, at the HQ of the German Army Group, Commanding Officer Crown Prince Rupprecht von Bayern has now gone through the reports of Hamel, and he records his own thoughts:

> According to the 2nd Army, the opponent attacked with one division north of the Somme and with two divisions south of the Somme, both attacks being accompanied by tanks. South of the Somme, the enemy succeeded in achieving a larger break-in into our positions at Hamel and in taking the height east of Hamel.[25]

Yes, Brigadier Pompey Elliott's men north of the Somme, using just 400 men, has been mistaken by the Germans for a full-blown Divisional attack of 16,000 men! So much so, that Rupprecht will be not long in writing: '*Eine neuerliche Weisung*, a new directive from Supreme Army Command about the leadership of the defensive battles, had an almost depressing effect on me . . . *Das ganze Schriftstück*, the whole document is *ein betrüblicher Beweis unserer Schwäche*, a sad proof of our weakness.'[26]

For now, though, Rupprecht is intent on winning back the ground lost, and at least content that a serious counter-attack will be put in overnight.

•

Yes, all day, the artillery observers atop Wolfsberg had been able to direct the Allied artillery onto any sign of a build-up of German troops in the *Vallée d'Abancourt*, which lies at its base. But, sure enough, now, that it is so dark *dass man die Hand vor Augen nicht sehen kann*, that you cannot see the hand before your eyes, the commander coordinating the German counter-attack on Wolfsberg, the 43rd Division's *Generalmajor* Wilhelm Theodor Knoch, is able to make reply.

First he gives the orders for his troops to move *en masse*, forward from the *Vallée*.

And now, at last, at 9 pm, the German guns which have survived unseen through the day start to belch their streaks of fiery fury. Just seconds later, precisely as *der Generalmajor* had planned, the defenders of Wolfsberg, the Australians and Americans dug into the newly claimed positions near the crest – and on the furthermost Australian positions 200 yards down its eastern side – are engulfed with shells as geysers of flame and dirt shoot skywards all around them.

Many of the shells that don't score direct hits on the trenches at least shatter the wire.

'*Und wie gefällt es dir?*' And how do *you* bastards like it?

The short answer is, 'not very bloody much, but we will cope the best we can'.

Which the men of the 44th Battalion do, at least those who survive.

Among them is Private Charles Manners, who is glad to see that their own side is not entirely without venom of their own.

'Our artillery and machine guns open up with the fury of the devil,' he would recount. 'There seems to be a curtain of steel and lead tearing through the air over our heads.'[27]

But equally no-one is under any illusions that it will stop the Germans.

'One will never forget this night,' Manners would recount. 'Hamel is now behind us, a burning ruin. The Germans are now pouring a few shells into the ruin. These shriek overhead and land with a crash. Now and again an occasional gas shell with its shriller shriek tears through the sky and bursts with a dull thud, the sound of which serves to put the wind up one and all, the more on account of its deadliness.'[28]

Up ahead of Manners and C Company, in the front-line trenches on Wolfsberg, they know only too well what is coming.

Suddenly, after the barrage has lasted an hour, at 10 pm it stops, and through the smoke come charging the unleashed *Schweinhunde* of hell – first a bombing party of aggrieved German soldiers of the 1st Battalion of the 202nd Reserve Infantry Regiment, followed by 400 soldiers of the Battalion proper, determined to take back that which had been taken from them. After grenades are hurled from both sides, as well as machine-gun fire, vicious fighting breaks out in the trenches themselves.

The thrust of the German attack has hit the trenches, as the 44th's Official History records, 'at the junction of A and B Companies sectors',[29] and in the end Fritz's counter-attack is indeed overwhelming.

'With artillery support,' the German Official History will recount, 'the three companies pushed into the east-trenches of Wolfsberg. [It was] *ihr Bemühen, die vom Feinde besetzte Stellung weiter aufzurollen*, their effort to roll up the position occupied by the enemy . . .'[30]

And yes, it is true, having secured some 200 yards of those trenches, killed several dozen Australians of the 44th Battalion, and taken some 15, mostly wounded, prisoners, they would have liked to extend their hold from there. Alas, they had '*infolge mangelnder Kräfte keinen Erfolg*, no success due to the lack of forces'.[31]

But they have taken a good swathe of Wolfsberg back, and that is really something. At least they have got a foothold.

•

Back at 44th Battalion HQ, now established in a cellar in Hamel, it does not take long to work out what has happened, and that the Germans have taken back at least 200 yards of their trenches on Wolfsberg.

Moving typically quickly, the 44th's Commanding Officer, Colonel James Clark, orders C Company, which has been held back in reserve to retake the line at dawn, to prepare for action soon. Unbeknownst to him, however, two of the officers up front do not even wish to wait that long. For, amidst the roar and tumult, they have decided there is only one thing for it. The surviving Australians of the 44th – those in the trenches on either side of the part that Fritz has taken, are going to have to *counter*-counter-attack, and get the brutes out again.

In the meantime, Manners makes his way back to join them.

'With every nerve on the alert, we creep up the Communication Trench and listen for voices . . .'[32]

He is there just in time to hear the key decisions being sorted out.

'Fritz was well established along about 200 yards of trench,' Captain Cyril Longmore would recount. 'So the plan is the two bombing parties start 200+ yards apart, and work their way towards each other till Fritz is squeezed out.'[33]

It is Lieutenant Dick Cornish of B Company and Lieutenant Rick Gaze of D Company who take the lead on the southern side of the German break-in, calling for volunteers. The hands of a dozen Diggers shoot up, together with the hand of one Yank.

And they are good men! Among them is a 'great Dane', Sergeant Jens Edvard Valdemar Karl Ingvarson, DCM, though known to one and all as 'Yak', who'd only arrived in Australia in 1913 – after jumping ship at Fremantle. Shortly thereafter he had become a naturalised Australian, joined up in 1916, and had since been one of the 44th's best soldiers. In the light thrown by a flare it gives Lieutenant Cornish some confidence just to gaze upon Yak: a 24-year-old with classic Nordic features, built like a blond Viking, with tattoos on both arms and a chin like a clenched fist. The equivalent wild man in the D Company group – a near six-footer – is Sergeant John Padgett, a 36-year-old stonemason from Perth, who had risen to the rank of sergeant three times! Twice before 'reduced to the ranks', for being absent without leave for a week at a time, and twice wounded in action, he had risen back both times by pure dint of the fact that there is no better man to have in action when the bullets are flying and the bayonets flashing.

Another that stands out is Private James Lynch of Gympie – an enormous 23-year-old axeman of great repute before the war, with a neck like the stump of an iron-bark tree, and arms like other men's thighs, with a scar on his right leg and two huge scars on his right arm from axe accidents. He, too, gives Lieutenants Gaze and Cornish confidence that Fritz is about to get a belting.

One American wants to be in it too, Corporal Thomas Pope, from Chicago.

Quickly, following the Lieutenants' urgings, the volunteers – Private Charles Manners among them – gather every grenade they can get their hands on.

Here, Digger, take this. And here are some more. And some more still, for you worthy Yank, and good on yer!

•

For the exhausted, bloodied soldiers of the 202nd RIR it has been one thing to take back this part of the trench of Wolfsberg, but the question is, will they be able to hold it? Certainly, if they'd had the 201st RIR with them, they would have been able to put the issue beyond doubt, but most of the 201st had been kept back in reserve – until the situation becomes clearer. As it is, they have just 300 men who have survived the attack to this point, and of them dozens are wounded, and unable to be evacuated, the same as the Australian prisoners they have taken. Things are grim.

•

Watches synchronised, the time to get going is now approaching. With Lieutenants Gaze and Cornish gathering their men at the southern end of the German intrusion, the seconds tick away until – exactly as it had been the night before – there is *just* enough light from dawn to let the dog see the rabbit. It is just gone 3.10 am on the morning of 5 July.

And . . . *now*.

With a cry, the Aussies are up, and, as Captain Cyril Longmore of the 44th would describe it, 'they went bald-headed at the Huns from both flanks'.[34]

And so it goes, bald-headed and growling like hungry animals cut loose to hunt their natural enemies, the Australians and American charge in the gloom.

Into the bastards, boys!

There is more riding on their attack than they can know. For, from the other end, on the north side, the attack by the men of A Company, under Captain Wilfred Stables, is getting nowhere as Fritz holds firm, giving at least as good as he gets and more. So it will be all up to Cornish and Gaze, with their great Dane, their wild American, their stonemason, their axeman, and a dozen other hard men to do the job.

•

One moment the Germans of the 202nd Reserve Infantry Regiment are nervously peering up and down Wolfsberg, and the next there are grenades exploding all around them, even as enormous men with flashing, slashing bayonets fall upon them. Even their tattoos are angry!

'They drove them from bay to bay in the trench,' Longmore would proudly describe it.

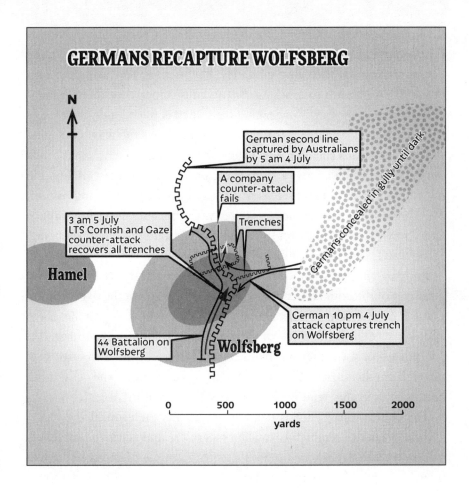

GERMANS RECAPTURE WOLFSBERG

N

German second line captured by Australians by 5 am 4 July

A company counter-attack fails

3 am 5 July LTS Cornish and Gaze counter-attack recovers all trenches

Trenches

Germans concealed in gully until dark

Hamel

German 10 pm 4 July attack captures trench on Wolfsberg

44 Battalion on Wolfsberg

Wolfsberg

0   500   1000   1500   2000

yards

In the confusion of it all, Manners loses his Skipper, who, as it happens is doing much the same, albeit in reverse.

'At last I see him forging right ahead with great agility for one of his stamp; then making a rush to reach his side before he gets out of sight again, I find myself entangled in the barb-wire. As German machine gun bullets are getting pretty thick, I get pretty annoyed and hasten to extricate myself from its coils. It is still dark, and I have a job to find the Skipper. I manage to discover him at last rushing at three Fritzies. On bailing them up, my bayonet drops off . . . !'[35]

And yes, there is serious resistance, but the Australians and their accompanying American are up for it. As expected, Yak and Padgett are outstanding from the first. But on this occasion, the one who is like the human version of an exploding grenade in a barrel of monkeys is Private James Lynch. For it is Lynch now *leading* the charge, down the German trenches, throwing grenades, bayoneting, and using the butt of his rifle as a club to crack German skulls. Once they meet Stables' A Company in the north – meaning the trench is theirs once more – it is again Lynch, 'irresistible throughout',[36] who shows the way. Changing direction, he leads the men down the communication trench that heads on the perpendicular away from the German front-line; this was the trench the Germans had used to first sneak into the Australian position. The German soldiers fly helter-skelter with the Wild West Australians and Crazy Brave from Illinois, 'after them, bombing, snap-shooting, and firing Lewis Guns from the hip'.[37]

And yet, though some Germans are fast – and faster still when they jump out of the communication trench to charge down the open ground of the hill – they are not fast enough for Lynch, who soon catches them and is instantly in the thick of them once more, until, oh, Christ . . .

Until a sole shot rings out from close quarters, and Lynch falls, shot through the head by a German officer, who has done the only thing he can to stop this wild bull of an Australian madman.

The courageous Lynch is dead 'afore he hits the ground.

Still, after the mighty Australian's heroics, and with the attackers swarming like a pack of dingoes – with a couple of coyotes thrown in – the Fritzes understand that now is not the time to be a hero and continue to flee, some of them, no doubt, 'incontinently'.

For his part, Manners is in two minds. With a few German prisoners nearby, the obvious temptation beckons.

'Perhaps if the Skipper had not rushed to new fields, I may have ratted the blighters. I had to follow the Skipper anyhow . . .'[38]

He'll have to be quick, as his Skipper and the others are now in full cry, chasing the Germans.

For the most part, the remaining Fritzes stay in the communication trench which they had used to get here in the first place, but when they get to a place where it is only two feet deep, they jump out and flatout flee across the fields, down the hill.

'The two parties followed, flinging bombs, bayoneting, sharp-shooting, and using two Lewis Guns (one per party) from the hip.'[39]

Going out hard – like foxes after chickens when their blood is up – the Australians and their American support are *still* closing on them, when, with a chattering shattering, one of the German machine-gun posts ahead of them opens fire the instant Fritz is past it.

Most of the Australians go to ground immediately, some because they are hit.

But there is an exception.

With a shout of, 'I see it!'[40] The Chicagoan, Corporal Thomas Pope – a fine soldier, though he doesn't know it yet – of E Company, 131st Infantry, leaps up and starts running straight at where he has seen the flashes of the machine gun in the gloom. Firing as he goes, he is soon able to leap into the pit and do the rest of his grisly work with his bayonet, killing several Germans in the process. Even now his work is not done, and as would be officially recorded, 'standing astride . . . the [German gun he] kept the remainder of the detachment at bay until the arrival of reinforcements . . .'[41]

(It is madness, absolute madness, but similar acts of Crazy Brave bravery are displayed by the Yanks through the day, as observed by the Australians. As one of the Diggers says afterwards, 'We are damned glad they are on our side.'[42])

In this case, Pope's derring-do hastens the German flood away from the attackers, as the Fritzes continue scrambling all the way back to *Vallée d'Abancourt* whence they had come.

In short order the 44th Battalion has once again secured the Blue Line on Wolfsberg.

All up, theirs is an extraordinary feat.

'Some Germans got away,' the 44th's History records, 'thirty were killed, many wounded, and one officer and seventy men, together with fifteen machine guns mounted in the trench, were captured. Also eleven out of the fifteen 44th men who had been taken the night before were [liberated]. And all this by two officers and fourteen men! It was a wonderful performance, watched by practically the whole battalion . . .'[43]

For its part, the Official History of the 202nd RIR would be a little less prosaic: 'The enemy again wrested away the conquered trench sections from the *sehr geschwächten*, very weakened 1st Battalion. The trenches at the east edge of Wolfsberg were lost, so that the enemy now had all of Wolfsberg in his possession.'[44]

It has been an extraordinary night for the survivors of both sides.

'Having had no sleep for 48 hours,' Private Charles Manners would record, 'at 8.00am on the 5th July, after dragging five or six dead bodies over the top and dumping them, I am very thankful to crawl into a bunk after an acceptable tot of rum, and fall asleep at once.'[45]

The day after, 5 July 1918, dawn on the thin Blue Line

And yet, if the ultimate failure of the German counter-attack on Wolfsberg in the early hours of 5 July will prove to be Fritz's last attempt to seize the trenches on foot, still there will prove to be plenty of venom left in his planes and artillery. They harass the new holders of the Blue Line throughout the rest of the day, and Monash's men are pounded unmercifully.

'The air was alive with German planes,' Cliff Geddes records. 'Where ours were I don't know, but I've never seen so many Huns up before . . . It's very exceptional for Fritz to be in the majority in the air. Wrote up my diary in morning & lay down in the bottom of our new trench, & had an uncomfortable sleep.'[46]

The Australians and Americans in the front-line have also been under severe bombardment. When they emerge, it is to find, first up, that Corporal Edward Bolus, the Company Clerk, has been badly wounded in the leg, while several others have such bad shell shock that they have to be evacuated. Worse, just to their right, a shell has made a direct hit, and two corporals, Charlie Mann and Marsden Holt, have been blown to pieces.

As experienced as he is in such dreadful matters, still Cliff is sickened as he gazes down upon the remains of Holty – what had been him is now missing one head and a leg.

'Good heavens, it's an awful business. You never know what a minute will bring forth.'[47]

Now, theirs is the sleep of the just, it is just not a sleep that lasts for long, as the German shelling continues throughout the day, and the only thing they can do is to sit, 'huddled up in the bottom of the trench, while these big iron foundries burst with a dreadful crash, & one wondered when he would be hit, & his torture ended. It was something cruel to be under, but I didn't feel very frightened, one sort of gets resigned to it.'[48]

Others are not so resigned, however, most notably a young signaller who shivers and shakes with every fresh explosion. And though he dutifully stays on his receiver, cabling the situation back to HQ, the constant shelling takes its toll on him. As one huge shell explodes close enough to send detritus falling down upon them, he shudders and says, 'I can't stand it much longer.'[49]

Still, Cliff remains calm, knowing that there can't be much left in this barrage, as among other things, Fritz must soon run out of ammunition that he will have hauled forward. And sure enough, soon enough, it does stop.

Both Cliff and the signaller are all right – and as a relative calm returns to the once tumultuous battlefield, the lull after the storm once more, it is clear that for the moment at least, the Germans have no other counter-punches left to throw.

For now, the battle is over.

Forever, alas, Cliff's friends, Mann and Holt, are dead, and the respite has come just a little too late for them.

Of course, they are only a small part of death's cruel harvest of the battle overall. Of the Australians, no fewer than 1400 will be casualties in this battle, of whom some 300 are killed. The Americans will suffer in similar proportions, with 176 casualties among their 1000 soldiers, of whom 45 are killed. British losses among their artillery, tank and flight crews were negligible.

German losses on the other hand, are heavy, with no fewer than 1605 Germans taken prisoner, and as many again killed and wounded. For the first time on the Western Front the defending side has suffered more losses than the attacking side. And not just a little more. The defenders have lost – in killed, wounded and captured – double what the attackers lost. These figures – 3200 Germans lost, against just 1600 Australians, British and Americans – are irrefutable proof of a brilliantly conducted attack.

For the Allies, it has been the first major offensive success in eight months, since the attack at Cambrai the previous November – also with tanks.

5 am, 6 July 1918, in the newly dug trenches on the Blue Line north of Wolfsberg, overlooking the Somme

Time to go, you blokes. Here with the 43rd Battalion, the plan has been for the Americans to leave after a big breakfast of Aussie stew, washed down by endless Aussie pats on the back, and, 'Good luck, cobbers!'

All up, it is extraordinary . . .

The Australians and Americans have only known each other for a week and in most cases don't even know each other's names. But the bond between them has the strength of the ages behind it. Ever and always, brothers in arms, who have fought side by side together, who have buried their dead together, who have come through two long nights, seen the dawn, and lived to fight again, have a bond that mere associations in peacetime, lasting even for years, cannot get close to.

'You'll do me, Yank,' one Australian would say to his new American mate, in a line that would be oft repeated, 'but you chaps *are* a bit rough.'[50]

The speeches that the officers make to each other, thus, are heartfelt, as are the cheers from both Australian and American soldiers – many of the latter still proudly wearing the colours of the 43rd!

Ah, but one more thing before you go . . .

Will Corporal Henry Zyburt please step forward?

It is with thanks, and recognition of your extraordinary courage in the taking of Hamel village, that we present to you and your regiment, this 'machine-gun . . . captured under exceptional conditions of bravery'.[51]

Cheers all around, a gracious nodding of the head from Corporal Zyburt as he accepts, on behalf of the Americans, the souvenir that will surely top 'em all.

As the Americans of Company E march off into the growing light of this 6th day of July, it is to the shouts of farewell from their Australian brothers, who, as one would express it, are 'very proud of our victory and our Yankee pals'.[52]

Another puts it this way, of the Americans: 'Very impetuous when the barrage was on, but none gamer.'[53]

The Americans feel much the same when it comes to the Diggers, with one recording: 'A tough bunch of guys, but they taught us a whole lot.'[54] And as Charles Bean notes in his diary, 'Several Americans put up the colours of the [battalion] they were with + are wearing them still.'[55]

Yet another American put it like this: 'It was over – that first fight – but it made an impression on us so that for a day we lived as men who had seen another world – and we had. Our senses fairly reeled with the experiences that had been crowded into those few days . . . For the first time in history the troops of America and the troops of the British Empire fought side by side against a common foe, and we were glad that it had been our privilege to gain this victory for world freedom on our own Independence day. We had heard the shriek of exploding shrapnel, the whistle and clatter of machine gun fire. We had seen the thousand sights of a bloody battlefield, some of which we would be glad to forget. And we realized too that under the little crosses we made from ammunition boxes, lay all that was mortal of some of our comrades.'[56]

Their officers, at least those who have participated and seen the action up close, are united in the view that the whole thing has been enormously beneficial in 'blooding' their troops, with one of them noting in his official report 'United States troops are now classified as Diggers.'[57]

Captain Gale spoke for many of them when he said that, 'more real good was done . . . by this small operation with the Australians than could have been accomplished in months of training behind the lines'.[58]

Captain Thomas White of the 13th Battalion couldn't agree more.

'The battle created a bond of friendship and sincere respect between Diggers and Yanks,' he would note in the 13th Battalion's Official History, 'that should last forever . . . When they said good-bye to us . . . we really felt it was like losing old comrades. The 90 minutes with us had made them soldiers more than all their previous training . . . In our friends those 90 minutes had changed parvenu seriousness into veteran sang-froid.'[59]

•

For his part, at the top level, General John Monash matches the warmth of his battlefield commanders in writing to America's General George Bell of the 33rd Division, whose troops he had had the honour of having under his command.

> *My Dear General*
>
> *I desire to take the opportunity of tendering to you, as their immediate commander, my earnest thanks for the assistance and services of the four companies of infantry who participated in yesterday's brilliant operations. The dash, gallantry and efficiency of these American troops left nothing to be desired and my Australian Soldiers speak in the very highest terms in praise of them. That soldiers of the United States and of Australia should have been associated for the first time in such close co-operation on the battlefield is an historic event of such significance that it will live forever in the annals of our respective Nations.*
>
> *Yours very sincerely*
> *John Monash*
>
> *Lieut-General*
> *Commanding the Australian Corps*[60]

•

Shortly afterwards, on this late morning of 6 July, the now blooded American soldiers of Companies A and G of the 132nd Infantry arrive back at their HQ, looking, to the eyes of one, 'dirty, tired, and wild-eyed'.[61]

Yes, things had gone well and they had won well. But now two days since the battle, and a few hours since leaving the Australians, the red mist has lifted, leaving only the horror of things they had seen and done; while the lost camaraderie of the Australians leaves only sorrow for their own fallen comrades who they will never see again.

'The men were quiet,' one of the American officers who had noted their arrival would chronicle, 'they seemed melancholy; the glory of battle was not in their faces. Everyone carried a souvenir – a cap, a button, a badge, a rifle from the enemy.'[62]

As a matter of fact, the first rifle captured by American soldiers in an attack on the Germans is now presented to the 33rd Division's Commanding Officer General Bell, who makes a speech praising them for their bravery and the honour they have brought to their country. And now other officers speak and, as it is noted, 'after a time, it was uncertain whether the staff or the men had done the fighting, for the affair developed into a holiday of glory for the officers'.[63]

Such is war, whatever the country.

While praise for the Australians is strong, they do not escape criticism, with it being rather crisply noted by one American officer, Captain Carroll Gale, in an official report:

> A tendency was noted on the part of the Australians [who had] an entire disregard for the personal property rights of prisoners of war, stripping them as a rule of anything of value. It is feared some of our own troops followed this example.[64]

Afternoon, 6 July 1918, Blue Line, holding on

Meanwhile, up on the Blue Line, Cliff Geddes and his mates from 13th Battalion are *still* out there, *still* holding, among the last to be withdrawn, and replaced by the fresh reserves, now coming forward to hold the Blue Line.

'Our sadly dwindling company lay down in the bottom of the trench, & had a sleep. Fritz poured shells galore in the open ground behind us during the day, & did make the dust fly. Thank goodness we're going out tonight, there are only 9 in our platoon left, [from the 30 we started with].'

They are relieved that night at 10 pm, and their part of the Battle of Hamel is over.

'We got back to dugouts about 11.30 p.m., & after the usual old hot stew, turned in wearily. Five of us were in one dugout, & the chaps salvaged a couple of mattresses from other dugouts, & we lay side by side, & had a bonza sleep. We were amused in the night, when a chap suddenly jumped up & crawled over us, must have been dreaming of the Huns.'[65]

•

The said Huns are not dreaming. They are having nightmares, the principal one that the Australians will come on, again.

One of them is a Private of 3rd Battalion, 201st Regiment, the only Battalion not yet called forward to try to stop or turn the Australians. On this night he takes time to write to a dear friend, aware that it might well be their last contact.

> Dear Paul,
> Received your letter today. We are now on the Somme. We are also having an exciting time. The English are here, opposite us. He has just made three attacks; he has taken our front line and collared our first and second battalions. Yesterday morning he nearly collared us. During the past night the whole company was withdrawn to the third line; we are to hold the third line and have left one platoon and one machine gun in the front line. If he attacks again now he will finish us. It would be better if he _did_ capture us.[66]

•

Truthfully? Many of the senior officers of the Australian Corps really are tempted to keep pushing east, to make their extraordinary advance even more spectacular. But General Monash is not remotely tempted. That is not part of the plan.

There are to be no more ad hoc advances. The battle is won in the planning. No plan, no battle.

There will be many more advances, but only when the time is right.

•

Now three days after the battle, on this morning of 7 July, Charles Bean happens to turn up at the 4th Division HQ at the Bussy-les-Daours quarry, just five miles from the newly captured village of Hamel, to find a crowd of officers and men gathered around 'a little square man in a neat brown sack suit and a crumpled little felt hat talking to them and smiling. He was most genial, in his element quite; laughing and smiling all the time and talking to them in English.'[67]

Yes, an important man . . .

So important that in the account of Colonel Arthur Hymen, a Gallipoli veteran who is also present, the 'officers and men of the 4th Brigade were specially withdrawn from the line to be introduced . . . and they came on the scene straight from the trenches in fighting kit and covered in mud'.[68]

For notwithstanding the fact that the men squiring this important man are none other than the Generals Sir Henry Rawlinson and Sir John Monash themselves, the man of the moment is, of course, the veteran politician, the one the French themselves call '*Le Tigre*'. Flanked by the French Minister for War and a retinue of senior French officers, Prime Minister Georges Clemenceau is in full cry, making an impromptu speech of gratitude to the Australian troops, on behalf of the French people, and delivering what John Monash will describe to his wife, Vic, 'a very fine and fiery oration, in very good English'.[69]

Take it away, *Monsieur le Premier Ministre*.

'I am glad to be able to speak at least this small amount of English,' he tells them, in his nevertheless thick accent, 'because it enables me to tell you what all French people think of you. They expected a great deal of you because they have heard what you accomplished in the development of your own country. I should not like to say that they are surprised that you have fulfilled their expectations. By that high standard they judge you, and admire you that you have reached it. We have all been fighting the same battle of freedom in these old battlegrounds. You have all heard the names of them in history. But it is a great wonder too, in history, that you should be here fighting on the old battlefields, which you never thought, perhaps, to see. The work of our fathers, which we wanted to hand down unharmed to our children, the Germans tried to take from us. They tried to rob us of all what is dearest in modern human society. But men were the same in Australia, England, France and Italy, and all countries proud of being the home of free people. That is what made you come; that is what made us greet you when you came. We knew you would fight a real fight, but we did not know that from the very beginning you would astonish the Continent with your valour. I have come here for the simple purpose of seeing the Australians and telling them this. I shall go back tomorrow and say to my countrymen: I have seen the Australians; I have looked into their eyes. I know that they, men who have fought great battles in the cause of freedom, will fight alongside us, till the freedom for which we are all fighting is guaranteed for us and our children.'[70]

The troops listen enthralled, and after he finishes there are a few moments of silent reverie at the beauty and emotion of the speech. It had been an oration, Colonel Hymen would note, given 'in such a way that only a great man, such as he undoubtedly was, could do. His sentences were broken, but were sharp and incisive, and most inspiring.'[71]

So inspiring the Diggers now break into tumultuous applause.

'Three cheers for France!'[72] roars a muddy Digger, and his call is met with wild hurrahs.

Delighted by their delight, Clemenceau wades into the soldiers, shaking hands, kissing cheeks and, beaming, refers to the gnarled Diggers as '*De jolis enfants*',[73] pretty children, as he starts to take his leave. And now, to mark the moment, one of the battalion bands that has been hastily formed up breaks into '*La Marseillaise*', causing the Prime Minister to stop on the spot, and stand to attention, as do all the Diggers and officers. He sings, they hum.

Aux armes, citoyens!
Formez vos bataillons!
Marchons! MARCHONS!

'After the last note of the French Anthem had died away,' Colonel Arthur Hymen would recount, 'M. Clemenceau rushed into the centre of the band and embraced the band leader, as only a Frenchman could. Then, waving his hand to us all, he stepped into his car and was gone.'[74]

The Australians have done well, as have their American brothers, and will not be forgotten in these parts.

Not even a hundred years on.

Bravo.

•

The success of the 'Battle of Le Hamel' changes everything. For an Allied military establishment, wearied and bloodied nearly to its knees by four years of a war where every 100 yards of advance had had to be paid for, all too frequently, by *thousands* of lives, the revelation that a formula had finally been found to crack the German line at minimal cost is as manna from heaven.

Never has the reputation of Australian soldiers been higher.

'It is unofficially (very) often stated that Gen'l Foch asked Haig for 40 divisions of British troops for a certain front,' one Digger, Private Sydney Young, notes in his diary on 15 July. 'Haig said it was impossible as we had not the men. Foch said Never mind let me have the 3rd & 4th Australian Divs.'[75]

Rah!

It means, among other things, that the most junior Corps commander of the lot, John Monash – who had been in his new role for just over a *month* – is suddenly the toast of the Allies.

'All England is talking about it and me, and France too,'[76] Monash soon writes home.

Not that he would have it all his own way, as there would be some effort by General Rawlinson to take more than his fair share of the credit for himself.

This would include writing a letter to his friend, Colonel Clive Wigram – Secretary and Equerry to the King – three days after the battle, claiming, among other things . . .

'I selected the date of Independence Day as it was the first occasion on which American troops had taken part in an actual attack alongside our own fellows and I was not a little put out when at the very last moment I got a direct order from Pershing that no American troops were to be employed. It was too late to withdraw them so I am afraid I had to disobey the order.'[77]

(In fact, it was Monash who selected the day, and if anyone had the wherewithal to 'disobey' the order it was also Monash, not the Englishman.)

Rawlinson goes on:

'I introduced several novelties into the attack. Firstly the Tanks which the Australians had no confidence in after their experiences at

Bullecourt where the tanks went wrong, did not turn up in time, ending by shooting at the Australians, so when I proposed using tanks this time the suggestion was not welcomed. However I made them do it.'[78]

(Hardly. In fact, Monash had embraced the tanks from the first.)

The rather more balanced observers, however, are in no doubt where the credit lies and those Allied Commanders and staff officers who wish to learn the secrets of the extraordinary success – and there are many – head not to Rawlinson, but to Sir John Monash.

As to the personal fame and veneration suddenly coming General Monash's way, however, he is nothing if not partial to it, as most Generals would be in such a situation, having risked mightily and . . . won big.

'You will see . . . that the French Press also has got very excited about the Australian Corps,' Monash writes to his wife, Vic, on 15 July. 'In fact we are very much now in the limelight, and I have been personally quite lifted out of the former anonymity of the War. All sorts and conditions of people, from up and down the Battle Line are coming to see me, to try to find out "how it was done".'[79]

To teach those who will be taught, Monash receives his visitors graciously and passes on everything he can. To disseminate his wisdom wider than those who could manage a personal audience, within just three weeks of the Battle of Hamel, a General Staff instructional pamphlet is issued which gives a precise model to the other 25 Corps Commanders on how to conduct an 'all arms battle'. In essence, the idea of the pamphlet is to encapsulate the musical score by which Monash had conducted his orchestra to such stunning effect, and to such a climax.

Among other things it insists that other Allied commanders observe some key points:

NOTE BY THE GENERAL STAFF. ·

1. The success of these operations was largely due to the secrecy with which they were prepared. Every precaution was taken not only to deceive the enemy and to do nothing to arouse suspicion, but also to prevent . . . own troops from knowing that an attack was intended.

2. The value of tanks in assisting the advance of the infantry was conclusively proved . . . It is important, in drawing deductions from this action, to bear in mind . . . that the objective was strictly limited and within the effective fire of the field and heavy artillery as sited for the attack.[80]

In short, courtesy of Monash, GHQ makes it official: the days of just sending waves of men at enemy trenches and hoping to overwhelm them by sheer force of numbers are mercifully gone. From now on, the key is to use 'fighting machinery'[81], the tanks, planes and guns to do much of the heavy lifting as, through rapid, co-ordinated attack against a surprised enemy, you overwhelm their resistance and use your soldiers to mop up and consolidate the ground won.

For Monash, Hamel made all the difference both to his men, and his own position.

'Its effect was electric,' he would claim, 'and it stimulated many men to the realization that the enemy was, after all, not invulnerable, in spite of the formidable increase in his resources which he had brought from Russia. It marked the termination, once and for all of the purely defensive attitude of the British front. It incited in many quarters an examination of the possibilities of offensive action on similar lines by similar means – a changed attitude of mind . . .'[82]

Never one to be accused of hiding his light under a bushel, he would equally note of the battle, 'no fighting operation that the Corps has ever undertaken, has been more brilliantly, cleanly and perfectly carried through . . . The psychological effect . . . was electric and startling. People came from far and near to hear all about it and find out how it was done.'[83]

He had been under no illusions that if it had gone wrong, the machinations of the likes of Murdoch and Bean would likely have seen him relieved of his command. Now, however, he is untouchable . . . and it is General Birdwood whose position is threatened. A month after Hamel, Billy Hughes even cables Cabinet: 'Re position of AIF . . . Birdwood ought not remain GOC AIF any longer.'[84] Hughes' proposal was to have Monash fill both roles, noting 'In view of what Monash has done in the field we feel that his claims cannot be overlooked . . .'[85]

Though the Cabinet did not act upon it, the point remains: in the wake of Hamel, all of Bean's and Murdoch's machinations had come to nought, and nothing they could do would change that.

'So much,' Bean would ruefully note many years later, 'for our high-intentioned but ill-judged intervention.'[86]

For, as he would also later note, 'Hamel was more than a parcel of separate experiments with tanks, Americans and aeroplanes, it was also a trial of a surprise offensive carried out with John Monash's methods of infinite care in co-ordination of the several arms – after preliminary discussion and his own lucid exposition in conference.'[87]

And no-one could dispute its striking success.

Still, at the time, Bean could not quite stop himself from sniping, at least in the privacy of his diary, noting of an episode as General Monash was handing out medals to his finest soldiers, something the photographer recording the moments had told him.

'When the old chap was taking the salute in front of Querrieu Chateau, he kept one eye cocked on the camera and when it was clearly preparing to open fire he made his salute – one of overpowering dignity.'[88]

Vindication!

Even a week after the triumph of Hamel, Keith Murdoch had not given up hope of seeing Monash replaced in the position as Commander of the Australian Corps by General Brudenell White.

So much so, in fact, that a furious White feels obliged to remonstrate with him, in 'a raging conversation'[89] in the chateau gardens at Fifth Army HQ at Upen d'Aval, when White realises that Murdoch is *still* agitating.

'It is highly improper,' White tells him straight, 'to try and interfere as a pressman or a publicist, in a decision made by the government of our country on the advice of its responsible authorities ... Monash deserved his post and cannot be removed without suffering a terrible blow to his prestige.'

And he does not want to hear Murdoch's remonstrations.

'Even if asked to become Corps commander,' he thunders, 'I would reply that I could not take the position unless it were with Monash's full approval, and [even then] I would only take it under protest.

I feel that it would be said that I had taken the position from Monash and I would not be able to look many of the officers in the face. The efforts of you and Bean are already being referred to as "an intrigue by White's friends" . . .'

For his part, Murdoch is underwhelmed.

'I describe the interview as wholly unsatisfactory,' he would report to Bean in a letter, 'because it really led nowhere. White is not nearly as strong in political thought as he is in military thought.'[90]

The same could never be said of Murdoch himself as, a week after Hamel, he writes to Monash in an effort to 'dispel any suspicion that may still lurk in your mind about an intrigue against you . . .'[91]

Perish the thought!

In the meantime, Monash is now too busy – and too powerful – to bother too much with such trifles. Not for nothing would the historian John Terraine later note that Hamel 'was a revolution, a text-book victory, a little masterpiece casting a long shadow before it'.[92]

For with the battle on 4 July now the model for how to proceed, it is no surprise that the Australian forces are thereafter at the forefront of so many battles for the rest of the war – making Monash ever stronger still – and the whole thing starts with one more extraordinary triumph.

On the evening of 7 August 1918, just a little more than a month after the battle of Hamel, General Monash takes Bean aside and tells him the big news. The next day, the Australians would be front and centre on a major offensive south of the Somme.

Sure enough, on 8 August 1918, the Battle of Amiens begins, under the command of Field Marshal Douglas Haig, but with a clear difference from previous battles. For all such attacks after 4 July used the model of what had happened at Hamel, a model specifically designed by Sir John Monash.

The Australians' role in the battle is to advance, with the Canadians on their right, from the very ground they had won in the Battle of Hamel, from their trenches on Wolfsberg. Using the same model as on 4 July, they attack the German lines in the darkness of 4.20 am, and promptly unleash tanks, soldiers, planes and artillery in a highly co-ordinated attack . . .

As, an hour before dawn on that day, 3640 guns of the British and French Army explode in unison, signalling the beginning of the battle, a member of General Monash's staff, Major Frank Berryman, turned to him.

'Sir,' he said, 'this is a most wonderful day for you.'

'No, Berry,' Monash replied, 'it is a very wonderful day for Australia and history will bear this out.'[93]

A 15-mile hole is created in the German line and they advance eight miles on just the first day. General Erich Ludendorff, the defeated adversary, would famously write that, '*Der 8. August*, the 8th of August, *ist der schwarze Tag des deutschen Heeres in der Geschichte dieses Krieges*, is the black day of the German Army in the history of this war.'[94]

As a mark of what had been achieved, four days after the battle, Monash is knighted by King George V 'in the field', at Chateau de Bertangles – effectively a rising in rank from his two previous knighthoods.[95] It is the first time a commander had been knighted on the field of battle by a British monarch since 1743, when King George II had knighted General John Ligonier on the battlefield after the British victory at the battle of Dettingen. Monash is given only 24 hours' notice that an entire ceremony has been devised just for him, and would take place on the steps of Bertangles Chateau, using a sword borrowed from a member of the HQ Staff – retrieved from his fiancée's keeping, some 80 miles away at Boulogne, and arriving just in time for the ceremony.

For the grand occasion – a guard of honour of 600 Australian troops line the drive, greeting King George V at his arrival – Sir John is clearly quite nervous. So nervous in fact that, after King George taps one shoulder with his sword, Monash is so eager to rise once more that the sovereign has to quickly tap him on the other shoulder to get the job done.

Gathering himself, Sir John asked the Australian troops to give 'three cheers for His Majesty!', but the response was 'ragged'.[96]

Underwhelmed, Sir John tried again with a 'Come on!',[97] only to get the same unenthusiastic result.

It was likely more sheer exhaustion than anything else, mixed with the wearying realisation that there remained much work to do. Still, another possible factor is that while King George V had graciously chatted to assembled Divisional commanders and other senior officers, he had, according to Bean, apparently taken 'not the least interest in the Diggers'.[98] Could it be that this has not sat easily with the Australian soldiers, and they are not disposed to cheer one who has not been cheery to them? For his part, the grumbling Charles Bean is *not* impressed with any of them, muttering that the whole thing is 'a lot of nonsense'.[99]

One addendum to the story is worth mentioning. In the course of his visit to Monash at Bertangles, King George notices that General Monash has an autograph book on his desk.

'By Jove, Monash,' the English sovereign says, after leafing through the extensive collection of notable signatures the Australian has collected in the course of the war, 'you have a wonderful collection here.'

'Yes, Sir,' replies the man from Jerilderie.

'Do you mind if I take this?'

'Not at all, Sir,' replies Monash, for what else can he say?

Without another word, His Majesty slips the deeply treasured book into his overcoat pocket and takes his leave. It would be a few weeks later before the denouement came. For again, the King would come and find Monash, this time casually handing back this most prized of Monash's possessions.

'I've brought you back your book, Monash,'[100] he says. And indeed he has. Leafing through it himself, Monash is thrilled to note that it now boasts not only the salutations of the King himself, completed with autography, but also the same from every member of the Royal family!

•

In the interim, of course, the General had been very busy. For the battle four days before he had been knighted by the King had begun the famed 100 days offensive, whereby Allied forces – led for much of it by Australians under the command of General Monash – would decide the war, and it is these same soldiers who will soon hear cheering as never before as they continue to push to the east.

For, 'feed your troops on victory',[101] had always been Monash's goal, and the Australian troops now feasted on it as never before, ever and always coming back for second and third helpings as, under the command of General Monash, they spearheaded the whole advance of the British Expeditionary Force. In Australian military history, the next 100 days will always stand out. Along with the Diggers' defensive battles around Villers-Bretonneux in late March and April earlier that year, it was the only time the Australian Army would find itself as the main force, on the main battlefield against the main enemy, and triumph!

After 8 August, at the hands of the Australians, the Germans were again defeated at Proyart and Chuignes. And then, from 31 August to 3 September, in Monash's finest hour, it is the Australian Corps under his tight and brilliant command which all alone smashes and shatters the German line at Mont St Quentin, quickly going on to capture even their heavily fortified city of Peronne, which German High Command had expected to hold through the winter of 1918–1919. That man, Monash! Any General with such an unprecedented record of success can expect more resources to be sent his way, and by late September and early October it was, once more, Monash's 200,000 strong Australian Corps – by now with 60,000 Americans under his command – which broke through the fabled Hindenburg Line, the last prepared German defensive position. The war was over in all but name, as from then on the Allied advance pushed through open country with no prepared German defensive positions to stop, or even slow them. Prince Max von Baden asked immediately for an armistice on behalf of the German government. In three months Monash had progressed from victory at Hamel to smashing a hole in the last German defensive system some 40 miles east of Hamel. It was an astonishingly fast triumph and a total one.

A war that had begun with Australia as a relatively minor player in the British-planned shemozzle of Gallipoli, ended with the Diggers at the pointy end of the spear driving towards the heart of Germany.

In no small part due to the exertions of Sir John Monash and his men, and the example they set at Hamel – which was then replicated many times over – the war was over within weeks. Germany sought peace terms from the Allies, and, with the Armistice at 11 am on 11 November 1918, the war ended.

Bravo, you brave bastards.

Lest we forget.

EPILOGUE

I would name Sir John Monash as the best general on the western front in Europe; he possessed real creative originality, and the war might well have been over sooner, and certainly with fewer casualties, had Haig been relieved of his command and Monash appointed to command the British Armies in his place.[1]

Montgomery of Alamein, in his *History of Warfare*, 1968

A war-winning combination had been found: a corps commander of genius, the Australian infantry, the Tank Corps, the Royal Artillery and the RAF.[2]

General Hubert Essame, British military historian, who in 1918 had been a 21-year-old Captain of the Northamptonshire Regiment, which fought with the Australians on the Western Front

The battle represented a quantum leap in tactical method that consigned the technique of 1 July 1916 to a bygone age and became a model for the British Expeditionary Force thereafter. In particular, the stroke on 8 August 1918, the German Army's 'black day', was simply Hamel on a larger scale. An understanding of the concept and the plan that emerged from it are crucial for grasping the texture of the attack.[3]

Peter Pedersen, author of *Hamel*, 2003

A Farmer Remembers the Somme

I have returned to these:
The farm, and the kindly Bush, and the young calves lowing;
But all that my mind sees
Is a quaking bog in a mist – stark, snapped trees,
And the dark Somme flowing.[4]

Vance Palmer

There remained just one last major military challenge for Monash: repatriation. The precious task was to get all of those Australians who had fought in foreign fields back to their homeland, on the other side of the planet. No fewer than 180,000 servicemen and women (and 7000 wives and children) were longing to head home, and Monash was determined that the massive logistical exercise be completed as quickly as possible, relying on every ship he could scrounge for their mass transport. But merely transporting them was not enough for Monash. With typical humanity, he did what he could to ensure that their prospects for employment would be maximised upon their return and so, while they waited for their ships to come in, to keep them occupied, he initiated the AIF Education Scheme. It was designed to equip all members of the AIF with the training, experience, skills, and even qualifications to significantly increase their capacity to re-enter the civilian workforce, often in different professions from those in which they were engaged on enlistment.

In the meantime, Monash threw himself into penning his memoir of the war and his role in it, *The Australian Victories in France in 1918*. Starting it on 1 September 1919, he had completed it just a month later, enabling him to submit it to Melbourne University as his thesis on how the science and discipline of engineering could be applied to warfare, to make it all but an art form. (On the strength of it, Monash was awarded a doctorate in engineering.)

Throughout his entire time in the capital of the British Empire, Monash found himself lionised by London society. Monash's key biographer, Geoffrey Serle – to whose work this book owes a great debt – would note just how celebrated he was by the best and brightest.

'At the Australian and New Zealand Luncheon Club,' Serle would record 'Hamilton, Churchill, Hughes and Birdwood all referred to him in their speeches; each time there was "vociferous applause" . . . During the finals of the British Empire Boxing Tournament at the Albert Hall, Prince Albert summoned him to the royal box and they chatted for half an hour. At the state banquet at Buckingham Palace for President and Mrs Wilson, he sat between the press proprietor Lord Burnham and Rudyard Kipling, who swapped autographs and told him anecdotes about himself. The company stood while the King and

Wilson made their speeches. Monash had five minutes with them and ten with the Queen after dinner, and he conversed with Lloyd George, Asquith, French, Balfour and Austen Chamberlain. It was "a thrilling function of unsurpassed splendour and brilliancy". He sat at Haig's right hand when the Secretary of State for War, Lord Milner, dined the army chiefs. The "blare and blaze of fame" was enveloping him.'[5]

Six months after the war was over, London honoured Monash and his Australians by hosting an Anzac Day march for 5000 Australian soldiers, starting at Hyde Park then going down to The Mall and to The Strand. Monash, of course, took pride of place, riding on horseback at the head of his beaming troops, as the pressing crowd cheered them three times through, while General Birdwood, as Monash's biographer put it, 'was relegated to the saluting base at Australia House with the Prince of Wales, Haig, Hughes and Chauvel'.[6]

(Despite all their Machiavellian machinations, Bean and Murdoch had been no more successful in removing Birdwood as Commanding Officer of the AIF than they had been in removing Monash from command of the Australian Corps.)

Overhead, those heroes of the Australian Flying Corps soared, shimmered, roared and rolled as the crowds cheered them even louder. As Sir Douglas Haig himself drove up in a closed car, a lusty shout rang out: 'Good-day, Doug!'

'Looking for the source of the easy greeting,' the *Times* would happily report, 'one discovered the Gladstone statue to be covered with Anzacs – the topmost of them hanging affectionately round the neck of a statesman who had never been so familiarly treated in his life-time.'[7]

And even then, the *Times* was only just warming up.

'Apologies,' the august chronicle of record would note, 'must be made for using such a word as "stroll" for such a display of marching as the Australians gave, when they saluted the Prince of Wales at Australia House ... but the Australian soldier has such a way of pleasantly and pertinaciously doing just what he chooses, and of persuading the London public, and even the London police, that because he is doing it just to please himself there can be no possible harm in it, that everything which these great, smiling, easy-going brothers of ours do seems to be entirely spontaneous and accidental. Their geniality, no less than their tremendous achievements in the field of battle, have made them the people's pets, and the people of London gave them a welcome in which affection was as strong as admiration.'[8]

No-one enjoyed that admiration and affection more than Monash himself, something that did not necessarily sit easily with General Birdwood, and over ensuing months the Englishman became ever more prickly. It was the Australian's conclusion that the issue was that Birdwood felt overshadowed by his former underling and things got so bad, with such words exchanged, that Monash would report that Birdwood 'behaved in a most discourteous and shabby manner towards me, and I find it quite difficult to be even polite to him'.[9]

Under such circumstances, thus, it was a curious circumstance which – at the behest of the Australian government – placed General Birdwood on the same ship as General Monash, when the latter finally made his return to his homeland, after brilliantly completing the task of organising the swift repatriation of the entire AIF to Australian shores.

For the reception accorded the two men was instructive.

In Great Britain, Monash had been rightly lionised as the most significant Corps Commander of the war. But in Australia, at least at official level, it was quite reversed and that curious streak in our national character, which is at its most content when deferring to things British, came into full play.

For as RMS *Ormonde* arrives at Fremantle on 19 December, it is the Englishman, Birdwood, front and centre, waving his Digger hat from the deck, making the headlines in the *West Australian*, and being toasted at the civic reception at Fremantle Town Hall, while also being given the honour of speaking first just as occurrs at two subsequent gatherings while they are in town.

Birdie! Our English General!

The *West Australian* knows who deserves the most tribute; and who is the secondary figure who stands by his side in reflected glory: 'No one has been more generous in recognising the qualities of our men that counted than the great soldier who came among us on Friday after guiding the destinies of the Australian army in the field for five years.

'An Englishman, he might have been as much an Australian as that other outstanding figure, Sir John Monash, who shared the spontaneous welcome of Friday . . . Our army was an army of the rank and file, and it was General Birdwood's good fortune, as it was the happy lot of the men he commanded and the people whose sons and brothers he had in charge, that he was one in spirit with the gallant battalions . . .'[10]

There is a similar lack of recognition for Monash's achievements when they arrive in Adelaide, though here, they are actually on land for no more than five hours.

Whatever the official snubbing, however, neither the government nor the higher echelons of the military have control over the *people*'s affection, and it is demonstrated in full, when General Monash finally sets foot back in Melbourne on Boxing Day 1919.

The *Age* captures the tumult singularly well: 'Imagine a bronzed khaki figure, slightly above middle height, with a rugged, florid face, the wrinkle of a smile near the eyes, a touch of grey in the hair beneath the gold-braided cap, stepping quickly on to St. Kilda pier – and there was the picture which thousands of returned soldiers recognised with a welcoming cheer yesterday morning. Officially he was Lieutenant-General Sir John Monash . . . formerly Commander of the Australian Army Corps in France. But to the crowd of soldiers on the pier he was simply "Monash" – the citizen soldier, who had fought his way to a brilliant field record in Gallipoli and France, a patriot who had worked indefatigably for his country even after the war had finished. And the people remembered . . .'

For as Monash makes his triumphant landing, it is to be met by the roared acclaim of *thousands* of returned soldiers who'd served under him in Gallipoli and the Western Front, and who have turned out now to greet him!

'For possibly the first time in his distinguished military career,' the *Age* reports, 'General Sir John Monash, one time leader of the Australian Army Corps, found himself completely outnumbered, outflanked – outmanoeuvred. Never, it seemed, was the higher strategy more futile in the face of such opposing odds. At the rear retreat was cut off by a wide expanse of water; ahead there were hundreds of smiling faces and a mayor in the flowing robes of office; at the flanks there were more excited people anxious to prevent his escape. And so, like a gallant leader, General Monash metaphorically tendered his sword and smiled pleasure at the welcome ... Along the whole length of the pier and across the beautiful grass lawns which skirt the Lower Esplanade he was carried shoulder high. Around him surged a body-guard of soldiers. From the promenade above came a thunderous and sustained roar of applause. In the van a barrage of cheers was thrown by groups of admirers. The General still maintained his position. It was the penalty of military greatness and popularity.'

The fact that he is Jewish?

The *Age* gives it a delicate nod.

'"Ain't he the general, eh?," somewhat aggressively demanded a stout, old lady with the pride of race in her eye.'[11]

A wonderful parade proceeds all the way into Melbourne town, the crowds getting ever bigger and more enthusiastic, until they arrive at their digs at the Menzies Hotel, where Monash's wife, Victoria – exhausted and ill – goes straight to bed, while the General gets straight into 'civvies'.

'He is still very much of a civilian and a democrat in his views,' the *Age* reports, 'and the military caste will never be able to claim [him] as one of its own.'[12]

Truthfully, as it turned out, if extraordinarily, the military caste did not *want* Monash as one of its own.

Just as there had been an exclusive professional military cabal before the war, led by Defence Minister George Pearce, so too was it still substantially intact when the war was over, and when the plum positions were to be handed out, few wanted the celebrated civilian-engineer-turned-celebrated-General to be anywhere near the front of the queue.

And while it may have been obvious for Monash to be given the highest position in the Australian Army, as Chief of the General Staff, no such position was offered to him.

Though not quite *persona non grata* in official circles, it was not far off.

Few things better illustrated how outrageous the official snubbing of Monash was when Edward, the Prince of Wales *himself*, arrived in Melbourne on 28 May 1920, to be greeted by dozens of dignitaries at the Victorian State Parliament, *not* including Sir John Monash, who was reduced to watching his arrival, as an anonymous punter among the pressing crowd in Swanston Street. Oh, the indignity! Not for nothing would the *Bulletin* thunder of the recently widowed hero – for Victoria had died of cervical cancer three months earlier, only a few weeks after arriving home – that 'military officialdom has done its best to snub Australia's citizen-soldier'.[13]

And it would continue.

In the Governor-General's speech at the opening of Federal Parliament, on 26 February 1920, Sir Ronald Craufurd Munro Ferguson intones: 'I record with pleasure the visit to Australia of General Sir William Birdwood, who commanded the Australian forces with such distinction throughout the war.'[14]

Standing in front of the British aristocrat as he says these words is another who commanded the Australian forces, with even greater distinction, in the person of Sir John Monash, but he is ignored.

For all that, Monash was not without strong support in the public domain, with one ex-Victorian minister writing in protest at the latest snub to Senator Albert Gardiner, who read it out in parliament: 'If evidence were required of Senator Pearce's subservience to-day to a military clique – shall I call it the seniority brigade – which is determined to prevent the utilisation of the best brains brought out by the war, you will find it in the studied insult to General Monash in the Governor-General's speech at the opening of Parliament, and in the fact that no citizen-officer, however brilliant, has been deemed as worthy of permanent military employment, as are permanent officers whose war records were far less successful. These military failures regard Senator Pearce as their last hope. They consistently flatter him and his vanity, which is in inverse ratio to his gifts ... You are at liberty to use this letter in any way you think fit.'[15]

Another letter that Monash himself received at this time, from one of his old soldiers, was emblematic of a broader anti-Semitism that Monash had to deal with, as he remade his civilian life: '[A general] said all over Melb. a year ago that your wife and her sister are whores and that you are a beastly dog of a Jew.'[16]

More than ever, it appears that the decision to make him Commander of the Australian Corps was an aberration, a brief exception to a general anti-Semitism that was abroad in the highest official circles of the military–political establishment.

With the military path now blocked to him, the best that Monash can find to soak up his organisational abilities is to become General Manager of the Victorian State Electricity Commission. As fine as he is in that role, still it appals many. The influential magazine *Smith's Weekly* – already on the record trumpeting its view that 'If the war had lasted one year more Monash would have been British Commander-in-Chief'[17] – was one outlet that was completely dismayed that it should have come to this.

'Who is Monash? The answer is brief and definite. He is the greatest brain in Australia for practical organisation. Tested in the biggest things, he proved to be one of the great practical brains of the world.'[18]

And yet, the best the country can do for him is give him a job as the Electrical Engineer of Victoria? After detailing Monash's staggering achievements in the war, *Smith's* cannot help itself.

'In this advance, Monash began the smashing of Germany. So he came back to Australia, which tooted its trumpets round Birdwood, and forgot its own soldier . . . He ought to have had the acclamations of the continent. But, above all, his genius should be made to "shine in use".'[19]

Well, he will be getting no sympathy from Birdwood, who later writes to John Baird (Lord Stonehaven, the Englishman who became Governor-General of Australia in 1925), noting that: 'Monash [was] not a professional soldier . . . [Now] in charge of all electric supply in Victoria – a very able administrator and mathematician – a Jew with all the faults of his race – thinks he won the war and tells everyone so. He might be useful, but a terrible self-advertiser.'[20]

No matter. As he was ever wont to do, Monash simply got on with it, and did a grand job in his new role – providing power for an entire state. By the beginning of the next decade the grid of the State Electricity Commission not only covered all of Victoria, but it was turning a profit. The project's chief technical engineer, Hyman Herman, would describe his boss as 'a genius at getting to the heart of any problem and finding its solution'.[21]

In the meantime, Monash also devoted his energies to such things as being the Vice-Chancellor of the University of Melbourne, President of the Australasian Association for the Advancement of Science, and organising the Anzac Day marches, as well as being the driving force for the establishment of the Shrine of Remembrance, and President of the Australian Zionist Federation.

So highly respected was he, in so many quarters – despite his snubbing by the military establishment – that when, in 1930, the Scullin administration prepared itself to embrace the revolutionary idea of having an actual Australian as the Australian Governor-General (don't get me started), Monash was strongly considered. Alas, his own deteriorating health ruled him out. After suffering a heart attack at his home, *Iona*, on Thursday 8 October 1931, he died at the age of 66.

And so who weeps now for the fallen old soldier? The answer is, an extraordinary number of people, and a huge number of them are his own soldiers who now mourn one of their own, a man they had respected, who had treasured and guarded their own lives more than most.

For 'neath appropriately sombre leaden skies, on Sunday 11 October 1931, no fewer than 300,000 people – a stunning one third of the entire population of Melbourne – form up in funereal garb to pay their last respects to the greatest General of the Great War, Australia's own Sir John Monash.

After Rabbi Jacob Danglow has completed a private service in the Queens Hall of the Victorian Parliament House – where Monash's body had lain in state with a 24-hour Honour Guard from the day after his death – at 1.30 pm on this sad day, Sir John begins his long journey to eternity. As the coffin is solemnly borne down the stairs of the parliament by the Honour Guard, his long-time mistress, Lizzie Bentwich, is standing opposite, before the Windsor Hotel, 'grieving uncontrollably'.[22]

The coffin, draped in the Union Jack, is placed on the gun carriage, and now seven horses draw it forward in slow march, closely flanked on either side by the pallbearers, whose numbers include the Victorian Premier, the Victorian Chief Commissioner of Police, General Sir Harry Chauvel, General Sir Brudenell White, and the 'Old Brig' himself, Brigadier General C. B. Brand. Just behind the carriage comes a riderless horse, Sir John's own charger with – as military tradition demands – his boots reversed in the stirrups.

From the parliament, the carriage makes its way between the crowds, along St Kilda Road to a podium that lies before the very Shrine of Remembrance that Sir John had been the driving force in creating. As part of a Returned Soldiers Memorial Service attended by 50,000 mourners, no fewer than 10,000 veterans – *once more unto the breach, dear friends, once more* – now march by. On and on they come, in ranks eight abreast, returned soldiers, sailors and airmen – some missing arms and legs, some being pushed along in wheelchairs, and nearly everyone now in civilian garb, but all . . . *eyessss right* . . . saluting as they come before their fallen General. And *still* they keep coming, marching proudly as in days of yore, all to the beat of muffled drums.

Now, if the beginning of history judging you well starts with your eulogy and your obituaries, then Monash got off to a very fine start.

For the eulogy, it is the deceased's long-time intimate, General Sir Harry Chauvel, who does the honours, in singularly honourable fashion, his voice ringing out over the immense crowd . . .

'We are gathered here this afternoon to pay a last tribute to a great soldier and a great citizen,' he rumbles in his stentorian tones, 'one whom a great number of you followed in the field, and who, since the war, has been a tower of strength to the returned soldiers' organisations. He was responsible for the great parade that takes place on Anzac Day. I do not say that he first suggested it, but it was he who worked it up from very small beginnings to the wonderful demonstration that it has been in the last few years. It is very fitting that we should hold this service at the Shrine of Remembrance, because Sir John Monash was also responsible for that. It was in the first instance his suggestion, and he, above all others, worked hard in the face of all kinds of difficulties, including financial difficulties, to have it erected. Now it is nearly finished, and will be a noble memorial to the soldiers who laid down their lives in the Great War. A great many tributes have been paid to Sir John Monash, and it is difficult for me to add to them.'[23]

But add to them he does, and the battles and victories the men know so well are listed and explained for those who do not know what they mean. Finally it is over and the funeral procession makes its way out onto St Kilda Road once more, and proceeds all the way to Brighton Cemetery, where the coffin is placed in the grave after a final farewell by the Rabbi is 'conducted in Hebrew ritual'.

As for his own memorial, his own tombstone, it is no flowery or grand tribute: it reads at his own request just this: 'John Monash'.

As to obituaries, there are, of course, many, but it is the great English historian Liddell Hart, writing for the London *Daily Telegraph*, who perhaps captures Monash's significance best.

'He had probably the greatest capacity for command in modern war among all who held command . . . If [the Great War] had lasted another year he would almost certainly have risen from commander of the Australian Corps to command of an army; he might even have risen to be Commander-in-Chief. If capacity had been the determining factor he would have done so . . .

'He was in some ways an utter contrast to the traditional idea of a great military commander. He, more than anyone, fulfilled the idea which gradually developed in the war – that the scale and nature of operations required a "big business" type of commander, a great constructive and organising brain. His views were as large as his capacity. Perhaps the strongest testimony to his capacity is the distance he went in spite of a tremendous compound handicap of prejudice . . .'[24]

And so say all of us.

•

Even Charles Bean, to a *certain* extent, albeit highly reluctantly, mellows on the subject of Monash – though it is in a rather half-hearted manner, as witness some of his notes, in his papers, with no date, but likely written shortly after Monash's death in 1931. The first is headed:

Confidential and Personal Only

Monash's account of events after they happened . . . can never be relied on . . . I am not sure that Murdoch and I were not wrong in trying to get [changes] made in the AIF command . . . What guided me was the knowledge that Monash's chief motive was ambition and that the lives of his troops and the greater interests of his side were not his paramount cares, or at any rate, his ambition, I believed, would weigh heavily in the scale whenever it came to a decision . . . I do not think he was the man to handle men – for all his great qualities he was not, I fancy, quite straight and courageous enough.[25]

In response, allow this author to note two things.

Firstly, I am in awe of the work of Bean across the board, and am under no illusions that it would be like my damn hide to presume to criticise conclusions he has come to. He was there, in the middle of it, knew the key players personally, and was right in the thick of the action from the first.

But in the case of Monash, there is no way around the fact that he got it completely wrong and made terrible errors of judgement. Neither he nor Murdoch had any business in trying to do him down, and it is impossible to believe they would have done so had his last name been Fotheringbottom, from a fine family of Anglos who attended The King's School. One particular conclusion Bean came to regarding Monash really does confuse me. Far from being cavalier with the lives of his troops, the conclusion of other people close to the action, including Colonel Thomas Dodds, General Thomas Blamey and Prime Minister Billy Hughes, seems to be quite the reverse, that Monash was more careful than most to spare their lives, to let the machinery do the heavy lifting and to come up with plans, like Hamel, where casualties would be kept to a minimum. In other writings, Bean is very positive about General Iven Mackay, who presided over the slaughter at Fromelles. And then, the following day, when hundreds of Australian soldiers lay wounded and dying out in No Man's Land, and the Germans were happy to agree to a truce, it was Mackay who refused to countenance it. Bean was there at Fromelles on the day this disgrace took place. And yet it is *Monash* who comes in for such harsh criticism that he does not care about his men?

In another handwritten note titled <u>Monash</u>, Bean addresses the rumours that Jerilderie's favourite son was, way back when, being groomed for the highest post of all.

'Monash,' he writes flatly, 'could not have taken Haig's place . . . he had little moral courage – he could not resist political pressure or that of powerful intrigues ... His ideals were not so high as Birdwood's and he really had a lower conception of his men. His military capacity consisted mainly in organising, but his conceptions were often widely wrong. He never really grasped the mentality of his men. His greatest feats were Hamel, Aug 8 ... and Mont St Quentin ...'

In the margin of this note is this: 'He was also never distinguished by personal bravery – his fight for his great scheme of electricity was finer than any he put up in the AIF.'[26]

(I am gobsmacked! The Victorian electricity grid more important than the seminal battles that Monash presided over?)

A third handwritten note is titled <u>Appointment of Monash</u>:

'Maclagan is the only one who possibly thought him inefficient – that is he thought Monash was lacking in military knowledge. The others recognised that at Hamel he had given proof of his capacity – he was comparatively speaking unknown before, but was reputed to have been successful sometimes and unsuccessful at others. They [the divisional commanders including Sinclair-Maclagan] agreed that no action should be taken to unseat Monash – if he lacked in anything the team could pull him through.'[27]

The one concession that Bean would make that he might have got it wrong all those years ago in his scheming with Murdoch to stop Monash keeping command of the Australian Corps is a notation in his old diary, where he had accused Monash of scheming to get the position.

'I do not now believe this to be true.'[28]

At least in his obituary for Monash, Charles Bean would pay tribute in his manner: 'It is quite certain that the AIF contained no brain better than that of John Monash ... In his capacities he probably had few equals, not just in the AIF but in the whole British Army.'[29]

Similarly, Bean would also praise the man he had tried to thwart.

'As a leader for the Australians he gave the Diggers at that time precisely what they wanted,' he would note in the *Sun*, 'an organiser who would never let them down by the failure of supplies or material. The Digger, trained almost to perfection, required someone behind whom he could trust to see that all such arrangements were perfect.'[30]

His praise would continue in his *Official History*, 'And for that purpose the whole British Army . . . would probably have picked one man above all others . . . John Monash. He was Australia's greatest military leader – "neither a hero nor a mighty strategical genius [but] probably the ablest and most successful British corps commander in France".'[31]

Amen.

One hundred years on from 'Monash's Masterpiece' of Hamel, the reputations of both the General himself, and the battle he planned and executed, are instructive.

In Australia, the name Monash is very well known, in part because of his presence on the $100 bill, and the fact that Monash University is so highly regarded, while there are at least 20 Monash Streets throughout the country. But among the broad populace, his specific deeds are not widely known and, when it comes to famous First World War Generals, most Australians would more likely go with General Herbert Kitchener and General Sir Douglas Haig and then change the subject. The fact that many qualified judges regarded our own Monash as the best of the breed, and many maintain that it was by a country mile – even out Jerilderie way – is known only to very few.

Ditto, the Battle of Hamel. The significance of what occurred, and Monash's role in it is known to very few. To begin with, Rawlinson's claims to take credit for the affair achieved some success, and it is to be noted that when, six decades later, Sir John Smyth penned his seminal work, *Leadership in Battle*, and devoted four pages to the Battle of Le Hamel, it was Rawlinson who was portrayed as the prime moving force and key innovator of the attack, while Monash . . . did not rate even a mention in passing! Beyond that, however, because it was only a little more than a Divisional attack, and casualties were so low, its significance is usually overlooked. The major factor, of course, is that like just about every other fine Australian effort over the last century, it has made very little headway against Gallipoli, which continues to dominate the popular imagination, despite the fact that much of what happened on the Western Front made Gallipoli look like a mere sideshow by comparison.

Nevertheless, at least among the highest echelons of the Australian Defence Force, both Monash and the Battle of Hamel are highly regarded, and every few years 'Exercise Hamel' is held to hone the battle skills of a combined arms force – infantry, tanks, artillery and aircraft. Monash would have oh so heartily approved.

•

The success of the Battle of Hamel and subsequent battles that ended the war relatively quickly would have ramifications far beyond that of the life of General Monash.

The quick and victorious finish meant the Allies could dictate terms on the way the post-war world would be organised, starting with meetings at the Palace of Versailles as the world leaders gathered in January 1919. Australia's representative was, of course, the ever-irascible **Billy Hughes** who, at one point, clashed with **President Woodrow Wilson** of the United States, on the issue they had first discussed in Washington the previous year, of which country should rule the former German protectorate of New Guinea. Wilson insisted on Japan, while Hughes was equally adamant that it was a matter of enormous strategic importance, and *right*, that it was now under Australian rule and should remain so. In one version of their legendary exchange, Wilson laid it on the line, banging the table: 'I would have you to know, Mr. Hughes, that I represent 90 million . . . Americans!'

'I'd have you to know, Mr. President,' Billy replied, 'that I represent 60,000 dead Australians!'[32]

Wilson: 'Do I understand that Australia in the face of the wishes of the world would insist upon having her own way?'

Hughes: 'That's about the size of it, Mr. President.'[33]

At this point, the British Prime Minister, Lloyd George, stepped in, trying to defuse the New Guinea tension, and asked, helpfully, of Hughes: 'Are you prepared to let missionaries have access to the natives?'

'Yes,' replied Billy equably, 'with the greatest pleasure.'

The mood in the room softens . . .

'Because I assure the President that on some days these poor devils don't get enough missionaries to eat.'[34]

It would be with some feeling that Wilson would go on to describe Hughes, as a 'pestiferous varmint'.[35]

•

More than a few British generals and Allied leaders had felt much the same, in their own terms, of **General 'Black Jack' Pershing.** And yet, despite his many critics, General Pershing did indeed attain his dream, in September 1918, to lead an independent United States Army of 2,000,000 men. He led the Americans for the rest of the war, and in 1919 was rewarded with a promotion to the position of 'General of the Armies of the United States', a position created just for him. A hundred years later, there has been only one other American military man to hold it, and that is none other than George Washington. The first President of the United States was promoted posthumously in 1976 so that his iconic stature would not suffer from being outranked by 'Black Jack'. When Pershing returned to America after the war, he took the 24-year-old Micheline with him, and in 1946 married her, when he was 88 and she was 52. He died just two years later, in 1948, and is buried at Arlington Cemetery, in section 34 under a simple white headstone:

> John J Pershing
> Missouri
> General of the Armies of the United States
> September 13 1860 July 15 1948

His grandson, who died in Vietnam in 1968, is buried next to him.

•

For his part, **General Sir Henry Rawlinson** led the Fourth Army through the Hundred Days Offensive that broke the Hindenburg Line, culminating in the Battle of Canal du Nord, which consolidated the Germans' defeat. He was showered with honours after the war, including a KCMG, a GCB and an elevation to the peerage, being made Baron Rawlinson of Trent. In 1920 he was made the Commander-in-Chief of the British forces in India, a post that was due to go to General Birdwood before Winston Churchill personally intervened to ensure

Rawlinson got the post. It was a command he still held in 1924 on his 61st birthday when he celebrated by playing polo and cricket, fell ill due to suspected appendicitis, and was operated on immediately. A twisted intestine was revealed and Rawlinson died soon after, to be succeeded by the now Field Marshal Sir William Birdwood.

•

After the war, **Captain Lawrence Wackett** married his high school sweetheart, Letty Woods, in London, and they went on to have a son and daughter. Returning to Australia, Lawrence became one of the 21 initial officers in the newly created Royal Australian Air Force in 1921 and within three years was placed in charge of their Experimental Section in Randwick, New South Wales, starting what would become his life's work: designing new aircraft for the RAAF. A distinguished figure in the history of Australian aviation, I have written a little on him previously, in my book on Charles Kingsford Smith, in regards to his vociferous criticism that the plane Kingsford Smith chose to attempt to fly the Pacific with, the *Southern Cross*, was a Fokker.

'What they're doing,' Wackett, the founding chairman, just the previous year, of the inaugural Australian branch of the Royal Aeronautical Society, told the press, 'is offering an insult to every returned Australian soldier, sailor and airman. Fokkers were used by the German Air Force to fight us, and many a good Australian died from bullets spewed from them . . .'[36]

When Kingsford Smith was told of Wackett's views by an American reporter, he was in San Francisco under the *Southern Cross* at the time. Enraged, he put down his tools, emerged from under the fuselage and told the reporter straight: 'That's crap. No-one loves Australia more than I do. I'm dealing with a plane, not with personalities or nationality. I'm dealing with a fine piece of machinery and engineering. You can quote me as telling Wackett to go to hell.'[37]

Retiring from the RAAF with the rank of Wing Commander in 1930, Wackett became General Manager of the Commonwealth Aircraft Corporation, supplying over a thousand planes to the RAAF, some his own design, during the Second World War. His only son, Wilbur, died while serving as a fighter pilot in the RAAF in 1944. Lawrence was knighted in 1954. When he suffered a fall in 1970 and became a near quadriplegic, he turned his inventive mind to designing equipment and aids for those who had been similarly crippled. He died on 18 March 1982, aged 86.

•

In recognition for his extraordinary bravery in the taking of Kidney Trench in the wee hours of 4 July, **Lance Corporal Jack Axford** was promoted to corporal ten days later, and a month later again it was announced that he had been awarded the Victoria Cross. His father, though on his deathbed in Kalgoorlie, was able to read the citation, just before he died, noting that his brave son's 'initiative and gallantry undoubtedly saved many casualties, and most materially assisted in the complete success of his company in the task assigned to it'.[38]

Receiving his award from King George V himself at Buckingham Palace on 26 September, Jack Axford was soon on his way home, arriving in Fremantle on HMAT *Sardinia*, on 16 December 1918.

One journalist who spoke to him upon his arrival in Perth could not get much out of the modest VC winner, who was still wearing a black armband in memory of his father.

'A typical Australian in looks,' the journalist recounted, 'and as reticent as most brave men, it was impossible to get much information from this hero regarding himself or his deeds.'

'It was my luck,' he said, 'to be seen. There are men here with us on this train who are entitled to the VC with as much or better right than myself.'[39]

When his train arrived in his home town of Kalgoorlie on Christmas Day 1918, half the city was there to greet him and though Jack did the best he could to escape them, and the fuss, too many locals knew him, and he was soon corralled by the mayor on the platform, and implored to speak.

'Tell them,' someone suggested *sotto voce*, 'how you are glad to be home.'[40]

All Jack could manage was, 'Thank you gentlemen,' though that drew cheers enough. He was then taken to Kalgoorlie Town Hall, where again the mayor did his best before the milling throng.

'In assuring Lance-Corporal Axford of the respect and veneration in which his family were held upon the gold fields I would ask the audience to give three hearty rousing cheers for "Axford, VC".'

Again the cheers were resounding, as was a collective rendition of 'For He's a Jolly Good Fellow'.

'Rounds of cheers were given in succession for "His Mother", "Harry Axford" and "His Brothers and Sisters".'

And now Jack Axford rises to respond, being obliged to wait till yet more cheers have died down.

'Well,' says he, 'I don't think there is anybody more pleased than myself to be back here, and I thank you all for the welcome.' And then he sat down.

'You are almost as bad as Carroll, VC,' the mayor notes, referring to Kalgoorlie's other winner of the military's highest honour. 'We could not get a word from him.' *(Laughter.)*

'Well,' said Jack, 'I've got nothing to talk about.'[41]

Despite the warmth of his welcome in Kalgoorlie, Axford would soon settle in Perth, where a job awaited . . . labouring. Yes, you can see him there, digging ditches around Perth through much of the next few years: 'Labourer Jack Axford VC, MM'.

There was occasional trouble for Jack, as in 1921 when he was charged with punching a police officer in a dust-up. Jack's claim was that he was trying to help a lady who had fallen and was in danger of being run over by the policeman's horse. Police said he was drunk and singing the socialist anthem, 'The Red Flag'. When the Magistrate realised he was a VC winner, Jack was let off with a caution.

In late 1926, at the age of 32, he married his sweetheart, Lily Maud Foster, in Perth – a fine woman who calmed him down more than somewhat – and from there he rose to the position of 'clerk, VC', for the Hugh McKay Sunshine Harvester Company.

He and Maud settled at Mount Hawthorn, in the inner suburbs of Perth, and went on to raise five children. Ah, but there were tough times, too, and never tougher than in the Depression, when – on a WA government scheme – Jack was obliged to take labouring jobs on farms far from Perth, just to feed his growing family. At one point, Jack and his mate from the 16th Battalion, Joe Cusack, did a long stint at Narembeen, 160 miles east of Perth. Alas, when at the end of the stint they went to the local bank to get their pay, some technicality prevented the money being handed over. There was an argument until Joe said, 'This here is Jack Axford. He has a VC. Do you know what he got it for? For killing ten men. Now, I don't think you want to take this any further, do you?'[42]

They were paid what was owed them, and Jack went home to Maud with enough money to keep the family going.

In the Second World War, Jack enlisted once more, serving as a Sergeant in the Western Australian Echelon and Records Office, and stayed on, even after the war was over, before finally being discharged once more in April 1947.

After the war Jack grew veggies and handed them out to anyone who needed them. 'Everyone who was in trouble,' his local newspaper would recount, 'knocked at his door.'

From time to time, his exploits would make the wider papers, as a new generation discovered his deeds – and the obvious question beckoned . . .

How on *earth* did he have the courage to do those amazing things?

He has no explanation.

'And I wasn't full of rum at the time,' he told one journalist from Perth's *Sunday Times* in 1950 with a quiet grin, 'for I've never had a drink in my life, though I did work in a brewery for eight years . . .'[43]

Jack Axford was ever and always his own man,

In 1954 when Queen Elizabeth II visited Perth, Jack and three other Victoria Cross winners were invited to sit on the dais with the royal party. Maud was not invited. Jack asked the official, 'Will the politicians be up there?'

'Yes.'

'Will their wives be with them?'

'Yes.'

'Can Maud come?'

'No.'

'Well in that case I'm not coming,'[44] said Jack.

What did he care? As he told the press, he had already been presented to three Kings of England so he wasn't that fussed.

Still, two years later at the age of 61, he was still hale and hearty enough to attend the VC Centenary Celebrations in London. In fact, nigh on 30 years later again, in October 1983, the just widowed Jack Axford – Maud had died three months earlier – was *still* going strong enough to attend a reunion of the Victoria Cross and George Cross Association held at London, when – in the company of another famous Australian soldier, Keith Payne, VC – he died on 11 October 1983, returning home on an aircraft between Dubai and Hong Kong.

(Amazing, isn't it? How different an ending for him, 65 years on, from the one that might have been imagined for him as he charged Kidney Trench with the 16th Battalion.)

He was 89 years old, and received a State Funeral. Over a thousand people attended, including a few old mates from 16th Battalion.

Vale, Jack Axford. In a very gracious gesture, in 1985, the five children of Jack and Maud Axford donated his Victoria Cross, and the other medals he'd been awarded, to the Australian War Memorial, Canberra, where they are now on proud display.

•

In late 1918, the mother of **Private 'Two Guns Harry' Dalziel**, living in Atherton, received word she was about to get a message from London about her lad. She was certain that it was news that he had been killed – she could feel it in her bones – but, in fact, it was notification that he had been awarded the Victoria Cross, as a matter of fact, the 1000th recipient of the medal. 'I don't care about that,' she replied quietly, 'as long as my boy is well.'[45]

Briefly released from his British military hospital on 13 December 1918, to receive his Victoria Cross from King George V, Harry was finally released in the New Year, whereupon he headed for home.

After recovering from his wounds in an English hospital, Harry would receive a hero's welcome upon his return to his hometown, with the mayor of Cairns decreeing no less than a municipal public holiday on the day the town's prodigal son, the one who had brought such glory upon their fair burgh, returned to their arms.

But, *shhh*, don't tell him yet!

The first Harry knows of it is when his ship *Kuranda* arrives at Cairns wharf on the morning of 30 April 1919, and he is greeted not only by his weeping mother, but also the Deputy Commissioner of the Railways, who personally drives him and his mother to his old workplace at Cairns railway station, where . . .

Well, where blessed bedlam breaks loose!

For, look at the crowd gathered outside the station, composed of all the railway employees, most of whom he used to work with! Listen to the cheering, and the raucous rendition by the Railway Band of 'See the Conquering Hero Comes . . .'[46] as Two Guns beams in amazement and his mother cries with pride until she can cry no more. Her boy, the conquering hero, home, *safe*! He had told her before departing for the war that she would have to 'get out the band' for his return, and now, here it is!

And this is *before* they are driven to the Town Hall, where the mayor and a packed civic reception await.

Two Guns Dalziel has done North Queensland proud, and they are intent on doing him proud in turn.

Later in life, Dalziel became a songwriter, honing a skill – composing verses – he'd first practised on his way back from Gallipoli in the hospital ship.

'He was far too ill to be able to sit up and write,' the *Brisbane Courier* would report, 'but he contented himself with committing his poems to memory.'[47]

One of his songs, a waltz, 'Old Sundowner', was judged good enough to be broadcast on the BBC. He would also write screenplays, and had eight of them submitted in the 'Commonwealth film contest'. Some of his songs, such as 'A Song of the Tableland' and 'Love Time, Merry Love Time', were published in England. He also found some commercial and critical success as an artist, and poet, and potter.

After marrying in 1921 a nurse, Ida Ramsay – they'd met when she'd been serving on the Western Front in the 17th Australian General Hospital – Dalziel and his bride bought a farm at Atherton, which Ida ended up running as Harry lived an itinerant life, earning money in a factory job in Sydney interspersed with gold mining in Bathurst, followed by being unemployed in Brisbane – a long way from home and happiness – during much of the Depression. Though still suffering from splitting headaches, Harry found that sculpting, painting and writing poetry, songs and screenplays helped to soothe his wounded mind, while also offering spiritual comfort. For all that, his marriage to Ida was not a happy one, and after they divorced in the early 1930s he remarried to Elsie Kanowski, another nurse, in 1935. This time it was a happy match that lasted.

When the Second World War began, Harry, a member of the Citizen Military Forces for the last six years, immediately applied for active service, but it was decided that his fame could contribute more than his ability to hold a rifle or, in his case, likely two pistols. Due to his advanced age, he was then 46 years old, he was not sent overseas to fight, but instead taken around Australia to help with recruiting by talking of his experiences and raising money through funding drives. When the Second World War was over, Harry was placed on a disability pension and able to truly settle down into a happy suburban life in Oxley, Queensland; with Elsie and their three children, David, Frank and Ann, just another family man who, nevertheless, long ago, on a battlefield on the other side of the world, did something extraordinary and received the Victoria Cross.

'He never made a big issue of it,' his son, David, would later recount. 'He would give it to me to take to school for show and tell.'[48]

The story about being shot in the head? Ever after, he would describe it as getting 'a wallop in the top story'.[49]

Yes, the skin grows over that hole in the head, and he can even comb his hair over the worst of it, but his kids can feel the extraordinary indent all right – like they could even give Dad's brain a poke without too much trouble. Two Guns is still no more fussed about it than he is by the hole in his hand he had taken with him as a souvenir from the Battle of Passchendaele. The only thing is, the kids can't rough-house with him, and when he swims, he never puts his head under water. Still, the headaches were bad, with only one upside – advertising! As he would tell his fellow Australians in the mid-1950s on billboards around the country, and in newspaper ads, 'Bex seems to be the only thing that relieves me of my severe headaches'.[50]

Throughout his life, despite his robust Australianness, Harry Dalziel was very proud to be a member of the British Empire – so much so that just before Prince Charles was born to Princess Elizabeth in 1948, he placed his hard-won Victoria Cross in an envelope and sent it to the young Princess, as a gift for her child.

In response, the Princess, who would become Queen Elizabeth II, graciously replied with a handwritten note on two pages of Buckingham Palace stationery:

> *Dear Sergeant Dalziel,*
>
> *I was most touched to receive your letter of 1st November and the Victoria Cross which you won on American Independence Day 1918. I know that it must be a very treasured possession, and I am deeply grateful for the honour of being offered this Victoria Cross as a gift. However, after consulting the King, and after much thought, I do not feel that it is right that I should accept such a present on behalf of my son. I do not wish you to think that I do this through any lack of appreciation, but it is because I feel most strongly that you should retain this mark of the King's, and the Commonwealth's, esteem for supreme valour in battle.*
>
> *In returning your Victoria Cross, I do so with profound understanding of the depth of loyalty and affection which prompted your action.*
>
> *I am yours sincerely,*
> *Elizabeth*[51]

(This time, let me say it: three cheers!)

In 1956 Harry made the trip to London for the centenary celebrations of the Victoria Cross. In his early 70s Harry suffered a stroke and died on 24 July 1965 at the Repatriation General Hospital, Greenslopes, Brisbane. He was cremated with full military honours.

His name lives on, and his home state of Queensland remains dotted with many things named after him, including Dalziel Street in Nundah, Brisbane, and Henry Dalziel Oval at Irvinebank, North Queensland, while the bar at the Atherton Returned Servicemen's Club is called The Harry Dalziel VC Memorial Bar.

Vale, Two Guns. I loved your story, Sir.

•

All three of the Geddes brothers survived the war and returned to Australia. Aubrey (Boo) went back to his job at the Bank of New South Wales, Stanley joined the Commercial Bank, while **Corporal Cliff Geddes** married Elsie Laura Gall in 1919, and they went on to have three children. Cliff became a real estate agent in Sydney, opening his own business in Rosebery, and played First Grade cricket for Gordon in the heart of the North Shore. By the account of his descendants, his life was not particularly easy thereafter and he had trouble with gambling debts among other things. Still, he struggled on, and while watching his beloved Gordon play in a First Grade cricket match at Chatswood Oval in 1947 he was sitting with his son Geoff, a promising cricketer, next to the Macartney scoreboard, when he suffered a stroke. Though he was rushed to hospital he died less than a month later.

•

Corporal Frank Shaw, the quiet son of the Adelaide Methodist minister, who had done so much to quell the Germans first in Hamel and then in the quarry beyond it, was awarded the Distinguished Conduct Medal in recognition for his inspirational courage.

Alas, just a month later, on 12 August, while being similarly courageous, he was killed in the battle of Amiens. The tragedy of his death renewed focus on his heroic act in the Battle of Hamel, and his superior officer, Captain Eustace Colliver, penned a missive to Shaw's parents affirming his view that their son deserved more:

> You will see by the actions of your hero son that my statement that he merited the VC. was correct, although higher authorities evidently did not think so. What I said to [his uncle] Mr Hambly, I again repeat. Frank was beloved of all for his sterling qualities and Christian manhood. He was never known to do anything that would pain or bring discredit to any of his loved ones. As he was a member of my platoon at the beginning I was greatly interested in his life and work. I well remember one day Frank was interviewed by Captain E. W. Bean, the

*war correspondent, regarding his exploit in the battle of Hamel, and
afterwards Captain Bean remarked to me that Frank was one of the
finest types of Australian he had met.*[52]

Vale, Frank. You did your people proud.

•

In recognition of the fine work done by the Americans, on 12 August
1918, some five weeks after the battle, General George Bell, Commander
of the 33rd Division, received scant notice that they were about to
receive an important visitor to their camp at Molliens-au-Bois – none
other than King George.

And, sure enough, at 10 o'clock in the morning 'a long limousine,
black and sleek, drew near', even as one American soldier noted loudly
to his comrades, 'So that's the big stiff.'[53]

Indeed!

None other than King George V himself emerges and graciously leads
a procession that includes the Generals Pershing, Rawlinson and Bell to
a podium by the chateau, where no fewer than four American officers
and 15 soldiers await, about to be recognised with such esteemed British
bravery decorations as the Military Cross, Distinguished Conduct Medal
and the Military Medal. Among them, of course, is the American hero
of the day, Corporal Frank Shaw's partner on the night, **Corporal
Henry Zyburt**. Fortuitously present for the occasion of the blooded
Americans receiving their first medals of the war, a reporter from the
Chicago Tribune would recount:

> Visiting an old chateau back of the lines today, I saw a squad
> of American soldiers standing in line under beautiful elms. The
> King of England, dressed in the uniform of a field marshal
> and accompanied by a staff in picturesque dress, was going
> from man to man pinning upon their breasts medals in recog-
> nition of their share in the recent glorious victories over the
> Germans.[54]

Zyburt survived the war and returned home to Chicago, dying there,
aged 72 in 1969.

•

Corporal Thomas A. Pope, who had so bravely rushed the German machine-gun nest in the early hours of 5 July – before being gassed later that day – to win back the ground lost on Wolfsberg, received the Distinguished Conduct Medal from King George V on 12 August 1918. Pope's own country, shortly afterwards, awarded him their Medal of Honor – the equivalent of the Victoria Cross. His was an extraordinary military career, in that despite the fact that he only ever saw two days of battle, he was to be commended for bravery by no fewer than four nations, including his own nation's highest honour. And no less than 60 years later, he was still alive to tell the tale of the battle of Le Hamel, and his part in it! As it turned out, Tom Pope was the last surviving soldier of the First World War to have won the Medal of Honor, and died on 14 June 1989, to be buried at Arlington Cemetery in Washington.

•

Corporal Michael Roach, who risked his life to shepherd the Americans of Company A of the 132nd Regiment back from the barrage, and was felled by shrapnel himself, was carried back to the Regimental Aid Post, but died shortly afterwards.

•

Private Isaac Betteridge was killed in action during the capture of Mont St Quentin, 1 September 1918. He was wounded in the stomach and arm, and survived until he arrived at the 8th Australian Field Ambulance, but died there. The diary from which material has been drawn was found on his body and posted to his grieving parents in Spring Bank, Victoria. He is buried at Assevillers New British Cemetery in the Somme, France.

•

Private Charlie Hubbard, the oldest man on the battlefield – or at least the oldest on the Australian side of the line – survived. After being evacuated to hospital in England, he recovered the power of arms and legs, as his paralysis proved only temporary, and shortly thereafter, returned to Australian and Northam. He lived out his days in a caravan and, as the local newspaper, the *Western Mail*, reported, 'when he gets tired of the scenery in one place his portable camp is attached to the car and away he goes'.[55] He died in Northam, 60 miles north-east of Perth, in November 1934, aged 81. As reported by the *Western Mail*, 'He was buried with semi-military honours, and several of his old comrades were at the graveside.'[56]

•

Ruth, the widow of **Bertie Englert**, the trumpeter who had been killed by the falling barn roof in the Allonville Disaster, never remarried, never had a child, and died alone in 1957.

(I know. I weep, too.)

•

As noted in my Great War trilogy, in the course of the war **Captain Charles Bean** filled the 226 notebooks which form the foundation stone for his work for the next 23 years after the war, as he compiled 12 volumes – of which he wrote the first six volumes – of the *Official History of Australia in the War of 1914–1918*, with the twelfth and final volume being published in 1942. In 1946, Bean released a separate single volume account of the war titled *Anzac to Amiens*.

Beyond his writings, Bean's other great legacy, of course, was the Australian War Memorial, for which he was the driving force, and its first Acting Director. The building itself opened its doors on 11 November 1941. He died aged 88 on 30 August 1968, survived by his wife, Ethel.

•

As I noted in my book on Gallipoli, I deeply admired Keith Murdoch for his role in evacuating the Australian troops from that disaster before winter truly set in. His role in this episode, however, I put down as a serious error of judgement. A little over two years after the war was over, Murdoch returned to Melbourne early to take a position as Editor-in-Chief of the Melbourne evening *Herald*. That paper became a stunning success, in part because Murdoch pioneered in Australia the tabloid form journalism he had studied so assiduously while in England. By both covering and *generating* political controversy, and always putting it on the front page, as well as providing heavy celebrity coverage, he lifted circulation by 50 per cent in just his first four years. Going from strength to strength, in 1928 he became Managing Director of the company that owned the paper the *Herald & Weekly Times*, the same year that the 42-year-old married the 19-year-old Melbourne beauty Elisabeth Joy Greene.

One of the writers he would call on occasionally – as he was wont to do, when he required specialists in their field to work on difficult subjects – was Charles Bean, 'our brilliant and painstaking war historian',[57] and the two remained close, within the limits of their singularly intense careers, and family lives.

Murdoch was particularly busy with both and, even while buying the exceedingly dull *Adelaide Register* before turning it into a tabloid, and then taking over the *Adelaide Advertiser* and the *Adelaide News*, he and his new bride soon formed a family with one son and three daughters.

Keith Murdoch's key breakthrough came in 1948, when he persuaded the *Herald* board to sell to him its holdings in the *Adelaide News*, and when he died in 1952, this was the key asset of his estate – allowing a posthumous dream to be fulfilled, with his son, Rupert, taking over. And the rest, as they say, really *is* history!

•

Though it is not certain, there is a good chance that a final stanza of the story of the Battle of Le Hamel was played out in the early 1990s. In the 1920s the idea was first proposed to exhume the remains of an Unknown Australian Soldier from the battlefields in France to be returned to the Australian War Memorial[58] to lie in the Hall of Memory in the Tomb of the Unknown Soldier. The body in question – complete with the Australian badges and accoutrements that confirm its nationality – was taken from the Adelaide Cemetery, situated by Villers-Bretonneux, and though the reasoning is long and complex, the likelihood is that he was killed either in the Battle of Villers-Bretonneux or Hamel.

Either way, Prime Minister Paul Keating's magnificent words, on the occasion of the interment of the Unknown Soldier at the Australian War Memorial in 1993, ring through the ages.

Lean in. Listen, please, as he speaks of all of those Diggers who never returned to our shores, never embraced their loved ones, returned to their marital beds, never conceived children or helped raise the ones they had, who had been waiting for them all those years.

'We do not know this Australian's name and we never will,' Mr Keating declares. 'We do not know his rank or his battalion. We do not know where he was born, or precisely how and when he died. We do not know where in Australia he had made his home or when he left it for the battlefields of Europe. We do not know his age or his circumstances – whether he was from the city or the bush; what occupation he left to become a soldier; what religion, if he had a religion; if he was married or single. We do not know who loved him or whom he loved. If he had children we do not know who they are. His family is lost to us as he was lost to them. We will never know who this Australian was.

'Yet he has always been among those we have honoured. We know that he was one of the 45,000 Australians who died on the Western Front. One of the 416,000 Australians who volunteered for service in the First World War. One of the 324,000 Australians who served overseas in that war and one of the 60,000 Australians who died on foreign soil. One of the 100,000 Australians who have died in wars this century.

'He is all of them. And he is one of us . . .'[59]

And I, for one, offer a humble civilian salute of the deepest respect for the accomplishments of the Unknown Soldier and his comrades.

Lest We Forget.

ENDNOTES

Frontmatter

1 Taylor, *The First World War: An Illustrated History*, London, 1963, p. 179.
2 Monash, *Australian Victories in France in 1918*, Naval and Military Press, Uckfield, 2005, p. 56.
3 Molkentin, *Fire in the Sky*, Allen & Unwin, Sydney, 2010, p. 272.

Prologue

1 Author's note: It included 52 tons of shrapnel shells, more than 3000 percussion fuses, and 4200 cases of Remington rifle cartridges. The point being *Lusitania* was carrying weapons of war for the Allies, in which case, from the point of view of Germany, she was a legitimate target.
2 Author's note: There were, in fact, 1257 passengers and 702 crew, together with three stowaways. Of the 1962 on board, 1191 lost their lives.
3 Schwieger, Walther, 'English Translation of His Majesty's Submarine U-20 War Diary', 1915 [reported speech].
4 AA Hoehling and Mary Hoehling, *The Last Voyage of the Lusitania*, Madison Books, Lanham, 1956, pp. 189–90.
5 Berg, *Wilson*, Simon and Schuster, London, 2013, p. 440.
6 Müller and Görlitz, *The Kaiser and his Court*, Macdonald, London, 1961, p. 255.

Chapter One

1 Sheffield, *The Chief*, Aurum, London, 2012, p. 138.
2 Pedersen, *Monash as Military Commander*, Melbourne University Press, Melbourne, 1985, p. 216.
3 Eden, *Another World, 1897–1917*, Doubleday, New York, 1977, p. 134.
4 Monash, *Australian Victories in France in 1918*, p. 37.
5 Monash, *Australian Victories in France in 1918*, p. 38.
6 Pedersen, *Hamel*, Pen & Sword Books, Barnsley/South Yorkshire, 2003, p. 34.
7 Monash, *Australian Victories in France in 1918*, p. 39.
8 Lt William Charles Thomas, 14 Battalion, D Company, AWM PR 82.002.
9 Geddes, diary, 6th May 1918, SLNSW, MLMSS 2763 / Item 1, p. 77.
10 Geddes, diary, 4th July 1918, SLNSW, MLMSS 2763 / Item 1, p. 80.
11 Geddes, diary, 4th July 1918, SLNSW, MLMSS 2763 / Item 1, p. 80.
12 Geddes, diary, 6th May 1918, SLNSW, MLMSS 2763 / Item 1, p. 80.
13 Geddes, diary, 2 May 1918, SLNSW, MLMSS 2763 / Item 1, p. 68.
14 Essame, *The Battle for Europe 1918*, Batsford, London, 1972, p. 52.
15 Bean, *Official History of Australia in the War of 1914–1918*, Vol. VI, Angus & Robertson, Sydney, 1942 p. 43. Author's note: There are two spellings of this French epithet for the Germans, '*Boche*' and '*Bosche*', with the former marginally the most common. As *Boche* was also the one most often used by the Diggers, I have used that spelling throughout for consistency.

16 Bean, *Official History of Australia in the War of 1914–1918*, Vol. VI, p. 43.
17 McMullin, *Pompey Elliott*, Scribe, Melbourne, 2008, p. 456.
18 Author's note: Irvine's action occurred after Haig commented on 3rd Australian Division. However, it is an excellent example of numerous instances of initiative shown by the Division that Haig is praising.
19 Records of CEW Bean, AWM38 3DRL 606/112/1 – May 1918, pp. 14–15.
20 Monash, *Australian Victories in France in 1918*, p. 38.
21 Monash, *Australian Victories in France in 1918*, p. 290.
22 Monash *Australian Victories in France in 1918*, p. 290.
23 Author's note: Monash's first knighthood was 1915, his second, up a level, was January 1918, and his third, the big one up to the top level, was August 1918.
24 Sheffield and Bourne (eds), *Douglas Haig: War Diaries and Letters*, p. 296.
25 Serle, *John Monash*, Melbourne University Press, Melbourne, 1982, p. 277.
26 Macdougall (ed.), *War Letters of General Monash*, Duffy & Snellgrove, Sydney, 2002, p. 127.
27 Serle, *John Monash*, p. 302.
28 Winter, *Haig's Command*, Viking, London, 1991, p. 163.
29 Bean, diary, 17 June 1916, AWM38 3DRL 606/47/1, pp. 15–16.
30 Terraine, *White Heat*, Guild Publishing, London, 1982, p. 316.
31 Bean, *Official History of Australia in the War of 1914–1918*, Vol. VI, p. 327.
32 Bean, *Official History of Australia in the War of 1914–1918*, Vol. VI, p. 15.
33 Seale, Graham, *Inventing Anzac*, University of Queensland Press, St Lucia, 2004, p. 25.
34 *The Sydney Morning Herald*, 26 January 1935, p. 13.
35 Records of CEW Bean, AWM38 3DRL 606/111/1 – May 1918, p. 20.
36 Gary Sheffield and John M. Bourne (eds), *Douglas Haig: War Diaries and Letters*, Weidenfeld & Nicolson, London, 2005, p. 364.
37 Diary of General Rawlinson, Churchill Archives Centre, Cambridge, RWLN 1/16, p. 1.
38 Bean, diary, AWM38 3DRL 606/111/1 – May 1918, p. 11.
39 Healy, *More Lives Than One*, Appleton, New York, 1944, p. 212.
40 Maynard, *The Unseen Anzac*, Scribe, Brunswick, 2015, p. 150.
41 Serle, *John Monash*, p. 329.
42 Author's note: Hobbs is London born but a resident of Perth, WA, for the last 32 of his 54 years, so he counts as an Australian in everyone's eyes.
43 Bean, diary, AWM38 3DRL 606/111/1 – May 1918, pp. 4–5.
44 Bean, diary, AWM38 3DRL 606/111/1 – May 1918, p. 6.
45 Bean, diary, AWM38 3DRL 606/111/1 – May 1918, p. 6.
46 Serle, *John Monash*, p. 320.
47 Bean, *Official History of Australia in the War of 1914–1918*, Vol. VI, p. 188 [reported speech].
48 Zwar, *In Search of Keith Murdoch*, Macmillan, South Melbourne, 1980, p. 50.
49 Bean, diary, AWM38 3DRL 606/90/1, October 1917, pp. 11–14 [reported speech].
50 Serle, *John Monash*, p. 322.
51 Sheffield and Bourne (eds), *Douglas Haig: War Diaries and Letters*, p. 413.
52 Maurice, *The Life of General Lord Rawlinson of Trent*, Cassell and Co., London, 1928, p. 216.
53 Maurice, *The Life of General Lord Rawlinson of Trent*, p. 217.
54 Personal diary of Field Marshal Lord William Birdwood, 1 January – 31 December 1918, AWM 3DRL/3376 1/4 Part 1, p. 40.
55 Emden, *The Soldier's War*, Bloomsbury, London, 2008, p. 323.
56 Sheffield and Bourne (eds), *Douglas Haig: War Diaries and Letters*, p. 414.
57 Sheffield and Bourne (eds), *Douglas Haig: War Diaries and Letters*, p. 296.
58 Monash, letter, 14 May 1918, Vol. 2, p. 134 (p. 404 of typescript).
59 Bean, diary, AWM38 3DRL 606/111/1 – May 1918, p. 18.
60 Bean, diary, AWM38 3DRL 606/111/1 – May 1918, p. 18.
61 Bean, diary, AWM38 3DRL 606/111/1 – May 1918, pp. 21–2.
62 Bean, *Official History of Australia in the War of 1914–1918*, Vol. VI, pp. 195–6.
63 Geddes, diary, SLNSW 863029, p. 92.
64 Geddes, diary, SLNSW 863029, p. 92.
65 Pearce to Birdwood, NA CRS (Commonwealth Record Series) A6006/5 roll 2.
66 Roberts, *Before Rupert*, University of Queensland Press, St Lucia, 2015, p. 93.
67 Roberts, *Before Rupert*, p. 78.
68 Letter, Monash to Murdoch, Papers of Sir Keith Murdoch, NLA MS 2823/ 2/ 9, p. 1.
69 Roberts, *Before Rupert*, p. 78.
70 Roberts, *Before Rupert*, p. 78.
71 Pedersen, *Monash as Military Commander*, p. 216.

72 Pedersen, *Monash as Military Commander*, p. 216.
73 *Weekly Despatch*, 16 June 1918, Arthur O'Connor, 'Monash: The new fighting General', in: Monash, Personal Files, Book 19, 4 June – 24 June 1918, RCDIG0000632, p. 71.
74 *Weekly Despatch*, 16 June 1918, Arthur O'Connor, 'Monash: The new fighting General', in: Monash, Personal Files, Book 19, p. 71.
75 Monash, *Australian Victories in France in 1918*, p. 294.
76 *Weekly Despatch*, 16 June 1918, Arthur O'Connor, 'Monash: The new fighting General', in: Monash, Personal Files, Book 19, pp. 72–3.
77 Corning, *The Yanks Crusade*, self-published, Chicago, 1927, p. 22.
78 Corning, *The Yanks Crusade*, p. 22.

Chapter Two

1 *Pittsworth Sentinel*, 15 October 1941, p. 2.
2 Monash, *Australian Victories in France in 1918*, pp. 43–4.
3 Carlyon, *The Great War*, Macmillan, Sydney, 2006, p. 626.
4 Sydney B. Young, diary, SLNSW, MLMSS 985/Item 6 March, p. 8.
5 Geddes, diary, 26 May 1918, SLNSW, MLMSS 2763, p. 102.
6 Monash, Personal Files, Book 18, 8 May – 25 May 1918, RCDIG0000630, p. 96.
7 Serle, *John Monash*, p. 321.
8 Monash, letter, 14 May 1918, Vol. 2, p. 133 (p. 403 of typescript).
9 Monash, letter, 14 May 1918, Vol. 2, p. 134 (p. 404 of typescript).
10 Macdougall (ed.), *War Letters of General Monash*, p. 188.
11 Serle, *John Monash*, p. 323.
12 Lt William Charles Thomas, diary, 1918, AWM PR 82/002.
13 Diary of General Rawlinson, Churchill Archives Centre, Cambridge, RWLN 1/16, p. 11.
14 *Washington Post*, 25 July 2016 (online).
15 Dehgan, *America in Quotations*, Macfarlane, Jefferson, 2003, p. 86.
16 Geddes, diary, SLNSW 863029, pp. 106–7.
17 Geddes, diary, SLNSW 863029, p. 107.
18 Geddes, diary, SLNSW 863029, p. 107.
19 Further reading: http://trove.nla.gov.au/newspaper/article/5583533.
20 Rule, *Jacka's Mob*, Angus & Robertson, Sydney, 1933, p. 283.
21 Rule, *Jacka's Mob*, p. 283.
22 Rule, *Jacka's Mob*, p. 283.
23 Bean, *Official History of Australia in the War of 1914–1918*, Vol VI, p. 110.
24 Red Cross Wounded and Missing, AWM 1DRL0428, files7588 and 7342 and http://www.cwgc.org/find-war-dead.aspx?cpage=5&sort=name&order=asc.
25 Bertie George Englert, Australian Red Cross Wounded and Missing Enquiry, AWM 1DRL/0428.
26 Geddes, diary, SLNSW 863029.
27 War Records of CEW Bean, AWM38 3DRL 606/113/1 – May – June 1918, p. 49 [reported speech].
28 War Records of CEW Bean, AWM38 3DRL 606/113/1 – May – June 1918, pp. 52, 53–4.
29 War Records of CEW Bean, AWM38 3DRL 606/113/1 – May – June 1918, p. 53.
30 War Records of CEW Bean, AWM38 3DRL 606/91/1 – October 1917, pp. 65–6.
31 War Records of CEW Bean, AWM38 3DRL 606/115/1 – June 1918, pp. 56–7.
32 Letter, Bean to Murdoch, 2 June 1918, AWM 38 3DRL 1722/30, p. 1.
33 Letter, Bean to Murdoch, 2 June 1918, AWM 38 3DRL 1722/30, p. 1.
34 Letter, Bean to Murdoch, 2 June 1918, AWM 38 3DRL 1722/30, p. 1.
35 Gunner Albert Williams manuscript, AWM MSS 1337, p. 216.
36 Bean, diary, AWM 3DRL606/113/1, p. 53.
37 Letter, Murdoch to Monash, Papers of Sir Keith Murdoch, NLA MS 2823/ 2/ 9.
38 Letter, Murdoch to Monash, Papers of Sir Keith Murdoch, NLA MS 2823/ 2/ 9.
39 Letter, Murdoch to Monash, Papers of Sir Keith Murdoch, NLA MS 2823/ 2/ 9, p. 1.
40 Letter, Murdoch to Monash, Papers of Sir Keith Murdoch, NLA MS 2823/ 2/ 9, p. 2.
41 Serle, *John Monash*, p. 324.
42 Serle, *John Monash*, p. 324.
43 Bean, diary, AWM38 3DRL 606/114/1 – June 1918, pp. 3–4 [reported speech].
44 Bean, diary, AWM38 3DRL 606/114/1 – June 1918, p. 4 [reported speech].
45 Bean, diary, AWM38 3DRL 606 114/1 June 1918, p. 7.
46 Bean, diary, AWM38 3DRL 606/114/1 – June 1918, inserted near p. 8.
47 Monash, John, *Australian Victories in France in 1918*, p. 17.

48 Monash, *Australian Victories in France in 1918*, p. 296.
49 *Journal of the Australian War Memorial*, Carl Bridge, Review of David Horner, *Blamey: the Commander-in-Chief*, Allen & Unwin, Sydney, 1998, p. 1.
50 Serle, *John Monash*, p. 319.
51 *Daily Examiner*, 1 January 1920, p. 4.
52 Blamey, *Reveille*, October 1931, p. 13.
53 Serle, *John Monash*, p. 319.
54 https://www.awm.gov.au/learn/understanding-military-history/official-histories/first_world_war/volVI_introduction.
55 Serle, *John Monash*, p. 389.
56 Sheffield and Bourne, *Douglas Haig, War Diaries and Letters*, p. 385.
57 Bean, diary, AWM38 3DRL 606/114/1 – June 1918, pp. 89–90 [reported speech].
58 Bean, diary, AWM38 3DRL 606/114/1 – June 1918, pp. 93 [reported speech].
59 Bean, diary, AWM38 3DRL 606/114/1 – June 1918, p. 93 [reported speech].
60 Corning, *The Yanks Crusade*, p. 25.
61 Judy, *A Soldier's Diary*, Judy Publishing, Chicago, 1930, p. 97.
62 Recouly and Jones, *Foch: The Winner of the War*, C. Scribner's Sons, New York, 1920, p. 112.
63 Edmonds, *Military Operations, France and Belgium, 1918, May–July*, Imperial War Museum, London, 1939, p. 166.
64 Edmonds, *Military Operations, France and Belgium, 1918, May–July*, p. 166.
65 Bean, *Official History of Australia in the War of 1914–1918*, Vol. VI, p. 240.
66 Author's note: The wood south-west of Hamel had two names. The northern half was Hamel Wood and the southern half Vaire Wood. I've decided to call the whole of it Vaire Wood.
67 Bean, *Official History of Australia in the War of 1914–1918*, Vol. VI, p. 243.
68 Monash, *Australian Victories in France in 1918*, p. 44.
69 Diary of General Rawlinson, Churchill Archives Centre, Cambridge, RWLN 1/16, p. 17.
70 Diary of General Rawlinson, Churchill Archives Centre, Cambridge, RWLN 1/16, p. 17.
71 Gunner Albert Williams, manuscript, AWM MSS 1337, p. 216.
72 Gunner Albert Williams, manuscript, AWM MSS 1337, p. 216.
73 Geddes, diary, 12 June 1918, SLNSW, MLMSS 2763, pp. 120–1.
74 Geddes, diary, 12 June 1918, SLNSW, MLMSS 2763, p. 121.
75 Geddes, diary, 12 June 1918, SLNSW, MLMSS 2763, p. 121.
76 Interview with Don Axford of Perth, Jack's grandson.
77 Betteridge, diary, AWM PR90.151, p. 10.

Chapter Three

1 Prior and Wilson, *Command on the Western Front*, Pen & Sword Books, Barnsley/South Yorkshire, 2004, p. 291.
2 Letter, Rawlinson to Bridges, National Army Museum, Rawlinson 1952, 01-33-76.
3 Serle, *John Monash*, p. 328.
4 Betteridge, diary, AWM PR90.151 P11.
5 Betteridge, diary, AWM PR90.151 P11.
6 Betteridge, diary, AWM PR90.151 P11.
7 Harris, *Men, Ideas and Tanks,* Manchester University Press, Manchester, 1995, p. 138.
8 Mitchell, *Backs to the Wall*, Allen & Unwin, Crows Nest, 2007, p. 202.
9 Diary of General Rawlinson, Churchill Archives Centre, Cambridge, RWLN 1/16, p. 2.
10 Laffin, *The Battle of Hamel*, Kangaroo Press, Sydney, 1999, p. 128.
11 Maurice, *The Life of General Lord Rawlinson of Trent*, p. 221.
12 Wodehouse, *Blandings Castle – and Elsewhere*, H. Jenkins, London, 1957, p. 29.
13 Pedersen, *Anzacs on the Western Front*, John Wiley & Sons, Melbourne, 2012, p. 150.
14 Pedersen, *Monash as Military Commander*, p. 18.
15 Maurice, *The Life of General Lord Rawlinson of Trent*, p. 221.
16 Bean, *Official History of Australia in the War of 1914–1918*, Vol. VI, p. 246.
17 Hickey, *Rolling into Action*, Naval and Military Press, Uckfield, 2007, p. 85.
18 Monash, Personal Files, Book 19, 4 June – 24 June 1918, RCDIG0000632, p. 87.
19 Geddes, diary, 20 June 1918, SLNSW, MLMSS 2763, p. 130.
20 Geddes, diary, 4th July 1918, SLNSW, MLMSS 2763 / Item 1, p. 150.
21 Terraine, *The Smoke and the Fire*, Sidgwick & Jackson, London, 1980, pp. 201–2.
22 Pedersen, *Monash as Military Commander*, p. 13.
23 *The Sydney Morning Herald*, 22 January 2001.

24 Courage, Letter to Monash, 20 June 1918, in: Monash, Personal Files, Book 19, 4 June – 24 June 1918, RCDIG0000632, p. 95.
25 Courage to Monash, Monash, Personal Files, Book 18, AWM 3DRL 2613, p. 94.
26 Courage, Letter to Monash, 20 June 1918, in: Monash, Personal Files, Book 19, 4 June – 24 June 1918, RCDIG0000632, p. 95.
27 Courage, Letter to Monash, 20 June 1918, in: Monash, Personal Files, Book 19, 4 June – 24 June 1918, RCDIG0000632, p. 96.
28 Courage, Letter to Monash, 20 June 1918, in: Monash, Personal Files, Book 19, 4 June – 24 June 1918, RCDIG0000632, p. 96.
29 Monash, *Australian Victories in France in 1918*, pp. 47–8.
30 Monash, Personal Files, Book 19, 4 June – 24 June 1918, RCDIG0000632, p. 98.
31 Molkentin, *Fire in the Sky*, p. 271 [reported speech].
32 Molkentin, *Fire in the Sky*, p. 271 [reported speech].
33 Corning, *The Yanks Crusade*, p. 30.
34 Corning, *The Yanks Crusade*, p. 31.
35 Corning, *The Yanks Crusade*, p. 31.
36 Corning, *The Yanks Crusade*, p. 31.
37 Pedersen, *Monash as Military Commander*, p. 226.
38 Diary of General Rawlinson, Churchill Archives Centre, Cambridge, RWLN 1/16, p. 21.
39 Bean, *Official History of Australia in the War of 1914–1918*, Vol. VI, p. 252.
40 Pedersen, *Hamel*, p. 47.
41 Chattaway, *History of the 15th Battalion*, W. Brooks, Brisbane, 1948, p. 209.
42 *The Northern Herald* (Cairns), 19 December 1918, p. 38.
43 *The Northern Herald* (Cairns), 19 December 1918, p. 38.
44 Pedersen, *Monash as Military Commander*, p. 219.
45 Bean, *Official History of Australia in the War of 1914–1918*, Vol. VI, p. 254.
46 Bean, *Official History of Australia in the War of 1914–1918*, Vol. VI, p. 254.
47 Monash, *Australian Victories in France in 1918*, p. 46.
48 Molkentin, *Fire in the Sky*, p. 271.
49 Molkentin, *Fire in the Sky*, p. 271.
50 Foott, Cecil, Letter to *Reveille*, in: Bean, Charles, AWM38 3DRL 606/276/1, War records, 1928–1937, p. 33.
51 Corning, *The Yanks Crusade*, pp. 36–7.
52 Corning, *The Yanks Crusade*, p. 37 [reported speech].
53 Corning, *The Yanks Crusade*, p. 37.
54 Monash, Personal Files, Book 19, 4 June – 24 June 1918, RCDIG0000632, p. 122.
55 Rawlinson, Letter to Wigram, National Army Museum (NAM) Rawlinson 1952, 01-33-73.
56 Diary of General Rawlinson, Churchill Archives Centre, Cambridge, RWLN 1/16, p. 22.
57 Bean, *Official History of Australia in the War of 1914–1918*, Vol. VI, p. 262.
58 Huidekoper, *The History of the 33rd Division, A.E.F.*, Vol. III, Illinois State Historical Library, Springfield, 1921, p. 352.
59 Bean, *Official History of Australia in the War of 1914–1918*, Vol. VI, p. 262.
60 Monash, *Australian Victories in France in 1918*, p. 52.
61 Corning, *The Yanks Crusade*, p. 40.
62 Diary of General Rawlinson, Churchill Archives Centre, Cambridge, RWLN 1/16, p. 22.
63 Roberts, *Before Rupert*, p. 78.
64 Author's note: In a later typed version of this letter the word 'pogrom' has been changed to 'intrigue'.
65 Serle, *John Monash*, p. 325.
66 Macdougall (ed.), *War Letters of General Monash*, p. 191.
67 Serle, *John Monash*, p. 414.

Chapter Four

1 Larres, *Churchill's Cold War*, University Press, New Haven, 2002, p. xxii.
2 Monash, *Australian Victories in France in 1918*, p. 56.
3 Hart, *1918 A Very British Victory*, Phoenix, London, 2008, p. 304.
4 No. 3 Squadron War Diary, AWM4 8/6/18 – June 1918, p. 9.
5 No. 3 Squadron War Diary, AWM4 8/6/18 – June 1918, p. 10.
6 *The Mercury* (Hobart), 24 September 1924, p. 10.
7 Sanborn, *131st US Infantry (First Infantry Illinois National Guard) in the World War*, p. 370.
8 Sanborn, *131st US Infantry (First Infantry Illinois National Guard) in the World War*, p. 371.

9 Laffin, *The Battle of Hamel*, p. 66.
10 Laffin, *The Battle of Hamel*, p. 66.
11 John Earnshaw, Lecture at Huddersfield Military History Society, 19 November 2014.
12 Wackett, *Aircraft Pioneer*, Angus & Robertson, Sydney, 1972, p. 73.
13 Monash, *Australian Victories in France in 1918*, pp. 150–1.
14 Serle, *John Monash*, p. 339.
15 Kieza, *Monash*, HarperCollins, Sydney, 2015, p. 457.
16 Clausewitz, *On War*, Princeton University Press, Princeton, 1976, p. 101.
17 Monash, *Australian Victories in France in 1918*, pp. 291–2.
18 Serle, *John Monash*, p. 387.
19 Monash, *Australian Victories in France in 1918*, p. 204.
20 Pedersen, *Hamel*, p. 55.
21 Wackett, *Aircraft Pioneer*, p. 73.
22 Pedersen, *Monash as Military Commander*, p. 217 [reported speech].
23 Pedersen, *Monash as Military Commander*, p. 217 [reported speech].
24 Bean, Charles, *Official History of Australia in the War of 1914–1918*, Vol VI, p. 205.
25 Courage, Letter to Monash, 20 June 1918, in: Monash, Personal Files, Book 19, 4 June – 24 June 1918, RCDIG0000632, p. 94.
26 Wackett, *Aircraft Pioneer*, p. 73.
27 Pedersen, *Hamel*, p. 50.
28 Monash, *Australian Victories in France in 1918*, p. 50.
29 Thompson, *On Lips of Living Men*, Lansdowne Press, Melbourne, 1962, p. 144.
30 Thompson, *On Lips of Living Men*, p. 144.
31 Yockelson, *Borrowed Soldiers*, University of Oklahoma Press, Norman, 2008, p. 76.
32 Yockelson, *Borrowed Soldiers*, p. 77.
33 Yockelson, *Borrowed Soldiers*, p. 77.
34 Yockelson, *Borrowed Soldiers*, p. 77.
35 Wackett, *Aircraft Pioneer*, p. 71.
36 Wackett, *Aircraft Pioneer*, p. 71.
37 Wackett, *Aircraft Pioneer*, p. 71.
38 Wackett, *Aircraft Pioneer*, p. 73.
39 Wackett, *Aircraft Pioneer*, p. 73.
40 Wedel, *Das Feldartillerie-Regiment 213*, Bernhard Sporn, Zeulenroda-Thür., 1930, p. 230.
41 Wedel, *Das Feldartillerie-Regiment 213*, p. 230.
42 *Port Adelaide News*, 26 July 1929, p. 4.
43 *Port Adelaide News*, 26 July 1929, p. 4.
44 Pedersen, *Hamel*, p. 23.
45 Rule, *Jacka's Mob*, p. 297.
46 Rule, *Jacka's Mob*, p. 297.
47 Geddes, diary, 29 June 1918, SLNSW, MLMSS 2763, pp. 140–1.
48 Bean, *Official History of Australia in the War of 1914–1918*, Vol. VI, p. 264.
49 Bean, *Official History of Australia in the War of 1914–1918*, Vol. VI, p. 260.
50 Peter Nunan, 'Diggers Fourth of July', *Military History Magazine*, August 2000, p. 26.
51 Peter Nunan, 'Diggers Fourth of July', *Military History Magazine*, August 2000, p. 26.
52 Bean, *Official History of Australia in the War of 1914–1918*, Vol. VI, p. 262.
53 Pedersen, *Hamel*, p. 60.
54 Pedersen, *Hamel*, p. 60.
55 Lt Henry Neaves, AWM 2DRL.0752, p. 125.
56 Rule, *Jacka's Mob*, p. 299.
57 Sheffield and Bourne (eds), *Douglas Haig: War Diaries and Letters*, p. 424 [reported speech].
58 Author's note: Charles Bean has a different view. He believes all ten US companies were originally promised, but through an oversight at first only four were sent. I believe the original documents, not available to Bean at the time, show my account to be correct.
59 Diary of General Rawlinson, Churchill Archives Centre, Cambridge, RWLN 1/16, p. 25.
60 Smithers, *A New Excalibur*, Leo Cooper, London, 1986, p. 104.

Chapter Five

1 Simpson, Private Record, AWM PR00733.
2 Monash, *Australian Victories in France in 1918*, p. 96.
3 Monash, *Australian Victories in France in 1918*, p. 49.
4 Geddes, diary, SLNSW 863029, p. 141.

5 Monash, *Australian Victories in France in 1918*, p. 49.
6 Geddes, diary, SLNSW 863029, p. 141.
7 White, *The Fighting Thirteenth*, Naval & Military Press and Imperial War Museum, 2009, p. 142.
8 Geddes, diary, SLNSW 863029, p. 142.
9 White, *The Fighting Thirteenth*, p. 142.
10 Monash, *Australian Victories in France in 1918*, p. 50.
11 Rawlinson, Henry S., diary, Churchill Archives Centre, Cambridge, RWLN 1/16, p. 24.
12 Rawlinson, diary, Churchill Archives Centre, Cambridge, RWLN 1/16, p. 25.
13 Pedersen, *Hamel*, p. 61.
14 Monash, *Australian Victories in France in 1918*, p. 50.
15 White, *The Fighting Thirteenth*, p. 142.
16 White, *The Fighting Thirteenth*, p. 142.
17 Geddes, diary, SLNSW 863029, p. 145.
18 Geddes, diary, SLNSW 863029, p. 143.
19 White, *The Fighting Thirteenth*, p. 142.
20 Monash, *Australian Victories in France in 1918*, p. 50.
21 White, *The Fighting Thirteenth*, p. 142.
22 Geddes, diary, 4 July 1918, SLNSW, MLMSS 2763 / Item 1, p. 143.
23 Bean, *Official History of Australia in the War of 1914–1918*, Vol. VI, p. 259.
24 Sanborn, *131st US Infantry (First Infantry Illinois National Guard) in the World War*, p. 52.
25 Rule, *Jacka's Mob*, p. 298.
26 Rule, *Jacka's Mob*, p. 299.
27 Rule, *Jacka's Mob*, p. 299.
28 Rule, *Jacka's Mob*, p. 299.
29 Lieutenant Callister quoted in: Carne, *In Good Company*, 6th Machine Gun Company (A.I.F.) Association, Melbourne, 1937, p. 319.
30 Geddes, diary, 13 May 1918, SLNSW, MLMSS 2763, p. 87.
31 Lieutenant Callister quoted in: Carne, *In Good Company*, p. 319.
32 https://www.awm.gov.au/journal/j35/blair/#66.
33 https://www.awm.gov.au/journal/j35/blair/#67.
34 https://www.awm.gov.au/journal/j35/blair/#65.
35 Pedersen, *Monash as Military Commander*, p. 230.
36 Rawlinson, diary, 1 July 1918, Churchill Archives Centre, Cambridge, RWLN 1/16.
37 Monash, Personal Files, Book 19, 23 June – 7 July 1918, RCDIG0000633, p. 43.
38 Monash, Personal Files, Book 19, 23 June – 7 July 1918, RCDIG0000633, p. 43.
39 Pedersen, *Monash as Military Commander*, p. 98.
40 Monash, Personal Files, Book 19, 23 June – 7 July 1918, RCDIG0000633, p. 42.
41 Monash, Personal Files, Book 19, 23 June – 7 July 1918, RCDIG0000633, p. 42.
42 Pedersen, *Hamel*, p. 37.
43 Terraine, *The Smoke and the Fire*, p. 198.
44 Bassett, MA Thesis ('Does the leadership and command method of General Sir John Monash remain relevant to the contemporary commander?'), U.S. Army Command and General Staff College, Fort Leavenworth, Kansas, 2009, pp. 68–9.
45 Pedersen, *Monash as Military Commander*, p. 176.
46 Monash, Personal Files, Book 19, 23 June – 7 July 1918, RCDIG0000633, p. 45.
47 Monash, Personal Files, Book 19, 23 June – 7 July 1918, RCDIG0000633, p. 45.
48 Monash, Personal Files, Book 19, 23 June – 7 July 1918, RCDIG0000633, p. 45.
49 Monash, Personal Files, Book 19, 23 June – 7 July 1918, RCDIG0000633, p. 45.
50 Letter, Coxen to Bean, War records of CEW Bean AWM38 3DRL 606/276/1 – 1928–1937.
51 Pedersen, *Hamel*, p. 58.
52 Australian corps general staff, defence of Amiens 1 July 1918, AWM 25 361/3 .
53 Bean, War Records, AWM38 3DRL 606/116/1 June–September, p. 9.
54 Edmonds, *Military Operations, France and Belgium, 1918, May–July*, p. 215.
55 Gross and Rudloff, *Infanterie-Regiment Herwarth von Bittenfeld (1. Westfälisches) Nr. 13 im Weltkriege 1914–1918*, Verlag von Gerhard Stalling, Oldenburg i.O./Berlin, 1927, p. 307.
56 Gross and Rudloff, *Infanterie-Regiment Herwarth von Bittenfeld (1. Westfälisches) Nr. 13 im Weltkriege 1914–1918*, p. 306.
57 Schulz, *Infanterie-Regiment Graf Bülow von Dennewitz (6. Westfälisches) Nr. 55 im Weltkriege*, Verlag der Meyerschen Hofbuchhandlung (Max Staercke), Detmold, 1928, p. 230.
58 Schulz, *Infanterie-Regiment Graf Bülow von Dennewitz (6. Westfälisches) Nr. 55 im Weltkriege*, p. 230.
59 Ulrich, *Res.-Inf.-Regiment 52 im Weltkriege*, Lausitzer Verlagsanstalt, Cottbus, 1925, p. 510.

60 Ulrich, *Res.-Inf.-Regiment 52 im Weltkriege*, p. 510.
61 Ulrich, *Res.-Inf.-Regiment 52 im Weltkriege*, p. 510.
62 Campbell, *The Ebb and Flow of Battle*, Oxford University Press, Oxford, 1979, p. 51.
63 Campbell, *The Ebb and Flow of Battle*, p. 59.
64 Campbell, *The Ebb and Flow of Battle*, p. 67.
65 Campbell, *The Ebb and Flow of Battle*, p. 69.
66 Geddes, diary, 18 June 1918, SLNSW, MLMSS 2763, p. 127.
67 Edmonds, *Military Operations, France and Belgium, 1918, May–July*, p. 217.
68 Bean, *Official History of Australia in the War of 1914–1918*, Vol. III, Angus & Robertson, Sydney, 1937, p. 537.
69 Bean, *Official History of Australia in the War of 1914–1918*, Vol. VI, p. 5.
70 *Reveille*, Vol. 5, No. 2, October 1931, p. 10.
71 *Richmond Guardian*, 6 April 1918, p. 5.
72 Grimwade, Harold, Letter to *Reveille*, in: Bean, Charles, AWM38 3DRL 606/276/1, War records, 1928–1937, pp. 1–2.
73 Monash, Letter to his wife, 4 July 1918, Vol. 2, p. 156 (p. 426 of typescript).
74 Sheffield and Bourne (eds), *Douglas Haig: War Diaries and Letters*, p. 425.
75 Rawlinson, diary, Churchill Archives Centre, Cambridge RWLN 1/16, p. 25.
76 Corning, *Yanks Crusade*, p. 42.
77 Corning, *Yanks Crusade*, p. 42.
78 Corning, *Yanks Crusade*, p. 42.
79 Bond, Personal Papers, Tank Museum Bovington, E2012.4678 p. 17 [reported speech].
80 Armitage, James Ramsey, Private Record, AWM PR00420, p. 16.
81 Campbell, *The Ebb and Flow of Battle*, p. 76.

Chapter Six

1 Terraine, *The Smoke and the Fire*, p. 188.
2 Diary of General Rawlinson, Churchill Archives Centre, Cambridge, RWLN 1/16, p. 22.
3 Letter, Murdoch to Monash, Papers of Sir Keith Murdoch, NLA MS 2823/ 2/ 9.
4 *Reveille*, Vol. 5, No. 2, October 1931, p. 10.
5 Serle, *John Monash*, p. 323.
6 Thompson, *On Lips of Living Men*, p. 141.
7 Kieza, *Monash*, pp. 446–7.
8 *The Age*, 5 July 1982, p. 11.
9 Geddes, diary, SLNSW 863029, p. 144 [reported speech].
10 Geddes, diary, SLNSW 863029, p. 144 [reported speech].
11 Geddes, diary, SLNSW 863029, p. 144 [reported speech].
12 Geddes, diary, SLNSW 863029, p. 144.
13 Geddes, diary, SLNSW 863029, p. 144.
14 Geddes, diary, 4 July 1918, SLNSW, MLMSS 2763 / Item 1, p. 145.
15 Geddes, diary, SLNSW 863029, p. 144.
16 Young, diary, SLNSW MLMSS 985/Item 6, p. 58.
17 Judy, *A Soldier's Diary*, p. 103.
18 Pershing, *My Experiences in the World War*, Hodder and Stoughton, London, 1931, p. 475.
19 Diary of General Rawlinson, Churchill Archives Centre, Cambridge, RWLN 1/16, p. 26.
20 Thompson, *On Lips of Living Men*, p. 132.
21 Hobbs, diary, SLWA, 5523A/4, Vol. IV, p. 23.
22 Serle, *John Monash*, p. 376.
23 Geddes, diary, 2 July 1918, SLNSW, MLMSS 2763 / Item 1, p. 144.
24 *The West Australian* (Perth), 19 June 1919, p. 7.
25 *The West Australian* (Perth), 19 June 1919, p. 7.
26 Fitzhardinge, *The Little Digger 1914–1952*, Angus & Robertson, Sydney, 1979, p. 321.
27 Thompson, *On Lips of Living Men*, pp. 140–1.
28 Geddes, diary, SLNSW 863029, p. 144.
29 Bean, diary, AWM38 3DRL 606/116/1 – June – September 1918, p. 12.
30 http://www.ww1westernfront.gov.au/villers-bretonneux/amiens-cathedral/billy-hughes-at-the-western-front-movie.php.
31 Geddes, diary, SLNSW 863029 p. 144.
32 Bean, diary, AWM38 3DRL 606/116/1 – June – September 1918, p. 12.
33 Walsh, Letter to his Brother, AWM, PR01801, pp. 1–2.
34 Bean, diary, AWM38 3DRL 606/116/1 – June – September 1918, p. 12.

35 Bean, diary, AWM38 3DRL 606/116/1 – June – September 1918, p. 12.
36 Geddes, diary, SLNSW 863029, p. 145.
37 Geddes, diary, SLNSW 863029, p. 145.
38 Bean, diary, AWM38 3DRL 606/116/1 – June – September 1918, p. 12.
39 Bean, diary, AWM38 3DRL 606/116/1 – June – September 1918, p. 12.
40 Bean, diary, AWM38 3DRL 606/116/1 – June – September 1918, p. 12.
41 Macdougall (ed.), *War Letters of General Monash*, p. 193.
42 Harold Shapcott memoir 'War Babies,' AWM, MSS1369.
43 Rawlinson, diary, Churchill Archives Centre, Cambridge, RWLN 1/16, p. 26.
44 Pershing, *My Experiences in the World War*, p. 475 [reported speech].
45 Hugher, Matthew Seligman, *Leadership in Conflict*, Pen & Sword Military, South Yorkshire, 1990, p. 26.
46 Rawlinson, diary, Churchill Archives Centre, Cambridge, RWLN 1/16, p. 26.
47 Judy, *A Soldier's Diary*, p. 15.
48 15th Infantry Battalion, AWM4 23/32, July 1918, Appendix 2, p. 1.
49 Corning, *The Yanks Crusade*, p. 43.
50 Corning, *The Yanks Crusade*, p. 43.
51 Geddes, diary, SLNSW 863029, p. 145.
52 16th Infantry Battalion War Diary, AWM 4 23/33/32 Part One, July 1918, Appendix 2, p. 22.
53 Bean, *Official History of Australia in the War of 1914–1918*, Vol. VI, p. 294.
54 *The Daily News* (Perth), 15 June 1914, p. 8.
55 Sheffield and Bourne (eds), *Douglas Haig: War Diaries and Letters*, p. 425.
56 Sheffield and Bourne (eds), *Douglas Haig: War Diaries and Letters*, p. 425.
57 Rule, *Jacka's Mob*, p. 302.
58 Longmore, *Eggs-a-Cook*, Imperial War Museum, London, 2009, p. 147.
59 Maynard, *The Unseen Anzac*, p. 153.
60 Monash, *Australian Victories in France in 1918*, p. 52.
61 Monash, *Australian Victories in France in 1918*, p. 46.
62 Geddes, diary, SLNSW 863029, p. 146.
63 Geddes, diary, SLNSW 863029, p. 146 (Wednesday, 3 July 1918).
64 Armitage, Private Record, AWM PR00420, p. 17.
65 Armitage, Private Record, AWM PR00420, p. 17.

Chapter Seven

1 Huntingdon, AWM PR00654, p. 8.
2 Hankey, *The Supreme Command*, Routledge, New York, 2014, p. 821.
3 Bean, *Official History of Australia in the War of 1914–1918*, Vol VI, p. 278.
4 Rawlinson, diary, Churchill Archives Centre, Cambridge, RWLN 1/16, p. 26.
5 Young, diary, SLNSW MLMSS 985/Item 6, p. 50.
6 Geddes, diary, SLNSW 863029, pp. 145–6.
7 Rawlinson, 'Wood and Wire' (Unpublished Memoir), AWM, MSS0770, p. 49.
8 Hickey, *Rolling into Action*, p. 97.
9 Hickey, *Rolling into Action*, p. 97.
10 Monash, *Australian Victories in France in 1918*, p. 53.
11 Monash, *Australian Victories in France in 1918*, p. 53.
12 Monash, *Australian Victories in France in 1918*, p. 53.
13 Monash, *Australian Victories in France in 1918*, p. 53.
14 Monash, *Australian Victories in France in 1918*, p. 23.
15 Bean, *Official History of Australia in the War of 1914–1918*, Vol. VI, p. 279 [reported speech].
16 Bean, *Official History of Australia in the War of 1914–1918*, Vol. VI, p. 279.
17 Monash, *Australian Victories in France in 1918*, p. 53.
18 Bean, diary, AWM38 3DRL 606/116/1 – June – September 1918, p. 18.
19 Monash, *Australian Victories in France in 1918*, pp. 53–4.
20 Monash, *Australian Victories in France in 1918*, pp. 53–4.
21 Maurice, *The Life of General Lord Rawlinson of Trent*, p. 222.
22 Bean, *Official History of Australia in the War of 1914–1918*, Vol. VI, p. 278 [reported speech].
23 Rule, *Jacka's Mob*, pp. 300–1.
24 Serle, *John Monash*, p. 390.
25 Bean, diary, AWM38 3DRL 606/116/1 – June – September 1918, p. 18.
26 Bean, diary, AWM38 3DRL 606/116/1 – June – September 1918, p. 18 [reported speech].
27 Sheffield and Bourne (eds), *Douglas Haig: War Diaries and Letters*, p. 425.

28 Sheffield and Bourne (eds), *Douglas Haig: War Diaries and Letters*, p. 425.
29 Rawlinson, diary, Churchill Archives Centre, Cambridge, RWLN 1/16, p. 26 [reported speech].
30 Rawlinson, diary, Churchill Archives Centre, Cambridge, RWLN 1/16, p. 26.
31 *The World's News*, 11 January 1919, p. 8.
32 *Newcastle Morning Herald*, 31 August 1918, p. 4 [tense changed].
33 *Newcastle Morning Herald*, 31 August 1918, p. 4 [tense changed].
34 *Newcastle Morning Herald*, 31 August 1918, p. 4 [tense changed].
35 *Newcastle Morning Herald*, 31 August 1918, p. 4 [tense changed].
36 Bean, *Official History of Australia in the War of 1914–1918*, Vol. VI, p. 282.
37 *Newcastle Morning Herald*, 31 August 1918, p. 4 [tense changed].
38 Bergeder, *Das Reserve-Infanterie-Regiment Nr. 202*, Verlag Tradition, Berlin, 1927, p. 144.
39 Schulz, *Infanterie-Regiment Graf Bülow von Dennewitz (6. Westfälisches) Nr. 55 im Weltkriege*, p. 230.
40 Jones, *The War in the Air*, p. 416.
41 *The Australasian*, 18 January 1941, p. 4.
42 Bovington Archive BB 2324 Ref: E2014.2882.
43 Private Percy Jarvis, Personal Papers, Tank Museum Bovington, E2014.2882, p. 1.
44 Hickey, *Rolling into Action*, p. 97.
45 Corning, *The Yanks Crusade*, p. 42.
46 Further reading: H. A. Jones, *The War in the Air: Being the Story of the Part Played in the Great War by the Royal Air Force*, Vol. VI, Oxford, 1937, p. 415.
47 Bond, Personal Papers, Tank Museum Bovington, E2012.4678, p. 18.
48 Bond, Personal Papers, Tank Museum Bovington, E2012.4678, p. 19.
49 *Observer* (Adelaide), 12 July 1919, p. 39.
50 *Observer* (Adelaide), 12 July 1919, p. 39.
51 *Observer* (Adelaide), 12 July 1919, p. 39.
52 Bean, *Official History of Australia in the War of 1914–1918*, Vol. VI, p. 281.
53 *Observer* (Adelaide), 12 July 1919, p. 39.
54 Rule, *Jacka's Mob*, p. 302.
55 Betteridge, diary, AWM PR90.151, p. 13.
56 *Newcastle Morning Herald*, 31 August 1918, p. 4.
57 Letter, private papers, Sydney Huntingdon AWM PR00654, p. 1.
58 Riebensahm, *Infanterie-Regiment Prinz Friedrich der Niederlande (2. Westfälisches) Nr. 15 im Weltkriege 1914–18*, Minden i.W., 1931, p. 346.
59 Letter, Lt Lionel Short, Personal Papers, AWM 2DRL.0045, p. 2.
60 Letter, Coxen to Bean, 1937, AWM38 3DRL 606/276/1 – 1928–1937, p. 2.

Chapter Eight

1 Orgill, *The Tank*, Heinemann, London, 1970, p. 65.
2 Harold Preston, 'John Leak's VC.', *Reveille*, 1 August 1935, p. 30.
3 Horniman, letter, AWM 1DRL.0357, p. 3.
4 Bean, *Official History of Australia in the War of 1914–1918*, Vol. VI, p. 283.
5 *Newcastle Morning Herald*, 31 August 1918, p. 4 [tense changed].
6 Bond, Personal Papers, Tank Museum Bovington, E2012.4678, p. 17.
7 Armitage, Private Record, AWM PR00420, p. 17.
8 Letter, Walter Coxen to Bean, War records of CEW Bean AWM38 3DRL 606/276/1 – 1928–1937, pp. 1–2.
9 *Newcastle Morning Herald*, 31 August 1918, p. 4 [tense changed].
10 Schulz, *Infanterie-Regiment Graf Bülow von Dennewitz (6. Westfälisches) Nr. 55 im Weltkriege*, p. 230.
11 Ulrich, *Res.-Inf.-Regiment 52 im Weltkriege*, p. 510.
12 Betteridge, diary, AWM PR90.151, p. 13.
13 Molkentin, *Fire in the Sky*, p. 273.
14 Horn, *Die deutsche Soldatensprache*, Alfred Töpelmann, Gießen, 1905, p. 136.
15 Huntingdon, 4th Machine Gun Battalion AWM PR00654, p. 1.
16 Letter, Lionel Short, Private Papers, AWM 2DRL.0045, p. 2.
17 Rule, *Jacka's Mob*, p. 302.
18 Mitchell, *Backs to the Wall*, p. 298.
19 Mitchell, *Backs to the Wall*, p. 298.
20 Tank Actions 1918, Hamel, Tank Museum Bovington, E2006.2439, p. 17.

21 Bartenwerffer and Herrmann, *Das Reserve-Infanterie-Regiment Nr. 232 in Ost und West*, Verlag Gerhard Stalling, Oldenburg/Berlin, 1927, p. 154.
22 *Newcastle Morning Herald*, 31 August 1918, p. 4.
23 Bean, diary, AWM38 3DRL 606/116/1 June – September, p. 19.
24 Gross and Rudloff, *Infanterie-Regiment Herwarth von Bittenfeld (1. Westfälisches) Nr. 13 im Weltkriege 1914–1918*, p. 307.
25 Geddes, diary, SLNSW 863029, p. 147.
26 Brahms, *Spirit of the Forty-Second*, Imperial War Museum, London, 1938, p. 82.
27 Geddes, diary, SLNSW 863029, p. 153.
28 Betteridge, diary, AWM PR90.151, p. 14.
29 Pedersen, *Hamel*, p. 40.
30 Longmore, *Eggs-a-Cook*, p. 147.
31 Huidekoper, *The History of the 33rd Division, A.E.F.*, p. 408.
32 Betteridge, diary, AWM PO90.151, p. 12.
33 Short, private papers, AWM 2DRL.0045, p. 2.
34 Betteridge, diary, AWM PO90.151, p. 12.
35 Betteridge, diary, AWM PO90.151, p. 13.
36 Betteridge, diary, AWM PO90.151, p. 13.
37 Short, private papers, AWM 2DRL.0045, p. 2.
38 Geddes, diary, SLNSW 863029, p. 147.
39 Harry Dalziel's story, 'My VC', courtesy of David Dalziel, Brisbane.
40 *Cairns Post*, 23 November 1918, p. 8.
41 http://www.storiesofthesomme.com/uploads/1/1/9/0/11904061/a_soldier_of_the_great_war_harry_dalziel.pdf, accessed: 27.7.2017.
42 *Cairns Post*, 23 November 1918, p. 8.
43 *The Sydney Morning Herald*, 14 November 2010, (online), http://www.smh.com.au/national/world-war-i-vc-to-go-up-for-auction-20101113-17rul.html#ixzz3h2wABspt.
44 Harry Dalziel's story, 'My VC', courtesy of David Dalziel, Brisbane.
45 *The Sydney Morning Herald*, 14 November 2010.
46 Bean, *Official History of Australia in the War of 1914–1918*, Vol. VI, p. 289.
47 *Cairns Post*, 23 November 1918, p. 8.
48 Huidekoper, *The History of the 33rd Division, A.E.F.*, p. 355.
49 Schulz, *Infanterie-Regiment Graf Bülow von Dennewitz (6. Westfälisches) Nr. 55 im Weltkriege*, p. 233.
50 16th Battalion history, p. 183.
51 Gross and Rudloff, *Infanterie-Regiment Herwarth von Bittenfeld (1. Westfälisches) Nr. 13 im Weltkriege 1914–1918*, p. 307.
52 Huidekoper, *The History of the 33rd Division, A.E.F.*, p. 358.
53 Shearer, diary, AWM 3DRL.3662 [no page numbers].
54 Shearer, diary, AWM 3DRL.3662 [no page numbers].
55 Chataway, *History of the 15th Battalion, Australian Imperial Forces*, p. 216.
56 Chataway, *History of the 15th Battalion, Australian Imperial Forces*, p. 216.
57 Shearer, diary, AWM 3DRL.3662 [no page numbers].
58 *Cairns Post*, 23 November 1918, p. 8.
59 *The World's News*, 11 January 1919, p. 8.
60 http://www.europeana1914-1918.eu/en/contributions/5392#prettyPhoto.
61 http://www.europeana1914-1918.eu/en/contributions/5392#prettyPhoto.
62 http://www.europeana1914-1918.eu/en/contributions/5392#prettyPhoto.
63 *Sunday Mail* (Brisbane), 28 April 1940, p. 2.
64 http://www.europeana1914-1918.eu/en/contributions/5392#prettyPhoto [reported speech].
65 P.L. Edgar, Australian Dictionary of Biography. http://adb.anu.edu.au/biography/axford-thomas-leslie-jack-12159.
66 Ferguson, *Experiences of a Forty-niner in Australia and New Zealand*, Gaston Reynard, Melbourne, 1979, p. 284.
67 Bean, *Official History of Australia in the War of 1914–1918*, Vol. VI, pp. 295–6.
68 Bean, diary, AWM38 3DRL 606/188/1, July 1918, p. 13.
69 Sanborn, *131st US Infantry (First Infantry Illinois National Guard) in the World War*, p. 52.
70 Sanborn, *131st US Infantry (First Infantry Illinois National Guard) in the World War*, p. 52.
71 Bean, diary, AWM 38 3DRL606/188/1, July 1918, p. 19.
72 Huidekoper, *The History of the 33rd Division, A.E.F.*, p. 354.

Chapter Nine

1 Lithgow *Mercury*, 22 May 1925, p. 7.
2 15 Battalion War Diary, AWM4 23/32/40, July 1918, Appendix 3, p. 1.
3 Yockelson, *Borrowed Soldiers*, p. 78.
4 Giese, *Geschichte des Reserve-Infanterie-Regiments 227 im Weltkriege 1914/18*, Halle, 1931, p. 493.
5 Bartenwerffer and Herrmann, *Das Reserve-Infanterie-Regiment Nr. 232 in Ost und West*, p. 154.
6 Bean, *Official History of Australia in the War of 1914–1918*, Vol. VI, p. 320 [tense changed].
7 Bean, *Official History of Australia in the War of 1914–1918*, Vol. VI, p. 323.
8 Bean, *Official History of Australia in the War of 1914–1918*, Vol. VI, p. 323.
9 Ellis, *The Story of the Fifth Australian Division*, Hodder and Stoughton, London, 1920, p. 316.
10 McMullin, *Pompey Elliott*, p. 459.
11 McMullin, *Pompey Elliott*, p. 459.
12 Riebensahm, *Infanterie-Regiment Prinz Friedrich der Niederlande (2. Westfälisches) Nr. 15 im Weltkriege 1914–18*, p. 346.
13 Riebensahm, *Infanterie-Regiment Prinz Friedrich der Niederlande (2. Westfälisches) Nr. 15 im Weltkriege 1914–18*, p. 346.
14 Riebensahm, *Infanterie-Regiment Prinz Friedrich der Niederlande (2. Westfälisches) Nr. 15 im Weltkriege 1914–18*, p. 346.
15 Schulz, *Infanterie-Regiment Graf Bülow von Dennewitz (6. Westfälisches) Nr. 55 im Weltkriege*, p. 230.
16 Schulz, *Infanterie-Regiment Graf Bülow von Dennewitz (6. Westfälisches) Nr. 55 im Weltkriege*, p. 231.
17 Harry Dalziel's story, 'My VC', courtesy of David Dalziel, Brisbane.
18 Harry Dalziel's story, 'My VC', courtesy of David Dalziel, Brisbane.
19 Harry Dalziel's story, 'My VC', courtesy of David Dalziel, Brisbane.
20 Colliver and Richardson, *The Forty-Third*, Rigby, Adelaide, 1920, p. 93.
21 Corning, *The Yanks Crusade*, p. 42.
22 *Commonwealth of Australia Gazette* No. 23 Date, 12 February 1919.
23 Longmore, *The Old Sixteenth*, Naval and Military Press, London, 2009, p. 183.
24 Bean, *Official History of Australia in the War of 1914–1918*, Vol. VI, p. 292.
25 Bean, *Official History of Australia in the War of 1914–1918*, Vol. VI, p. 292.
26 Geddes, diary, 4 July 1918, SLNSW, MLMSS 2763 / Item 1, p. 147.
27 Bond, Personal Papers, Tank Museum Bovington, E2012.4678, p. 18.
28 Geddes, diary, SLNSW 863029, p. 148.
29 Geddes, diary, SLNSW 863029, p. 148.
30 Australian Red Cross Society Wounded and Missing Files, 7063 Corporal Michael Joseph Roach, AWM 1DRL/0428.
31 Australian Red Cross Society Wounded and Missing Files, 7063 Corporal Michael Joseph Roach, AWM 1DRL/0428.
32 Australian Red Cross Society Wounded and Missing Files, 7063 Corporal Michael Joseph Roach, AWM 1DRL/0428 [Reported Speech].
33 *The Australian* (Perth), 4 November 1921, p. 2.
34 Betteridge, diary, AWM PO90.151, p. 13.
35 Betteridge, diary, AWM PO90.151, p. 13.
36 Bean, diary, AWM38 3DRL 606/116/1, June – September 1918, pp. 19–20.
37 Rule, *Jacka's Mob*, p. 303.
38 Bean, diary, AWM38 3DRL 606/188/1, July 1918, p. 13.
39 15th Infantry Battalion, war diary, AWM4 23/32/40 appendix 3, p. 12.
40 Harry Dalziel's story, 'My VC', courtesy of David Dalziel, Brisbane.
41 Members of the Intelligence Staff (eds), *The Forty-First*, Australian Commonwealth Military Forces (no publisher given), 1919, p.106.
42 *Newcastle Morning Herald*, 31 August 1918, p. 4.
43 Betteridge, diary, AWM PO90.151, p. 13.
44 Riebensahm, *Infanterie-Regiment Prinz Friedrich der Niederlande (2. Westfälisches) Nr. 15 im Weltkriege 1914–18*, p. 346.
45 Riebensahm, *Infanterie-Regiment Prinz Friedrich der Niederlande (2. Westfälisches) Nr. 15 im Weltkriege 1914–18*, p. 346.
46 Horn, *Die deutsche Soldatensprache*, p. 135.
47 Riebensahm, *Infanterie-Regiment Prinz Friedrich der Niederlande (2. Westfälisches) Nr. 15 im Weltkriege 1914–18*, p. 347.

48 Riebensahm, *Infanterie-Regiment Prinz Friedrich der Niederlande (2. Westfälisches) Nr. 15 im Weltkriege 1914–18*, p. 347.
49 Riebensahm, *Infanterie-Regiment Prinz Friedrich der Niederlande (2. Westfälisches) Nr. 15 im Weltkriege 1914–18*, p. 346.
50 Geddes, diary, 4 July 1918, SLNSW, MLMSS 2763 / Item 1, p. 148.
51 Geddes, diary, 4 July 1918, SLNSW, MLMSS 2763 / Item 1, p. 148.
52 *Australian Christian Commonwealth*, 7 March 1919, p. 15.

Chapter Ten

1 Hassett, Personal Papers, Tank Museum Bovington, E2007.632, p. 67.
2 Hassett, Personal Papers, Tank Museum Bovington, E2007.632, p. 80.
3 *Newcastle Morning Herald*, 31 August 1918, p. 4 .
4 Campbell, *The Ebb and Flow of Battle*, p. 78.
5 Monash, *Australian Victories in France in 1918*, p. 50.
6 Huidekoper, *The History of the 33rd Division, A.E.F.*, p. 364.
7 Mitchell, *Backs to the Wall*, p. 299.
8 Mitchell, *Backs to the Wall*, p. 299.
9 Geddes, diary, 4th July 1918, SLNSW, MLMSS 2763 / Item 1, p. 149.
10 Geddes, diary, 4th July 1918, SLNSW, MLMSS 2763 / Item 1, p. 149.
11 Geddes, diary, 4th July 1918, SLNSW, MLMSS 2763 / Item 1, p. 149.
12 Geddes, diary, 4th July 1918, SLNSW, MLMSS 2763 / Item 1, p. 149 [reported speech].
13 Geddes, diary, 4th July 1918, SLNSW, MLMSS 2763 / Item 1, p. 150.
14 Geddes, diary, 4th July 1918, SLNSW, MLMSS 2763 / Item 1, p. 150.
15 Geddes, diary, 4th July 1918, SLNSW, MLMSS 2763 / Item 1, p. 150.
16 Geddes, diary, 4th July 1918, SLNSW, MLMSS 2763 / Item 1, p. 150.
17 Rule, *Jacka's Mob*, p. 305.
18 Rule, *Jacka's Mob*, p. 305.
19 Rule, *Jacka's Mob*, p. 305.
20 Rule, *Jacka's Mob*, p. 305.
21 Harry Dalziel's story, 'My VC', courtesy of David Dalziel, Brisbane.
22 Harry Dalziel's story, 'My VC', courtesy of David Dalziel, Brisbane.
23 Harry Dalziel's story, 'My VC', courtesy of David Dalziel, Brisbane.
24 *Newcastle Morning Herald*, 31 August 1918, p. 4.
25 Bean, *Official History of Australia in the War of 1914–1918*, Vol. XI, Angus & Robertson, Sydney, 1941, p. 305.
26 Bean, *Official History of Australia in the War of 1914–1918*, Vol. XI, p. 305.
27 Ulrich, *Res.-Inf.-Regiment 52 im Weltkriege*, p. 512.
28 Huidekoper, *The History of the 33rd Division, A.E.F.*, p. 355.
29 *Western Mail*, 16 November 1933, p. 20
30 *Western Mail*, 16 November 1933, p. 2 [reported speech].
31 Molkentin, *Fire in the Sky*, p. 274.
32 Molkentin, *Fire in the Sky*, p. 274.
33 Molkentin, *Fire in the Sky*, p. 274.
34 Ulrich, *Res.-Inf.-Regiment 52 im Weltkriege*, p. 513.
35 Monash, Letter, AWM 3DRL/ Series 1, 23162, Vol. 2, 4 July 1918, p. 156 (p. 426 of typescript).
36 Short, private papers, AWM 2DRL.0045, p. 2.
37 Pedersen, *Hamel*, p. 86.
38 *The Australasian*, 18 January 1941, p. 4, http://trove.nla.gov.au/newspaper/article/142428114/.
39 *The Australasian*, 18 January 1941, p. 4, http://trove.nla.gov.au/newspaper/article/142428114/.
40 Corning, *The Yanks Crusade*, p. 43.
41 Corning, *The Yanks Crusade*, p. 44.
42 State Library of NSW, MLMSS 187/Item 1 Blanc's war yarns 1914–1920, p. 15.
43 Headquarters, 33rd Division, American Expeditionary Forces, *33rd Division A.E.F.: From its Arrival in France until the Armistice with Germany*, p. 3.
44 Rule, *Jacka's Mob*, p. 298.
45 *Chicago Daily Tribune*, 5 July 1918, p. 1.
46 *Chicago Daily Tribune*, 5 July 1918, p. 1.
47 Giese, *Geschichte des Reserve-Infanterie-Regiments 227 im Weltkriege 1914/18*, p. 493.
48 Geddes, diary, 4 July 1918, SLNSW, MLMSS 2763, p. 150.
49 Riebensahm, *Infanterie-Regiment Prinz Friedrich der Niederlande (2. Westfälisches) Nr. 15 im Weltkriege 1914–18*, p. 348.

50 *Newcastle Morning Herald*, 31 August 1918, p. 4.
51 *Newcastle Morning Herald*, 31 August 1918, p. 4.
52 *Newcastle Morning Herald*, 31 August 1918, p. 4.
53 Montgomery-Massingberd, Papers, King's College London, Liddell Hart Centre for Military Archives, Montgomery-Massingberd 7-24-1, [no page numbers].
54 Geddes, diary, 4 July 1918, SLNSW, MLMSS 2763, p. 151.
55 Geddes, diary, 4 July 1918, SLNSW, MLMSS 2763, p. 152.
56 Geddes, diary, 4 July 1918, SLNSW, MLMSS 2763, p. 152.
57 Geddes, diary, 5 July 1918, SLNSW, MLMSS 2763, p. 155.
58 No. 3 Squadron war diary, AWM4 8/6/19 July 1918, Part 2 Appendix, p. 39.
59 No. 3 Squadron war diary, AWM4 8/6/19 July 1918, Part 2 Appendix, p. 39.
60 No. 3 Squadron war diary, AWM4 8/6/19 July 1918, Part 2 Appendix, p. 62.
61 No. 3 Squadron war diary, AWM4 Subclass 8/6/19 Part1, July 1918, p. 5.
62 *Newcastle Morning Herald*, 31 August 1918, p. 4.
63 Monash, AWM 3DRL/2316, Personal Files Book 19, 23 June – 7 July 1918, p. 67.

Chapter Eleven

1 Young, diary, SLNSW 422340, p. 11.
2 Hankey, *The Supreme Command*, p. 729.
3 Hankey, *The Supreme Command*, p. 822.
4 Pershing, *My Experiences in the World War*, p. 474.
5 Diary of General Rawlinson, Churchill Archives Centre, Cambridge, RWLN 1/16, p. 30.
6 Pershing, *My Experiences in the World War*, p. 475.
7 Bean, diaries and letters AWM38 3DRL 606/116/1 – June – September 1918, p. 21.
8 *The West Australian* (Perth), 19 June 1919, p. 7.
9 *The West Australian* (Perth), 19 June 1919, p. 7.
10 *Newcastle Morning Herald*, 31 August 1918, p. 4.
11 Gross and Rudloff, *Infanterie-Regiment Herwarth von Bittenfeld (1. Westfälisches) Nr. 13 im Weltkriege 1914–1918*, p. 307.
12 Giese, *Geschichte des Reserve-Infanterie-Regiments 227 im Weltkriege 1914/18*, p. 494.
13 Bergeder, *Das Reserve-Infanterie-Regiment Nr. 202*, p. 145.
14 Bergeder, *Das Reserve-Infanterie-Regiment Nr. 202*, p. 145.
15 Bergeder, *Das Reserve-Infanterie-Regiment Nr. 202*, p. 145.
16 Bergeder, *Das Reserve-Infanterie-Regiment Nr. 202*, p. 145.
17 Bergeder, *Das Reserve-Infanterie-Regiment Nr. 202*, p. 145.
18 Manners and Manners, *Never a Dull Moment*, Mannwest, Subiaco, 2002, p. 147.
19 Manners and Manners, *Never a Dull Moment*, p. 148.
20 Riebensahm, *Infanterie-Regiment Prinz Friedrich der Niederlande (2. Westfälisches) Nr. 15 im Weltkriege 1914–18*, p. 347.
21 Geddes, diary, 4 July 1918, SLNSW, MLMSS 2763, p. 152.
22 Geddes, diary, 4 July 1918, SLNSW, MLMSS 2763, pp. 152–3.
23 *Newcastle Morning Herald*, 31 August 1918, p. 4.
24 Diary of General Rawlinson, Churchill Archives Centre, Cambridge RWLN 1/16, p. 27.
25 Rupprecht, *In Treue Fest (Steadfast in Loyalty)*, Deutscher National-Verlag, Munich, 1929, Vol. II, p. 418.
26 Rupprecht, *In Treue Fest (Steadfast in Loyalty)*, Vol. II, p. 419.
27 Manners and Manners, *Never a Dull Moment*, p. 144.
28 Manners and Manners, *Never a Dull Moment*, p. 146.
29 Longmore, *Eggs-a-Cook*, p. 148.
30 Bergeder, *Das Reserve-Infanterie-Regiment Nr. 202*, p. 145.
31 Bergeder, *Das Reserve-Infanterie-Regiment Nr. 202*, p. 145.
32 Manners and Manners, *Never a Dull Moment*, p. 147.
33 Longmore, *Eggs-a-Cook*, p. 148.
34 Longmore, *Eggs-a-Cook*, pp. 148–9.
35 Manners and Manners, *Never a Dull Moment*, p. 143.
36 Bean, *Official History of Australia in the War of 1914–1918*, Vol. VI, p. 317.
37 Bean, *Official History of Australia in the War of 1914–1918*, Vol. VI, p. 317.
38 Manners and Manners, *Never a Dull Moment*, p. 143.
39 Longmore, *Eggs-a-Cook*, p. 149.
40 Willbanks, *America's Heroes*, ABC, Santa Barbara, 2011, p. 268.
41 *New York Times*, 17 October 1918, p. 1.

42 Maurice, *The Life of General Lord Rawlinson of Trent*, pp. 222–3.
43 Longmore, *Eggs-a-Cook*, pp. 148–9.
44 Bergeder, *Das Reserve-Infanterie-Regiment Nr. 202*, p. 145.
45 Manners and Manners, *Never a Dull Moment*, p. 147.
46 Geddes, diary, 5 July 1918, SLNSW, MLMSS 2763, p. 155.
47 Geddes, diary, 5 July 1918, SLNSW, MLMSS 2763, p. 155.
48 Geddes, diary, 5 July 1918, SLNSW, MLMSS 2763, p. 155.
49 Geddes, diary, 5 July 1918, SLNSW, MLMSS 2763, p. 155.
50 Bell, *33rd Division American Expeditionary Force*, Diekirch, Luxembourg, March 5, 1919, p. 3.
51 Sanborn, *131st US Infantry (First Infantry Illinois National Guard) in the World War*, p. 53.
52 Bean, *Official History of Australia in the War of 1914–1918*, Vol. VI p. 332.
53 *The Argus*, 3 July 1943, p. 4.
54 *The Argus*, 3 July 1943, p. 4.
55 Bean, Diary No. 188, July 1918, AWM38 3DRL606/188/1, p. 20.
56 https://archive.org/stream/stusinfantryfir00malsgoog/stusinfantryfir00malsgoog_djvu.txt.
57 Bean, *Official History of Australia in the War of 1914–1918*, Vol. VI, p. 332.
58 Bean, *Official History of Australia in the War of 1914–1918*, Vol. VI, p. 331.
59 White, *The Fighting Thirteenth*, p. 146.
60 Sanborn, *131st US Infantry (First Infantry Illinois National Guard) in the World War*, p. 248.
61 Judy, *A Soldier's Diary*, p. 104.
62 Judy, *A Soldier's Diary*, p. 104.
63 Judy, *A Soldier's Diary*, p. 104.
64 Judy, *A Soldier's Diary*, p. 106.
65 Geddes, diary, SLNSW, MLMSS 2763 pp. 157–8.
66 4th Aust Division General Staff Headquarters, War Diary July 1918 AWM4 1/48/28 pt 2, staff war diary Appendix 21, p. 59.
67 Bean, diaries and letters AWM38 3DRL 606/116/1 – June – September 1918, p. 21.
68 *Maryborough Chronicle*, 3 January 1930, p. 9.
69 Macdougall (ed.), *War Letters of General Monash*, p. 194.
70 Monash, *Australian Victories in France in 1918*, p. 63.
71 *Maryborough Chronicle*, 3 January 1930, p. 9.
72 *Barrier Miner*, 1 February 1919, p. 11.
73 Bean, diaries and notebooks, AWM38 3DRL 606/116/1 – June – September 1918, p. 23.
74 *Maryborough Chronicle*, 3 January 1930, p. 9.
75 Young, diary, 2 February – 1 September 1918, 20 July 1918, SLNSW, MLMSS 985, Item 6 March, p. 61.
76 Monash, Letters, AWM 3DRL/2316 15 July 1918, p. 1 .
77 Rawlinson to Lt Col Clive Wigram: 07Jul1918. National Army Museum (NAM) Rawlinson 1952 – 01-33-73, p. 1.
78 Rawlinson to Lt Col Clive Wigram: 07Jul1918. National Army Museum (NAM) Rawlinson 1952 – 01-33-73, p. 1.
79 Monash, Letters, AWM 3DRL/2316 Vol. 2, 4 March 1917 – 28 December 1918, p. 158 (p. 428 of typescript).
80 General Staff Fourth Army, *Operations by the Australian Corps against Hamel*, in Tank Actions 1918 Hamel, Bovington Tank Museum, E2006 2439, p. 1.
81 Pedersen, *Hamel*, p. 51.
82 Monash, *The Australian Victories in France in 1918*, p. 57.
83 *The Daily News* (Perth), 28 December 1934, p. 6 .
84 NA CRS (Commonwealth Record Series) A6006/5 roll 2.
85 NA CRS (Commonwealth Record Series) A6006/5 roll 2.
86 Bean, Charles, *Two Men I Knew*, Angus & Robertson, Sydney, 1957, p. 173.
87 Bean, Charles, *Official History of Australia in the War of 1914–1918*, Vol VI, p. 332.
88 Bean, AWM38 3DRL 606/116/1 – June – September 1918, p. 29.
89 Wray, Christopher, *Sir James Whiteside McCay: A Turbulent Life*, Oxford University Press, Melbourne, 2002, p. 218.
90 Letter, Murdoch to Bean, Papers of Sir Keith Murdoch NLA MS 2823/ 2/ 12.
91 Letter, Murdoch to Monash, Papers of Sir Keith Murdoch NLA MS 2823/ 2/ 9.
92 Terraine, *Douglas Haig*, Cassell, London, 2005, p. 450.
93 Thompson, *On Lips of Living Men*, Cassell, London, 2005, p. 142.
94 Ludendorff, *Meine Kriegserinnerungen*, E.S. Mittler und Sohn, Berlin, 1919, p. 547.

95 Author's note: In 1915 Monash was made Companion of the Order of the Bath, the lowest level of knighthood of that order. At Bertangles, in August 1918, he was raised to the highest level, Knight Commander of the Order of the Bath.
96 Serle, *John Monash*, p. 351.
97 Serle, *John Monash*, p. 351.
98 Bean, diary, 12 August 1918, AWM38 3DRL 606/116/1 June to Sept 1918, p. 78.
99 Kieza, *Monash*, p. 484.
100 *Sydney Morning Herald*, 26 January 1935, p. 13 .
101 Monash, *Australian Victories in France in 1918*, p. 290.

Epilogue

1 Serle, *John Monash*, p. 379.
2 Essame, *The Battle for Europe*, p. 104.
3 Pedersen, *Hamel*, p. 8.
4 Les Murray, *The New Oxford Book of Australian Verse*, Oxford University Press, Oxford, 1996, p. 256.
5 Serle, *John Monash*, p. 404.
6 Serle, *John Monash*, p. 416.
7 *The Times*, reprinted in: *The Mercury*, 21 June 1919, p. 11.
8 *The Times*, reprinted in: *The Mercury*, 21 June 1919, p. 11.
9 Serle, *John Monash*, p. 420.
10 *The West Australian* (Perth), 22 December 1919, p. 6.
11 *The Age*, 27 December 1919, p. 7.
12 *The Age*, 27 December 1919, p. 7.
13 Serle, *John Monash*, p. 429.
14 *Kilmore Free Press*, 11 March 1920, p. 2.
15 *The Sydney Morning Herald*, 3 May 1920, p. 7.
16 Serle, *John Monash*, p. 424.
17 *Smith's Weekly* (Sydney), 7 August 1920, p. 1.
18 *Smith's Weekly* (Sydney), 7 August 1920, p. 1.
19 *Smith's Weekly* (Sydney), 7 August 1920, p. 1.
20 Letter, Birdwood to Stonehaven, Papers of Viscount Stonehaven, NLA MS 2127, Series 1, Folder 1.
21 http://dra.org.au/news/14283/the-legacy-of-monash-in-the-australian-army-of-today.
22 Serle, *John Monash*, p. 526.
23 *The Sydney Morning Herald*, 12 October 1931, p. 10.
24 Serle, *John Monash*, p. 377.
25 Records of CEW Bean AWM38 3DRL 606/274B/1 – 1918–1939.
26 Records of CEW Bean AWM38 3DRL 606/274B/1 – 1918–1939.
27 Records of CEW Bean AWM38 3DRL 606/274B/1 – 1918–1939.
28 Records of CEW Bean AWM38 3DRL 606/274B/1 – 1918–1939.
29 *Reveille*, Vol. 5, No. 2, October 1931, p. 2.
30 *The Sun* (Sydney), 8 October 1931, p. 14.
31 Bean, *Official History of Australia in the War of 1914–1918*, Vol. VI, p. 207.
32 *The Advertiser* (Adelaide), 12 August 1933, p. 8.
33 Heater, *National Self-Determination*, Macmillan, Basingstoke, 1994, p. 92.
34 *The Evening News*, 15 November 1933, p. 10.
35 *Worker* (Brisbane), 5 August 1946, p. 6.
36 McNally, *The Man on the Twenty Dollar Note*, A. H. & A. W. Reed, Sydney, 1976, p. 60.
37 McNally, *The Man on the Twenty Dollar Note*, p. 60.
38 *Kalgoorlie Miner*, 26 December 1918, p. 4.
39 *Tambellup Times*, 28 December 1918, p. 2.
40 *The West Australian* (Perth), 25 December 1918, p. 5.
41 *Kalgoorlie Miner*, 26 December 1918, p. 4.
42 Interview with Pam Caddy.
43 *Sunday Times* (Perth), 13 August 1950, p. 8.
44 Interview with Pam Caddy.
45 Interview with David Dalziel.
46 *The Brisbane Courier*, 29 April 1919, p. 9.
47 *The Brisbane Courier*, 24 January 1935, p. 1.
48 *The Courier Mail* (Brisbane), 23 July 2016, p. 6.
49 *The Courier Mail* (Brisbane), 26 April 1952, p. 1.

50 *The Truth*, 7 August 1957, p. 5.
51 *The Courier Mail* (Brisbane), 23 July 2016, p. 6.
52 *Australian Christian Commonwealth*, 7 March 1919, p. 15.
53 Evans, *Somme 1914–18*, History Press, Stroud, 2010, p. 251.
54 *Chicago Tribune*, 14 August 1918, p. 1.
55 *Western Mail* (Perth), 14 June 1934, p. 2.
56 *Western Mail* (Perth), 27 December 1934, p. 2.
57 Roberts, *Before Rupert*, p. 228.
58 http://www.abc.net.au/news/2013-11-11/
    what-do-we-know-about-australias-unknown-soldier/5081574.
59 Sally Warhaft (ed.), *Well May We Say . . . The Speeches that Made Australia*, Text, Melbourne,
    2014, pp. 137–8. Reproduced with permission of Hon. P.J. Keating. Author's note: I note that
    I have quoted Keating's wonderful words before to end my book *Fromelles & Pozières, In the
    Trenches of Hell*, but on this subject, no other words will do.

BIBLIOGRAPHY

Australian War Memorial (AWM)

Mitchell Library (ML)

National Army Museum (NAM)

National Library of Australia (NLA)

State Library of NSW (SLNSW)

State Library of Western Australia (SLWA)

Tank Museum Bovington (TMB)

Books

Bartenwerffer, Erich von; Herrmann, Alfred, *Das Reserve-Infanterie-Regiment Nr. 232 in Ost und West: Nach den amtl. Kriegstagebüchern, persönlichen Aufzeichnungen und Erinnerungen bearbeitet* (*The RIR No. 232 in East and West: Based on the official war diaries, personal accounts and memories*), Part II, Verlag Gerhard Stalling, Oldenburg/Berlin, 1927

Bean, Charles, *Official History of Australia in the War of 1914–1918*, Vol. III ('The Australian Imperial Force in France, 1916'), 12th edition, Angus & Robertson, Sydney, 1941

Bean, Charles, *Official History of Australia in the War of 1914–1918*, Vol. V ('The Australian Imperial Force in France during the Main German Offensive, 1918'), 8th edition, Angus & Robertson, Sydney, 1937

Bean, Charles, *Official History of Australia in the War of 1914–1918*, Vol. VI ('The Australian Imperial Force in France during the Allied Offensive, 1918'), 1st edition, Angus & Robertson, Sydney, 1942

Bean, Charles, *Official History of Australia in the War of 1914–1918*, Vol. XI ('Australia During the War'), 7th edition, Angus & Robertson, Sydney, 1941

Berg, A. Scott, *Wilson*, Simon and Schuster, London, 2013

Bergeder, Fritz, *Das Reserve-Infanterie-Regiment Nr. 202: Auf den Schlachtfeldern des Weltkrieges 1914–1918* (*The Reserve Infantry Regiment No. 202: On the Battlegrounds of the World War 1914–1918*), Verlag Tradition, Berlin, 1927

Brahms, Vivian, *Spirit of the Forty-Second*, Imperial War Museum, London, 1938

Bundesarchiv, *Der Weltkrieg 1914–1918* (*The World War 1914–1918*), Vol. XIV: '*Die Kriegführung an der Westfront im Jahre 1918*' ('Warfare at the Western Front in the Year 1918'), E.S. Mittler und Sohn, Berlin, 1944

Campbell, Patrick James, *The Ebb and Flow of Battle*, Oxford University Press, Oxford, 1979

Carlyon, Les, *The Great War*, Macmillan, Sydney, 2006

Carne, William A., *In Good Company: An Account of the 6th Machine Gun Company A.I.F., In Search of Peace 1915–1919*, 6th Machine Gun Company (A.I.F.) Association, Melbourne, 1937

Chataway, Thomas, *History of the 15th Battalion, Australian Imperial Forces, War 1914–1918*, W. Brooks, Brisbane, 1948

Clausewitz, Carl von, *On War*, Princeton University Press, Princeton, 1976

Colliver, Eustace; Richardson, Brian, *The Forty-Third: The Story and Official History of the 43rd Battalion, A.I.F.*, Rigby, Adelaide, 1920

Corning, Walter D., *The Yanks Crusade: A Book of Reminiscences*, self-published, Chicago, 1927

Coulthart, Ross, *Charles Bean: If People Really Knew: One Man's Struggle to Report the Great War and Tell the Truth*, HarperCollins Publishers, Sydney, 2014

Dehgan, Bahman, *America in Quotations*, Jefferson, McFarland, 2003

Eden, Anthony, *Another World, 1897–1917*, Doubleday, New York, 1977

Edmonds, Sir James, *Military Operations, France and Belgium, 1918: May–July, the German Diversion Offensives and the First Allied Counter-Offensive*, Imperial War Museum, London, 1939

Ellis, Arthur D., *The Story of the Fifth Australian Division*, Hodder and Stoughton, London, 1920

Emden, Richard Van, *The Soldier's War: The Great War through Veterans' Eyes*, Bloomsbury, London, 2008

Essame, Hubert, *The Battle for Europe, 1918*, Batsford, London, 1972

Evans, Martin, *Somme 1914–18: Lessons in War*, The History Press, Stroud, 2010

Ferguson, Charles D., *Experiences of a Forty-niner in Australia and New Zealand*, Gaston Reynard, Melbourne, 1979

Fitzhardinge, Laurence F., *The Little Digger 1914–1952: William Morris Hughes, A Political Biography* (Vol. 2), Angus & Robertson, Sydney, 1979

Fuller, John F. C., *Memoirs of an Unconventional Soldier*, Nicholson & Watson publishers, London, 1936

Giese, Franz, *Geschichte des Reserve-Infanterie-Regiments 227 im Weltkriege 1914/18: Nach amtlichen Kriegstagebüchern des Reichsarchivs, sowie Aufzeichnungen und Schilderungen von Mitkämpfenden* (*History of the Reserve Infantry Regiment 227 in the World War 1914/18*), Verein ehemaliger Angehöriger des R.I.R. 227 (Association of former members of the R.I.R. 227), Halle, 1931

Gross, Carl; Rudloff, Werner von, *Infanterie-Regiment Herwarth von Bittenfeld (1. Westfälisches) Nr. 13 im Weltkriege 1914–1918* (*Infantry Regiment Herwarth von Bittenfeld (1st Westphalian) No. 13 in the World War 1914–1918*), Verlag von Gerhard Stalling, Oldenburg i.O./Berlin, 1927

Hankey, Maurice, *The Supreme Command, 1914–1918*, Vol. II, Routledge, New York, 2014

Harris, John, *Men, Ideas and Tanks*, Manchester University Press, Manchester, 1995

Hart, Peter, *1918: A Very British Victory*, Phoenix, London, 2008

Headquarters, 33rd Division, American Expeditionary Forces, *33rd Division A.E.F.: From its Arrival in France until the Armistice with Germany, November 11, 1918*, self-published by 33rd Division, 1919

Healy, Tim, *More Lives Than One: My Days of Hazard*, Appleton, New York, 1944

Heater, Derek B., *National Self-Determination: Woodrow Wilson and His Legacy*, Macmillan, Basingstoke, 1994

Hickey, David, *Rolling into Action*, Naval and Military Press, Uckfield, 2007

Hoehling, Adolph A.; Hoehling, Mary D., *The Last Voyage of the Lusitania*, Madison Books, Lanham, 1956

Horn, Paul, *Die deutsche Soldatensprache*, Alfred Töpelmann, Gießen, 1905

Huidekoper, Frederick, *The History of the 33rd Division, A.E.F.*, Vol. III, Illinois State Historical Library, Springfield, 1921

Jones, H. A., *The War in the Air: Being the Story of the Part Played in the Great War by the Royal Air Force*, Vol. VI, Clarendon, Oxford, 1937

Judy, Will, *A Soldier's Diary*, Judy Publishing, Chicago, 1930

Kennedy, John J., *The Whale Oil Guards*, James Duffy and Co, Dublin, 1919

Kieza, Grantlee, *Monash – The Soldier Who Shaped Australia*, ABC Books HarperCollins, Sydney, 2015

Laffin, John, *The Battle of Hamel: The Australians' Finest Victory*, Kangaroo Press, Sydney, 1999

Larres, Klaus, *Churchill's Cold War: The Power of Personal Diplomacy*, Yale University Press, New Haven, 2002

Longmore, Cyril, *Eggs-a-Cook! The Story of the Forty-Fourth: War as the Digger Saw It*, Imperial War Museum, London, 2009

Longmore, Cyril, *The Old Sixteenth: Being A Record of the 16th Battalion A.I.F. during the Great War, 1914–1918*, Naval and Military Press, London, 2009

Ludendorff, Erich, *Meine Kriegserinnerungen, 1914–1918* (*My War Memories, 1914–1918*), E.S. Mittler und Sohn, Berlin, 1919

Macdougall, A. K. (ed.), *War Letters of General Sir John Monash*, Duffy & Snellgrove, Sydney, 2002

Manners, Ron; Manners, Charles; Manners, Nancy, *Never a Dull Moment: Kalgoorlie's Golden Years Through to the Seventies, Including Life in the WW1 Trenches*, Mannwest, Subiaco, 2002

Maurice, Sir Frederick, *The Life of General Lord Rawlinson of Trent from his Journals and Letters*, Cassell and Co., London, 1928

Maynard, Jeff, *The Unseen Anzac: How an Enigmatic Explorer Created Australia's World War I Photographs*, Scribe, Brunswick, 2015

McMullin, Ross, *Pompey Elliott*, Scribe, Melbourne, 2008

McNally, Ward, *The Man on the Twenty Dollar Note: Sir Charles Kingsford-Smith*, A. H. & A. W. Reed, Sydney, 1976

Members of the Intelligence Staff (eds), *The Forty-First*, Australian Commonwealth Military Forces, 1919

Mitchell, George, *Backs to the Wall: A Larrikin on the Western Front*, Allen & Unwin, Crows Nest, 2007

Molkentin, Michael, *Fire in the Sky: The Australian Flying Corps in the First World War*, Allen & Unwin, Sydney, 2010

Monash, Sir John, *Australian Victories in France in 1918*, Imperial War Museum, London, 2009

Müller, Georg A. von; Görlitz, Walter, *The Kaiser and his Court: the Diaries, Notebooks and Letters of Admiral Georg Alexander von Müller Chief of the Naval Cabinet 1914–1918*, Macdonald, London, 1961

Murray, Les, *The New Oxford Book of Australian Verse*, Oxford University Press, Oxford, 1996

Orgill, Douglas, *The Tank: Studies in the Development and Use of a Weapon*, Heinemann, London, 1970

Pedersen, Peter A., *ANZACS on the Western Front: The Australian War Memorial Battlefield Guide*, John Wiley & Sons, Melbourne, 2012

Pedersen, Peter A., *Hamel*, Pen and Sword Books, Barnsley (South Yorkshire), 2003

Pedersen, Peter A., *Monash as Military Commander*, Melbourne University Press, Melbourne, 1985

Pershing, John, *My Experiences in the World War*, Hodder and Stoughton, London, 1931

Prior, Robin; Wilson, Trevor, *Command on the Western Front: The Military Career of Sir Henry Rawlinson*, Pen & Sword Books, Barnsley/South Yorkshire, 2004

Recouly, Raymond; Jones, Mary C., *Foch: The Winner of the War*, C. Scribner's Sons, New York, 1920

Riebensahm, Gustav, *Infanterie-Regiment Prinz Friedrich der Niederlande (2. Westfälisches) Nr. 15 im Weltkriege 1914–18: Nach den beim Reichsarchiv in Potsam vorhandenen Kriegsakten und privaten Aufzeichnungen (Infantry Regiment Prince Friedrich of the Netherlands (2nd Westphalian) No. 15 in the World War 1914–1918)*, Bund ehemaliger Angehöriger des Infanterie-Regiments Nr. 15 (Association of former members of the Infantry Regiment No. 15), Minden i.W., 1931

Roberts, Tom D.C., *Before Rupert: Keith Murdoch and the Birth of a Dynasty*, University of Queensland Press, St Lucia, 2015

Rule, Edgar J., *Jacka's Mob*, Angus & Robertson, Sydney, 1933

Rupprecht von Bayern, Kronprinz, *In Treue Fest: Mein Kriegstagebuch (Steadfast in Loyalty: My War Diary)*, Vol. II, Deutscher National-Verlag, Munich, 1929

Sanborn, Joseph B., *131st US Infantry (First Infantry Illinois National Guard) in the World War: Narrative, Operations, Statistics*, Chicago, 1919

Schulz, Walter (et al.), *Infanterie-Regiment Graf Bülow von Dennewitz (6. Westfälisches) Nr. 55 im Weltkriege (Infantry Regiment Count Bülow von Dennewitz (6th Westphalian) No. 55 in the World War)*, Verlag der Meyerschen Hofbuchhandlung (Max Staercke), Detmold, 1928

Serle, Geoffrey, *John Monash: A Biography*, Melbourne University Press, Melbourne, 1982

Sheffield, Gary, *The Chief: Douglas Haig and the British Army*, Aurum, London, 2012

Sheffield, Gary; Bourne, John M. (eds), *Douglas Haig: War Diaries and Letters, 1914–1918*, Weidenfeld & Nicolson, London, 2005

Smithers, Alan J., *A New Excalibur: The Development of the Tank, 1909–1939*, Leo Cooper, London, 1986

Smyth, Sir John, *Leadership in Battle*, David and Charles, New York, 1975

Taylor, A. J. P., *The First World War: An Illustrated History*, London, 1963

Terraine, John, *Douglas Haig: The Educated Soldier*, Cassell, London, 2005

Terraine, John, *The Smoke and the Fire: Myths and Anti-Myths of War 1861–1945*, Sidgwick & Jackson, London, 1980

Terraine, John, *White Heat: The New Warfare 1914–1918*, Guild Publishing, London, 1982

Thompson, John J.M., *On Lips of Living Men*, Lansdowne Press, Melbourne, 1962

Ulrich, Herbert, *Res.-Inf.-Regiment 52 im Weltkriege Zusammengestellt aus Berichten, Tagebüchern und eigenen Erlebnissen (Res. Inf. Regiment 52 in the World War: Compiled from Reports, Diaries and Personal Experiences)*, Lausitzer Verlagsanstalt, Cottbus, 1925

Wackett, Lawrence J., *Aircraft Pioneer: An Autobiography*, Angus & Robertson, Sydney, 1972

Warhaft, Sally (ed.), *Well May We Say . . . The Speeches that Made Australia*, Text Publishing, Melbourne, 2014

Wedel, von, *Das Feldartillerie-Regiment 213: Nach amtlichen Unterlagen, Tagebüchern und persönlichen Notizen bearbeitet von verschiedenen Angehörigen des Regiments (The Field-Artillery Regiment 213: Edited based on official Documents, Diaries and Personal Accounts by various Members of the Regiment)*, Bernhard Sporn, Zeulenroda-Thür., 1930

White, Thomas A., *The Fighting Thirteenth: The History of the Thirteenth Battalion, A.I.F.*, Naval & Military Press and Imperial War Museum, 2009

Willbanks, James, *America's Heroes, Medal of Honor Recipients from the Civil War to Afghanistan*, ABC, Santa Barbara, 2011

Winter, Denis, *Haig's Command: A Reassessment*, Viking, London, 1991

Wodehouse, Pelham G., *Blandings Castle – and Elsewhere*, H. Jenkins, London, 1957

Woodward, David R., *The American Army and the First World War*, Cambridge University Press, New York, 2014

Yockelson, Mitchell A., *Borrowed Soldiers: Americans under British Command*, University of Oklahoma Press, Norman, 2008

Zwar, Desmond, *In Search of Keith Murdoch*, Macmillan, South Melbourne, 1980

Diaries, Letters, Manuscripts and Records

4th Australian Division, AWM28 1/213, Part 3, 24.9.1917 to 30.9.1917

4th Australian Division (General Staff, Headquarters), AWM4 1/48/28, Part 2, July 1918, Appendix 21, RCDIG1010815

15th Infantry Battalion, AWM4 23/32/40 – July 1918, RCDIG1004294

16th Infantry Battalion, AWM4 23/33/32, Part 1, July 1918, Appendices 1–2, RCDIG1004831

16th Infantry Battalion, AWM4 23/33/32, Part 2, July 1918, Appendices 3–22, RCDIG1004832

Armitage, James R., AWM, PR00420, Private Record, Memoir, 1917–1918

Australian Corps General Staff, defence of Amiens, 1 July 1918 AWM25 361/3

Bean, Charles, AWM38 3DRL 606/47/1, June 1916, Official Record/Diary, RCDIG1066856

Bean, Charles, AWM38 3DRL 606/90/1, October 1917, Official Record/Diary, RCDIG1066658

Bean, Charles, AWM38 3DRL 606/91/1, October 1917, Official Record/Diary, RCDIG1066659

Bean, Charles, AWM38 3DRL 606/111/1, May 1918, Official Record/Diary, RCDIG1066557

Bean, Charles, AWM38 3DRL 606/113/1, May – June 1918, Official Record/Diary, RCDIG1066559

Bean, Charles, AWM38 3DRL 606/114/1, June 1918, Official Record/Diary, RCDIG1066560

Bean, Charles, AWM38 3DRL 606/115/1, June 1918, Official Record/Diary, RCDIG1066561

Bean, Charles, AWM38 3DRL 606/116/1, June – September 1918, Official Record/Diary, RCDIG1066562

Bean, Charles, AWM38 3DRL 606/188/1, July 1918, Official Record/Note book, RCDIG1066804

Bean, Charles, AWM38 3DRL 606/274B/1, 1918–1939, Official Record/Papers, RCDIG1066714

Betteridge, Isaac H., AWM, PR90.151, Private Record, Diary, 1917–1918

Birdwood, Lord William R., AWM, 3DRL/3376, Series 1 ('Field Marshal Lord William Birdwood's Personal Diaries, 1915–1920'), Personal Diary, 1 January – 31 December 1918

Birdwood, William R., Letter to Stonehaven, NLA, MS 2127, Series 1, Folder 1, 'Papers of Viscount John Lawrence Baird Stonehaven, 1893–1941'

Bond, Edwin, TMB, Personal Papers, E2012.4678

Coxen, Walter in: Bean, Charles, AWM38 3DRL 606/276/1, 1928–1937, Official Record/Papers, Letter to Bean, 1928, RCDIG1066716

Dalziel, Harry, 'My VC' (unpublished memoir, from 1942), courtesy of David Dalziel, Brisbane.

Englert, Bertie G., File 7342, in: Australian Red Cross Society, AWM, 1DRL/0428, Private Record, Wounded and Missing Enquiry Bureau Files, 1915–1919

Geddes, Clifford, SLNSW, MLMSS 2763, Item 1, Diary (May – July 1918)

Hassett, John, TMB, Personal Papers, E2007.632

Hobbs, Joseph J. T. ('Talbot Hobbs'), SLWA, 5523A/4, Vol. IV, Diary, 1919

Horniman, Lancelot V., AWM, 1DRL/0357, Private Record, Papers, 1928

Huntingdon, Sydney L., AWM, PR00654, Private Record, Letters (copies), 1918

Jarvis, Percy, TMB, Personal Papers, E2014.2882

Monash, Sir John, AWM 3DRL/2316, Series 1 ('Personal Letters, 1914–1918'), Vol. 1 ('War letters of General Monash: 24 December 1914 – 4 March 1917'), typescript, https://www.awm.gov.au/collection/C2077749

Monash, Sir John, AWM 3DRL/2316, Series 1 ('Personal Letters, 1914–1918'), Vol. 2 ('War letters of General Monash: 4 March 1917 – 28 December 1918'), typescript, https://www.awm.gov.au/collection/C2077751

Monash, Sir John, AWM 3DRL/2316, Series 3 ('First World War Papers, 1914–1918'), Papers, 1914–1919; Personal Files Book 18, 8 May – 25 May 1918, RCDIG0000630, https://www.awm.gov.au/collection/C1375981

Monash, Sir John, AWM 3DRL/2316, Series 3 ('First World War Papers, 1914–1918'), Personal Files Book 19, 4 June – 24 June 1918, RCDIG0000632, https://www.awm.gov.au/collection/C1422883

Monash, Sir John, AWM 3DRL/2316, Series 3 ('First World War Papers, 1914–1918'), Papers, 1914–1919; Personal Files Book 19, 23 June – 7 July 1918, RCDIG0000633, https://www.awm.gov.au/collection/C1375981

Montgomery-Massingberd, Sir Archibald, Papers, King's College London, Liddell Hart Centre for Military Archives, Montgomery-Massingberd 7-24-1

Murdoch, Keith, Letter to Bean, Papers of Sir Keith Arthur Murdoch, 1908–1967, NLA, MS 2823/2/12

Murdoch, Keith, Letter to Monash, Papers of Sir Keith Arthur Murdoch, 1908–1967, NLA, MS 2823/2/9

Neaves, Henry, AWM, 2DRL/0752, Private Record; Copy, Diary, Documents, ca. March 1916 – March 1919

No. 3 Squadron, Australian Flying Corps, AWM4 8/6/18, June 1918, Official Record, 1918, RCDIG1004224

No. 3 Squadron, Australian Flying Corps, AWM4 8/6/19, Part 2, July 1918, Official Record, 1918, RCDIG1004226

O'Connor, Arthur, *Weekly Dispatch* (handwritten), 'Monash: The new fighting General', 16 June 1918, in: Monash, Sir John, AWM 3DRL/2316, Series 3 ('First World War Papers, 1914–1918'), Personal Files Book 19, 4 June – 24 June 1918, RCDIG0000632, https://www.awm.gov.au/collection/C1422883?image=71, https://www.awm.gov.au/collection/C1422883?image=72, https://www.awm.gov.au/collection/C1422883?image=73

Powell, George W., File 7588, in: Australian Red Cross Society, AWM, 1DRL/0428, Private Record, Wounded and Missing Enquiry Bureau Files, 1915–1919

Rawlinson, Henry S., Diary, Churchill Archives Centre (Cambridge), RWLN 1/16

Rawlinson, Henry, NAM, Rawlinson, 1952, 01-33-73, Letter to Wigram

Rawlinson, Henry, NAM, Rawlinson, 1952, 01-33-76, Letter to Bridges

Rawlinson, Frank R., AWM, MSS0770, Manuscript, Papers, 'Wood and Wire' (unpublished memoir), 1917–1962

Roach, Michael J., File 7063, in: Australian Red Cross Society, AWM, 1DRL/0428, Private Record, Wounded and Missing Enquiry Bureau Files, 1915–1919

Schwieger, Walter, 'English Translation of His Majesty's Submarine U-20 War Diary', Diary, 1915, National Archives (USA), ID 833792, Series: Subject Files, ca. 1924 – ca. 1946, Record Group 45: Naval Records Collection of the Office of Naval Records and Library, 1691–1945, https://catalog.archives.gov/id/833792?q=lusitania

Shapcott, Harold S., AWM, MSS1369, Manuscript, 'War Babies' (unpublished memoir, typescript), ca. 1934

Shearer, James H., AWM, 3DRL/3662, Private Record, Diary, 1916–1919

Short, Lionel G., AWM, 2DRL/0045, Private Record, Letters/Papers (copies), 1916–1919

Simpson, Roland H., AWM, PR00733, Private Record; Book, Letters, Papers, Souvenir, 1916–1919

Tank Actions 1918 – Hamel, Booklet, TMB, E2006.2439

Thomas, William C., AWM, PR82/002, Private Record, Diary, 1918

Walsh, Ulric K, AWM, PR01801, Private Record; Letters, Photograph, Postcard; 1915–1919

Williams, Albert J., AWM, MSS1337, Manuscript, 'A Soldier Looks Back' (submitted war novel, typescript), ca. 1935

Young, Sydney B., SLNSW, War Diary, 2 February – 1 September 1918, MLMSS 985, Item 6

Newspapers

Australian Christian Commonwealth
Bendigo Advertiser
Cairns Post
Chicago Tribune
Daily Examiner
Kalgoorlie Miner
Maryborough Chronicle
Newcastle Morning Herald and Miners' Advocate
Observer (Adelaide)
Pittsworth Sentinel
Port Adelaide News
Richmond Guardian
Smith's Weekly (Sydney)
Sunday Mail (Brisbane)
Sunday Times (Perth)
Tambellup Times
The Advertiser (Adelaide)
The Age
The Argus
The Australasian
The Australian (Perth)
The Brisbane Courier
The Courier Mail (Brisbane)
The Daily News (Perth)

The Evening News
The Mercury (Hobart)
The New York Times
The Northern Herald (Cairns)
The Sun (Sydney)
The Sydney Morning Herald
The Telegraph (Brisbane)
The Truth
The West Australian (Perth)
The World's News
Washington Post
Weekly Times (Melbourne)
Western Mail (Perth)
Worker (Brisbane)

Journals and Magazines

Commonwealth of Australia Gazette, No. 23, 12 February 1919
Journal of the Australian War Memorial
Military History Magazine, Vol. 17, Issue 3, August 2000
Reveille, Vol. 5, No. 2, 31 October 1931
Reveille, Vol. 8, No. 12, August 1935

Websites

Commonwealth War Graves Commission, http://www.cwgc.org/find-war-dead.aspx?cpage=5&sort=
    name&order=asc
http://dra.org.au/news/14283/the-legacy-of-monash-in-the-australian-army-of-today
http://www.abc.net.au/news/2013-11-11/what-do-we-know-about-australias-unknown-soldier/5081574
http://www.europeana1914-1918.eu/en/contributions/5392#prettyPhoto
http://www.storiesofthesomme.com/uploads/1/1/9/0/11904061/a_soldier_of_the_great_war_harry_
    dalziel.pdf
http://www.ww1westernfront.gov.au/villers-bretonneux/amiens-cathedral/
    billy-hughes-at-the-western#name?
https://archive.org/stream/meinekriegserinn00lude?ref=ol#page/546/mode/2up
https://archive.org/stream/stusinfantryfir00malsgoog/stusinfantryfir00malsgoog_djvu.txt.
https://www.awm.gov.au/exhibitions/1918/soldier/sammy/
https://www.awm.gov.au/learn/understanding-military-history/official histories/
P.L. Edgar, Australian Dictionary of Biography. http://adb.anu.edu.au/biography/
    axford-thomas-leslie-jack-12159

Interviews

Williams, Peter D., Interview with David Dalziel, 27 April 2017
Williams, Peter D., Interview with Don Axford (Jack's grandson), 7 May 2017
Williams, Peter D., Interview with Pam Caddy, 7 May 2017

Other

Bassett, Colin, MA-Thesis ('Does the leadership and command method of General Sir John Monash
    remain relevant to the contemporary commander?') U.S. Army Command and General Staff College,
    Fort Leavenworth, Kansas, 2009
Bell, George, 33rd Division American Expeditionary Force, Diekirch, Luxembourg, 5 March 1919
    (Pamphlet)
Cabinet Papers, 1918, National Archives of Australia, CRS (Commonwealth Record Series), A6006/5,
    Roll 2
Earnshaw, John, Lecture at Huddersfield Military History Society ('The Battle of Hamel:
    4th July 1918'), 19 November 2014, https://www.slideshare.net/JohnHEarnshaw/
    the-battle-of-hamel-4th-july-1918-nov-14
Foott, Cecil, Letter to *Reveille*, in: Bean, Charles, AWM38 3DRL 606/276/1, War records, 1928–1937
Grimwade, Harold, Letter to *Reveille*, in: Bean, Charles, AWM38 3DRL 606/276/1, War records,
    1928–1937

INDEX